46629

£14.95 ✓

M$_P$$_S$

Managing
Total Qual

D0727722

RETURNED

The Manufacturing Practitioner Series

Stop Wasting Time: Computer-Aided Planning and Control:
   Norman Sanders
Just-in-Time Manufacturing in Perspective: Alan Harrison

Managing for
Total Quality

From Deming to Taguchi and SPC

N. Logothetis

Prentice Hall

New York   London   Toronto   Sydney   Tokyo   Singapore

First published 1992 by
Prentice Hall International (UK) Ltd
Campus 400, Maylands Avenue
Hemel Hempstead
Hertfordshire, HP2 7EZ
A division of
Simon & Schuster International Group

Typeset in 10/12pt Times
by Mathematical Composition Setters Ltd, Salisbury

Printed and bound in Great Britain by
Hartnolls, Bodmin

Designed by Lesley Stewart

Library of Congress Cataloging-in-Publication Data

Logothetis, N.
    Managing for total quality : from Deming to Taguchi and SPC / N.
Logothetis.
        p. cm. — (Manufacturing practitioner series)
    Includes bibliographical references.
    ISBN 0–13–553512–3
    1. Total quality management.   2. Manufactures—Management.
I. Title.   II. Series.
    HD62.15.L64 1992   92–9278
    658.5'62—dc20   CIP

British Library Cataloguing in Publication Data

A catalogue record for this book is available from
the British Library

ISBN 0–13–553512–3

1 2 3 4 5 96 95 94 93 92

To the memory of my father

Contents

Preface

Excellence is not an act, but a habit.
Aristotle

There is a quality challenge facing European companies. There is a new economic age, created by Japan and continuously affected not only by Japan but also by other Eastern countries such as Korea, Taiwan, Hong Kong and Singapore (known as the gang of four), as well as by the United States. In fact, American company managers have ceased to suffer from the 'not invented here' syndrome and, like their Japanese counterparts before them, have developed an eagerness to adapt, to become proficient with and to develop further ideas and methods which have arrived from overseas. Many Eastern and American 'quality gurus' have emerged and have advocated principles and techniques that already have a major impact on the improvement process of the manufacturing and service industry of their countries.

It is now Europe's turn. It is time to listen, to adapt, to (re)learn, to become comfortable with, to develop further. There is nothing wrong with this process. It has been working for years. It worked for the Japanese, it is working for the Americans – there is no reason it should not work for Europeans. After all, there is nothing to be ashamed of: the European continent is not just the cradle of the everlasting principles of democracy and civilization itself; it is also the origin of many of the methodologies and philosophies which form the backbone of the recent advances in quality-achieving techniques such as those of statistical analysis and experimental design, which the Japanese borrowed in the first place. Their usefulness and potential is now being rediscovered by Europe. The quality tools are returning to their cradle. The circle is complete.

Europe's strategic position on the globe, the multiplicity, diversity and wealth of its cultures, its traditions, ancient histories and political systems, and the opportunities provided by the economic integration of 1992 and the re-emergence of the East European economies make the European continent the ideal place for an enterprise to function and prosper. It also makes it a highly competitive and ruthless arena where one soon realizes that Darwin's law of survival of the fittest (company) applies without exception. Moreover, Europe is not immune to the universal truth of our times that, when it comes to quality, the consumer is no longer at the mercy of the producer; rather, it is the other way around.

But awareness is on the increase. The economic 'threat', especially from Japan, has already made many European companies aware of the need to improve the quality and reliability of their products and services, to optimize their processes, increase their productivity and minimize their costs. Efforts to discover the Japanese secret of industrial success have revealed the management principles of Dr W. Edwards Deming, an American statistician to whom the Americans would not listen in the early post-war years.

Deming's philosophy advocates widespread use of statistical ideas, with the top managers taking a strong initiative in building quality into all products, processes and services. This requires the minimization (through statistical techniques) of variability, something which will always lead to less waste, errors, costs and reworking and to high reliability, reputation and market share.

For controlling and reducing variability during production (on line), the method of statistical process control (SPC) ranks very highly among the programmes relating to quality improvement; furthermore, SPC is also seen in a wider context as being relevant to any department or any section of an organization, whether it be manufacturing, service, education or any other.

If one of Dr Deming's main contributions has been to convince people to shift quality improvement efforts from mass inspection to process control (through SPC), Dr Genichi Taguchi's has been to take the further step back from production to design. The design stage is the off-line stage. For dealing with variability at a pre-production stage and building in quality at a very early phase of the product or process development, Taguchi's techniques for off-line quality control are currently attracting a fast-growing interest in the West, with many successful applications being reported throughout Western industry. To safeguard the quality gains obtained through off-line control, SPC can be applied subsequently, thus completing the total quality loop.

Deming's and Taguchi's statistically minded scientific approach had as a beneficial effect the long overdue importing of statistical techniques into industry. Professional statisticians, passive by discipline, are now knocking on managers' doors with less timidity than before, strongly arguing that the use of statistical methods by everyone provides one of the most promising strategies for achieving excellence. However, for excellence to be attained, the gap between the managerial/engineering and statistical worlds has to be bridged; professionals on both sides need to understand each other's language, so that a common language is eventually routinely used and a common goal is eventually reached. Hence the scope of this book.

In this book, an attempt is made to show how Taguchi's approach and SPC can help to further the Deming ideals for an organization committed to improving quality in a total sense, at the off-line and on-line stages, in manufacturing and service, in management practices and workforce activities.

Although the book draws heavily on what Deming and Taguchi have to say, it also covers notable alternatives recommended by other quality gurus. Chapters 1–5 and 8–11 are primarily written for the attention of practising managers and/or students of management; education and practical involvement should start from the top for the quality initiative to have any chance of success. The book is also written for engineers (Chapters 8–15) and scientists with management ambitions, and for members of the business community. But it should not be viewed as a text just for managers. As a total quality approach is a necessity for every aspect of business, it is sincerely hoped that this book will appeal to every individual in an organization, from the top manager to the shop-floor engineer, or indeed to any employee who is in need of some guidelines for a better management of his/her activities, whether in manufacturing, service, health, education or any other.

An effort has been made to keep the technicalities to the minimum necessary. But inevitably, as is the case with any quality tools and techniques, some statistical issues (Chapters 6–7) could not be avoided. Some were included for completeness and can be overlooked at a first reading. It is hoped that the technical nature of some of the sections will not deter the reader from revisiting them at a later stage. If nothing else, such sections could be viewed as a reference manual for future use.

In an effort to help in the bridging of the existing gaps between theory and practice, between off-line and on-line quality control, between manufacturing and service industry applications, between the Japanese approach and Western standards, and, most importantly, between management and workforce, the present author, it is hoped representative of his own (European) educational and cultural traditions, will attempt to make some sense of the different ideas, and perhaps, less modestly, to provide some recommendations for the future.

N.L.
June 1991

Acknowledgments

Unless otherwise indicated, every practical example or case-study included in this book is the result of an actual study undertaken within the General Electric Company (GEC), UK, or within British Telecom (BT). I am deeply grateful to all the members of the different GEC and BT sites who allowed experiments or studies to take place and to be completed. I consider myself very fortunate to have been employed in these two great British institutions at a time when the 'quality evolution' was catching up with Western industries; my working environment could not have been better for allowing for innovation, for assimilation of the new ideas and for their utilization. I would especially like to thank Dr Derek Roberts, former deputy Managing Director of GEC, and Dr Cyril Hilsum, GEC's Director of Research, for their active support and help in the establishment of off-line quality control techniques within GEC. I am also grateful to all the members of BT's Management Science Consultant Unit (MSCU) – a truly TQM unit – and in particular Ted Gregory, MSCU's General Manager, John Allen and Dr John McKenzie, principal consultants, for actually proving to me how effective quality management can be, irrespective of the size of the company or the department.

As with any revolutionary movement, the total quality movement would not have started in the UK if it were not for the efforts and endless enthusiasm of two men: Dr Henry Neave, the founder of the British Deming Association, and Professor Tony Bendell, the founder of the Taguchi Club, the first quality societies of this type in Europe. I am grateful to them for the many stimulating discussions we have had together.

The American Supplier Institute Inc, Dearborn, Michigan, USA, is gratefully acknowledged for granting permission for the reproduction of some of the orthogonal arrays and triangular matrices from *Taguchi Methods: Orthogonal arrays and linear graphs; tools for quality engineering*, by G. Taguchi and S. Konishi (1987).

I would finally like to thank my wife Elena and my son Yiannis for being so inspirational during the writing of this book.

List of Case Studies

1 | Introduction

The problem is not to increase quality;
increasing quality is the answer to the problem.

Myron Tribus

■ 1.1 Total quality management: a new culture

It is being increasingly recognized that a high quality of product and service and their associated customer satisfaction are the key to survival for any enterprise. The nature of the current worldwide competition generally demands from any corporation the following four types of ability characteristic:

1. To understand what the customer wants and to provide it, immediately on demand, at the lowest cost.
2. To provide products and services of high quality and reliability consistently.
3. To keep up with the pace of change, technological as well as political and social.
4. To be one step ahead of the customer's needs; that is, to predict what the customer will want one year or ten years from now.

Of course, as Deming says: 'You don't have to do this; survival is not compulsory!' But the fact is that any company which lags behind in terms of any of the above characteristics will inevitably be overtaken by a competitor.

The attainment of those abilities requires an organized approach to management – an approach of managing for total quality, of managing for effectiveness and competitiveness, involving each and every activity and person at all levels in the organization. This is the total quality management (TQM) approach. Usually this approach will demand a total transformation of the existing management culture. There will be no room for complacency or half-hearted measures. There will be no alternative. If the quality revolution is to take root and succeed, a brand new culture will be required. TQM is such a culture – a culture advocating a total commitment to customer satisfaction through continuous improvement and innovation in all aspects of the business.

The customer in the TQM culture is not intended to mean only the final recipient of the corporation's end-product or service. The customer is also

1

every individual or department within the organization, which is now viewed as a chain of which only the final part is the external customer. Every person or departmental activity affects another, and in turn is affected by others. There is always a recipient of the output from every process – any activity, operation, action, single task or decision that is taking place. This makes everyone a customer of, and a supplier to, someone else, with quality inputs and outputs demanded and expected at every part of the chain. In the complex businesses of today, many different skills are involved (for just a single output), all heavily relying on each other. Hence the need for a proper method of communication and a common language, which TQM can supply.

Having as a basis the above definition of a customer, the actions required for the achievement of customer satisfaction become the everyday duties of every individual or division within the organization. Some of those routine duties could be as follows:

- To monitor performance and customer satisfaction levels.
- To identify improvements necessary in the customer interface.
- To deliver improved customer products and services at the lowest cost.
- To assess and agree the customer's requirements.
- To tailor output to the customer's demand.

When appropriate company policies have firmly been established, so that activities such as the above and the TQM definition of the customer become second nature for every employee in the company, the TQM culture will have been established.

Inevitably, the TQM culture will vary from company to company, in the same way that cultures vary from country to country. However, the essential principles are the same and equally useful, not only among the different organizations, but also among the different divisions of the same organization, such as procurement, accounting and finance, research and development, design, production, distribution, sales and marketing. They require the achievement and maintenance of quality on a total scale. This involves everyone in a common effort of improving every functional procedure which can be analysed by an examination of its inputs and outputs.

Major achievements include cost reduction and corporate success. But removal of waste, reduction of costs, improvement of reputation and increased market share are not the objectives; they are simply the natural consequences. Continuous improvement and innovation are the objectives, if, that is, one can give such a name to a non-static, updating and never-ending process. It is an objective without a completion date, because nothing can ever be immune from further improvement; new technologies, methods and attitudes or the presence of innovators and advocates of change will make sure of that.

In a TQM culture, the top managers are themselves the advocates of change. They must be, because no improvement can ever materialize without a change in the old management attitudes and, in particular, in the attitude embodied in the maxim, 'Stick to what you know!' You can never reach a stage when 'what you know' is enough. Progress and breakthrough have always been due to those advocates of change who did not want to adjust their actions to fit in with their environment; to those who eventually succeeded in making the environment fit with their beliefs and actions – actions which turned out to be correct. Progress and success for a company, therefore, can materialize only when a committed management accepts the challenge of change, and becomes the leader in defining a (new) total quality policy and in creating the conditions to enable everybody to fit into this policy.

Clearly, the process of change is not an easy one to manage. It is not only the commitment and the technical change (new methods and techniques for quality improvement) that need to materialize; more importantly, there is also the social change. One should be concerned with the social effect that any deviance from the norm usually has. Abandoning old habits and attitudes in favour of new ones can be an awesome task requiring, among other things, a large amount of faith and commitment. It is, indeed, difficult to change a corporate culture, which, by nature, usually evolves over a very long period of time. The basic values, the assumptions, the goals and beliefs which guide the way a company operates, and which probably still reflect the values of the company's founders, are what determines the face the company presents to the outside world. Old attitudes die hard and can be an obstacle to change. The greatest resistance usually comes from those who see the change as a threat to their status in the company. There are also those whose actions are always governed by a fear of failure, or even those who worry about the extra responsibility any new knowledge might bring. A manager who tries to change others will also have to be a behavioural scientist, an expert in human motivation, and proficient in the concepts of the existing culture, such as prevailing attitudes, beliefs, habits and practices. It is important, of course, that one should be careful not to create a culture vacuum by demolishing the old culture. For somebody genuinely to accept the change, a viable alternative should be on offer. The TQM culture provides such an alternative.

TQM provides an environment where fear is eliminated, where all the employees take pride in their work, where they feel respected and accepted, where they feel part of the same team, and where they strive not only for their own interests, but also for the interests of the whole organization. This probably sounds utopian and alien (by Western standards), but it is not impossible to achieve. It needs the establishment of the following three fundamental characteristics:

1. Commitment (to never-ending quality improvement and innovation).
2. Scientific knowledge (of the proper tools and techniques for the 'technical' change).
3. Involvement (all in one team, for the social change).

The above characteristics are so important that they can be considered as the axioms of the TQM culture. They are of equal significance, something that can

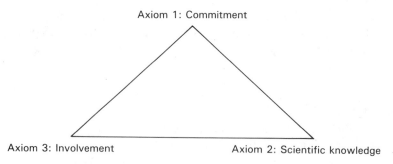

Figure 1.1 The TQM triangle

be expressed by putting them on the corners of an isosceles triangle, as Figure 1.1 shows. We will be revisiting the TQM triangle many times in the course of this book. The name of the triangle might change (into the 'Joiner triangle', the 'Deming triangle', the 'Crosby triangle' etc.), but the axioms behind it will basically remain the same.

The importance of the TQM axioms can never be overemphasized. Every principle, rule, modern technique or teaching from every quality guru to date can fit into one of the corners of the TQM triangle; and no statement about quality is complete unless all three axioms can somehow be read between the lines. A typical example can in fact be found in the publications of the UK government's Department of Trade and Industry:

> Modern Quality Management means adopting a total approach to quality. A vital ingredient is a commitment at the highest level to improving quality [need for Axiom 1].... This requires a company or organization to arrange every aspect of its activities in a cost effective way which ensures that a product or service is designed, built and delivered to meet the final customer's needs and expectations [need for Axiom 2]. A vital part of this is making every member of the organization aware of the importance of their role in achieving it [need for Axiom 3]. (Department of Trade and Industry, 1986)

It is worthwhile elaborating further on these TQM fundamentals.

■ 1.2 The TQM axioms

There is no such thing as a long-term, sustainable, competitive advantage without a sustainable effort for continuous improvement. The essence of the strategy should be the establishment of a TQM culture, through the realization of its three axioms. The interdependence of those axioms makes it easy to characterize the TQM environment fully, as well as to define clearly and in brief what we mean by TQM:

Total quality management is a culture; inherent in this culture is a total commitment to quality and an attitude expressed by everybody's involvement in the process of continuous improvement of products and services, through the use of innovative scientific methods.

The justification of this definition becomes apparent when we expand on each of the three TQM axioms.

1.2.1 Commitment

A management commitment to continually improving the quality of products and services sounds an obvious necessity, but it is not an easy commitment to adhere to. For some organizations this might require a complete shift from the old style of management, a total cultural transformation in the company. But there is no alternative, no easy way out. Quality is the major determining factor in the choice of the consumer, who is not prepared any more to accept second best, however attractive the price.

Improvement in everything can assist and enhance innovation, an absolute necessity in the competitive markets of today. The customer's ever-increasing expectations demand the urgent reconsideration of current practices and the development of a new strategy driven by a management-led focus on total quality. Senior managers should be the ones to plan, initiate and coordinate the quality improvement process and keep up the momentum when the initial enthusiasm dies down. This inevitably requires appropriate and adequate training and education, not just for the workforce but also for the managers themselves, who should be the first to demonstrate their commitment by active participation in quality improvement projects.

Management participation and demonstration by example are the best ways of convincing the workforce that the managers are serious about quality and that the same should be expected of everybody. Commitment should be demonstrated by actions from the very beginning, perhaps with the publication of signed quality policies and the formation of quality steering committees and quality councils involving top managers and directors. Actions are needed, not just words and declarations.

Slogans demanding quality from everyone are not likely to achieve anything but frustration, anxiety and isolation. Posters and exhortations do not usually say anything that the employee does not know already. Everybody wishes to do an excellent job, and a slogan is unnecessary even as a reminder. The majority of the workforce is already committed, provided the conditions are there for encouragement and help. It is the management's responsibility to create the right conditions and the appropriate environment for quality to flourish and be maintained. Only then can quality become an inseparable aspect of everybody's activities. It is not the fault of the shop-floor engineer when a product consistently turns out to be defective if the materials, originally purchased on the basis of a (low) price tag, were not the appropriate ones. No amount of patronizing posters demanding zero defects will improve the output if the input was wrong in the first place. A worker can function as well as the system allows; beyond this lies the management's responsibility. And it is the manager who should ensure that the worker is motivated and not handicapped by the system. Only then do the tasks become challenging and meaningful, only then is the hidden potential of the workforce utilized to the full.

Proper working conditions, adequate education and training, good communication and cooperation, modern leadership rather than strict supervision, good incoming materials and equipment, appropriate quality tools and job satisfaction are some of the ingredients of a system that can motivate. Such a system needs a change in attitudes and culture, something that is impossible unless there is real commitment to quality and innovation from the senior management. Such a change cannot be made to materialize by merely creating a 'quality department' and then forgetting about it. The quality problem will not be made to go away by passing the responsibility to somebody else and by having a scapegoat to blame when things go wrong. And things are certainly going to go wrong if just one person, the quality manager, is responsible for quality.

But if the top managers' responsibility is to plant the seed of the quality tree (company quality policy, demonstration of commitment) and to provide the appropriate soil and environmental conditions (creation of a system appropriate to a TQM culture), the middle managers' responsibility is equally important in ensuring that the quality tree is continuously nourished and strengthened. They will be the ones to ensure that the TQM principles are being communicated and spread adequately throughout the company so that the TQM culture is maintained and eventually brings results. They will also act as the link between the top management and the workforce so that the hidden potential of the latter is recognized, paid the attention that it deserves and rewarded accordingly. TQM will then become a common language, helping to break down all barriers and making it easier for the management's commitment (to total quality) to become everybody's commitment.

High quality and innovation are achievable by every individual, assuming the appropriate TQM structure is in place. This requires, among other things, a commitment to education, training and retraining on well-established and up-to-date, innovative quality improvement techniques. Everybody is in need of proper education, from the top manager down, and not just a one-off course, but continuous training. This, of course, assumes a willingness on the part of the management to invest in the future development of the workforce; a willingness to regard the workforce as an asset, not as a commodity; a commitment to long-term survival and growth, not just to short-term profits; a faith that there will be a future. But no future is possible without the attainment of the appropriate knowledge – scientific knowledge.

1.2.2 Scientific knowledge

There is no excuse any more for passing the responsibility for quality to others. Tools do exist; tools for the manager, tools for the technician, tools that can be utilized by both the manager and the technician. There is a scientific theory supporting each of those tools, something that validates them beyond doubt. Their value has already been proved in practice, in a way that can convince even the most difficult unbeliever. There is no excuse any more not to use them.

The majority of the scientific methods are applicable to both manufacturing and service industry, and equally usable by a manager and a shop-floor engineer. Apart from providing a common language throughout the organization, they help in the assignment of responsibilities; they provide exact boundaries which fairly separate everybody's duties and obligations concerning quality, so that the vicious circle of blame, unjust recrimination and apathy is eliminated. The workers can now know where their responsibilities for quality end, and where those of the management begin; this knowledge is not contaminated by meaningless slogans, unjustified opinions, emotions or unrealistic expectations.

There is a quality tool for everybody, something that inevitably makes the current practices of a quality control department obsolete. And so it should be, especially in cases where outdated methods of mass inspection are still in use, because no amount of inspection of the end-product can improve quality or compensate for bad quality. What is needed is emphasis on continuously improving the process that produces the product, perhaps from as early on as its design stage. This is something that everybody could be responsible for, given the right conditions; because, everybody, one way or another, is involved in some kind of a process which produces a product or service.

Of course, a quality department does not have to become redundant; only its outdated practices. The role of a TQM quality department should be that of coordination, education and support of scientific quality tools throughout the organization. Additional duties should include continuous research on and development of innovative methods or further development of existing ones. Its best role should be that of the source of scientific knowledge and the advocate of the belief that everybody should be responsible for quality. Given the necessary scientific tools, every individual can pinpoint a cause of bad performance and take care of it as soon as possible, thus perhaps preventing a major problem, rather than relying on the quality control department to act at a point that is probably too late. Then, the value of prevention becomes obvious; because avoiding major errors and thus cutting down on fire-fighting and waste can in fact contribute far more to company profits than, say, an expensive marketing and advertising campaign. 'Prevention rather than cure' is the basis of the philosophy for a company striving for 100% efficiency.

But prevention needs predictability, and statistical techniques can provide it. They can be utilized to determine the current process capability and what is attainable, so that reasonable quality targets can be set. There are techniques for keeping attained quality in control, and others for achieving further break-throughs. Innovation naturally becomes the next stage, and new processes can more easily be developed in order to take care of customer requirements a year or ten years from now. There are methods for building quality in the process at the earliest stage of its development, so that 'Do it right first time' is not just another unjustified exhortation.

Scientific knowledge helps in the creation of the proper conditions so that all employees can take responsibility for the quality of their own tasks and accept ownership of certain quality problems as they arise. Employee flex-ibility and adaptability then become a way of life. Quality output is seen as an expected reward rather than a forced obligation. Job satisfaction, with pride in one's work, is then one of many consequences; company survival is another. Indeed, as H.G. Wells says (in Chapter 15 of *The Outline of History*): 'Human history becomes more and more of a race between educa-tion and catastrophe.' Certainly, one way to avoid economic catastrophe is through quality education.

A commitment to quality without the proper means to make it a reality can only be a short-lived commitment. A quality programme launched by ceremonies and fancy declarations of faith to TQM ideas can only lead to frustration, low morale and bad feelings unless the words are accompanied by the provision of the appropriate tools; these tools should be matched to the TQM structure, one of senior management's responsibilities. The result of a successful matching will be the creation of a learning culture, the refinement of total quality and the redistribution of knowledge throughout the organiza-tion; eventually, the bridging of the gap between what the customer wants and what the customer gets.

One of the main advantages of scientific knowledge is that it provides a common language which can facilitate communication between the different departments and between individuals. A common language, supported by the necessary commitment, can certainly facilitate the realization of the third TQM axiom – involvement.

1.2.3 Involvement

If Axiom 1 and Axiom 2 are concerned respectively with structural and techno-logical aspects, Axiom 3 is concerned with the social aspect. No TQM initiative has any chance of bringing about a TQM culture unless the social factor is properly addressed, because total quality is not about a particular process or department, or about the responsibilities of a particular quality manager. It concerns everybody in the company and it requires a new social attitude and a new network of relationships. A management commitment to improvement will remain a mere commitment unless the workforce is motivated enough to get involved in the effort. Any initiative concerning, say, the introduction of new scientific methods will fail unless the methods are adaptable to the needs of the people who use them.

Higher salaries and monetary rewards can motivate only on a short-term basis; taking pride in one's work and being involved in the achievement of excellence are the real motivators for the long term. There is no doubt that the majority of the people basically want to feel respected and accepted by others. They genuinely want to feel part of a team striving for a common goal and sharing in the successes and failures. They value the trust shown in them and are stimulated to greater effort if they know that they can actually influence other activities with their own action, and understand that somebody else depends on them. Given the choice, they would rather contribute to a common effort than become outsiders, feeling isolated and useless. They will continue to contribute if they know that genuine effort will be properly appreciated, despite the fact that they may not always be successful in their endeavours; this is because teamwork provides a strong basis to absorb occasional failures. After all, nobody is perfect, and two can certainly achieve more than one can; many problems are beyond the capabilities of just one individual or even just one department. Many problems are common to every department, and cooperation is the only way forward.

Everyone has a part to play, because the chain of conformity to the customer's requirements is always built up from many related processes, each of equal importance. Indeed, the teamwork argument is so compelling that one is surprised to see that many organizations are still not making better use of it. Of course, achievement of a real team spirit presupposes absence of fear and mistrust, absence of communication barriers, absence of secrecy and competitive feelings, absence of individualism and isolation. Such a climate can only be created when top management changes the system accordingly. Only then is the enormous potential of the workforce released for the benefit of the individual as well as of the company as a whole.

The capability for solving problems increases many times when there is a common effort. When problems are discussed in brainstorming sessions, they are more likely to be examined critically and in detail. Team members help each other to rule out mistakes and to provide many potential solutions. A team brings together a vast amount of skill in problem solving and idea generation. In the end, there is more chance for a right solution to emerge from averaging out many potential solutions.

Involving everybody in the common pursuit of quality will ensure that all interdependent processes can function to their maximum capacity, and can be seen to do so right the way through. Maximum efficiency can only be achieved by the utilization of the valuable experience of the people nearest to the process. This experience, shared through open, honest and adequate communication, and helped by modern quality improvement techniques, can achieve results far superior to the ones obtained through isolated efforts or through a campaign of unsupported slogans and exhortations. Demanding excellence without providing the means to achieve it promotes passive resistance, individualistic competitiveness and lack of team spirit, which can only impede any efforts for overall quality improvement.

Of course, competitive instincts can never be eliminated. But this does not have to be a negative aspect. When a natural commitment to teamwork is ingrained deeply enough to withstand or even benefit from competitive efforts, innovation will be taking place more naturally and eagerness to change will be the norm. When such a healthy situation is allowed to develop normally, encouraging the emergence of competing unit cultures within the same company might help the business units to be more responsive to fast-changing markets. Models can then be created so that other units can learn from the culture of the firm's most successful division. But top managers should be extremely careful of how they control the evolution of a healthy competitive element within the company; this has to follow naturally the evolution of a controlled and healthy TQM culture, or it will be the cause of the company tearing itself apart.

To control an evolution, which, when it comes to changing a culture, amounts to a revolution, one should be a firm and knowledgeable leader, but also an evolutionary part of the process itself. It is essential that active participation and communication are promoted by the actual involvement of senior managers, who should help quality improvement projects to get started, and who should encourage the open discussion of problems. It is also essential that adequate resources for training are provided and adequate time is allowed for planning, brainstorming sessions and team meetings. This will in turn require that recommendations (resulting from the brainstorming sessions) are accepted, proposed changes are implemented, constraints on operator control are removed, process ownership and greater responsibility are allowed, continuous monitoring of the improvement process takes place and the momentum is maintained.

All these requirements may sound awesome, but they can easily materialize when management commitment is there; which brings us back to Axiom 1.

■ 1.3 Consequences of total quality

In the line of their duties, many senior managers define objectives that they wish to be met in the short or long run. They focus on general issues or specific targets, such as customer satisfaction, meeting specifications, larger market share, higher productivity, zero defects, $x\%$ increase in sales, $y\%$ decrease in costs etc. By embedding a quality ethic in all aspects of the organization, all the above objectives can become mere consequences. They can be achieved naturally and painlessly by continuously striving towards a single objective: total quality attainment. In a TQM culture, the customer is the most important part of the process line, and if process quality is attained, customer satisfaction is guaranteed. Quality products and services ensure not only the customer's future return, but also fewer complaints and lower warranty costs, higher profits, improved reputation and hence increased market share.

Decreases in costs under warranty are not the only cost reduction to be achieved. Continuous process improvement will make zero defects a reasonable expectation. The higher the improvement, the lower the number of inferior products. Energy and working hours can then be saved, because materials have to be replaced less often, machines have to be stopped for adjustment less frequently, and less effort needs to be allocated for inspection of the final output. This can only lead to prompt deliveries and higher productivity levels, and simultaneously to lower costs for repair and reworking.

Reduction in costs can allow the setting of lower, more competitive prices on the end-product or service, which proves that investment in process quality does not necessarily mean higher prices for the process output. But even if price reduction is not possible, quality should not be compromised, because the consumer these days is willing to pay more for quality, and is no longer prepared to subsidize inferior products or services.

It is clear, therefore, that any investment in quality will eventually pay off. Corporate success will be the outcome of this investment. This success will be measured not only by customer satisfaction, profits and market share, but also by improved employee morale, certainty and efficiency in operations, innovation (a necessity for future survival), teamwork and effective communication, respect for the management as well as the workforce and, consequently, fewer complaints, a happier working environment and improved industrial relations. On the whole, investment in continuous total quality improvement will guarantee the survival and prosperity of the business, the protection of the initial investment, future dividends and more jobs.

So, total quality should be the objective; everything else follows as a result. One of the certain results is the reduction of the costs of quality, a favourite measure of success in many corporations.

■ 1.4 Costs of total quality

Quality costs are generally any costs associated with the discovery (appraisal costs) and fixing (failure costs) of poor quality, and also the costs associated with preventing poor quality (prevention costs). Because of the quality costs involved in every quality improvement project, many people still regard quality improvement efforts as a cost burden, which inevitably will have to be shouldered by the customer.

This may be the case (and still is in many organizations) when the only actions involved in the quality programme are increased efforts for mass inspection, reworking of defective items, reinspection, performance evaluation, frequent quality audits, checking the quality of received goods and capital investment in new machinery. Most of these actions are negative in terms of quality attainment. They are not likely to contribute anything to the improvement process. They encourage the belief that defects are inevitable, and so the only way to avoid poor quality reaching the customer is to put more effort into the discovery and fixing of the defective item. This attitude encourages passivity and complacency, and in fact contributes to the increase of poor quality and total costs; mass inspection is never foolproof, reworked items are more likely to go wrong etc. Moreover, rising quality costs are often a reflection of company bureaucracy, rather than the true cost of improvement and innovation. No wonder that the customer eventually has to pay more — not necessarily for better quality.

But it does not have to be so. If enough effort is put into proper education in the use of quality tools for preventing poor quality, the two negative components of the quality costs, failure and appraisal costs, will be reduced as a result. The positive component, prevention costs, is a necessity, and so, if anything, should be expected to increase. But the total quality costs will decrease, as a mere consequence of the total quality initiative.

At the initial stages of the quality initiative, monitoring quality costs might serve a purpose in raising the level of awareness of quality problems. It might be helpful in the appreciation of the size of the non-value-added activities, and thus motivate efforts for improvement. However, when a TQM culture is firmly in place, calculating the costs of quality does not serve any purpose; after all, on many occasions, the most important costs might be incalculable or unknowable. Most importantly, monitoring quality costs accounts only for where the costs fall, not where they are caused. The outcome of this monitoring might even be the result of fiddling with the figures, dishonesty or unnecessary cost cutting. There is a danger of it eventually becoming at best a non-value-added activity, and at worst a failure cost in its own right.

Let us not forget that reduction of quality costs is a consequence and does not have to be an objective to aim for continuously. One thing is certain: take care of quality, and quality costs will take care of themselves!

■ 1.5 Valuable tools for quality

The tools for quality attainment can be broadly classified in the following two main categories:

1. Management tools for quality.
2. Statistical tools for quality.

It should be stressed, however, that the tools of category 1 are not for the sole use of management, and those of category 2 are not for the sole use of the technician or operator. Both types are tools for the process, with process being any activity. There are tools for managing the process, and there are tools for technically improving the process: both types can be used by anybody, from the top manager to the shop-floor engineer. In a TQM culture, everybody has a responsibility for managing as well as technically improving his/her activities. Both types have a common aim: the attainment of quality. Of course, although scientific knowledge means adequate knowledge of both types of tool, it is inevitable that the first category will be most useful to managers, whereas the second will be so to the people concerned with the technical side of the process.

There are many valuable techniques advocated by various quality gurus, and a fair number of them will be described in this book. But in the opinion of this author, there are certain principles and techniques which are outstanding; for category 1, these are the principles and management rules advocated by Dr W. Edwards Deming, and for category 2, the techniques under the banner of statistical process control (SPC) and the methods advocated by Dr Genichi Taguchi. Their usefulness has already been demonstrated in practice in a plethora of situations, and their theoretical value has been recognized beyond doubt.

Deming provides a philosophy of management, a theory of management and specific, powerful rules capable of transforming any company culture into a true TQM culture. On the other hand, the innovative techniques advocated by Taguchi and SPC provide the means for technically improving any process in a total sense; that is, its every stage, from design to production and maintenance, and also for keeping improved processes under control. It is worthwhile outlining briefly the main points of these techniques:

1.5.1 The Deming approach

Dr W. Edwards Deming has been called the founder of the third wave of the Industrial Revolution. His name has become synonymous with the reason for Japanese industrial success in the second half of the twentieth century. The successful implementation of his approach has greatly contributed to Japan's high reputation for quality and reliability, and therefore to its industrial success. Japan's highest industrial award is named after him: the Deming Prize is awarded annually to the one company or individual who has contributed most to the enhancement of statistical techniques, and to their improved application in design, research and development, manufacturing or service.

Deming advocates the implementation of a statistical quality management approach. He considers it critically important that top managers acquire knowledge, or at least a clear appreciation, of the usefulness of statistical tools for achieving enhanced quality and increased productivity. His philosophy is encapsulated in his fourteen points for management, which will be described in detail in Chapter 2. The essential elements of his process-oriented approach can be represented by only three main principles, which B.J. Joiner puts at the corners of an equilateral triangle (hence the name 'Joiner triangle' – see Figure 1.2), and which are as follows:

1. **Obsession with quality:** The key to improved quality is focusing on efforts for continuous improvement of all processes. Numerous processes need improvement, including those which are not normally thought of as being under control and those which are not usually thought of as processes, such as the training of employees, the purchasing of materials, customer services etc. Preoccupation with quality should be the business of the day, every day, in an obsessive manner so that nothing else takes priority.

2. **Use of the scientific method:** The use of the scientific approach – not opinion or emotion – is the best way forward for improving processes. Statistical data-based techniques help managers to focus their attention on the process system rather than on individuals, and take decisions based on facts and unprejudiced information and not on subjective gut feelings or unrealistic expectations. Statistical methods can help in the deep understanding of the nature of variation, the enemy of quality. They can be utilized to determine the source of variation and then help to control or eliminate it. Through them, one can successfully exploit the information generated by the processes, which information can in turn be used to anticipate, identify and correct mistakes, thus improving quality and achieving excellence.

3. **All in one team:** This describes the achievement of a feeling among employees that they are all part of one team working towards a common goal, towards self-improvement as well as long-term company success. There is no place for barriers, isolation and fear; no place for departmental competition and conflict, usually the result of management-set arbitrary targets and numerical goals. The top managers should play a major role in the establishment of a team spirit, by being themselves actively involved in the quality improvement effort. The team spirit should extend outside the company, to cover even the subcontractors and the suppliers, in an atmosphere of cooperation and trust.

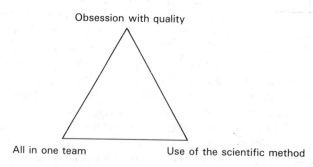

Figure 1.2 The Joiner triangle

It is quite obvious that the Joiner triangle is equivalent to the TQM triangle mentioned in Section 1.1. It is therefore clear that the Deming path to quality management is implicit in a TQM culture.

Dr W.E. Deming, having helped the Japanese to rebuild their industries after World War II, has made it his mission to spread the same ideals to the Western world. These ideals, embodied in his fourteen points for management (see Chapter 2), stress the importance of commitment by everybody to continuous improvement in products, processes and services, with the help of the scientific method. The key has been to adopt predictive quality control techniques which quickly identify and solve problems before they become the cause of costly output of waste. Statistical process control (SPC) is such a technique, and it has already been proved that it makes a vital contribution to improved quality and efficiency in every area of an organization. This valuable tool and its connection with Deming are briefly described next (see also Part III).

1.5.2 Deming and SPC

Deming himself would have summarized the whole of his philosophy in just two words: Reduce variation. These two words are fundamental to the principle of continuous improvement and to the achievement of consistency, reliability, uniformity. In other words, trustworthiness, competitive position and success. Reducing variation was also the purpose of the work of Walter Shewhart, the inventor of the control chart, the main tool of SPC. Shewhart's work in the 1920s was initially focused on the reduction of variability in the performance of the telephones at Bell Laboratories. However, Deming soon realized that Shewhart's ideas were capable of much wider application, not only in the manufacturing but also in the non-manufacturing environment.

The basis of measurement is a performance indicator, either individual, group or departmental, calculated over time (hourly, daily, weekly etc.). Plotting the performance measures on a chart may produce a pattern, on the basis of which appropriate action can be taken. SPC involves a scientific step, which is to carry out the necessary calculations so that performance-based lines, the control limits, can be put on the chart. While the sample results remain randomly between the upper and lower limit, the process is deemed to be under control. Non-random behaviour or departures outside the limits require immediate corrective action to bring the process back to a stable state. This stable state is what in SPC terminology is called a state of statistical control, a state where the variation, although still existent, is controllable and predictable.

Measuring performance and determining whether or not it conforms to the requirement of statistical control is not the only function of SPC. It is also intended to lead action on the processes at the appropriate time, so that the process variation is minimized and major problems are prevented in the future. The timing and type of, and the responsibility for, these actions depend on whether the causes of variation are controlled (common) or uncontrolled (special).

Special and common causes

In Shewhart's terminology, uncontrolled variation is due to assignable causes, while controlled variation is due to unassignable, chance or random causes. Deming refers to them as special and common causes respectively.

Violation of the limits in a control chart, or the presence of a specific pattern within the control limits, indicates the existence of special causes of variation which are often easily recognizable: changes of operator or shift, changes in raw material, breakages, misreading of scales, occasional wrong settings of the machines etc. These causes are not common to all the operations involved, and so their discovery and removal requires local action by someone who is directly connected with the operation.

Common causes are the many sources of variation within a process that is under statistical control. These could be uncontrollable environmental conditions, the inflexibility of aged machines, variability in purchased materials, component tolerances, or other non-obvious causes of variation which may or may not be present at any one time, but which, when taken together, produce random results. They behave like a constant system of chance causes. The resolution of common causes of variation requires action on the system; this is usually the responsibility of management because it requires change to the process itself, in the way it has been designed and built or set up.

Misinterpreting either type of cause as the other and acting accordingly not only fails to improve matters, it can actually make things worse. It would be very wrong, for example, to take local action (such as readjusting a machine) when management action on the system was required (such as selecting suppliers that provide consistent input materials — one of Deming's management principles).

The benefit of the techniques of SPC lies in their ability to provide a common language which can help everybody in an organization to avoid tampering with the process, and to distinguish correctly between special and common causes, thus avoiding unnecessary blame and recrimination. Proper decisions can then be taken as to what sort of action is required and whose responsibility this action should be. Industrial experience suggests that only about 15% of process troubles are due to special causes and therefore correctable locally by people directly connected with the operation. The majority of the problems — the other 85% — are correctable only by management action on the system.

One thing should be clear: control limits are not specification limits. Control limits do not depend on any demands, prespecified requirements or economic necessities; they only depend on how the process is actually performing at the time. This makes the control chart a valuable operator's tool: through it the process is talking to the operator, at any time the operator cares to listen. It is also a valuable management tool: managers making decisions on processes in statistical control stand a much better chance of actually affecting the company's future.

An ideal tool that can help in the effort to deal with any kind of variation, and in particular variation arising from common causes (the most difficult to determine and remove), is briefly outlined next.

1.5.3 From Deming to Taguchi

If Deming's teachings inspire a revolution in the old management culture, Taguchi's approach is an inspired evolution; an evolution of valuable statistical techniques which have their origins in the practices of Roland Fisher at the Rothamstead Agricultural Centre in the 1920s.

Much of the work derives from the management principles propounded by W.E. Deming (see Chapter 2), in particular Point 3: 'Cease dependence on inspection to achieve quality.' In other words, eliminate the need for mass inspection by building quality into the product and process at the design stage. This idea was taken up by Dr Genichi Taguchi, director of the Japanese Academy of Quality and four-times recipient of the Deming Prize. His quality improvement approach uses experimental design methods for efficient characterization of a product or process, combined with a statistical analysis of its variability. The technique allows quality considerations to be included at an early stage of any new venture: in the design and prototype phase for a product; before full production commences; during installation and commissioning of a manufacturing process; or even during routine maintenance. As the method allows quality to be improved and maintained independently of the production line, it belongs to the group of techniques under the banner of off-line quality control.

It is worth listing the main components of Taguchi's philosophy (see also Part IV).

Quality and the loss function

Taguchi defines quality in a negative way as 'the loss imparted to society from the time the product is shipped'. This loss includes the cost of customer dissatisfaction, which may lead to a loss of reputation and goodwill for the company. Taguchi uses his loss-function approach to establish a value base for the development of quality products. The function recognizes the need for average performance to match customer requirements, and for the variability of this performance to be as small as possible. According to Taguchi, a product causes a loss not only when it is outside specification, but also whenever it deviates from its target value; this loss is proportional to the square of the deviation from the target. So one should always attempt to attain the target by minimizing variability.

Objective

The objective of the method is process and product-design improvement through the identification of easily controllable factors and their settings, which minimize the variation in the product response while keeping the mean response on target. By setting those factors at their optimal levels, the product can be made robust to changes in operating and environmental conditions or, generally, to the effects of uncontrollable factors. Thus, more stable and higher-quality products can be obtained, and this is achieved by removing the bad effect of the cause rather than the cause of the bad effect. If the 'cause' is uncontrollable, there is indeed no alternative. Furthermore, since the method is applied in a systematic way independently of the pre-production stage (off line), it can greatly reduce the number of time-consuming tests needed to determine cost-effective process conditions, thus saving on costs and wasted products.

Background of the method

There are two main aspects to the Taguchi technique. First, the behaviour of a product or process is characterized in terms of factors (parameters) that are separated into two types as follows:

1. Controllable (or design) factors – those whose values may be set or easily adjusted by the designer or process engineer.
2. Uncontrollable (or noise) factors – those often associated with the production or operational environment. The overall performance should, ideally, be insensitive to their variation.

Second, the controllable factors are divided into those which affect the average levels of the response of interest – referred to as target control factors – and those which affect the variability in the response – the variability control factors. It is this concentration on variability which distinguishes the Japanese approach from traditional tolerance methods or inspection-based quality control. The aim is to reduce variability by changing the variability control factors, while maintaining the required average performance through adjustments to the target control factors.

Careful experimentation is required to achieve satisfactory product or process characterization. However, by using the methods of statistical experimental design, it is possible to study the effects of many factors within relatively few appropriately selected trials. The results of these trials are then used to compute certain statistical measures, called performance measures, which quantify quality. Analysis of these will provide the means to estimate and minimize the effect of the noise factors on the product's performance.

The technique is a straightforward, well-integrated system for implementing statistical experimental designs; it has already been proved capable of improving both simple and complex processes and products with the minimum of experiment at an off-line stage. It encourages proper experimentation and closer association between statisticians and engineers, and increases statistical awareness in industry. If one of Deming's main achievements has been to convince companies to shift quality improvement backwards from inspection to SPC, Taguchi's has been to take the further step back from production to design, in an attempt to make the design robust (at the off-line stage) against variability downstream in both production and the user environment. This is in complete agreement with Deming's belief that reducing variation is the key to improving quality, to decreasing quality costs, and therefore to survival in this new economic age.

■ 1.6 The Japanese factor

If one attempts to identify the strategies behind Japan's industrial success, the TQM principles are bound to surface: never-ending programmes of quality improvement, actively supported by management and involving everybody in the organization. There is a Japanese word describing the approach of gradual process improvement involving everybody – *kaizen*. In Japan, *kaizen* is everybody's business, and many systems have been developed to make managers and workers *kaizen*-conscious. In the words of Masaaki Imai, the author of *KAIZEN: The key to Japan's competitive success*: 'KAIZEN is the simple truth behind Japan's economic miracle and the real reason the Japanese have become the masters of "flexible manufacturing" technology – the ability to adapt manufacturing processes to changing customer and market requirements, and do it fast.' Imai advocates that *kaizen*, which means step-by-step gradual improvement in the nature of refinements or enhancements, doing little things better, continuously setting and achieving ever-higher standards, is as important as breakthrough innovations. Indeed, the whole of the Japanese business philosophy is based on a successful combination of two strategies: *kaizen* and innovation.

The innovation strategy favoured by the United States in the post-war years was the only strategy in a period of low-cost resources, expanding markets and low international competition. At that time, quantity was more important than quality, and management was more concerned with increasing sales than with reducing costs. Western industry believed this would last for ever and ignored the quality-based teachings of experts such as W.E. Deming and Joseph Juran (see Chapter 3), who, consequently, decided to turn their attention to the East.

Japan, having been burned to the ground during the war, encouraged a climate of change from the start. Japanese managers took seriously the warnings about forthcoming changes in the customer's perception of quality and about the future demands for faster development of customer-oriented products and services. So they successfully combined the strategy of innovation with that of continuous quality improvement; this brought a reduction in costs, faster development times, prompt deliveries, customer satisfaction and enormous competitive advantage internationally. *Kaizen* was the element of the overall company strategy that was missing from Western industries. The Western approach was always based on the belief that innovation alone was enough for survival and growth. This has already been proved wrong on many occasions.

Many people, trying to explain the Japanese success, still attribute it to cultural factors. But if this were the case, why did Japan appear on the quality map only during the second half of the twentieth century and not before? The difference-in-culture approach is the easy excuse offered by those managers in the West who do not want to admit their own guilt for the quality mess their company is in, or by those who want to avoid the responsibility of actually doing something about it. The fact is that the Japanese success has much to do with good management practices and little to do with national cultural factors. The distinction is not one of national culture; it is one of company culture, something that top management has absolute responsibility for. *Kaizen*, a customer-oriented approach to improvement, became the foundation on which the whole structure of successful Japanese management was built. It unifies the philosophy, the systems and the problem-solving tools which have helped Japanese products and services to obtain the quality reputation they currently enjoy.

There are two distinct features inherent in the *kaizen* philosophy, as follows:

1. There is an urgency about the never-ending efforts for improvement and gradual change for the better. Repetitiveness is considered as negative and as an inhibitor to progress.
2. There is an emphasis on the process rather than on the output. 'Build quality into the process' was and still is a popular Japanese phrase, based on the realization that mass inspection of the output is a non-value-added activity, incapable of improving quality.

Kaizen obviously has a lot in common with Deming's philosophy. In fact, *kaizen* is based on Deming's teachings to the Japanese in the early 1950s. Since then, other concepts, systems and tools have been developed, such as QC circles, *kanban* (just-in-time), zero defects, total quality control (TQC) etc., which are all incorporated under the umbrella of *kaizen* (see also Chapter 5). But Deming's process-oriented way of thinking, based on the principle of continuous quality improvement and involving people at all levels of the organization, is what the *kaizen* message is all about.

A personal thought

It is indeed ironic to observe, yet again, how much Western ideas have contributed to the birth and development of an Eastern economic superpower, with the West being left behind. But it is never too late to relearn. Our Western intellectual wealth awaits rediscovery. Once this is achieved, we can develop further and move in front, once again. During the journey of rediscovery, some old principles and techniques will be appreciated for the first time, perhaps after a delay of over half a century. But better late than never.

This appreciation will probably be due to the fact that the true value of these methods has already been demonstrated by the Japanese. Indeed, if the East has to thank the West for their discovery, the West can thank the East for proving their validity in practice. But development is made up of two complementary components: discovery and validation. In that sense, it was a partnership on a global scale, with East and West contributing towards a common goal, the development of valuable tools for quality. So up to now, nobody has lost; both sides have benefited from each other. And it does not have to be any different in the future. Global team spirit can develop in the same way as company team spirit can. The rapid development of global telecommunications makes this even easier. It all depends on whether the desire for global cooperation exists to make it also inevitable. Whether this will happen nobody can tell, but the future looks exciting enough!

PART I
Management Tools
for Quality

> *Management is like sex or politics or religion: all of us do it, most of us are convinced that our way is the best, few of us bother to ask if we have met the other's needs and expectations.*
>
> R.J. Mortiboys

In this part of the book (Chapters 2–5) we examine the management principles propounded by certain experts in the field of quality management. The approaches of these quality gurus have had a major influence in the management culture of many organizations worldwide, in both the manufacturing and service sectors.

Most of the original quality gurus who have emerged, mainly in the second part of the twentieth century, are Americans. The most notable among those are W. Edwards Deming (see Chapter 2) and Joseph Juran (see Chapter 3), who in the early 1950s preached the importance of quality to the Japanese, thus contributing to the birth of an Eastern economic superpower. The list of other important quality experts includes the Americans Philip Crosby, examined in Chapter 4, and Armand Feigenbaum (see Chapter 5), and also the Japanese Masaaki Imai, Kaoru Ishikawa, Taiichi Ohno and Shigeo Shingo, who are all mentioned in Chapter 5.

It is apparent that quality expertise seems to originate from either the United States or Japan. But whether the quality guru is an American or Japanese does not matter. It does not even matter what the definition of quality actually is; after all, there is no such thing as a universally accepted definition. There are many interpretations of quality, depending on the different situations and circumstances one has to deal with. What really matters is a genuine aspiration to improve products and services in order to satisfy the customer – the most important part of the production line. This is the main unifying element in the teaching of all quality gurus to date.

There is certainly no such thing as an American, Japanese or European concept of quality, and there is not much point trying to establish one. It matters little if an industrial sector develops its own sense of quality criteria as long as, at the end of the day, these criteria can contribute to the customer's satisfaction. Those who attempt to develop a European concept of quality are usually those who want to establish themselves as authorities or European gurus in an effort to cash in on the commercial advantages that this concept might bring in a post-1992 unified Europe. It is actually tampering with the learning process if everybody tries to develop new definitions of quality or a new set of fourteen rules, when Deming's well-proved fourteen points, Juran's diagnostic and remedial tools and Crosby's quality treatments already exist to teach us the best way of managing a business – a way that is not dependent on any national or continental boundaries and borders. The benefits of quality (whatever its definition) and the tools for attaining them are universal. This immediately becomes clear when one studies in depth the (true) teachings of the original quality gurus. Relaunching old products under new names never led anywhere.

The next four chapters may sometimes appear repetitive. This only demonstrates that the similarities in the teachings of these men are greater than their differences.

The question, of course, arises as to what should be the best choice of a quality guru whose teachings one should learn and adopt. A simple answer does not exist. There is no such thing as a quick-fix solution to quality problems, and the application of certain management tools as advocated by a certain expert should not become an end in itself. What matters, first of all, is to promote quality awareness throughout the company; this requires, among other things, awareness of what all eminent quality experts have to say. Having adequately appreciated and understood the various messages and management tools the main quality gurus have to offer, a good first step would be to attempt to implement the principles that are common to the teachings of all of them. Since the common elements in the various quality philosophies constitute a majority rather than a minority, the question as to which of the quality gurus is right for your company becomes completely irrelevant, and does not even deserve an answer.

As far as the differences in those teachings are concerned, one should set them in perspective and realistically assess their relative merit. An unbiased decision for adopting one instead of another can only be taken if all these differences are studied in depth, with all the views of the gurus (about their individual merits) being taken into consideration. In this way, one might even find that most of these differences are actually complementary aspects of the same (valid) principle; or that the difference is really in style rather than in substance. For example, Juran prefers to start his quality efforts from where the management currently is, whereas Deming preaches about the stage where the management ought to be; Juran's teachings also have a more technical flavour than Deming's. These things do not make Deming and Juran different. They both have many valuable messages to offer, and the teachings of both can be accommodated in the company's culture perfectly well.

But it can never be overstated that, whatever the management programme followed, it should not be regarded as an end in itself, but as a means to an end: the creation and continuance of a company-wide TQM culture.

2 The Deming Approach to Management

You do not have to do this;
survival is not compulsory!
W. Edwards Deming

The threat of worldwide competition has made many organizations aware of the need to improve their products and services. At an increasing rate, Western management is now attempting to follow the Japanese example by adopting a consistent approach to quality, which is currently considered as the most vital ingredient for corporate success. However, it so happens that the quality management principles mostly followed in Japan are those pioneered by Dr W. Edwards Deming, a Western statistician. The successful implementation of his statistical approach by Japanese industry has been the main contributor to Japan's attainment of its worldwide reputation for quality products and services. Inherent in this approach is the principle that a statistical analysis and control of all processes and systems are as vital as any other of the management duties, such as administration, marketing, sales, training or service operations.

Dr Deming provides a framework for action with his fourteen points for management which will be presented in this chapter, and which, if properly appreciated and accepted, can lead to a permanent change (for the better!) in the thinking of top management, and to a beneficial transformation of the whole company culture.

Perhaps Joiner's three points, presented in Section 1.5.1, provide one of the best ways for quickly revisiting the essential elements of Deming's important message. But it is worth remembering that Deming advocates change on a grand scale. Such change requires full appreciation and understanding of all the appropriate management tools and actions, as well as elimination of certain long-established bad management practices. Hence Deming's fourteen points for management, a comprehensive study of which could reveal the necessary steps to take on a route that can lead to an effective implementation of a programme for total quality management and long-term success. Some of the points might appear radical and some intuitively obvious. One thing is certain: if Deming's philosophy is truly understood, every point, if implemented, can create improvement individually, and all of them together can lead to tremendous benefits for the organization.

■ 2.1 Historical background

William Edwards Deming was born in Sioux City, Iowa, on 14 October 1900. After obtaining a bachelor's degree in physics at the University of Wyoming, he gained his PhD in mathematical physics at Yale in 1928. He worked for eleven years, until 1939, at the US Department of Agriculture as a mathematical physicist. This eleven-year period coincided with one of great development in the theories and practices of statistical science, thanks to the efforts of R.A. Fisher at the Rothamstead Agricultural Centre in England. So Deming's interest in statistics is not surprising, and this interest helped him to appreciate fully the potential in the work of Walter Shewhart, the originator of the concept of statistical quality control. Shewhart's original message was based on the idea of gaining control over the variability in the manufacturing processes. Deming extended this message to cover the systematic approach to problem solving in any sector, manufacturing or not. He immediately saw the value of the Shewhart type of analysis, which is mainly concerned with the understanding of the nature of variation and particularly its division into controlled and uncontrolled variability due, respectively, to unassignable (or, as Deming calls them, common) causes, and to assignable (or special) causes.

In order to bring a process into statistical control and hence make it stable and predictable, the special causes of variation (estimated to be around 15% of all causes) should be eliminated. Achieving control is usually within the capability of the process operator, and hence within the responsibility of the workforce. This leaves the management accountable for at least 85% of the problems, which can be dealt with only if the management changes the system appropriately. As Deming insists, 'When a worker gets his output into statistical control, he can do no more!' He views the control chart as the ideal tool for 'assigning the responsibilities' for quality improvement, basically according to the ratio 15 : 85 for workforce : management. (In fact, during the 1980s, Deming revised this ratio to 6 : 94!)

During the period 1939–45, the American Bureau of Census and the US weapons industry were greatly benefited by his advice on the techniques of sampling and statistical control, with manifold productivity increases and cost savings. However, despite Deming's initial efforts and successes, the importance of correctly diagnosing the most important sources of variation, and then controlling or eliminating them as the best way of improving quality, was not appreciated enough by American managers. This was perhaps because the management did not want to accept such a high level of responsibility (at least 85%!) for the quality improvement effort, as Deming insisted; or perhaps because, after World War II, there was an open market for everything produced, and no particular attention was paid to high quality.

This made Deming turn his efforts to teaching the Japanese, who listened to him eagerly. He first visited Japan in 1946, as a representative of the Economic and Scientific Section of the US Department of War, and returned there in 1948. Thousands of scientists and engineers attended Deming's courses on statistical process control, which started in 1950 after an invitation from the Union of Japanese Scientists and Engineers (JUSE). Deming spoke directly to the leaders and top industrialists of Japanese companies, who immediately took his philosophy seriously and applied his teaching enthusiastically. Nowadays, Dr Deming's managerial and technical methods are widely accepted as being responsible for the turnaround of Japanese industrial fortunes.

Each year since 1951, Japanese industry has awarded the highly valued Deming Prize to a company or individual that or who has actively contributed to the spread and development of statistical techniques for quality improvement. Recipient companies include Nissan, Toyota, Hitachi and Nippon Steel. Florida Power and Light became the first non-Japanese company to win the Deming Prize (in 1989), and companies like Texas Instruments, Nashua Corporation, Ford Motor Company, AT & T, Dow Chemicals and General Motors are changing their ways to fit with Deming's principles. Dr Deming holds the Second Order Medal of the Sacred Treasure, bestowed on him by the late Emperor Hirohito in 1960, for valuable contributions to Japan's economy. He has received numerous other awards, honorary doctorates and medals, including the National Medal of Technology from the US president. He has been credited as being the father of the third wave of the Industrial Revolution. But despite all this fame, Deming still modestly prefers to be known as a consultant in statistical studies.

As well as manufacturing industries, Deming's clients included telephone companies, consumer researchers, hospitals, law firms, government agencies and universities. But despite his enormous success and reputation in Japan, he was relatively unheard of in the United States until 1979, when William Conway, president of Nashua Corporation, having heard of Deming through Japanese contacts, approached him. Conway was soon convinced by Deming, and decided to adopt his management principles throughout Nashua; as a result, a dramatic increase in profits soon followed. Awareness about Deming was also helped by an American television programme, on 24 June 1980, in which Conway and Deming were interviewed at length.

In the decade that followed, after a delay of over thirty years, Deming's philosophy was, at last, spread in the West. Numerous Deming user-groups in America, the MANS Foundation in Holland, the Deming Institute in New Zealand, the British Deming Association and the Association Française E. Deming have been formed to promote awareness and understanding of Deming's work, and to help group members towards the implementation of his principles. His teachings are currently attracting a greater number of

followers than ever before, and he is increasingly recognized as bei
with the most profound influence on the world's industrial histc

■ 2.2 Deming's fourteen points for management

Deming does not consider it as sufficient merely to solve problems, big or
small. He seeks a major transformation in the current practices of Western
management. He suggests that a basis for this transformation is provided by
his fourteen points, whose adoption and implementation would be a sign that
'the management intend to stay in business and aim to protect investors and
jobs'. The fourteen points also provide the basis for a theory of management.
There is no excuse any more for ignoring or misusing the science of managing
for quality; an applicable theory does exist, a theory that has already been
successfully put into practice by the Japanese. Deming's theory of management defines the steps required for transforming a company's quality culture,
but also extends to the definition of what he calls the deadly sins and diseases
that are crippling virtually every company in the West.

What has to be clearly appreciated before any attempts are made at
implementing Deming's philosophy is the level of corporate cultural change
required. The quality initiative has to start at the top, and many traditional
views have to be substantially altered. A management commitment to a complete transformation of the current (bad) practices is absolutely necessary for
survival and competitive success in this new economic age. This necessity is
revealed by almost all Deming's fourteen points, which we will now examine
in detail.

Point 1: Create constancy of purpose for continual improvement of product and service

Set the course today in order to be in business tomorrow, to become more
competitive, and to provide more jobs. Provide for long-term needs rather
than short-term profits. Investment on preventive maintenance today can
avoid major operational problems tomorrow. Investment in quality and
innovation now is certain to ensure the existence and competitiveness of the
company ten, twenty or thirty years from now, because quality in processes
and products always results in less scrap, less reworking, reduced inspection
and warranty costs, and higher productivity and customer satisfaction. On the
other hand, innovation guarantees the consumer's repeated return and the
company's enhanced reputation and market share.

Long-term constancy of purpose for continuous improvement and
innovation is an obligation that management should accept as a number one
priority. Management must confront any deviations from this direction and
immediately deal with them. Resources have to be allocated for long-term

planning with the faith that there will be a future. This faith has to be demonstrated continuously on a day-to-day basis by top management in order to motivate employees and convince them of the seriousness of their efforts. Convincing can become easier if genuine long-term aims about quality are properly communicated, in the form of clear policies which leave no doubt about their long-term purpose. In this way, nobody will be in any doubt about why the company is in business and what the future holds in store. If the thinking is only short term, decline is guaranteed.

Of course, short-term problems are important and their solution assures today's survival. But Deming warns of the danger of staying 'bound up in the tangled knot of the problems of today'. The right balance has to be found in the allocation of efforts for dealing, on the one hand, with the problems of today and, on the other, with the problems of tomorrow. While you fire-fight for the sake of today, your competitor does not stand still.

Investment in innovative methods and techniques, in new skills and materials, in research and education, and in continuous improvement in the design of products and services are the elements that can demonstrate constancy of purpose for survival, today and tomorrow. Constancy of purpose for competitive success is demonstrated by continuous consumer research; without it, a manufacturer can hardly hope to stay ahead of the competition. As Deming says, it is not enough merely to satisfy the customer. If you do not want to lose the customer to a competitor, you must completely delight him/her with your product or service, so that s/he can boast about it and bring more customers. Investigating what the customer needs or will need tomorrow should be an integral part of production activities. Consumer research has to continue after a product has been sold, in order to investigate whether the product fulfils its purpose, what the user thinks of it and, perhaps more importantly, why the non-user has not bought it. Valuable information thus gained could make all the difference between future success or failure for the company. This information can make it easier to make predictions, a necessity for proper future planning. But no prediction is possible without stability.

Stability combined with innovation leaves the consumer more satisfied and the manufacturer assured both of new customers and of the old customers' willingness to return. But only top management can initiate the long process of researching, discovering and then meeting or predicting the customer's needs and expectations. It is their responsibility to create and maintain the constancy of purpose for never-ending improvement and innovation, and to provide the road map that the rest of the organization can follow.

Statistically speaking, the problem of establishing constancy and maintaining consistency of purpose can be related to the problem of, respectively, achieving the mean (target) and minimizing the dispersion (variability) around the mean. Indeed, simply establishing constancy of purpose is equivalent to setting the course towards the target and achieving it; this is a necessary condition for business success but is not sufficient. Maintaining long-term consistency is equivalent to striving for a reduction of the spread around the course so that the target is consistently achieved. This, of course, as with any problem about variability – the cause of non-quality – is usually the more difficult to resolve. But one should always keep trying.

Point 2: Adopt the new philosophy for economic stability

A change is necessary in the old management methods, which are no longer effective for today's business environment. Without innovation you can never lead. If you just try to meet the competition, you will not survive in the new economic age. This new age has been created by Japan. We can no longer live in the days when quantity was more important than quality; but what has to be realized is that higher quality costs less. Western management must fully appreciate the Eastern challenge and accept the obligation for change; accept change in order to become (economically) stable. We do not live any more in the 1950s and 1960s, when Western-manufactured goods dominated the world market. Today's business environment is much more complex and unpredictable, more competitive and more than ever in need of constant innovation. Markets are now global; people have a choice. Deming regards the current style of management as totally unsuited to the new world of dependence and interdependence that we are in now; if this style is not changed, the cost is bound to be 'loss of competitive position and destruction of the individual!'.

Of course, the change cannot happen overnight. There must be a constant movement in the direction of the philosophy of ever-improving quality in all systems and processes. To start with, the current management system, style and operating attitudes have to be realistically examined in order to determine whether they support or inhibit continuing improvement in quality and productivity. When the damage caused by current practices is appreciated, top managers have to be bold enough to accept that a total transformation is needed in their current style of management.

Managers also have to be humble enough to admit that the days when the management only needed to think, and the workforce only needed to do, have passed. A company trying to survive on the intelligence of only a handful of managers has no chance in the new economic age. A mobilization of every bit of all the employees' intelligence is definitely needed. The breaking down of barriers through adequate communication can achieve this mobilization. Top managers have to face up to a new philosophy of pulling together the intellectual resources of all the employees for the benefit of the company.

The new management philosophy is not just an additional new technique to supplement existing ones. It is a radical philosophy advocating a complete change. As Deming says, a completely new strategy is needed to halt the continued decline of Western industry. This fact needs to be accepted as a first step in the right direction.

Point 3: Cease dependence on inspection to achieve quality

Build quality into the product at the development/design stage through off-line quality control (see Part IV), and maintain it or improve further during normal production through on-line quality control of the process that produces the product (see Part III). Insist that the same procedures are being followed by the company's subcontractors and suppliers to ensure trustworthy incoming materials and supplies. Mass inspection cannot compensate for useless incoming materials, bad design or less than optimal process maintenance. If possible, everything has to be made right first time so that there is no need for rectification later. But 'do it right first time' should not be just a slogan, targeting only the workforce. It should be supported by genuine management efforts in improving supplier–customer relationships, and the system of education and maintenance. Only then will the importance of inspection schemes eventually diminish, so that 'right first time' can become a reality.

Unfortunately, mass inspection is still a way of life in most industries. But this implies that defects and mistakes should always be expected. It is an attitude born out of a failure to control and continually improve the process. According to Deming, routine 100% inspection is the same thing as planning for defects, an acknowledgment that the process cannot function correctly, or that the specifications made no sense in the first place. It focuses on the negative, without offering any means for quality improvement, as though it is part of a programme of managing for failure, not for success. There is a need to replace the practices of mass inspection and defect detection with practices of defect prevention and continuous improvement. Statistical evidence can be utilized to build in quality in both manufacturing and purchasing functions. Statistical techniques for process quality control (which involve the necessary level of sampling inspection at the right point of the process) can achieve consistent high standards before or during production, so that confidence in the process's capability is increased, thus reducing the importance of and necessity for a final mass inspection.

Of course, an amount of inspection might always be necessary. In small-scale production, inspection might not be costly. On certain occasions full inspection, for example before shipping an important product, might be an absolute necessity. But every important item consists of parts and components which are massively produced; and mass inspection of those parts, with rare exceptions, is unreliable, ineffective and does not guarantee quality.

It is a waste of time and effort simply to check goods with no consideration of how to make them better. Such an activity is often unreliable, as it is prone to mistakes and to variability in accuracy from the many inspectors involved, due to boredom and fatigue. The usual reaction to the inspection problems is to put on more inspectors, and to increase the inspection effort yet again – a certain cause of even more problems. Deming calls this the fallacy of divided responsibility. Indeed, many inspectors can be the cause of complacency: each inspector usually relies on all the others to do what should be done; eventually nobody does it properly! Divided responsibility is actually reduced responsibility.

All this effort can instead be directed towards a continuous on-line examination and improvement of the processes (see SPC in Part III) through a defect prevention programme for which everybody should be responsible; this in the long run costs much less, results in high-quality end-products and minimizes the need for inspection or after-sale service.

Point 4: End the practice of awarding business on price tag alone

Like every individual in all managerial ranks, the purchasing managers have a new job to perform in the new economic age. They must end lowest tender contracts; instead, they should always require meaningful measures of quality for the supplies. Supplies which do not meet with statistical evidence of quality should not be used. It is not the fault of the process operator if faulty output is produced when the supplied materials (a management responsibility) were cheap and faulty in the first place. A spirit of partnership with suppliers has to replace confrontation, conflict and mistrust.

Initial specifications and the price of incoming materials do not tell the whole story about performance. The suppliers that should be trusted are the ones that can provide evidence of sustained statistical control. An SPC chart (see Part III) showing past and current performance levels can provide this evidence; it can also prove that the supplier under consideration is actually using the appropriate quality tools, and therefore can be trusted.

The savings that can result from a relationship with a reliable supplier can by far outstrip the savings attainable by merely going for the lowest price. The objective should be to reduce the total costs, not just the initial costs. Total cost should include the cost of subsequently using the incoming materials in addition to their initial purchase price. Indeed, the long-term costs incurred as a result of using cheap, unreliable and low-quality input are possibly incalculable. A lowest tender contract might eventually turn out to be the most expensive of all the proposed contracts. It is common practice for a dishonest supplier to offer a low bid with the sole purpose of ensuring the business; after this has been achieved, at a convenient time when it is too late for the purchaser to make other arrangements, an excuse will be found for the price of the materials, regrettably, to double!

It is probably worthwhile to stick to a single supplier for any one item, in a long-term business association of loyalty and trust. Looking forward to long-term business with the purchaser, the supplier will be encouraged and more easily convinced to adopt a philosophy of continuing improvement, open and honest communication and feedback, and prompt delivery for quality supplies at a price reflecting the true value of the materials. If necessary, the supplier should be appropriately trained in quality techniques at the purchaser's expense. This expense is justified if one views the supplier as the initial, and thus very important, part of the whole manufacturing process.

The advantages of a single, reliable, cooperative supplier are many. This option, apart from decreasing the administrative and material-inspection costs, also minimizes the variability otherwise caused when different suppliers deliver parts which, even if they are within specifications, are not the same. Many components from different suppliers, however good they are individually, when combined can produce a mediocre result due to their inflated (combined) tolerance. Deming's advice is to choose a single supplier for each item on the basis of statistical evidence from the supplier's process feedback loop. In this way, what is bought is not only the outcome product, but also the process that produces it! A measure of quality is also bought. As Walter Shewhart says, price has no meaning unless a measure of quality is purchased at the same time.

Point 5: Improve constantly and for ever the system of production and service

Search continually for problems, in order to improve quality and productivity constantly and decrease costs. Always try to reduce the variability of products and services, in order to achieve the highest quality at lowest cost. Never be satisfied with simply meeting current standards or specifications.

It is management's job to work continually on the system (design, research and development, incoming materials, maintenance, process improvement, training, communication and supervision) and not turn a blind eye to chronic problems or let things ride until they become problematic, by which time it is usually too late. Always anticipate trouble and never be content. Seek out potential problems and solve them before they cause harm. Prevent rather than fire-fight.

Testing and retesting for quality should always take place in the laboratory, even during production. Statistical techniques exist to help in any area, manufacturing or not. A programme of total quality control for products, processes and services should be initiated and should take place continually. The process of quality improvement should never stop, and it should spiral towards a specific objective: the customer's absolute satisfaction with the purchased product, and the customer's return. This can be achieved not by simply meeting the customer's current expectations, but by predicting and exceeding the customer's future needs. Innovation is as important as improvement.

The main responsibility of the management is constantly to improve the system so that innovation can materialize more easily. This itself is not easy, because the system covers everything: choice of suppliers, procurement, transport, funding for research, design, engineering, tools and techniques, maintenance and improvement, capital investment, allocation of human effort, training and retraining, selection of new employees, sales and methods of distribution, supervision and internal communications, accounting and payroll, contact with and service to customers. Every part of the system is prone to deterioration and waste as soon as the efforts for improvement cease. Effort is required just to maintain the attained quality level, let alone to improve it.

There is always a variability around every target, and this is why there is always room for further improvement. This is a departure from the traditional supposition that, as long as the product meets the specification limits, there is nothing to worry about. But the effects of uncontrollable factors in the user's environment can very easily cause the product, whose components were too close to the specification, to fail. So the inadequacy of the attitude 'conformance to spec' can very easily slip through the manufacturing operation to the customer. And when the customer suffers, the whole company will eventually suffer; because the customer is the most important part of the process. On the other hand, preventive maintenance and continuous process improvement, in the form of minimization of variability around the target, are the best ways to achieve and sustain the highest quality at the lowest cost.

Point 6: Institute training on the job

A continuous programme of on-the-job training needs to be instituted, and this should include managers. If top managers make themselves subject to education and training, they can provide an example for the rest of the employees to emulate. Efficient and modern methods of training help a company to make better use of all its employees. Training and education are the corner-stones of greater consistency. Investment in proper training of all new employees will ensure that the newcomers will immediately start contributing to their full capacity, knowing exactly what is expected from them.

Management must understand and fully appreciate the concept of variation and its negative consequences; also the ways to tackle it. This requires training in statistical techniques which can deal with the reduction and control of variability. Many changes are taking place in methods, materials, machinery and design; adequate training at the appropriate time helps to keep up with any new developments, and to provide the basis for advancing the state of the art in any area.

Unfortunately, training is often regarded as non-productive by many managers, and is either overlooked or is the first to be cut when finances become tight. How wrong this attitude is becomes very obvious if one calculates how small the cost of some proper training is in comparison to the total costs associated with an employee over the years. Frequently, even when training is taking place, due to pressures from above to catch up with the work piled up, the new material learned is not immediately put into practice; consequently, it is quickly forgotten, with the initial effort and training cost being wasted. Management should remove the barriers which inhibit the effective implementation of the lessons learned.

Of course, the bad practices associated with the concept of training do not originate only from top management: many shop-floor supervisors often rely only on their past knowledge and experience and are reluctant to accept new ideas and innovations concerning process improvement methods. Deming suggests that the only past knowledge that is valid and useful is that gained through the application of simple statistical techniques before and during production, and is based on unbiased process data and real information, not gut feelings or prejudiced expectations.

The majority of the techniques needed are extremely easy to learn and implement immediately. They can provide a basis for action, indicate clearly what the next step should be, and supply the necessary experience for the future. They can also provide the basis of what Deming calls a System of Profound Knowledge, a necessity in the training curriculum of any manager. The four ingredients of the system of profound knowledge that it is necessary to learn and practise are as follows:

1. **Knowledge of (or appreciation of) the system and the theory of optimization:** Emphasis should be given to the optimization of the system rather than the suboptimization of the subsystems. According to Deming, any system that results in an I win–you lose structure is less than optimal. The aim should be for everybody to gain (win–win) in the long run – company, employees, customers, suppliers, shareholders, the community and the environment. Proper appreciation of the system can only come from adequate understanding of the capability of the system, and that in turn can only come from the second ingredient.

2. **Some knowledge of statistical theory (or the theory of variation):** Adequate knowledge of uncertainty and its different sources (special and common) will reveal whether the system is stable or not, what the system's controlled and uncontrolled components are, and how stability can be attained. Then the capabilities of the system can be assessed and reliable predictions can be made. All these can only be achieved with the aid of statistical theory; which brings us to the need for the third ingredient.

3. **Some theory of knowledge:** There is no knowledge without prediction and without theory. Experience may provide the answer, but the question can only come from theory. Experience and examples are of no help in management unless studied with the aid of theory. Transformation can come with the aid of theory, which can also teach the management about the psychology of change and the difficulties associated with it. This reveals the need for the fourth ingredient.

4. **Some knowledge of psychology:** When it comes to managing people, one needs some knowledge of psychology, which can help one to understand people and the interactions between one person and the other (all people are different), and between a person and the system. This knowledge, like

any other associated with the system of profound knowledge, can only be attained through appropriate training. As Deming says: 'We don't install Knowledge – I wish we could.'

Indeed, there is no substitute for knowledge. Top management has to appreciate that proper training always equips the employee with a better understanding of the job and its requirements. This can only lead to the job being completed in better time and more adequately, to the company's advantage, with the worker not only gaining the satisfaction of doing a good job but also acquiring the incentive to continue improving even further.

Point 7: Adopt and institute modern methods of supervision and leadership

Efforts should be focused on helping people and machines to do a better job. Supervisors must ensure that immediate action is taken on reports of defects, poor tools and conditions detrimental to quality.

In this new economic age, supervisors should be more than just overseers; they should also be teachers of the latest developments in their area of responsibility. They should counsel, not judge. They should be actively involved in the effort to improve the system that they and their people work in. They should be aware of the perils of variation, and they should appreciate that the best way to diminish variation between people is to improve the system. They should be supportive, sympathetic, encouraging and helpful to everyone. This is the only way to ensure continual improvement in the work that the employees are doing, which in turn will assure a level of high quality in products and services.

Leadership and supervision should concentrate on making the workers take more interest in their work. An interested worker will want to do the job well and will accept advice, training and help towards doing it better. If this is achieved, the worker's interest will increase further. On the other hand, insisting through patronizing posters and slogans that workers deliver the impossible without any indication of how this could be achieved, results in a bad job being done, in a loss of interest and in demotivation; this results in a yet poorer job, and so on in a vicious circle.

Modern leadership means continually ensuring that quality, productivity and the performance of people and processes are improved; it requires awareness and respect for differences between individuals. Variety among different people should be regarded as an asset (and taken advantage of) rather than as an inhibiting factor; their various abilities should be identified and properly utilized for the benefit of the company. Today's leaders should lead and motivate by example rather than fear, teach and counsel rather than judge and supervise, use mistakes to learn from rather than to blame, understand the difference between random and special variation (so that people in need of special help are recognized), promote teamwork and mutual trust, and provide innovative methods to accomplish the improvement.

Point 8: Drive out fear

Two-way communication should be encouraged so that fear is driven out of the organization. Ideas should be actively sought and eagerly listened to. In this way everybody may work more effectively and more productively for the company. This can only be achieved if a secure environment is created, where uncertainty, ambiguity and randomness in management practices are eliminated. Those working in fear of their superiors try to withdraw from attention, with the aim not to be noticed. In this way, people's true potential is lost for ever. Fear is a barrier to improvement and innovation. Successful joint working relationships, based on mutual respect and cooperation, can achieve much more than isolated individual efforts.

Deming believes that an atmosphere of fear makes the implementation of most of his other management points impossible. In other words, he does not believe that any real improvement is possible unless fear, the cause of enormous waste, is eliminated and replaced by mutual respect, trust and cooperation. An atmosphere of fear is always counterproductive, a stumbling block to continuing improvement, and always reduces positive competitiveness and innovation. In an environment of fear, new and promising ideas will never surface, and the necessary questions will never be asked. A fear of failure induces both resistance to innovation and an attitude embodied in the maxim, 'Stick to what you know.' If they fear being blamed by their own superiors, some supervisors might even paint a false picture of success for their processes, hiding their inadequacies and defect rates, which will thus continue to multiply. A fear of appearing ignorant makes many managers reluctant to undertake further education. Some even fear the possibility of an added responsibility that the new knowledge may bring.

Some managers prefer to create a climate of fear. They create a fear motive in their suppliers through an emotional and complaints-oriented attitude, in the hope of gaining a price advantage. Some believe that they will appear more important if their employees are afraid of them. They also believe that workers will perform better if they feel insecure or anxious about their jobs, so they introduce the fear of redundancy.

The truth is that the weapon of fear or anxiety is an automatic admission of a failure to manage. The result is demotivation, stress, work being done deliberately wrongly, fiddling of the figures, time wasted in looking and applying for other jobs, and valuable personnel being lost, usually to a competitor. Efforts and actions are directed more towards personal survival rather than towards the achievement of business objectives. Management by fear does not serve the best interests of the company. It leads to a reduction in efficiency and in decision quality. Time and energy are then wasted trying to bury the evidence, rather than solving the problem and learning from past mistakes.

This can lead to premature release of untested designs and products which may well turn out to be defective. On the whole, a combination of fear and ignorance is a well-proved formula for stagnation and failure.

Point 9: Break down barriers between departments and individuals

Every individual from research and development to production and sales must work as a team, so as to foresee problems before they arise or to tackle them if they happen to arise. Destructive competition within the same company has to be replaced with cooperation. This will help to solve individual problems which can actually be very common in their nature.

The performance of any individual department should be evaluated in terms of its contribution to the company as a whole, not for its individual profit or any other measure that promotes competitiveness. Lack of proper communication inhibits the company-wide development of the innovative idea, which thus remains just an idea. The common language of simple statistical techniques is extremely effective in enabling people to appreciate each other's problems and contribute to their solution. For example, a chart showing the monthly performance of a quality characteristic has exactly the same structure irrespective of whether the quality characteristic is monthly sales or monthly defects. And it does not require a genius to appreciate that monthly defects do affect the monthly sales; or that the number of defects is directly proportional to the effort put into process control and to the quality of the incoming purchased materials. Everybody is a customer of somebody else along the process line, and the sooner this is fully appreciated, the better the chance for team spirit to flourish.

Deming believes that the common causes of problems which affect everybody amount to more than 85% of the total causes. They are part of the system and affect every individual and division irrespective of the nature of the work. They can be dealt with by management action on the system itself; this action should start by eliminating inner conflict and by encouraging communication. If the power of a common (statistical) language is adequately appreciated and made use of, management will be more capable in breaking down the barriers to communication. This will in turn enable the workforce to contribute more to the actual solution of problems for the benefit of the company. Of course, for this to happen, the 'fear of communicating' has to be driven out, which makes Deming's Point 9 closely allied to Point 8.

The close cooperation of many diverse organizations within the same company is imperative for the eventual market success of a particular product. The apparently different departments contributing to the development of just a single product could include those of market research, product planning and design, materials purchasing, engineering and manufacturing, quality control and improvement, sales and marketing, advance product planning and research. The people involved in all the above need to realize that they each have much to contribute to the common goal of satisfying the customer's needs and expectations, and eventually to the success of their company. They can do so in a barrier-free atmosphere of mutual trust and cooperation.

Point 10: Eliminate the use of slogans, posters and exhortations

Eliminate slogans which demand zero defects and new levels of excellence without providing the methods. People should be given the means to 'work smarter, not harder'. Arbitrary objectives not accompanied by a road map to help in their accomplishment can be counterproductive.

If there are problems of high defect rates and low productivity, slogans such as 'Zero defects', 'Do it right first time' and 'Increase productivity by 10%' are not going to achieve anything; they never helped anyone to do a better job. Most of the causes of low quality and unsatisfactory productivity are beyond the power of the workforce. They belong to the system and can be dealt with by changing management practices. How, for example, can somebody make something right first time if the incoming material, probably purchased on the basis of its (low) price tag, is defective, or if the equipment is in need of better maintenance and calibration? Verbally insisting that somebody should be a quality worker is at best patronizing and at worst the cause of frustration and resentment, especially when it is obvious that the insistence does not originate from a quality manager.

Deming believes that people are already doing their best. No substantial improvement, apart from the elimination of some obvious special problems (a minority of all problems) can result from management gimmicks. Given the chance, the workers will gladly do things right first time; but most of the time, a handicapping system does not give people a chance.

People can only improve through proper training. There is no substitute for knowledge. Productivity can only improve through the provision of statistical aids for quality, better equipment, trustworthy materials and adequate time. Provide the appropriate tools; only then can reasonable requests for improvement be made. Unreasonable requests through hectoring slogans and posters, without the provision of the necessary tools for those requests to be met, can only create adverse relationships, mistrust towards management, isolation and increased anxiety.

Point 11: Eliminate work standards and numerical quotas

Eliminate management by objective (MBO), by numbers and by numerical goals. Focus on quality not quantity. The attainment of a target must not be viewed as the ultimate success, because there is always room for further improvement. MBO neglects the variation in the processes and it is an invitation to short-term thinking. The only way to increase quality and productivity (and joy in work) is to replace work standards with competent leadership.

40

With respect to prespecified targets, one of the following could happen:

1. If the target is reasonable and is eventually achieved, the individuals involved will probably become complacent and have a well-earned rest, and no greater efforts are likely to be made for further improvement – an attitude that has no place in today's competitive world.
2. If the target is unreasonable, then either it will not be attained (resulting in unfair blame, increased anxiety and demoralization), or it will be attained by cutting corners, by fiddling the figures or by lowering quality standards – something that is bound to affect the customer and eventually the future of the whole company.

So what is the use of numerical targets? Numerical goals can never be right except (very occasionally) by accident. The focus should be on continuous improvement and on customer satisfaction. Numerical targets and goals mean only concentrating on short-term results and are inhibitors to long-term, lasting success. Most of the time, MBO expects a performance which exceeds the true, but unknown, capability of the system. It is not difficult to find out what the system is capable of; but before this is done, arbitrary objectives can only damage the system.

Of course, Deming does not tell us to manage without numbers. After all, individuals must have goals, aspirations, aims and intentions; companies need budgets, forecasts etc. for planning and allocation of resources. But they should not be arbitrary, nor should they become so. Only statistical data, properly selected and analysed, can show what is achievable, and what the next step should be for further improvement. Simple statistical methods and charts can immediately show the manager the current capabilities of the processes, of the system and of the existing procedures, and what can be reasonably expected of the workforce.

One should never forget the frequently demonstrated truth of the ratio 15:85 concerning the workforce: management's responsibilities for quality improvement. One of the goals that can reasonably be expected of the workforce is to bring a process into statistical control (that is, to take care of the special causes of variation – 15% of all causes). Once this stability is achieved, the workers can do no more. Even if they tried they would only tamper with the process. Targets will never help, because a stable process will only deliver tomorrow whatever it delivered today and yesterday. The situation is predictable; nothing more or less can be expected. For further improvement, the management must act on the system in order to take care of the common problems (85% of the total) which inhibit progress in all processes. So in a stable system, targets do not make sense, because one can only get what the system can deliver. In an unstable system there is no point setting a target either; because such a system is incapable and unpredictable, and there is no way of knowing what the next effort will bring. Any action usually distorts the system even further, and causes extra trouble elsewhere. Any success can only be temporary and unrepresentative of the system's true capability. Such a success can cause illusions of improvement; figures can easily appear to improve after a certain amount of fiddling.

According to Deming, 'management by numerical goal is an attempt to manage without knowledge of what to do, and in fact is usually management by fear.' Indeed, it would be better if MBO or MBR (management by results) were replaced with MBIO: management by improvement objectives. If there is an objective to be set, it should be that of constancy of purpose for continuous quality improvement of products, processes and services, an objective which is not specific in detail in the form of a numerical target in isolation. This objective should always be a real consensus rather than a top-down mandate, and should be supported by continuous training and sustained cooperation involving everybody from the top manager down.

Point 12: Remove barriers that rob the hourly worker of the right to pride in workmanship

It is widely accepted that eliminating physical and mental obstacles facilitates communication, encourages cooperation and improves the overall morale of employees. The most serious of mental obstacles are those which do not allow pride in workmanship. Management by objective is one of them; the annual merit rating (performance appraisal) is another. Admittedly these practices are so ingrained in the culture of the majority of organizations that any attempt to abolish them in one go would instantly provoke resistance and would probably generate a vacuum. Some other obstacles are not so difficult to overcome, such as absence of communication, poor incoming materials, inappropriate tools and inadequate training. But the fact remains that the main consequence of these obstacles is to rob hourly workers of the right to be proud of their work, a birthright as far as Deming is concerned.

Indeed, one cannot expect workers to be proud of their output when it consistently turns out to be defective because of faulty purchased materials, faulty equipment or poor working environment, the provision of which is a management responsibility. Everybody wants to do a good job and feel proud of it. But how can one improve an inadequate process if no time is allowed for improvement activities, no quality tools are given, no adequate documentation is provided to show employees what is expected from them, or no appropriate training is offered for self-education and development? How can the hidden potential of the workforce reveal itself if no one dares to bring into the open valuable ideas for improvement from fear of being laughed at, or of being considered as a subversive element wishing to stir things up? It results in frustration and loss of interest and pride when a brilliant suggestion, already admitted by many to be useful, goes unnoticed and wasted because of poor communication channels to the higher management. And no one can feel proud of his/her work if, in order to meet an arbitrary target or an unreasonable management objective, he/she is obliged to cut corners, hide the truth or manipulate the final figures. These kill pride in workmanship; and without pride there is no joy in work. No one can feel proud of work which is deliberately done in a particular way so that it is well appraised at the end of the year. This brings us to the worst mental obstacle of all: the yearly performance appraisal.

Deming strongly recommends the abolition of the annual merit rating, because it destroys teamwork, fosters mediocrity, increases variability in the performance of the appraisee, and focuses on the short term. Indeed, the practice of merit rating is so subjective and such a serious cause of isolation and negative competitive feelings that it ceases to be of any use at all. It is an admission that the whole career of an employee depends on the personal opinion of the employee's immediate superior. This opinion may be due to reasons completely irrelevant to the true value of the employee. The final appraisal might in fact depend on the current level of friendliness between the appraiser and the appraisee, or it might depend on a current rating system, for the validity of which there is no guarantee. Some people may even be over-rated, just because the appraiser wishes to show that all is well in his/her department; after all, the appraisers have to survive a performance appraisal on themselves!

Even assuming an objective system of merit rating, there are other problems associated with it, as in the following examples:

1. It causes excessive internal competition and isolation. Of course, some healthy competition is always desirable, but this assumes a healthy team spirit. The chances are that, in the presence of a strict and secretive merit-rating system, any team spirit or cooperation among departments, and even among individuals, is lost for ever.
2. It reduces initiative and risk-taking. People prefer to stick to what they know, because otherwise the fear of failure becomes more acute. They spend their time dealing with easy to achieve objectives, so that they have something successful to report at the end of the year. The aim is to get a high merit grade; the work itself ceases to be important.
3. It increases variability in performance. Every employee has a different way of achieving a personal objective. If those with a low rating in one year try to adjust their actions to emulate those with high ratings, a chaotic situation could arise (tampering with the process yet again). The resulting variability effectively obscures the true value of the appraisee.
4. It focuses on short-term results, which are not representative of long-term performance. Some companies even have an appraisal every three months. There is a great temptation to cut corners or take short-term decisions in order to show profits at all costs.

The appraisal procedure should be replaced by proper leadership and communication and by a counselling and development procedure, whose main purpose would be to identify, sustain or develop further the employee's contributions towards the continuous improvement of the organization as a team. Personal contact and personal knowledge can easily identify those who demonstrate abilities as leaders, to whom opportunities for promotion should be offered.

Statistical theory can help in the identification of those in need of special aid (not punishment). Poor contributions should be studied with the sole purpose of determining what is wrong with the whole system which caused failures to happen. One should work on causes, not on consequences. Everything should start with the understanding that at least 85% of the problems are system related, and individuals should not be blamed for these. Rather than merely judging people, management should be concerned with the task of improving the system within which the people work.

An open communication between the employee and supervisor, supported by continuous training and counselling, and by opportunities for personal skills enhancement, can allow pride in workmanship, can maximize contribution to the company and can help in development and motivation to a degree far higher than the one hoped to be achieved by a frequently unreliable (and embarrassing) appraisal system.

Point 13: Institute a vigorous programme of education and retraining

Encourage continual training to keep up with new developments, changes in product design and machinery, and innovative techniques. Things change fast; managers should be aware of this change and should themselves be appropriately trained to take advantage of it. Otherwise the competitor will. Self-improvement for everyone should always be encouraged and ever-broadening opportunities for the workforce should always be provided.

This point might look similar to Point 6, 'Institute training on the job'. Deming makes a clear distinction between these two in that Point 6 refers to the foundations of training for management and new employees to assist them to perform well in their current job, whereas Point 13 refers to continual re-education and self-improvement for everyone. The simple truth, common to both points, is that without adequate training (initially and subsequently), there is no guarantee of innovation or any improvement in the company's competitive position. Retraining is a necessary investment in the most important asset of a company: its people. It also helps in giving the employees a sense of security. People are better motivated towards self-improvement when they see that their company believes in them, because it invests in them.

With this point Deming, perhaps indirectly, asks for a commitment to life-time employment. Continuous re-education and retraining are based on the understanding that new skills are continuously required to keep up with developments in the new economic age. Re-education assures the employees that, should the position they are currently holding become outmoded, they would be able to change into a more valuable post within the company. So the most that can happen is reassignment, not redundancy. The company itself has a lot to gain from this policy: less brain-drain from the competitors, and less waste of effort. When employees do not feel safe in their job, apart from losing their motivation to work for the benefit of their company, they waste a great deal of time and effort looking for another job with (who else?) a competitor.

Many Japanese companies provide excellent examples of commitment to the development of their people. There is a wide variety of courses available to all employees throughout their careers. The companies view this as the best way of mobilizing the full potential and intelligence of the workforce, which might otherwise be hidden and lost for ever. They treat re-education as an investment, not an expense, and they treat their people as an asset, not a commodity.

Point 14: Define top management's permanent commitment to ever-improving quality and productivity

Management should immediately take action to accomplish the transformation by implementing all the preceding thirteen points (the action plan Deming recommends is outlined in Section 2.4.2 below). All employees must understand and be committed to the new philosophy. Senior managers must lead the way by fully committing themselves to continuous quality improvement and innovation, and by practising whatever they preach.

A permanent management structure has to be created at the top to help towards the achievement of the transformation. Without full management belief, progress will be at best temporary; no real change will ever take place, even if everybody from the middle management down believes in it. The support of somebody at the 'top' is imperative. The actions that affect the whole company can only be initiated by people in authority, who must be the first to admit that they also have much to learn and be prepared to learn it. There is no other way. As Deming advocates: 'Quality is made in the Board Room ... [however] ... limitations on quality are also made in the Board Room.' Having learned of the above thirteen points, and having agreed on their meaning and the direction to take, managers in authority must explain to the rest of the employees the necessity for change. Everybody must accept their new responsibilities, which will differ depending on their position in the organization.

Deming's principles provide a starting point and a road map to success. Once a manager fully understands Deming's philosophy, s/he will be able to identify inhibiting management practices, and will become capable enough of coordinating actions for continuous improvement.

Leadership in statistical methodology must predominate in any attempt to achieve the transformation. This is simply because quality is what counts these days, and proper implementation of statistical techniques always leads to quality improvements and innovations. It is the ability of statistical theory to provide a common language which makes statistical knowledge the most important asset in all management practices. Deming believes that no general manager can actually succeed in running a company unless s/he is equipped with an ability in statistical methodology, or has assigned at least one professional statistician as a member of the board of management.

Everybody should be encouraged to contribute to the process of innovation and continual improvement of quality. Management must promote a team spirit by eliminating communication barriers and by providing the appropriate training in statistical tools and techniques so that a common language is established. Everybody should be involved in the team, which should be extended to include the suppliers, the subcontractors and even the customers. If some efforts fail to bring the desired improvement, the efforts should start again afresh, utilizing the experience gained.

There is a relentless battle for company survival in this new economic age of increased competition and expanding world markets. Who is capable of responding to the challenge? Deming has the answer: 'Actually, the problem will solve itself. The only survivors will be companies with constancy of purpose for quality, productivity, and service.'

■ 2.3 Deadly sins and diseases

The implementation of Deming's fourteen points can transform the Western style of management. This transformation can fully materialize only when certain bad practices, called by Deming unforgivable sins or deadly diseases (DD), are eliminated. These diseases are crippling practically all large organizations in the West, and their cure requires a complete shake up in the current managerial culture, style and attitudes.

As with most diseases, a simple diagnosis of their causes can lead towards their permanent cure. As far as Deming is concerned, the causes of all major diseases that affect Western industry can be traced back to the ranks of senior management. This belief does not sound so controversial if one considers the diseases Deming is talking about.

DD1: Lack of constancy

Deming advocates constancy of purpose in his very first point. Even his last point urges an absolute and constant commitment on the part of senior management to quality, productivity and innovation. He views lack of constancy as the most crippling disease. Deming justifiably wonders: 'How can a company remain in business and provide jobs if there is a lack of constancy of purpose to plan product and service that will have a market?'

Continual improvement of processes will raise the quality and reliability of the product and service, will decrease costs, will protect investment, will assist in innovation, and will create a larger market and more jobs. It will positively affect everything and everybody, from the management and the workforce within the company to the consumer, the country's economy and society as a whole. If absence of constancy of purpose for quality has such a bad effect on the whole of society, to do nothing about it is an unforgivable sin.

DD2: Short-term profits

Short-term thinking defeats constancy of purpose to stay in business with long-term growth. A company should always plan for the future. Pursuit of the quarterly dividend and of short-term profit is an admission that there is a lack of faith in the future, and an inability to plan for long-term and sustained progress.

Admittedly, this is an extremely hard disease to cure. In all Western private industries, there is a need to satisfy the shareholder. On many occasions, due to a fear of takeover, many company owners are primarily interested in showing a short-term profit; they do so by cutting corners, closing down plants, encouraging 'voluntary' redundancies, cutting down on training or on any other investment originally intended for the benefit of the employees. The sad truth is, of course, that such actions are more likely to make the company the subject of a takeover, rather than avoid it. Long-range planning provides the only chance for long-term survival and growth.

DD3: Performance appraisals

The effects of the performance appraisal or any other form of merit rating could be devastating. It encourages rivalry and isolation, it nourishes fear and demolishes teamwork and mutual respect. It concentrates on the short term, it focuses on the outcome rather than the cause of this outcome, it is extremely subjective and it can cause embarrassment, bitterness and depression lasting for weeks after the rating. It may ascribe to individuals faults that may well be caused entirely by the system within which they work. Eventually, it rewards the people who have performed well as far as the system's indexes are concerned. It does not matter if these indexes are ridiculous, such as number of contracts at lowest cost negotiated in a year, or amount of successful fire-fighting performed quarterly etc. There is no guarantee that the individuals performed well with respect to other (perhaps more realistic) terms of reference.

In fact, a well-established tradition of merit rating becomes the current system's most valuable weapon for its own survival. People who attempt to change the system (for the better) have no chance of recognition.

DD4: Job-hopping

Mobility of management causes instability. It results in decisions being made by people who do not know the exact character or the specific problems associated with the company they have just moved into. It inhibits commitment to any policy of improvement, especially when such a policy is viewed as one of the predecessors' ideas. It also destroys teamwork, since not enough time is provided for team spirit to flourish.

It takes time to become familiar with the various parts of an organization. Blind application of experience gained elsewhere does not usually bring the expected results, because the whole business, with its people, problems and customers, is different from company to company. It could be different even between the subsidiaries of the same company.

It is actually very easy for a new manager to succeed in a system affected by the three diseases mentioned above, because it is not difficult to show profits by eliminating or reducing, say, training and research — in other words by cutting corners on the investments for the future. In an industry run on quarterly dividends, a new manager can easily achieve profits (at all costs), leaving a path of destruction in the process, then move on to destroy yet another company.

DD5: Use of visible figures only

Anyone can manipulate the figures at the end of a quarter to show a picture which could not be further away from the truth. One can ship everything on hand, regardless of quality, or mark it shipped even if the product has never left the store-room. One can cut down on research, education, retraining and quality improvement efforts in order to show some extra quarterly profits. Deming strongly believes that 'he who runs his company on visible figures alone will in time have neither company nor figures!'.

The only figures to be trusted are those which represent properly selected statistical data. The management should systematically seek unbiased data about customer satisfaction and employee perceptions about the company, and use these data to drive its processes and motivate its people. Dr Lloyd Nelson, director of statistics in Nashua Corporation, once said that the most important figures for management are likely to be unknown and unknowable. Indeed, how can you measure the customer's dissatisfaction and your loss of market share due to unreliable and defective goods, or employees' loss of interest and pride in their work due to inadequate equipment or poor incoming materials, or the loss of brilliant ideas due to the absence of proper communication channels, or the lost potential of the workforce because of inadequate retraining etc? Making no attempts to estimate or even appreciate the existence of these invisible figures usually causes their (invisible) multiplication — a source of further contamination.

The above diseases are in need of cure if any quality initiative is to have any effect. The cure must come from senior managers, who will need to alter many of their traditional, but outdated, views. The main fact they should appreciate is that the system is responsible for at least 85% of the problems, and for 95% of the company's performance. This indirectly means that managers not taking care of the system (their responsibility), are the cause of at least 85% of the problems that inhibit progress. It is hardly surprising, therefore, that Deming views as unforgivable sinners those managers who, although capable of acting on the system (by first getting rid of the deadly diseases), choose not to.

■ 2.4 Implementing the Deming philosophy

There is no magic solution waiting to be revealed by opening a Deming box of tricks. It has already been noted that there is a need to understand clearly the level of corporate cultural change required before any attempts are made towards implementation of the Deming philosophy. Few, if any, of the fourteen points can be immediately adopted by an organization currently ruled by old-style management. Besides, all fourteen points are generally interlinked and overlapping. For example, to scrap inspection suddenly because of Point 3 would be disastrous! You first need to improve the upstream systems and processes (Point 5) using better incoming materials (Point 4) and modern scientific tools and techniques which need to be learned (Points 6 and 13). One can never just do the fourteen points and then proceed to do other things. The fourteen points are a long-term direction and aim, not a set of rules. They certainly involve a lot of doing but, before this, they also involve a great deal of education, understanding of why the recommended changes are needed, and a commitment to the effort to adopt every one of the fourteen (interlinked and overlapping) points. Although improvements can obviously be attained by partial adoption of Deming's teachings, the massive breakthroughs can only happen by complete adoption.

Some of the points may understandably seem controversial, simply because they are being compared to current beliefs which are too well ingrained in the company's culture to be easily disregarded in favour of new ones, so hasty actions in implementing the Deming philosophy, without a proper understanding of it, can only harm the process of implementation and make some of the points look less credible. Deming does not advocate immediate abolition of inspection or of performance appraisals before the necessary groundwork is laid down to enable the transformation to be made. No company culture can change in one day; the change needs to take place progressively, with proper planning of every step in advance. As Deming says: 'A big ship, travelling at full speed, requires distance and time to turn around.' To start with, the inadequacies of the current culture have to be identified so that the effort for change is focused on wherever it is needed the most. When confidence is built up, the pace of change can perhaps be accelerated, the direction being steered positively with a clear emphasis on customers, internal or external. Proper appreciation of the Deming principles can fuel the acceleration of change.

2.4.1 Essential first steps

A well-planned programme for implementing a philosophy which, perhaps, is currently viewed as alien or controversial should start with the creation of an awareness of the harm caused by the absence of this philosophy. So a first step for implementing the Deming philosophy could be to appreciate the damage caused by the five unforgivable sins of Section 2.3. The fact remains that in many organizations the title of Section 2.3 can easily be replaced by the heading: 'Company's current practices'! These practices are so ingrained in the company's culture that they are not seen as diseases in need of immediate cure.

However, besides the deadly diseases, there are other obstacles which inhibit progress, but which are easier to overcome; so, perhaps, the improvement efforts could start by first appreciating and taking care of those obstacles. The main ones are as follows:

Hope of instant pudding

A Greek proverb reads as follows: 'A single swallow does not bring the spring.' This expresses a simple truth which is also applicable to quality improvement efforts. A day with a quality consultant or a competent statistician will not solve the company's quality problems. The supposition that quick results can be expected without consistent effort and sufficient education is an absolute fallacy.

The quantification of improvement

There is a common supposition that every improvement result must be quantified. But how can one quantify the improvement in employees' morale, their pride in their work, the customer's satisfaction with a quality product? Management must accept that the most serious improvements might in fact remain invisible, and thus unquantifiable. There is also a supposition that every improvement should show a large monetary benefit. But every contribution to quality improvement is important, however small; and let us not forget the existence of the unknown and unknowable (monetary) figures – usually the most important of all.

Search for examples

A quality improvement effort can bring results in any organization, however small or large. It does not require examples of success from other, similar organizations. The principles and techniques of quality and productivity improvement are common and applicable to any company, manufacturing or not. The necessary factor is to understand the theory and to be committed to its application. Case-studies can then be generated from within, without having to be imported. It is a hazard to copy; if you just copy, you will always lag behind.

Our problems are different/Our culture is different

This is the classic excuse of Western management for refusing to accept the principles and techniques that have made Japan an economic superpower. Particular problems might indeed be different, but the principles for solving them and for satisfying the customer are universal. Japanese managers did not discover any difference in the essence of their problems or culture when they utilized the (Western) statistical ideas and techniques which brought them quality and productivity improvements; in fact, they accepted them and developed them further. It is now the turn of Western industries to do the same. National culture has nothing to do with it. If it had, why did the Japanese win the quality battle only in the second half of the twentieth century and not before? Only management culture is relevant, and indeed has a lot to do with it!

Poor teaching of statistical methods

There is a need to appreciate the power of statistical techniques for improving quality in products, processes and services. Adequate teaching in these methods in industry is of paramount importance, but equally important is *proper* teaching in them. Provision of one-off crash courses by inexperienced external consultants is not the answer. Statistical theory should be taught by competent statisticians on an ongoing basis, and supplemented by immediate implementation so that experience is immediately gained.

We installed quality control

This is the classic excuse of management for not getting personally involved in the quality improvement effort. But the current activities of a quality control department in Western industries are usually the provision of simple information on current defect rates, costs of inspection and warranty etc.; in other words, non-value-added activities. The existence of such a department hardly ever helps in the solution of quality problems. Innovation and improvement of quality and productivity must be an ongoing process involving everybody, with the top management taking the lead.

Specifications and the fallacy of zero defects

There is a very common supposition that whatever conforms to the specifications can guarantee zero defects. This a dangerous fallacy that does not take into consideration the effect of uncontrollable factors in the user environment, the ever-increasing loss associated with every departure from the target value, the added variability that the (specified) component tolerances bring in the performance of the end-product, and the fact that merely satisfying the customer with conformance to the required specifications cannot guarantee the customer's return. There is not much difference between a product just inside the spec and a product just outside it; Taguchi's loss function (see Part IV) can confirm that both products score almost the same as far as 'loss to society' is concerned. 'Meeting the spec' should not be the end of the improvement effort; on the contrary, this is where the serious effort should begin. Only consistent satisfaction of the nominal, rather than merely of the specification, limits can guarantee the customer's delight and repeated return.

Inadequate testing of prototypes

Most of the problems that arise during production can be avoided if adequate testing takes place at the design stage of the product. As soon as a prototype is produced, appropriate testing should be performed, considering all possible eventualities. Noise from uncontrollable factors that could affect the performance of the end-product (or the process that produces the product) should be experimentally simulated in a controlled environment, and ways should be found to achieve robustness against this noise. Quality is thus built into the product and process as early as at the prototype or the design stage (off line), which is the most convenient and flexible stage for the appropriate experimentation and testing to take place. The important concept of achieving insensitivity to noise is considered extensively in Part IV.

It has already been noted that the above obstacles are easier to overcome than the deadly diseases. Overcoming the obstacles will clear the way for the implementation of Deming's philosophy and the elimination of the diseases. To help with this process, Deming recommends an action plan comprising seven steps, which should be taken in the order presented in the following section.

2.4.2 Deming's action plan

Step 1. Top managers will struggle over the fourteen points, the deadly diseases and the obstacles; then they will agree on their meaning, their implications and the direction to take.

Step 2. Top managers will adopt the new philosophy and the new responsibilities with pride and a determination to break with the old traditions.

Step 3. Through seminars and other means of communication, top managers explain to the rest of the company employees why a change in everybody's current practices is necessary. The fourteen points, the deadly diseases and the obstacles will have to be understood and appreciated by everyone.

Step 4. Every activity is seen as a stage in a process. Every stage is the customer of the previous stage and the supplier of the next one. This implies that continual improvement will be taking place at every stage so that its customer is always satisfied. All stages will be working together towards quality that the ultimate, external customer will boast about.

Step 5. The process is set up for the construction of an organization to guide continual quality improvement. The Deming or Shewhart cycle, described in Section 2.4.3 below, is recommended by Deming as a helpful procedure to follow for improvement of any stage.

Step 6. Everybody takes part in a team effort with the aim of improving the input and output of any stage. Every team member should contribute ideas and plans, irrespective of whether or not these ideas will lead anywhere. What is important is the effort and not the result. The most innovative ideas are often the simplest.

Step 7. With the participation of knowledgeable statisticians, embark on the construction of an organization for quality. The serious implementation of the fourteen points will ensure the establishment and permanence of a real quality ethos.

While taking each of the above seven steps, it would be helpful always to keep in mind the Deming triangle (see Figure 2.1), which, in the same format as the Joiner triangle or the TQM triangle, represents the three fundamental principles that Deming's philosophy is all about.

Management commitment to improvement

Wake up to the challenge of the new economic age (Point 2). A culture transformation is needed, and this is everybody's business; but top management

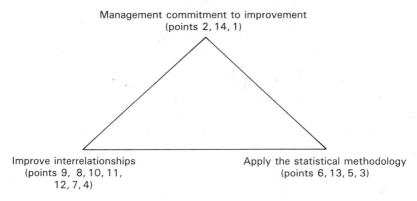

Figure 2.1 Deming's triangle

needs to take the lead (Point 14). Management is responsible for achieving competitiveness, for staying in business and for providing jobs; but these can only be achieved by being continuously obsessed with quality, and through the creation of a constancy of purpose for innovation and never-ending improvement of products, processes and services (Point 1).

Apply the statistical methodology

We live in a world full of variation. We need to understand its sources and we need a scientific method for predicting it, for reducing it and for controlling it. Statistical thinking is an essential part of this scientific method. Statistical theory is the only way to deal with variation. Continuous improvement means continuously solving the variation problem. But this relies on a successful marriage of theory and practice; experience is insufficient without theory. This theory needs to be taught. There is no substitute for knowledge.

Initial training (Point 6) and subsequent retraining and education (Point 13) on statistical theories and techniques is the best investment for the future. Only statistical methods can guarantee at all times the necessary ongoing improvement in quality and productivity (Point 5); only through these techniques can one build quality into the product and the process at the earliest stage possible, thus preventing subsequent errors, minimizing costs and eliminating the need for mass inspection (Point 3).

Improve interrelationships

Improve internal relationships and encourage team spirit by breaking down the barriers between the departments (Point 9), driving out fear (Point 8), cutting out slogans and exhortations (Point 10) and eliminating arbitrary targets, work standards, quotas and management by objective (Point 11). Abolish barriers to pride in workmanship (Point 12) and substitute mere supervision with modern leadership (Point 7). The effort should be directed towards improving people rather than controlling them through systems of merit rating (Point 12). Improve external relationships with suppliers and subcontractors so that quality incoming materials are assured (Point 4).

All efforts should be directed towards the complete satisfaction and delight of the final external customer, through quality and innovation; because, as Deming insists, the consumer is the most important part of the process. The process could be any individual activity, however small; or it could represent the whole company system, which, according to Deming, is a series of interdependent functions that work together towards the aim of the organization. The system covers every stage, from procurement of incoming materials to final distribution of the company's products or services, as Figure 2.2 shows. It is indeed evident from Deming's chain reaction in Figure 2.2 that everything starts and finishes with the customer. And so it should.

54

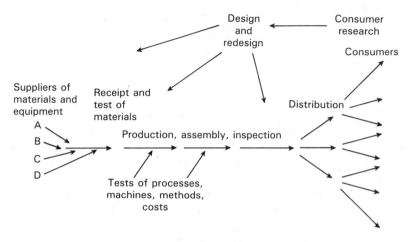

Figure 2.2 Deming's 'chain reaction'

2.4.3 Essential ongoing activities

There is an ongoing cycle of activities that Deming suggests as a procedure to assist in the establishment and long-term existence of a quality organization. The cycle, called the Deming cycle (or as Deming prefers, the Shewhart cycle), consists of four main stages, one following another in a specific order which is repeated continuously (see Figure 2.3). The name PDCA cycle is often used as an acronym for all four stages: plan, do, check, act. It reflects the basis of a self-sustaining quality programme. It is the classic problem-solving and loop-learning model.

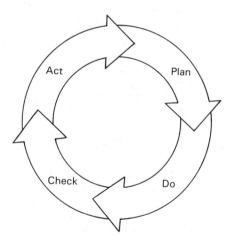

Figure 2.3 The Deming cycle

The PDCA cycle should drive any process or activity in the company, however small. In fact, it should drive the whole system itself, perhaps as Figure 2.4 shows.

Plan

The process of improvement should start in carefully planning the route of action. This could involve a great deal of understanding, documenting, evaluating and assessing the tools to be used for an effective quality programme. The understanding of Deming's principles can help greatly in setting up and gaining consensus for an effective plan, in order to avoid illusions of progress later. Change should be gradual, and not for change's sake. At this stage, decisions should be taken on the objectives to aim for, the changes that are needed, the types of performance measure to be used, and who should be responsible for what. Also, a determination should be made of the availability of resources or data, the possible implications of the actions and the contingency measures to be taken when something goes wrong.

Do

Implementation of the plan should follow, with the involvement of everybody. This will include training in scientific methods, survey of the customer's needs and expectations, identification of core processes, collecting of statistical information, understanding of process control and variation, identification of

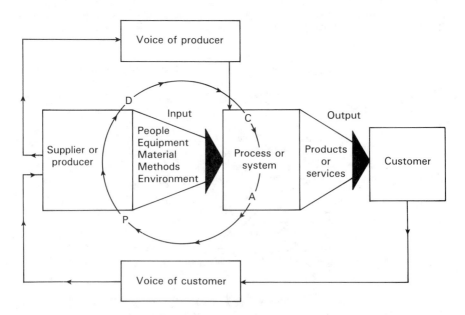

Figure 2.4 The PDCA cycle and the system

projects with improvement objectives, formation of project teams and communication of resulting successes. At this stage, small-scale implementation of any planned change or test will take place and the resulting data will be collected.

Check

Checking how the plan is evolving is an important part of the cycle. This involves measuring and observing the 'effects' of any change or test carried out at the do stage, analysis of results, feedback and review. Using actual data (and not gut feelings or emotions), deviations from original expectations should be evaluated and investigated. This is why the existence of a proper performance measure (decided in the plan stage) is so important. Problems should come out in the open and be realistically assessed, avoiding unjustifiable blame and recrimination. Breaking down the barriers and eliminating fear will prompt people to declare openly what is going wrong and what should be done from there on.

Act

Corrective action can follow, based on the lessons learned so far. Changes should be adopted or abandoned in line with the results of the previous stage. A study of the current situation should take place, standardizing any improvements and properly documenting any good new processes and innovative ideas. The review at the checking stage can be used as a learning process, so that knowledge is built into a new plan, which is now broadened with enough information to prevent mistakes from occurring again, and is developed further, utilizing the valuable experience gained so far. Planning requires prediction; the results of any change at the action stage can enhance the ability to predict and belief in the future. The Deming cycle of

Planning, Implementation, Checking, Action, (New) Plan

is thus ready to start again. This should never stop. One should always remember the requirement: continuous improvement and innovation. This can *never* end!

■ 2.5 Deming on management

Here are some uncompromising quotations and opinions from W. Edwards Deming concerning current management practices:

It would be a mistake to export American Management to a friendly country. America is the world's most underdeveloped nation!

Only transformation of Management and Government relations with Industry can halt the decline.

The prevailing system of management has smothered the individual, and has consequently dampened innovation, applied science, joy in learning, joy in work.

The wealth of a nation depends on its people, management and government, more than its natural resources.

The right Quality and Uniformity are foundations of commerce, prosperity and peace.

The workers are handicapped by the system, and the system belongs to the management.

The big problem for management may be the difficulty in making any kind of change. This difficulty may in fact amount to total paralysis!

Defects are not free; somebody makes them and gets paid to make them!

When will management learn that they have a moral obligation to protect investment and safeguard jobs?

Management By Walking Around (MBWA) can only be effective when the manager who walks around has a good idea of what questions to ask and pauses long enough to get the right answer.

A quality program launched by ceremonies, speeches, raising of flags, beating of drums, badges and heavy applause, is a delusion and a snare!

Experience without theory teaches nothing about quality and competitive position. Experience will answer a question, but the question comes from theory.

Learn the theory, then improve on it.

Hopes without a method to achieve them will remain mere hopes.

Management needs training to learn about their company.

He who would run a company on visible figures alone, will in time have neither a company nor figures.

The job of Management is not supervision but leadership.

It is difficult to overthrow the law of gravitation and laws of nature. Some managers forget an important mathematical theorem, that, if 20 people are engaged on a job, 2 will fall in the bottom 10% no matter what!

The important problem is not the bottom 10%, but who is statistically out of line and in need of help.

The big problem in leadership and training arises from a standard of what is acceptable work and what is not.

'SECURE': 'se' comes from Latin meaning 'without'; 'cure' means 'fear' or 'care'; 'secure' means 'without fear'. No one can give his best performance unless he feels secure in his job.

Putting out fires is not improvement.

Specification limits are not Action limits.

When managers visit other companies seeking examples, one can only hope that they will enjoy the ride; because this is the only thing they will be getting out of it!

The question is not whether a company is successful or not, but why.

It is a hazard to copy.

Problems are different, but the principles that will help to solve them are universal.

Requirement for innovation: faith that there will be a future.

Absenteeism is a function of poor management. If people feel important to a job, they will come to work.

Slogans, exhortations and posters with targets to be met (without providing the means to meet them), are directed to the wrong people. They take no account of the fact that most of the trouble comes from the system.

Devoid of ideas by which to improve productivity, but desperate to do something, management's course of action may be publication of new goals and new work standards.

What do 'targets' accomplish? Nothing. Wrong: their accomplishment is negative.

A work standard is a fortress against improvement of quality and productivity. It is a manifestation of inability to understand and provide adequate supervision.

Focusing on outcome is not an effective way to improve a process or an activity.

Useless and meaningless slogans:
    BE A QUALITY WORKER
    ZERO DEFECTS
    TAKE PRIDE IN YOUR WORK

DO IT RIGHT FIRST TIME
SAFETY IS UP TO YOU
TARGET FOR THIS MONTH: 95% SUCCESS
INCREASE PRODUCTIVITY
INCREASE SALES BY 10%
WE BELIEVE IN QUALITY
QUALITY IS OUR MOTTO

Useful and constructive announcements:
BETTER MAINTENANCE
BETTER TRAINING
BETTER PURCHASED MATERIAL
MORE STATISTICAL AIDS
NEVER-ENDING IMPROVEMENT
LONG-TERM SURVIVAL, NOT ONLY SHORT-TERM
   PROFITS
WORK SMARTER NOT HARDER!

What people require in their careers, more than money, is ever-broadening opportunities to add something to society, materially or otherwise.

There are cheaper ways to produce 7% defective product, if that were your aim!

Abolish the distinction between major and minor defects. A defect will be a defect.

The central problem in management, leadership and production is failure to understand the nature and interpretation of Variation.

Quality and innovation are inseparable: necessary ingredients for achievement of quality are innovation and profound knowledge of variation.

Quality is generated in the boardroom; limitations on quality are also made in the boardroom.

Good operations on the factory floor are essential, but good operations don't ensure quality.... Best efforts will not ensure quality. Hard work will not ensure quality. Experience will not ensure quality.

There is no process, no capability and no meaningful specifications, except in statistical control.

A usual stumbling block in most places is management's supposition that quality is something you install, like a Dean or a new carpet.

A company can do well with poor management – for a while!

Management too often suppose that they have solved their problems of quality by establishing a Quality Control Department and forgetting about it.

He who has a rule to give his business to the lowest bidder deserves to get rooked.

The price tag is easy to read, but understanding of quality requires education.

Who would buy a tyre for their automobile at lowest price?

The consumer is no longer willing to subsidize the waste.

It will not suffice to meet the competition; he who hopes only to meet the competition is already licked!

Customer? What does he know about it? If you wait until the customer knows what he wants, you will lose the customer!

Charles Darwin's law of survival of the fittest holds in free enterprise as well as in natural selection.

The management is at fault for terms of reference that are outmoded.

People get rewarded for 'conforming'. No wonder we are on the decline!

We have learned to live in a world of mistakes and defective products as if they were necessary to life.

There are many unforgivable sins, obstacles and deadly diseases that cripple the Western Industry; their cure requires a complete shake-up of style of management.

You do not have to do this; survival is not compulsory!

3 | Juran on Quality

Quality does not happen by accident;
it has to be planned.

Joseph Juran

Dr Joseph Juran is a Balkan-born charismatic American who does not actually know his own age. Since 1924, he has pursued a varied career as an engineer, industrial executive, government administrator, university professor, corporate director and management consultant. His *Quality Control Handbook* in 1951 led him to international fame. This and his other books on quality, namely, *Quality Planning and Analysis* and *Management of Quality*, have been translated into thirteen languages. In fact, Juran has made the greatest contribution to the management literature of any quality professional. He is altogether the author of twelve books, among them *The Corporate Director*, *Managerial Breakthrough*, *Upper Management and Quality* and more recently (1988) *Juran on Planning for Quality*. He has pioneered training manuals for junior management and foremen/women, and lectured to over 30,000 senior managers and specialists in over thirty countries on all continents.

Like Deming, Juran was invited to Japan by the Union of Japanese Scientists and Engineers in the early 1950s, to conduct seminars for top- and middle-level executives. He has served various industrial companies, governmental agencies and other institutions as a consultant. He is the recipient of over thirty honorary medals including the highest Japanese decoration, the Second Order of the Sacred Treasure, awarded to him by the Emperor of Japan for 'the development of Quality Control in Japan and the facilitation of US and Japanese friendship'.

In this chapter we will outline the main principles of Juran's message, which are focused on planning, organizational issues, the importance of creating beneficial change (breakthrough) and of preventing adverse change (control), and the management's responsibility for organizing a proper structure for quality attainment.

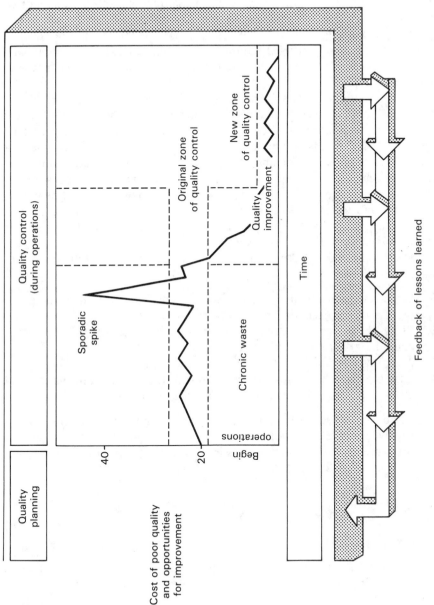

Figure 3.1 The Juran trilogy

■ 3.1 Developing a habit of quality

In the early 1980s, Juran recognized that a quality crisis had been spreading throughout Western industries. Moves to raise quality awareness, supported by company-wide campaigns, slogans and exhortations, did not result in any quality breakthroughs or any changes in the company's culture towards quality. Juran attributed this failure to the fact that the habit of making annual improvements in quality and reducing costs was never properly developed.

Juran defines quality as fitness for use, which demands quality of design, quality of conformance, availability and adequate field service. He believes that objectives should be set yearly for increased performance and decreased costs. To develop the habit of always striving for these yearly goals, a company needs quality planning and a quality structure – a responsibility of top management. Simplistic slogans and exhortations do not constitute a structure. There are no short cuts to quality. The emphasis should be put on the results and the experience gained from those results, not on the campaign itself. Juran insists that 'the recipe for action should consist of 90% substance and 10% exhortation, not the reverse!'.

He recommends a formula for results which comprises four important stages, as follows:

1. Establish specific goals to be reached – identify what needs to be done, the specific projects that need to be tackled.
2. Establish plans for reaching the goals – provide a structured process for going from here to there.
3. Assign clear responsibility for meeting the goals.
4. Base the rewards on results achieved – feed back the information and utilize the lessons learned and the experience gained.

All the above four stages have a lot to do with planning. Planning for quality is seen by Juran as an indispensable part of the quality trilogy: quality planning, quality control and quality improvement (see Figure 3.1).

■ 3.2 Juran's quality trilogy

Quality planning

Juran insists that quality does not happen by accident; it must be planned. Special training must be provided in how to plan for quality. Juran's 'quality planning road map' consists of the following steps:

1. Identify the customers and their needs. By customer, Juran does not mean only the end-recipient of the final product, but also the internal customer who relies on the output of a particular internal process.

2. Translate the customer's needs into a language everybody can understand, and develop a product which can respond to those needs. A common language can facilitate this development.
3. Optimize the product by developing and optimizing the process which produces this product.
4. Once the operating conditions have been established and proved as the optimal, transfer the process to operations.

In parallel with any of the above steps, cost considerations will play an important role in the planning, and every opportunity for improvement, quality-wise and cost-wise, should be taken.

As soon as a level of quality has been attained, it is immediately subject to negative influences and hence prone to deterioration. This brings us to the second important part of the quality trilogy.

Quality control

Control is the process of detecting and correcting adverse change, as soon as it happens, so that the status quo is maintained.

Conforming to quality specifications and adhering to standards and procedures requires prompt corrective action of any sporadic problems, so that the status quo is restored. Companies establish various ways of sounding the alarm when standards are not met: audits, special watchdogs, statistical control limits etc. Acting on the sporadic special problems takes the form of fire-fighting, but it is crucial that it is done so that the process returns to a state of control. Only a process in control is predictable and hence receptive to efforts for further improvement. These efforts will aim to reduce chronic waste (see Figure 3.1), usually the result of causes which are common to all company processes, and hence inherent in the current system, which it is management's responsibility to take care of.

Juran is in complete agreement with Deming when he says that chronic quality losses amount to more than 80% of all losses, and are management controllable through management action on the system itself. Therefore, always, 'the majority of the current quality problems are the fault of poor management rather than poor workmanship on the shop floor'. No amount of exhortation or slogans demanding zero defects (from the workforce) will solve them; only management action on the system will help to bring about the third stage of the quality trilogy.

Quality improvement

A quality breakthrough is needed to reduce substantially the chronic waste and achieve a new improved zone of quality control (see Figure 3.1). By definition, breakthrough is an improvement which takes us to an unprecedented level of performance; it is an organized creation of beneficial change. Indeed, organized procedures must be found to reduce the incidence of chronic defects and their associated costs. Clear priorities for projects have to be decided and clear responsibility for guiding the projects has to be assigned. Juran believes that no amount of desire for improvement will get results unless projects are chosen and given priority, and unless responsibilities are clear.

Unfortunately, many managers do not regard themselves as responsible for making improvements. Instead, they resort to cascades of exhortation and publicity-based programmes urging the workforce to become 'involved'. The quality campaign is then 'completed' with the creation of a quality department, which is assigned all the responsibility for quality. This is a misdirected approach, hardly ever effective in reducing chronic waste. The fact remains that the management is the major influence on quality matters, not the workforce. The workers can only contribute as much as the system allows them to. The majority of field failures and company defects have their origin in matters which are inherently beyond the capacity of the workforce.

The system consists of long-range policies, company-wide training, interdepartmental communication and coordination, purchased materials etc. When these are taken care of by management, the system itself improves, the workforce can participate and better utilize their education and creativity, and breakthroughs are a natural consequence. In this way, many valuable lessons can be learned which can then be fed back to improve quality planning in the next repetition of the quality trilogy stages.

■ 3.3 The universal breakthrough sequence

Juran believes that in this new economic age, it is imperative to develop the habit of making annual improvements in quality and annual reductions in quality costs. If this habit is not developed, ground will be lost to those competitors who already have it.

What is needed is a continuous effort to achieve a breakthrough. This in turn requires an organized sequence of activities, because, as has already been stated, breakthrough is the organized creation of beneficial change. Juran suggests an organized action and education programme which can assist the management in acquiring this habit. The main ingredients of this programme are as follows:

■ Accept the responsibility for making improvements.
■ Understand the universal sequence of events for making the improvements – Juran calls this 'the universal breakthrough sequence', to be outlined below.
■ Become familiar with the key concepts and techniques by which this universal sequence is carried out.
■ Apply the universal sequence to actual company problems.

The first of the above ingredients is crucial because one usually finds that most managers do not regard themselves as responsible for making improvements. The approach usually followed is the exhortation cascade, making sure that everyone 'gets the message'. This is the wrong approach; nothing really happens after an exhortation campaign, despite the fact that no one is against quality. What is really needed is actual involvement in specific projects, with emphasis on the assignment of clear responsibilities. If there are no specific programmes for quality improvement on a project-by-project basis, there is no hope for any (specific) breakthroughs.

But, as all breakthroughs follow the same sequence, the breakthrough sequence is universal. It can be seen as a road map to success, and it follows certain stages in a particular order, as follows:

- Proof of the need.
- Project identification.
- Organization for improvement.
- The diagnostic journey.
- Remedial action.
- Breakthrough in cultural resistance to change.
- Holding the gains − control at the new level.

These stages will now be examined in detail.

3.3.1 Proof of the need

People have learned to live with waste. Scrap is not regarded as abnormal as long as it does not exceed a specific level. When a faulty process is deemed normal, just because the defect rate is consistently kept below a particular defect level (chronic waste), this indicates that the alarm signals have been disconnected. The only way to make the alarm sound is to convert the chronic waste into money lost. Even a rough estimation of the monetary losses will suffice. The language of money is well understood by top management.

Of course, there are other common languages to be utilized; for example, statistical language, or even the local dialect used by the various specialized departments: personnel, sales, quality control, manufacturing. It is the responsibility of middle managers to learn to understand all the local dialects as well as the language of money, to enable them to communicate with the upper management as well as with the workforce. Juran views it as imperative that middle managers are bilingual. They will be the ones to prove to top management that quality improvement is necessary for survival. And the proof of this need is easily provided by quantifying the chronic problems in the language of money wasted. A rough estimation of quality costs can indicate areas in need of improvement and can increase the awareness of opportunities of cost savings. (Note that this approach is substantially different from Deming's, which completely ignores any efforts at quality costs calculation, on the basis that the most important cost figures are probably invisible.)

3.3.2 Project identification

General awareness of opportunities needs to be converted into specific projects for action. There is no other way of achieving a breakthrough. An agreed project provides a licence for action. It helps to secure the needed budgets, facilities, permission to conduct experiments, needed tools and techniques, and adequate personnel. It provides a forum for communication and participation, which increase the likelihood of constructive action on the findings.

The priority projects can be decided by utilizing the Pareto principle. In the words of Juran, this principle suggests that any natural assortment of species follows the rule of the 'vital few and trivial many'. For example, relatively few of the customers (about 20%) might account for most of the sales (about 80%) – see Figure 3.2. A Pareto analysis of the scrap problems in monetary terms will serve to separate the vital few problems from the trivial many.

The vital few problems are usually automatically selected to become the projects to be nominated as the first to be tackled. From all the nominations, the priority projects will be the ones which score highly on their monetary return on the effort invested, the amount of potential improvement in quality and product saleability, their urgency, ease of technology involved, and level of acceptance by management and workforce. As soon as the priority projects have been determined, the next step is to organize adequately in order to carry out these projects successfully.

3.3.3 Organization for improvement

This stage requires that clear responsibilities are established for three levels of activity:

1. Steering or guiding the overall improvement programme.
2. Steering or guiding each project individually (project-by-project improvement).
3. Diagnosing or analysing each project.

First, a broad committee or a team of upper managers has to be created to guide the overall improvement programme and to commit funds, personnel and facilities. When the priority projects are numerous and complex, multiple subcommittees or task forces need to be set up to guide the individual projects. The choice of the subcommittee members should depend not on rank but on

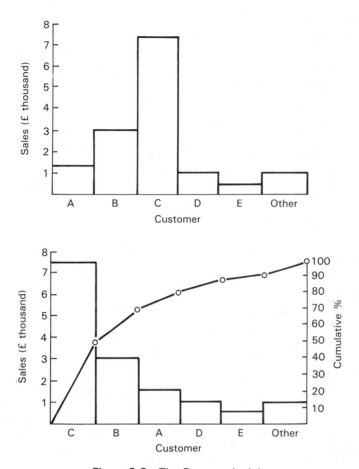

Figure 3.2 The Pareto principle

skill and capacity to make a useful contribution. If the problem tackled affects more than one department, the committee should be representative of all the affected company sections.

Written policies or charters need to be provided, so that legitimacy as well as direct and clear responsibilities are established for the members of the subcommittees. These are responsibilities for guiding, and responsibility and authority for analysis and diagnosis – necessary for making the journey from symptom to the cause of the problem. It is important that the line managers involved in the subsequent remedial actions are also involved in the steering activities. Whoever is fully involved in the diagnosis proceedings has a greater incentive for acting on the findings of the diagnosis.

When the company is small enough, or the projects are few and relatively simple, there is no need for formalities such as written charters. The team of upper managers can personally guide not only the broad improvement programme but each of the projects as well. So the need for formality should depend on the size and complexity of the problems.

After the completion of the organization for improvement, the diagnostic journey is ready to begin. This is the journey from symptom to cause, the more difficult of two necessary journeys, the other being that from cause to remedy.

3.3.4 The diagnostic journey

The journey from symptom to cause is an essential stage in the breakthrough sequence. It is a difficult stage to manage because it is not clear whose responsibility it is, and the skills for recognizing causes are rather difficult to find. The causes may remain hidden among many conflicting theories, and without diagnostic skills, agreement could be lacking.

Diagnostic skills are the ability to design experiments or data-sampling schemes, to collect the appropriate data without bias, to interpret the results, and to test any theories or propositions on offer scientifically. Apart from these skills, objectivity (to ensure a factual approach) and adequate time to conduct the diagnostic tasks (experiments, analysis etc.) are also needed.

Before any attempts are made to discover the causes of defects, one should keep in mind that there are two types of defect:

■ Operator-controllable defects.
■ Management-controllable defects.

The bulk of defects are the management-controllable ones – over 80% of the total (and remember, Deming now puts this figure at 94%!). These have to do with the system, which is controllable by the management. The operators can be said to be in a state of 'self-control' and to have all the means needed to 'control' any resulting defects when the following are true:

1. The operators know what is expected of them (they have adequately documented instructions, clear and unequivocal specifications, long-standing practices).
2. They know what their actual performance is (that is, whether or not they are fulfilling their current responsibilities).
3. They have the means to regulate (that is, to change their current practices to achieve conformance).

If any one of these points has not been met, it is because the management's job has not been completed and, hence, the resulting defects are management controllable.

Diagnosis of management-controllable errors requires a study of current management practices and current technology. A successful diagnosis can take place by conducting the following:

■ An analysis of symptoms (with 'autopsies' conducted to measure and examine the defects – to identify the failure modes).

- A systematic formulation of theories for the causes of the symptoms (through brainstorming, involving as many managers as possible).
- Thorough testing of the theories (by analysing prior in-house data – see Part II; by studying current operations and processes – see Part III; and by conducting off-line experiments – see Part IV).

As long as all the criteria 1–3 above are being met by the management, any occurring defects are controllable by the workforce.

But one frequently notes that, despite the fact that all the means for doing good work are provided, errors still occur. Attempts to motivate the workforce towards the zero defects concept have failed in the past, because this concept wrongly assumed that the bulk of defects were operator controllable and denied the old adage that 'to err is human'. Diagnosis of operator-controllable errors requires a study of current work habits, practices and priorities. One can then discover that there are many species of operator-controllable error, and lack of motivation is only one of them. In fact, according to Juran, there are three main types, as follows:

1. **Inadvertent errors:** These are unintentional, unpredictable errors, occurring randomly, which the operator is unaware of making.

    A remedy for this type of error consists of making the job more interesting (for example, through job rotation) or making it easier for the operator to retain attention (with templates, masks, overlays etc.). Another remedy is to reduce the extent of dependence on human attention; for example, through automation, alarm signals, cut-offs or fail-safe designs.

2. **Technique errors:** These arise from lack of knowledge of an essential new technique. They are unintentional, specific and unique to certain defect types, unavoidable (through the operators not knowing what to do differently) and consistent (they consistently occur to those operators who do not possess the technique).

    On many occasions, a small change in the method currently used can account for a large difference in the results. This difference constitutes the knack. This knack can be determined by studying and comparing the techniques used by the best and worst performers. It is then management's responsibility to enable the inferior performers, through proper training, to know what they should do differently in order to reach the level of the best. If possible, management should also change the current technology and operations, so that the process itself embodies the knack.

3. **Wilful errors:** These are the errors that the operator makes intentionally and persistently and is aware of making. These errors exhibit consistency (as opposed to randomness), they cannot be remedied by some special knack, and the majority of them are management initiated.

For example, fear induced by management may cause the operator not to reveal the true levels of scrap and current defect rates in order to avoid being blamed for them; thus, valuable information about past mistakes is deliberately hidden, so opportunities for prevention of future mistakes are lost. Certain standards may be violated in order to meet other (easier) ones. The workforce may cut corners in order to meet arbitrary targets imposed by the management. Frustrated by a lack of communication and a plethora of patronizing slogans demanding that everybody should do a better job (without providing the means), the workers may question management's sincerity and indeed be led to adopt an antisocial attitude of indifference, isolation and deliberate error-making.

Juran suggests that wilful errors can be remedied as follows:

(a) depersonalize the order ('one should not give orders to another; both should take orders from the situation');

(b) establish accountability and traceability (there is a need to know who the worker is, because anonymity is a temptation to irresponsibility — people behave more responsibly when their identity is known);

(c) provide balanced emphasis (if there are multiple standards to meet, some have to receive higher priority than others, and management has to take a definite decision on priorities);

(d) conduct periodic quality audits;

(e) provide assistance to the workers (to identify the principal operator-controllable defects, to discover for each defect the decisive knack and record it to serve as a basis for training);

(f) improve communications (to promote the mutual interests of and understanding between the workforce and the management);

(g) create positive competition with non-financial incentives;

(h) reassign the work (separate critical work from the rest so that selective assignment becomes feasible);

(i) motivate (by allowing participation and involvement in the company's future, by proper training and provision of the proper tools and techniques, by making the jobs inherently interesting, and by allowing the workers to take pride in their job by helping them to acquire a state of self-control).

3.3.5 Remedial action

In the preceding section some remedial actions have already been mentioned concerning the operator-controllable errors. However, the most important remedial actions are those associated with the management-controllable problems, the majority of all company problems. These actions are, of course, the responsibility of middle and top managers, who should embark on the remedial journey through the following phases.

Choice of alternatives

Once a problem has been diagnosed, there may be many alternative remedies to choose from. The choice can be considerably helped by quantifying for each alternative the cost impact to the company. An optimization of company costs and customer costs has to take place.

Activities that add no further value as far as the customer is concerned should be avoided. Non-value-adding activities include perfectionism and hair-splitting. A balance should be reached between extra value added and further cost consequences. The impact of different cost factors has to be taken into consideration. These factors include materials usage, productivity, energy consumption, market research expenditure etc. No individual department should attempt to optimize itself on its own, at the expense of other departments.

Preventive maintenance

When a problem has already caused some harm, solving it is simply fire-fighting; instead of working productively, managers are trying to rectify what has gone wrong, trying to make defective work good — a wasteful and disruptive activity. On the other hand, preventive maintenance of machines, tools, instruments and computers is always a value-added activity. Process designs should be directed at preventing the errors arising in the first place. Even the most automated process engineered to be in a state of self-control (by sensing the actual product quality and by regulating itself accordingly) needs a formal system of preventive maintenance added.

Communications

Adequate, open communication and feedback between the different departments are of paramount importance. Good communications require a standardization of language. Glossaries should be constructed for key words, phrases, code numbers and specifications. Procedures, instructions, corporate policies and objectives should be adequately and clearly documented, and frequently referred to, so that they remain the standard despite changes in materials, product configurations, formulations and test requirements.

When the quality of communication is low, many errors in the final product can be traced back to the information process rather than the manufacturing process. Error patterns can often indicate the need to improve the communication structure. Employees should be encouraged to pass information through that structure, to provide comments and queries, and to expect to receive answers. Incomplete communication and feedback are a breeding ground for errors; for example, at times of change in workshifts, when there is incomplete information about what has already been done (and how) and about what remains to be done.

Allocation of responsibility

There is a need to establish clear responsibilities for quality-oriented decisions and actions. The people available to make the decisions and take the actions should be identified. Agreement should be reached on who should do what, and any difference in opinions should be talked out and resolved as early as possible.

Inspection and test

Juran realistically sees the activity of inspection as a necessary evil, which, until the time comes when we can do without it, is in desperate need of improvement.

Errors in defect detection can be reduced by minimizing human errors, usually due to distraction and inability to focus properly all the time, especially when the number of quality characteristics under simultaneous inspection is large. The majority of human errors result when inspection is passive; that is, when the checker is not forced to maintain attention. Simple techniques can be employed to transform, where necessary, a state of passive checking into a state of active checking. For example, covering masks and overlays can help workers to concentrate, while sense multipliers can provide alarm signals in the presence of defects. To break up monotony and fatigue, reorganization of work, job rotation, rest periods etc. are recommended.

Fully automated inspection, providing feedback of process information and summary of faults (without human interference) is, of course, the ideal type of inspection. However, the certainty provided can be no better than the reliability of the equipment involved; this should be properly maintained and frequently calibrated.

But the fact remains that mass inspection and its associated costs cannot be reduced unless the chronic defect rate is reduced. Sampling inspection can replace 100% inspection; this presupposes adequate prior knowledge of process capability and stability, reliability of incoming materials, knowing how to react to the findings and when to take action etc. Under proper conditions it is feasible for process operators to undertake the job of sample inspection during full production, utilizing SPC tools and other diagnostic techniques (see Parts II and III).

Separation of problems

An application of the Pareto principle (see Part II) to the diagnosed problems can help in their separation into the following two categories:

1. **The vital few:** the minority of the problems which account for most of the defects. These should be tackled first in vital projects which can guarantee a good return on a relatively modest investment.

2. **The trivial many:** the many problems which account for a relatively low amount of defectiveness and cost. These should be tackled either collectively or individually.

Collective treatment of trivial problems is feasible when different problem types are essentially alike, having emerged from a process common to all (for example, different types of fault on printed circuit boards of varying size from the same flow soldering process). In such cases, optimization of the common process could solve the fault problems irrespective of the fault types.

Source utilization on a large scale for tackling trivial problems individually is not usually economically justifiable. For their solution one should rely on an ongoing effort, on a project-by-project basis, involving the workforce. In Japan, this idea has resulted in the establishment of quality control circles (see Chapter 5), a movement which greatly contributed to the solution of numerous trivial problems, and to the proof of the value of the ideas the workforce can offer on a routine basis, given the chance, the respect they deserve and the appropriate conditions.

3.3.6 Resistance to change

One obstacle inhibiting the beneficial application of the remedies for dealing with poor quality is resistance to change. This can take the form of delaying tactics or outright rejection of the remedy. The source of this resistance can be traced not only to the management ranks, but also to the workforce, to supervisors and even to unions.

Juran believes that resistance to a technological change is due to social and cultural factors. Anybody who is contemplating a technological change should first evaluate the potential impact the change can have on the company's culture. One should always be aware of the existence of a cultural pattern – a tight system of beliefs, habits, traditional practices – which will inhibit the implementation of any change which is seen as a threat. An essential ingredient of management development should be awareness of any cultural resistance and of the current practices that are usually threatened whenever a change is advocated.

Juran recommends certain actions to take in order to deal with cultural resistance. The main ones are as follows.

Provide participation

All those affected should be allowed to participate both in the planning and in the execution of the change. This, apart from avoiding feelings of resentment for being left out, provides the opportunity to evaluate the merits of the plan, its impact and the threat to current practices, and also to appreciate fully the resulting benefits once the change is implemented. For the advocates

75

of change it provides the opportunity to appreciate the other's point of view.

The recognized leadership of the culture should be the first to get involved. Every participant should be treated with dignity, so that a favourable social climate is developed, which can make the change more acceptable.

Provide enough time

Adequate time should be allowed for the change to be accepted. Indeed, it takes time to evaluate and accommodate the merits or threats of a change. Impatience and feelings of frustration about the delays in implementing a change never help; in fact, they might cause the resistance to become more acute.

Conducting a small-scale try out (at an appropriate time) reduces the risks and provides the needed proof not only for the unbelievers but also for the advocates themselves, who should not hesitate to drop their proposal if the evidence does not support it. In this way, the consequences of the change become predictable and surprises are avoided.

3.3.7 Holding the gains

The final step in the breakthrough sequence is to hold the gains achieved so far. This requires that the operating forces engage in control, which consists of evaluation of current performance, comparison of this performance with the desired (already gained) one, and corrective action when the comparison shows an out of control situation (a large difference).

For the operating forces to be able to engage in the control activity, they need to know what they are supposed to do, they need knowledge of their actual performance, and they need the ability to regulate – to take the corrective action when required. Management can assist the operators to achieve a state of self-control (and thus hold the gains) by successfully transferring the remedy from laboratory conditions to operating conditions. This can be achieved only if the management provides the following:

1. **A process capable of holding the gains:** Any recommended process changes should be designed to be irreversible. This is the only way that a revised process can work under operating conditions as well as it worked under laboratory conditions, when the associated project was guided well, causes of problems were diagnosed and remedies were designed. If the remedies are not consistently adhered to, the process may easily reverse back into its original (unsatisfactory) state.

2. **Established new standards:** The new operating standards and procedures need to be well defined and documented so that the operators know exactly

what is expected from them from now on. Confusion and uncertainty on this front always result in a failure to hold the gains.

3. **Training:** Changes in standards and procedures require training of the operators so that they know what exactly has been changed, what new decisions and actions will be required to make the changes effective, whose responsibility these are, the new tools and techniques, and the consequences of the changes.

4. **Established system of controls:** A well-established system of controls can consist of early warning signals, training prior to operations, systematic (statistical) techniques for analysis of data, a feedback loop of evaluation, assessment and action, automatic sensors and regulators where possible, and rules for decision making and reporting.

When a breakthrough into new levels of performance has been achieved and the resulting gains have been held and established as the new standard, the universal breakthrough sequence of events is ready to start again.

■ 3.4 Juran vs. Deming

Broadly speaking, the teachings of Juran and Deming are most of the time complementary, though sometimes substantially different; but many of their fundamental principles are basically the same. Their background is similar, too: they both studied under Shewhart, they were both invited to teach the Japanese in the early 1950s, are both world authorities in matters of quality. But what is apparent in their approaches is that Deming is concerned with education, whereas Juran is more concerned with actual implementation; this might have something to do with the fact that, while Deming was professionally mainly involved with academia and consultancy, Juran was more associated with professional management.

In general, Deming provides the philosophy, whereas Juran provides the specific structure which can help in the materialization of these principles. Indeed, it has been said that, 'If Deming is the Old Testament prophet of quality, Juran is the high priest of quality.' But the similarities in the fundamental principles advocated by the two men are many, especially in the following issues:

■ The role of top management. The main responsibility for guidance towards quality lies with the senior managers. After all, they are the ones responsible for more than 80% of the company problems (Juran prefers to use the realistic 80 : 20 ratio for the management-controllable versus the operator-controllable errors; Deming has recently revised this ratio to 94 : 6).

- The existence of a quality crisis.
- The importance of the customer: external and internal.
- The necessity of quality. Juran refers to the habit of quality, Deming to an obsession with quality, in order to satisfy the customer and survive in the competitive world markets of today.
- The importance of continuous improvement. Juran uses the word 'breakthrough', whereas Deming prefers 'innovation'.
- The need for scientific knowledge. Scientific tools and techniques must be used, in order to control the attained quality levels and improve further.
- Distinction of the causes of problems. Juran's sporadic and chronic parallel Deming's special and common causes.
- Dislike of unsubstantiated quality campaigns and exhortations demanding zero defects. Without the provision of the appropriate tools, exhortation cascades are always counterproductive.
- Training: investment for the future.
- Active participation in the efforts towards the solution of problems: the best way to utilize the hidden potential of the workforce.

Deming is supportive of many of Juran's ideas and frequently refers to them in his own books. In fact, Deming is closer to Juran than to any other quality guru. Both men's ideas have developed over time, and they are both working towards the same ends, with perhaps different strategies and starting points. Deming is more general in his approach, and Juran much more specific. Deming paints a picture of where you need to get to, whereas Juran suggests the specific tools and the precise road map to follow. Juran is not as hard on management as Deming, partly because he has risen up through management ranks. Deming strongly recommends a total transformation of current management practices as the only solution to the current crisis; he has not gone down the commercial track and does not worry too much about being confrontational. Juran prefers to take a more subtle approach, taking the existing management culture as a starting point and building on it; he puts emphasis on improving management performance rather than transforming management. For example, Juran discusses the pros and cons of management by objective (MBO), the setting of targets and goals, the provision of rewards and incentives, calculation of the costs of quality (the language of management) etc., whereas Deming dismisses them as bad practice.

Each uses different terminology and stresses different aspects. Deming's key issues are variation, continuous improvement, optimization of the total system. Juran concentrates on the quality trilogy (planning, control and improvement) and on a goal-setting approach towards increased conformance, guided by the costs of quality. Deming concerns himself with educational concepts and fundamental truths; Juran with building blocks and details of implementation. Deming stresses the evil of variation as the source of all problems, but Juran is not so profoundly influenced by it; instead, he believes in an organized structure for solving problems and making improvements on a project-by-project basis, something that Deming views as 'essential but not important'.

Deming puts emphasis on the management of the process rather than on the outcome, unlike Juran, who focuses on the results (see Section 3.1 for his formula for results), but with an emphasis on feedback loops as a model for managerial control. Juran also allocates responsibility among the company members differently from Deming. He places more of the quality responsibility on middle management and quality professionals, with top management's role restricted to guidance and policy making, and with the workforce's role being minimal. On the other hand, Deming believes that quality management and improvement responsibilities fall on all the company's employees, from top management to the hourly-paid worker; quality attainment has to become a religion for top managers, and (given adequate training) an everyday objective for the rest of the employees.

On the whole, there is a lot in Deming's philosophy that is not present in Juran's. Perhaps this is because Juran tries to accommodate his teachings, as far as is possible, to current management practices; but this obliges him to talk in the language of the old culture. The new economic age demands a new language, and the courage to break with tradition. This is where Deming comes in.

If there are aspects of Juran's philosophy that are viewed as wrong by Deming's standards, it is because they currently form a normal part of orthodox and deeply ingrained management practices; unlearning them would automatically help in coming to terms with Deming. Until this unlearning is complete, many of the other down-to-earth elements from Juran's approach can be utilized to soften the blow and fill any vacuum caused by the implementation of some of the more controversial aspects of Deming's philosophy; after a while, these aspects will not seem so controversial after all.

Crosby and the Quality Treatment

The determined executive has to have a brain transplant where quality is concerned.

Philip Crosby

Philip B. Crosby is another of the American quality gurus who rose to international fame mainly thanks to his teachings on quality management. Before he became a management consultant, he had worked his way up from line inspector to corporate vice-president and quality director of ITT. The author of *Quality is Free, Quality without Tears* and *The Art of Getting Your Own Sweet Way*, Crosby has taught thousands of company executives, and he is best known in relation to the concepts of zero defects (ZD), and 'Do it right first time.' He is the chairman of Philip Crosby Associates and the director of Crosby's Quality College in Winter Park, Florida.

In this chapter we will outline the main principles of Crosby's philosophy, pinpointing along the way the similarities to and some distinct differences from Deming's principles. Crosby's quality treatment largely sounds like a doctor's prescription: the aim is, of course, to prevent or cure the illness of low quality.

■ 4.1 Crosby's diagnosis of a troubled company

Crosby sees a troubled company as a patient in need of a quality vaccine. Trouble with quality inside always results in trouble with the customers outside. Customer dissatisfaction with the end-product or service may be the final and most obvious symptom of a diseased company, but there are also other symptoms, the appearance of which always indicates trouble with quality. One symptom is usually the consequence of another, something that perhaps facilitates their simultaneous cure. Some of the main symptoms are listed below, and their interrelationship is obvious:

1. The company has an extensive field service for reworking and corrective actions. But service under guarantee and readjustment or reworking of the product the customer has already bought may be the main cause of losing

the customer for ever. Investing heavily in such a service is an admission that faulty output is inevitable and should always be expected as a way of life; an admission that no process can ever be defect-free. Another version of this symptom is the presence of an extensive programme of mass inspection. Of course, the reason for the extensive inspection or field reworking service is usually the presence of the next symptom.

2. The outgoing product normally deviates from the customer's requirements. In many situations, non-conformance is so heavily embodied in the company culture that it has become the norm. Defects are seen as a necessary evil, tackled only by mass inspection or the reworking service. But this is something that normally costs much more than the effort required to prevent defects arising in the first place. Deviation from the desired target is usually the result of ignorance about quality standards, which brings us to the third symptom.

3. Management does not provide a clear performance standard, so the employees develop their own. It is management's responsibility to provide the conditions in which quality can flourish, and to establish a culture where continuous improvement is the standard. If this is not done, the workforce defines its own standards, based, justifiably, on the current capability of the processes. But in the absence of a quality ethos and of a management commitment, these processes will always function below their potential, something that will drive employees, through no fault of their own, to commit themselves to a specific level of incompetence! The absence of management commitment and involvement is always apparent from the next symptom.

4. Management denies that it is the cause of the problem. Managers tend to blame the workers in order to hide their inability to improve the system. As Deming and Juran state, more than 80% of the problems are traceable to the system, which it is the management's responsibility to take care of. Denial of this responsibility invariably means that management causes and will continue to cause the majority of the problems. Costly fire-fighting then becomes their only line of action, something that gives rise to the fifth symptom.

5. Management does not know the price of non-conformance. A determination of the cost of quality at this stage could alleviate this symptom. It might reveal how much it costs to the company to do things wrong, to fire-fight, to mass inspect, to rework and reinspect. It might reveal the usefulness of prevention and of proper training; training on the appropriate tools for achieving quality, first time, every time. As long as management prefers to remain ignorant about the costs of non-conformance, extensive field service will always be necessary; which brings us back to symptom 1.

The above symptoms are indicative of a company that always has problems with quality. Crosby also recognizes interrelated symptoms which characterize a company with a poor track record in the quality improvement effort, the most obvious of which are as follows:

1. The improvement effort is aimed at the lower level of the organization, as though senior management should not be responsible for and are not serious about, quality.
2. The effort is called a programme rather than a process. This gives the impression of something temporary, soon to be replaced by something else, rather than the impression of the never-ending which requires constant attention.
3. There are many temporary activities, uncoordinated from above, which always result in cynicism and self-defeating admission of the fact that defects are inevitable, and that the economics of quality require errors.
4. There is an apparent management non-involvement in the quality effort, which results in an ignorance of what tools are required and of how long one needs to allow for the process of quality improvement to have an effect. This in turn causes management to become impatient for results, and to proceed with spontaneous actions for short-term solutions which do more harm than good.

■ 4.2 Crosby's quality vaccine

The main ingredients of the 'Crosby vaccination serum' are based on integrity and dedication to customer satisfaction, and on a company-wide system of policies and operations designed to achieve and communicate quality improvements.

The major part of the vaccine should be integrity – an honest effort on the part of the senior executives so that hassle and bureaucracy are avoided, management performance is always improving and customer requirements are always satisfied in the most effective way (Right first time). Quality should be in the forefront of any policy and operation regarding the system of education, management, finance and cost evaluation, with an emphasis on defect prevention and on learning from past experience. Communicating information about identified errors, opportunity for improvements, quality progress and recognition is also of paramount importance for the quality vaccine to be effective. The communication should extend to suppliers, who should be supported and educated so that an atmosphere of trust and cooperation is developed, which will guarantee prompt delivery of quality incoming materials.

This last point very much resembles Deming's management Point 4 (see Chapter 2). But the resemblance of Crosby's serum ingredients to Deming's principles do not end there. For example, other similarities are in Deming's obsession with quality and with an education system based on the scientific approach, and also his dislike of performance appraisals, viewed by both men

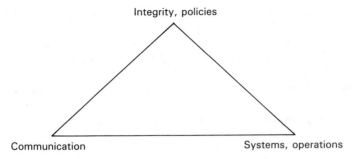

Figure 4.1   Crosby's triangle

as counterproductive and demotivating. Crosby believes that, in the majority of cases, performance reviews are not truthful, usually painting a better picture than people actually deserve; something that shows lack of integrity, an important ingredient of the quality vaccine.

But the main principle shared by Crosby and Deming is the responsibility of management. Crosby believes that the administration of the quality serum requires three distinct management actions or attitudes, as follows:

1. Determination – awareness that the management needs to take the lead in the new economic age. The times of cheap energy, low labour rates, captive markets and inexpensive materials are gone.
2. Education – for the managers, who should themselves become the educators and modern leaders, rather than mere supervisors.
3. Implementation – concentrating on the effort of creating a hassle-free and motivating working environment, providing adequate guidance on the never-ending road to quality improvement, and involving everybody.

The similarities of Crosby's principles to those of Deming, and indeed to those of a TQM culture, give rise to another quality triangle, this time with reference to Crosby's quality ingredients. Crosby's triangle is shown in Figure 4.1.

■ 4.3 Crosby's absolutes for quality management

First Absolute: The definition of quality is conformance to requirements, not goodness

The definition of quality can never make any sense unless it is based on exactly what the customer wants. A product is a quality product only when it conforms to the customer's requirements; of course, these requirements should be made known to the workforce, which should be provided with adequate tools to achieve them. Consequently, the management has the following three tasks to perform:

1. Establish the requirements to be met and communicate them to the employees.
2. Provide the appropriate tools and techniques, and the necessary training in them.
3. Provide continuous support and encouragement.

Second Absolute: The system of quality is prevention

The secret of success is to study the process and perform some sort of risk analysis; that is, identify opportunities for error. Something can then be done so that the error is avoided. Contingency plans can also be drawn up, so that if a problem materializes, the damage is controlled and restricted to the minimum possible.

A company which relies on mass inspection of the final output to improve quality is doomed to stagnation. The only prerequisite of prevention is an understanding of the process; implementation of SPC (see Part III) can provide the understanding needed. One can then immediately know what to do to prevent rather than inspect, appraise or test.

Third Absolute: The performance standard is zero defects

It is important that a feeling of determination exists throughout the company to do things right first time, on time, every time. Determination, coupled with a system of management which provides the communication needed and the tools for prevention, can succeed in making zero defects (ZD) a reality. However, it is important that the concept of ZD is not seen as a motivation programme, but only as a management performance standard, simply indicating that there is no room for imperfection, complacency or the attitude that 'that's close enough!' Crosby admits that many managers misunderstood the concept of ZD and used it as a slogan, imposing an arbitrary target on the workforce. As Deming emphasizes, unless the right conditions are created and the techniques are provided to reach this target, such a treatment of this concept can only create anxiety, frustration and mistrust towards management.

But error-free products are possible, and Japanese industry has proved it. It is not, therefore, unreasonable to expect a level of zero defects, and the quality tools for achieving it do exist. For example, the technique advocated by Taguchi (see Part IV) regards the mere satisfaction of specification limits as not good enough; this is because any deviation from the target, however small, causes a loss to society and will keep causing it until zero deviation (or ZD) is accomplished.

Fourth Absolute: The measurement of quality is the price of non-conformance

In order to attract the attention of senior management, quality has to be measured in financial terms. This is how quality can become a management function, and not just a technical one. If one measures the cost consequences involved in doing things wrong (due to rejects, reworking, warranty costs etc.), these can very well represent 20–40% of the total operating costs. This is the price of non-conformance (PONC), mainly the result of not doing things right first time.

When a rough calculation of the PONC is done initially, it can be so alarmingly high that it will surely prompt top management to do something about quality. What will become apparent is the need for professional quality functions, prevention efforts and quality education. The cost of these efforts is the price of conformance (POC) – money well spent.

■ 4.4 Crosby's fourteen steps for quality improvement

The quality improvement process is never-ending. To keep the momentum going, the appropriate culture and attitude about quality have to be embedded throughout the organization. Crosby has laid down fourteen steps to assist in the establishment of a quality ethic. The order is not too important, as most of the steps can run in parallel. However, it is evident that Steps 1–6 have to be made by management and should naturally come first.

Step 1: Management commitment

Senior management has to demonstrate a commitment to quality. This is the only way to convince the workforce that management is not only serious about quality, but also prepared to be involved in the process. A corporate policy on quality should be issued. This needs to be clear and unambiguous, and should ideally be based on the important premise of defect-free delivery of products and services, on time. Quality should be the first item on the agenda of all management meetings, and in all the activities that top managers are involved with. Management commitment should continuously be demonstrated and tested until it can be assumed.

Step 2: The quality improvement team

A team needs to be set up to guide the process of quality improvement. This team will require a definite direction and leadership, and should have clear access to top management. The idea is not to use this team for corrective actions or fire-fighting. Its main initial task will be to change the attitudes and practices of those who run the company; also to set up the educational activities required, and subsequently to coordinate and support the whole effort. In short, the quality improvement team will be the group of people (ideally from management ranks) which will assist in the changing of the system to enable quality to flourish.

Step 3: Measurement

To avoid frustration and hassle, one needs a clear method of measurement. Every part of any activity, its input, process work and output, lends itself to measurement. The type of measurement can be easily decided upon, by the people associated with the particular activity. Once this decision is taken, a level of reference is created, reasonable targets can be set, progress can be monitored and comparisons can be made. There is no other way to communicate in definite terms.

Step 4: The cost of quality

Calculating how much poor quality is costing the company can be beneficial in getting management's attention, in providing an incentive for improvement, in setting up priorities and in showing up trends. But Crosby himself admits that the whole concept of the cost of quality, if it is not handled properly, can be counterproductive and can actually cause more trouble rather than save money. This opinion is also shared by Deming, who actually believes that the most important cost figures are incalculable anyway. Nevertheless, Crosby believes that the quality costs need to be identified objectively, pulled together and fed into the regular management process formally, and treated as a positive rather than a threatening item. Only then can the concept serve as a good stimulus for the quality improvement process itself.

Step 5: Quality awareness

An adequate system of communication is vital for a company. Through this, awareness about quality should spread throughout the organization and be adapted to the company's culture. People should be continuously reminded about the management commitment to quality, the associated policies and the training facilities on offer. Crosby is not against slogans or posters about 'Zero defects' or 'Do it right first time' as a reminder to the workforce of the importance of quality; something that Deming strongly disagrees with.

Step 6: Corrective action

The main purpose of corrective action should be to prevent errors or identify and eliminate causes of problems for ever. Unfortunately, many companies regard corrective action as an activity composed of reworking, fire-fighting or replacement of the non-conforming item with a conforming one. But such an activity is always non-value-added. Corrective activities need to be based on analyses of past data so that the causes of problems are determined and taken care of permanently.

Step 7: Zero defects planning

Proper planning is required for the concept of ZD to become properly embedded in the company culture. It will have to start with a ZD commitment on the part of top management. This is the only way that the concept will be taken seriously and recognized as a dignified ideal.

Step 8: Employee education

An investment in quality education can result in quantum leaps in improvement. A proper education system requires time and money, class-work and assignments, explanatory videos and workshops, homework and team discussions in order to personalize the subject to the company concerned. Crosby summarizes the entire education process in what he calls 'the six Cs':

- Comprehension (understanding of what is necessary, abandonment of the old way of thinking and of outdated practices).
- Commitment (management-led dedication to cultural change).
- Competence (methodical and scientific implementation of the improvement process).
- Communication (complete cooperation throughout the production process, including suppliers and customers).
- Correction (elimination of all causes of problems and prevention of new ones arising).
- Continuance (never-ending effort for improvement).

Step 9: Zero defects day

Another point of difference with Deming's teachings is the matter of zero defects day. Crosby recommends that a ZD day is planned to reward serious efforts, and is celebrated at least annually with speakers representing senior management, the customers, the unions and even the city or region. This will then act as a reminder of the importance of quality and as a demonstration of the commitment towards the ZD principle. Deming opposes unsubstantiated ZD campaigns and exhortations as counterproductive; if a ZD day is part of a quality effort which lasts only for a single day, without being supported by any quality action in the rest of the year, it will only make the workforce question management's sincerity, and create a negative atmosphere of indifference.

Step 10: Goal setting

Goal setting is the immediate consequence of measurement. There is no point in measuring something unless there is a target to be met. When it comes to quality, the ultimate goal is that of zero defects, and all intermediate goals should move in that direction. Of course, Deming would argue that arbitrary targets do not serve any purpose whatsoever.

Step 11: Error cause removal

The permanent removal of the causes of error requires a team effort. Adequate means of communication will ensure the sharing of the necessary information, which can help not only in the identification of the common sources of error and their permanent elimination, but also in the prevention of the same problems arising in the future.

Step 12: Recognition

Crosby considers recognition as a necessary reference point and as a guideline to help the improvement efforts in the right direction. The recognition process needs to be planned carefully and developed gradually; it should not be rushed. When a 'Beacon of Quality' is awarded to somebody who deserves it, it does not have to be in monetary terms. It can act as an incentive to others and an example to emulate.

Step 13: Quality council

All quality professionals can be brought together in one group under the name of the quality council. These will be the people who will define the mission, vision, values and policies necessary for managing the improvement process. They can learn from each other, and their coordinated expertise can be more effective in supporting the quality improvement teams in their efforts towards the elimination of hassle and the achievement of zero defects.

Step 14: Do it all over again

The process of learning, participating, experimenting with new methods and improving should never end. Quality improvement has to become the culture of the company, and this can only happen if the effort is a continuous one. The process can then gain speed and permanence. The momentum should never be allowed to slow down. Continuous re-education and involvement, actively supported by top management, are the keys in making quality attainment an enduring way of life.

A final word from Crosby:

> Every ingredient involved in setting up a permanent system to eliminate hassle and to cause quality improvement requires special attention. When management respects the rights of the customer exactly the way it respects the rights of the banks and stockholders, then quality will happen all the time. When honoring the right of the employees to be free of hassle is considered as important as increasing sales, then hassle will be eliminated.
>
> What needs to be done first, is to educate people and at the same time to formalize the management commitment, the measurement and the awareness. Quality is to be first among equals, and it should be first on the agenda.
>
> Quality will never cease to be a major problem until management believes that there is absolutely no reason that we should ever deliver a nonconforming product or service to our customers. The producing of defect-free products and services on time, is mostly caused by the minds of those who hold the strings. If something you want to happen is not happening, follow the string back to its origin. It might terminate in the office of someone you know. Perhaps even yourself!

5 | Imai's *Kaizen*

Quality is not any single thing but an aura, an atmosphere, an overpowering feeling that a company is doing everything with excellence.
John F. Welch, General Electric Company

Masaaki Imai is the chairman of the Cambridge Corporation, an international management consultancy and executive recruiting firm, based in Tokyo, which he founded in 1962. Imai has brought together the management philosophies, theories and tools that have been popular in Japan over the years, as a single concept – *kaizen*. This chapter is based on Imai's view of *kaizen*, which, as he says, has been responsible for Japan's economic success.

There are, of course, many quality gurus whose principles and teachings formed the basis and contributed to the development of the *kaizen* concept. Some outstanding ones (Deming, Juran) have already been studied in detail earlier in this book. But there are more; the main contributions of some of those (Feigenbaum, Ishikawa, Ohno, Shingo) will also be covered in this chapter.

■ 5.1 The concept

In a working environment, *kaizen* means continuous process improvement involving everybody. But more generally, the *kaizen* philosophy advocates ongoing improvement, not only in working life, but also in personal life, home life and social life.

The type of improvement *kaizen* signifies is the constant and gradual improvement, no matter how small, which should be taking place all the time, in every process, involving everyone from all the ranks of management and workforce. When a new standard is achieved, the management should make certain it is maintained and that the conditions are there to ensure the attainment of even higher standards. The *kaizen* improvement is by definition a long-term and long-lasting improvement, the result of a team effort; it is process-oriented and actually requires little investment, but great effort, to maintain.

■ 5.2 *Kaizen* and innovation

The *kaizen* improvement contrasts sharply with the type of drastic improvement which is usually the result of innovation. This is a short-term, dramatic improvement, the result of a technological breakthrough based on individual ideas and efforts. It normally requires a large initial investment but little effort to maintain, since it is usually a one-off phenomenon.

Kaizen and innovation are two complementary aspects that both lead to improvement. Top management's responsibility is to maintain a balance between the two. They are both necessary for the survival and competitive success of an organization. Their main difference lies in the fact that *kaizen* is process-oriented, whereas innovation is results-oriented.

This same distinction generally epitomizes the difference between the Japanese and the Western way of thinking. In particular, the US economy, fast-growing during the post-war years, chose the innovation path in order to satisfy the ever-increasing market demands of the times. Many technological innovations and new products appeared, something that led to immediate profits and instant recognition. As a consequence, the seemingly minor benefits of gradual improvement were not rated as important. Emphasis on short-term profits led to a climate unfavourable to the idea of a slow and patient effort towards long-term quality attainment. On the whole, efforts towards continuous improvement were not rewarded by Western managers, who appraised individuals only on the basis of results. Such a management policy inevitably leads to individualism, competitive feelings and isolation.

This was not the policy of Japanese management, which always promoted and supported team efforts towards gradual improvement of the processes. This is the basis of *kaizen*; a process-oriented approach, where efforts for process improvement are properly rewarded. It is a people-oriented approach which promotes discipline, participation and involvement, skill development, morale and communication. The strategy does not exclude efforts for innovation and new ideas. But whenever a new breakthrough is achieved, *kaizen* efforts maintain it and improve it. This does not only help to keep the gains, it also creates the conditions to upgrade the standards and to achieve further breakthroughs more easily.

Keeping the gains is as important as upgrading the standard. Everything deteriorates as soon as it has been established, and if there is no effort for improvement, loss of gains is inevitable. *Kaizen* efforts are needed to maintain as well as achieve new levels of excellence. There is a sense of urgency in *kaizen*, an ongoing effort for change. There is no room for complacency or overconfidence. Everything is considered imperfect and therefore subject to further change. At the same time, perfection is viewed as a utopia, hardly ever achievable, which means that the efforts for further improvement should never stop.

Constant innovation is one of the two prerequisites for achieving and sustaining superior company performance, according to Tom Peters, one of the youngest American quality gurus. The second prerequisite is exceptional care for the customer, through superior service and quality for the external customer, and through proper leadership for the internal customer. A simple model for achieving excellence is shown in Figure 5.1. Peters does not see any viable alternative for long-term competitive advantage to adhering to the four basic principles depicted in Figure 5.1. He justifies this as follows.

Constant innovation

We start with the established condition of a messy world. The only way to advance is to experiment; but the best way for the experimenters to act is through independent groups. The management objective should be the development of the appropriate climate so that the experiments for innovation can bring results.

The ingredients for innovation are obvious: persistence, passion, effort, creativity, small research groups. Failure can also be an ingredient; but this is natural. One learns from failure. No failure usually means no innovative efforts, no experimenting in new areas.

Care of (external) customers

The consumer should not be viewed simply as the object of an instant sale, to be forgotten soon after. What is important is the long-term total satisfaction of the customer, and this should be a priority. Clearly this satisfaction can only come with a quality product that fully conforms to the customer's expectations, and with a proper after-sale service. Customers' complaints

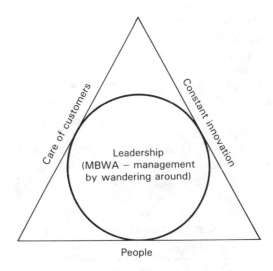

Figure 5.1 Peters' model

should be viewed as an opportunity for improvement, and in no case should be ignored. The customer should not be ignored: doing so amounts to thinly disguised contempt – the greatest obstacle to improvement. Treat the customer with respect: sell on quality, not on price. First concentrate on achieving quality, then on reducing costs. After all, when quality is there, profits, market share and low production costs will also be there.

People

There is a golden rule: take care of your customers, and your people (internal customers) and market forces will take care of you. The members of the workforce should be viewed as associates. And, as with any association, the following four rules should be adhered to:

1. Fairness: to control destructive conflict.
2. Freedom: to allow the experience of failure.
3. Commitment: the power behind the power to succeed.
4. Discretion: to avoid behaviour that could damage the company.

The secret of success is teamwork and ownership. Treat your people as business people; make everybody owners, involve them in important decisions. Indeed, when the members of a team feel that they own their job, they perform many times better than the rest and are committed to the company's success.

Leadership

This is the element that connects all the others in the model. Peters suggests a list of characteristics that a leader (not just a manager) should possess, as follows: vision, enthusiasm, love, trust, obsession, consistency, attention, care, implicit or explicit use of symbols, facilitation, creating heroes at all levels, shaping values, coaching, passion for excellence, effectively wandering around – in other words, being present at all levels of the organization. These provide a completely different model from the old (or current) one of the professional manager; that of administrator, referee, fire-fighter, decision maker, pronouncer.

The most important obligation of a leader is to take care of people – external or internal. It is simply a matter of paying attention. Attention can be regarded as symbolic behaviour; as a result of it, others become engaged. Productivity can go up simply because attention is being paid to the workforce; quality can go up simply because there is a focus on the importance of quality.

The leader must have a vision of where the company is heading, and should be able to communicate (dramatize) this vision consistently. The vision should be challenging, but at the same time realistic and achievable.

For successful leadership one needs the following: an ability to turn work into pleasure; small victories (creation of winners, feelings of ownership); and an ability to debureaucratize, to teach, to coach, to support, to advise, to confront problems. But most importantly one needs management by wandering around (MBWA). It is a duty to walk around and at the same time to listen, to teach and to help. Every manager should be out of his/her office 75% of the time, of which 50% should be spent with the production people, and the rest with (external) customers, suppliers and people in other levels of the organization. Contact through MBWA can always help in the better appreciation of everybody's performance, and it is the only way to discover what is happening, what goes wrong, so as to lead and convey values effectively.

■ 5.3 The *kaizen* management practices

A management-oriented *kaizen* is crucial if the morale and the momentum are to be kept up. The *kaizen* practices outlined below have been developed over the years, and can be attributed to various quality specialists, some of whom (and their main contributions) are also acknowledged below. The common element in these practices is that they are clearly management responsibilities, and most of the time involve managers from different departments working together as a team.

5.3.1 Total quality control

The practice of total quality control (TQC) is viewed as the high road to *kaizen*. If we search for the originator of the TQC concept, we will discover Dr Armand V. Feigenbaum. His books, *Total Quality Control* and *Quality Control: Principles, practices and administration*, were discovered by the Japanese as early as 1950–1.

Feigenbaum

Feigenbaum advocates a total approach to quality, involving everybody in any process, manufacturing or not. He argues the benefits of preventive maintenance as opposed to fire-fighting, and of the efforts for an early-stage build-in of quality as opposed to relying on inspection. To him, quality is simply a way of managing a business organization, and needs a customer-oriented, cost-effective quality management programme that all the people in a company can relate and commit themselves to.

All the above remind us of the Deming ideals, but it is clear that Feigenbaum also relates to Juran when he suggests the four steps of an effective quality control system:

1. Setting quality standards.
2. Appraising conformance to these standards.

3. Acting when standards are exceeded.
4. Planning for improvements in the standards.

He stresses the need for quality-mindedness throughout the organization; this needs a serious programme of quality education and participation, aimed at stimulating and building up operator responsibility and interest in quality. This programme should have the complete support of the top management, and should be allowed to develop gradually within the company.

Feigenbaum has a very serious, money-oriented approach to the management of quality. His major contribution to the subject of the cost of quality was his recommendation that quality costs should be categorized and separately managed. He identified three major categories: failure costs, appraisal costs and prevention costs. The underlying principle was that investment in proper quality planning and prevention activities can lead to a substantial reduction in failure costs (scrap, reworking, fire-fighting etc.) and even in appraisal costs (inspection, audits etc.).

Feigenbaum gives an excellent definition of a total quality system which encapsulates most of the principles he believes in:

> Total Quality System is the agreed company-wide and plant-wide work structure, documented in effective, integrated technical and managerial procedures, for guiding the co-ordinated actions of the people, the machines and the information of the company and plant, in the best and most practical ways to assure customer quality satisfaction and economical costs of quality.

Ishikawa

Within a Japanese organization, TQC also refers to company-wide quality control (CWQC), a concept strongly associated with Professor Kaoru Ishikawa, the pioneer in Japan of certain quality tools such as the cause and effect diagram (see Part II), and movements such as quality circles (see Section 5.3.3 below). Ishikawa strongly believed in the provision of a proper quality control education, initially to factory foremen/women and supervisors, and subsequently to grass-roots workers. He has produced down-to-earth textbooks for quality circle members, concentrating on simple statistical techniques for data collection and presentation, which would help in the sorting out and documentation of possible causes of variation and their interrelationships. Such a tool is the cause and effect diagram (or Ishikawa or fishbone diagram), which Ishikawa first developed in 1943. An important requirement for an effective application of this technique is open group communication and participation, things that Ishikawa viewed as critical.

Ishikawa is also associated with the company-wide quality control movement which started in Japan in the years following the visits of Deming and Juran, and which was concerned with company-wide participation in the pursuit of quality and its control, from top management to lower-ranking employees. Efforts were concerned with controlling and improving the quality not only of the final product, but also of the management, the after-sales service and the company itself.

Kaizen consciousness with TQC

Part of the TQC activities is to build quality not only into the product or process, but also into people, who will then become *kaizen*-minded. However, *kaizen* consciousness can only be established when management changes the corporate culture. Changing the attitudes towards TQC requires the cooperation of everybody, from top management to the least-skilled worker, in all areas, from market research, purchasing, product planning and design, to manufacture, inspection, scheduling (delivery), field service, training and finance. The company-wide coordination required to realize and deploy the policy goals (policy deployment) of a TQC programme is a management responsibility, and in *kaizen* terminology is called cross-functional management. Only a firm and effective cross-functional management can ensure that TQC becomes a company-wide problem-solving system of continuous improvement.

TQC is process-oriented, advocating the use of simple statistical techniques which utilize real process data in order to identify the sources of the problems. Improvement can then be attained during production (on-line QC) or even independently of the production line (off-line QC). Unbiased information about the true capability of the process can be gathered, and can be used by top management to define reasonable targets for productivity and quality. So TQC is not seen simply as a technical tool for the operator, but also as an indispensable tool for management decision making. The resulting management decisions are not profit oriented, but quality oriented, with the understanding that profit is a natural consequence of quality. Total quality is being achieved through adequate education and training, by proper communication, by treating next-process workers as customers, and by having as the ultimate objective the complete satisfaction of the recipient of the end-product or service.

Deming's PDCA (plan, do, check, act) cycle is in complete agreement with the TQC ideal. The Deming cycle reflects a never-ending, systematic attempt to improve everything. Every effort is first planned properly (P), then applied carefully (D), checked to see if it has brought the desired improvement (C) and acted upon (A) to ensure that past mistakes are prevented and the lessons have been learned. Then the whole procedure starts all over again in order to improve on the improvement and upgrade to new standards. TQC provides the discipline necessary to ensure that an improved standard is strictly observed and maintained, and an even better standard is continuously sought.

5.3.2 *Kanban* (just-in-time) systems

Kanban means signboards or labels, something that is being left behind at a specific stage of the process to signify that a collection of a quantity of parts is taking place. When all the parts have been collected, the same *kanban* is sent further back to an earlier stage of the same process or to a preceding process, at which time it becomes an order for more parts. So *kanban* can be viewed as an instruction requiring the operator to perform a given task, that is, to produce more product or move material. The underlying principle is that all necessary parts are received and delivered promptly only when they are needed, cutting down on waste, storing space and inventory.

The importance of the *kanban* communicating procedure has made it synonymous with the 'just-in-time' (JIT) production system, first employed by Toyota Motor Corporation. Inherent in the JIT principle is the understanding that the people responsible for a particular process are the suppliers of those responsible for the next process, and the customers of those of the preceding process. This means that just-in-time collection, production and delivery for a particular process can be achieved only if the same can be achieved for the preceding or following process. Management needs to identify the non-value-added activities and the waste movement of the materials which inhibit continuous operation. *Kanban* helps in changing the plant and machinery layout for better efficiency. If necessary, the whole factory space is redesigned to fit the layout. The idea is to reduce warehouse and storing space, stock on the line and excess inventory. But for this to happen it is necessary that quality materials are being processed at all times. This in turn requires the existence of a reliable supplier, and the provision of the proper tools and facilities, which can maximize process quality and efficiency and minimize effort.

A major step nearer to JIT can be made by modifying or eliminating unnecessary equipment and activities which contribute nothing to quality. An example is mass inspection of incoming materials and final products. This can be avoided if statistical evidence of quality is readily provided by a reliable supplier (Deming's Point 4), and if final inspection is replaced by ongoing, but limited, on-line inspection for faster feedback. The technique of statistical process control (see Part III) is ideal for this purpose.

Space should be reserved only for storing in-process stock, not for stock which might (or might not) be used one day. The idea is to store for just in time not for just in case. Ideally, there should be no warehouse in the factory; the parts needed for the assembly line should be unloaded from the back of a waiting truck at the exact time of production and at the point of use in the process, while another truck waits to load the finished product for delivery to the shop where it will be sold.

Taiichi Ohno, the pioneer of the *kanban* system in Toyota's plant, has identified many categories of waste which are avoidable: overproduction, waste in motion and transportation of units, waste in processing and machine time, waste in taking inventory and waste resulting from defects. Ohno demonstrated that most of the above waste can be eliminated if the following procedure is put in motion. The exact number of units required are transported to the next stage of the production process only when they are needed, not as soon as they are ready; the operator of each stage has the responsibility for the collection of the units from the previous stage. A *kanban* (signpost) is attached to the box of parts as they go to the assembly line, and the same *kanban* is returned when the parts are all used, to serve as an order for more and as a record of work done. The same procedure can be extended to sub-contractors and external suppliers, who will then be involved in a joint effort towards coordination and efficiency. Only enough production to meet demand (that is, small lots) should be allowed; speculative, just-in-case production should not. Eliminating wasteful interruptions and reducing the lot sizes will allow for better responsiveness to the customer's exact timing requirements.

Ohno combined the *kanban* system with another structural feature called *jidohka* (or autonomation), whereby an automatic mechanism stops the entire production system whenever a defective part is found along the process line. Appropriate adjustments then take place so that major problems are prevented from arising in the future. This concept, apart from adhering to the principle of prevention rather than cure, can substantially save on work allocation times, since the worker only needs to attend to the machine when it stops because of a problem, not at any other time.

The autonomation idea is equivalent to one pioneered by a Japanese quality specialist, Shigeo Shingo. In the early 1960s Shingo developed the concept of *poka-yoke* (or defect = 0), meaning mistake-proofing: source inspection is employed actively to identify process errors before they become defects; when an identification takes place, the process is stopped until the cause is determined and eliminated. Monitoring potential error sources takes place at every stage of the process, so that errors (leading to defects) are detected as soon as possible and corrected at source, rather than at a later stage.

Needless to say, Ohno's and Shingo's techniques can be effective only if a certain (high) level of quality has already been built into the process as early as possible. This can be achieved through the use of appropriate statistical tools by the workers, who should be allowed the initiative to eliminate bottle-necks and interruptions; also through proper cooperation with the suppliers of the process components. Otherwise, *jidohka* or *poka-yoke* will cause a prohibitively large number of stoppages, and just-in-time production will never materialize.

5.3.3 Small group activities – QC circles

These are the activities of informal groups whose members meet occasionally on a voluntary basis, with the main purpose of problem solving. Comprising these groups are people from management and the workforce, as well as from suppliers and subcontractors. These people work together on an equal basis; this strengthens team spirit, helps in the setting and attainment of reasonable targets, improves morale and communication, promotes initiative and substantially develops the ability to solve problems.

Over the years, there have been many types of group, with names representing their objectives, such as safety groups, productivity committees, zero-defects movements, quality control (QC) circles, mini-think-tanks etc. The most widely used name is 'QC circle', pioneered in Japan in 1962 by Professor Ishikawa. Initially, as is the case for many other groups, QC circles represented study groups, typically consisting of six to ten people, aiming towards the educational development of their members. In this particular case, study of statistical techniques on quality control led to workshops with an emphasis on problem solving and quality improvement.

The members of these groups were initially subjected to a training course lasting from 20 to 40 hours. The course consisted of the following three parts:

1. Study of simple problem-solving techniques (Pareto analysis, brainstorming, cause and effect diagrams, frequency histograms, control charts etc. − see Part II).
2. Study of reports of improvement projects carried out by other QC circles.
3. Participation in an actual project and implementation of the lessons learned.

Subsequently, the members were supposed to meet weekly or fortnightly, under the supervision of a circle facilitator, to solve work-related problems which they themselves had selected. They would select the appropriate data, apply the scientific tools in a systematic way and, having evaluated the cost-effectiveness of the solutions, present their findings to senior management for approval. The selected solution would be implemented and the effects would be monitored, ideally by the same individuals who had contributed to this solution. In this way, the people taking part learned new skills and developed their initiative and their abilities in problem solving. A supportive atmosphere and a spirit of trust and respect were also developed among the members and among different QC circles, something that helped the promotion of team spirit company wide.

The existence of QC circles was not restricted to manufacturing industry; thousands of QC circles flourished in the service sector, administration, sales, office-work etc. Their growth in Japan has been phenomenal. Joseph Juran has estimated that by the end of the 1970s, around 10 million workers were involved in the QC movement, completing over 15 million projects, some of modest value, but some quite large. Apart from substantial benefits for the company, this movement has allowed the employees to participate fully in company affairs and to use their education and creativity on job-oriented problems. There are currently over 170,000 quality circles officially registered with JUSE (Union of Japanese Scientists and Engineers), which allows easy access, communication and exchange of ideas and experiences among the QC circles of different industries. This national interrelationship expands the principle of teamwork nationwide.

5.3.4 Suggestion systems

The hidden potential of the workforce can be utilized for the benefit of the company (as well as the individual) through a suggestion system. This is an integral part of individual-oriented *kaizen* and can be the source of numerous opportunities for improvement on a continuous basis. It encourages communication and can also become a morale-booster for the workforce, especially when valuable suggestions materialize as activities which bring results.

Top management must ensure that a dynamic suggestion system is firmly in place, so that individual contributions are properly recognized and utilized. Many benefits can result, from improvement in one's own work, through cost savings in energy and resources, to process quality and innovative ideas. The most useful of the suggestions are those which come with supporting statistical data, an implementation plan and perhaps estimates of costs and savings. Of course, this does not mean that minor suggestions should be overlooked. After all, the whole scheme will inevitably have to start with primitive recommendations. But proper employee education can help in the quality of suggestions and, in the case of group suggestions, in the better estimation of their economic impact.

5.3.5 Total productive maintenance

While TQC aims to improve overall management quality, total productive maintenance (TPM) aims to maximize equipment effectiveness through preventive maintenance. In Japan TPM is as distinguished a practice as TQC, with 'plant maintenance' awards given yearly to companies that have successfully introduced TPM. This is because better utilization of existing equipment can be an important cost-saver: further capital investment on new machines can be avoided, and many breakdowns, tool replacements, repairs and other causes of inefficiency can be prevented.

Simple rules, such as the frequent cleaning and oiling of the equipment and making sure that everything is in order and in place, apart from enhancing the equipment's life expectancy, also improve the plant environment, thus making 'visitors' plant tours' a marketing tool. More sophisticated maintenance jobs, such as machine-setting optimization and overall performance improvement, can be made easy, utilizing the statistical techniques advocated by Taguchi (see Part IV). But the success of a TPM practice is based on the principle of preventive maintenance. In this way, minor abnormalities are never allowed to become serious problems, so that major breakdowns and replacements are avoided. The easiest way of spotting abnormalities in the everyday performance of the equipment is through the use of a simple tool, the control chart (see Part III). This versatile tool, apart from assisting in the identification and elimination of sources of potential problems, can also provide at any time an indication of the current capability of the equipment, and thus help in its further improvement, in a true *kaizen* spirit.

■ 5.4 *Kaizen* and Deming

There are many principles in *kaizen* that are identical to certain of Deming's management rules; for example, the obsession with never-ending quality improvement, the responsibility of management, the relationships with suppliers, the process-oriented approach, total quality attainment, striving for long-term and sustained benefits rather than short-term profits, the PDCA cycle, the importance of communication, education, development and involvement of all employees in quality-related activities etc. In fact, it is difficult to distinguish most of the *kaizen* principles from the Deming ideals. But this is not surprising. *Kaizen* represents the basis of the Japanese business philosophy, and the Japanese business philosophy was inspired by Deming's teachings.

Sources of Further
Information (Part I)

Crosby, P.B. (1979), *Quality is Free: The art of making quality certain*, McGraw-Hill: New York.

Crosby, P.B. (1984), *Quality without Tears*, McGraw-Hill: New York.

Cullen, J. and Hollingum, J. (1987), *Implementing Total Quality*, IFS Publications: Kempston.

Dale, B.G. and Plunkett, J.J. (1990) (eds), *Managing Quality*, Philip Allan: London.

Deming, W.E. (1982), *Quality, Productivity and Competitive Position*, MIT Center of Advanced Engineering Study: Cambridge, MA.

Deming, W.E. (1986), *Out of the Crisis*, MIT Center of Advanced Engineering Study: Cambridge, MA.

Department of Trade and Industry (1986), *Quality Counts*, DTI: London.

Department of Trade and Industry (1989), *The Quality Gurus*, DTI: London.

Edosomwan, J.A. (1988), *Productivity and Quality Improvement*, IFS Publications: Kempston.

Feigenbaum, A.V. (1983), *Total Quality Control*, McGraw-Hill: New York.

Fine, C.H. (1985), *Managing Quality: A comparative assessment*, Booz Allen and Hamilton: New York.

Hopper, K. (1985), 'Quality, Japan and the US: the first chapter', *Quality Progress*, **18**, pp. 34–41.

Imai, M. (1986), *KAIZEN: The key to Japan's competitive success*, Random House: New York.

Ishikawa, K. (1965), 'Recent trends of quality control', *Reports of Statistical Application Research: JUSE*, **12**, pp. 1–17.

Ishikawa, K. (1976), *Guide to Quality Control*, Asian Productivity Organization: Tokyo.

Ishikawa, K. (1985), *What is Total Quality Control? The Japanese Way*, Prentice Hall: Englewood Cliffs, NJ.

Juran, J.M. (1964), *Managerial Breakthrough*, McGraw-Hill: New York.

Juran, J.M. (1980), *Quality Planning and Analysis*, McGraw-Hill: New York.

Juran, J.M. (1981a), *Juran on Quality Improvement*, Juran Enterprises.

Juran, J.M. (1981b), *Management of Quality*, 4th edn, Juran Institute: Wilton, CT.

Juran, J.M. (1981c), *Upper Management and Quality*, 3rd edn, Juran Institute: Wilton, CT.

Juran, J.M. (1988a), *Juran on Planning for Quality*, Free Press: New York.

Juran, J.M. (1988b) (ed.), *Quality Control Handbook*, McGraw-Hill: New York.

Juran, J.M. (1989), *Juran on Leadership for Quality*, Free Press: New York.

Juran, J.M. and Gryna, F.M. (1988) (eds), *Juran's Quality Control Handbook*, 3rd edn, McGraw-Hill: New York.

Main, J. (1986), 'Under the spell of the quality gurus', *Fortune*, **18**, pp. 24–7.

Mann, N.R. (1985), *The Keys to Excellence: The story of the Deming philosophy*, Prestwick Books: Santa Monica.

Mortiboys, R.J. (1990), 'Quality management for the 1990s', Chapter 3 in Dale and Plunkett, 1990.

Neave, H.R. (1987), 'Deming's 14 points for management: framework for success', *The Statistician*, **36**, pp. 561–70.

Neave, H.R. (1990), *The Deming Dimension*, SPC Press: Knoxville, TN.

Oakland, J.S. (1989), *Total Quality Management*, Heinemann: Oxford.

Peters, T. and Waterman, R.H. jn (1982), *In Search of Excellence*, Harper and Row: New York.

Peters, T. and Austin, N. (1985), *A Passion for Excellence: The leadership difference*, Fontana/Collins: Glasgow and Random House: New York.

Scherkenback, W.W. (1986), *The Deming Route to Quality and Productivity: Road maps and roadblocks*, CEEP Press: Washington, DC.

Shingo, S. (1981), *Study of 'Toyota' Production System*, Japan Management Association: Tokyo.

Shingo, S. (1986), *Zero Quality Control: Source inspection and the poka-yoke system*, Productivity Press: Stamford, CT.

Shingo, S. (1988), *Non-Stock Production*, Productivity Press: Stamford, CT.

Smith, S. (1986), *How to Take Part in the Quality Revolution: A management guide*, P.A. Management Consultants: London.

PART II
Technical Tools
for Quality
Techniques for General Use

Statistical thinking will one day be as necessary for efficient citizenship as the ability to read and write.

H.G. Wells

This part of the book (Chapters 6–8) has been written as a supporting package of guidance and reference information on the various technical procedures for quality management and quality improvement to be described later. Some important statistical topics are outlined in detail, to facilitate understanding of the analyses of the various case-studies that follow. A few of the topics are not directly relevant to the case-studies, but are closely related to the rest of the ideas outlined and were included for the sake of completeness. The material can thus be used as an overall statistical education pack, with each chapter as a stand-alone item, for use by project teams, in training events and team briefings.

Chapters 6 and 7 cover the statistical subjects of experimental design and analysis, particularly useful for the support of the ideas covered in Part IV of the book. Chapter 8 covers techniques with almost no statistical content. These are common-sense tools, designed to become part of a manager's everyday toolkit; they are particularly useful in the early stages of any improvement project.

All the techniques described in this part are tools, not rules; the aim is to avoid turning a particular analysis into paralysis!

Basic Techniques
for Statistical Analysis

I know of scarcely anything so apt
to impress the imagination,
as the wonderful form of cosmic
order expressed by the LAW OF
FREQUENCY OF ERROR. The law would
have been personified by the Greeks
and deified, if they had known it.

Sir Francis Galton

■ 6.1 Introduction

Everything varies. No two things are ever the same, no matter how similar they seem to be. If variability did not exist, statistical science would not have been developed. It is the fundamental reason behind the statistical treatment of any problem. Any process, no matter how precise, is always subject to random disturbance. Each of those disturbances viewed individually might not be significant; but taken in combination, they could be the cause of a large deviation of the process performance from the optimum.

It is actually very common to describe a process performance by its average level; but unless some measure exists describing its spread around this average, only a very limited idea of the real performance can be obtained. Two processes with the same average response could be substantially different in their overall performance if their dispersion characteristics differ. Measures of *central tendency* and *dispersion* are extremely useful and necessary for decision making. However, in large *populations* of items under study (such as 'all employees in a large company', 'all telephone lines working properly', 'all products in a large batch', 'all batches in the production line' etc.), it might be extremely difficult to obtain such measures. The most that one can do is to hypothesize about their possible value, on the basis of information obtained from the study of a small number of items (*observations*) – called a *sample* – collected as randomly as possible from the parent population. The members of the sample are viewed as representatives of a population of many more items, and the aim is to use the sample to gain information about the population as a whole. The process of 'inferring' something about a population from a sample drawn from that population is called *statistical inference*. The number of observations in a sample is called the *sample size*, and the measures computed from the sample observations are called *sample statistics*.

We can regard the members of a sample as 'events' taking place deliberately with the purpose of obtaining valuable information. In describing events, it is natural to use single letters rather than lengthy verbal descriptions. We can go further and attach numbers to events and record them rather than the events themselves. During repetitions of the events we shall see the numbers changing. The quantity describing these repetitions is called a *random variable* and is usually denoted by a capital letter X, Y etc. The mathematical formulation is then to say that, for an outcome w in the sample space, we create a number $X(w)$. For example, if we toss a coin three times and observe (heads, tails, heads) as one of the eight possible outcomes, and if X is the quantity describing the number of heads, then for this outcome $X = 2$. *The X in this case is* discrete; that is, it takes a finite (or more generally countable) set of values. For other cases, a variable could be of a *continuous* nature, that is, capable of taking an infinite number of values, as, for example, when $Y = $ weight.

The specification of the behaviour of X is called the *distribution* of X. The random variables we find occurring naturally can often be assumed to belong to certain families of distributions. Section 6.6 describes some of the most important.

Most of statistical theory is based on the assumption that samples are drawn *at random*, that is, each member of the population has an equal chance of being chosen. Random sampling reduces the risk of bias in the sample but, in practice, the collection of sample data is very often subject to certain restrictions on randomization. However, assuming that the proper statistical rules are observed and adhered to, these restrictions are deliberate and their aim is to make the sample results more informative. For example, when systematic experimentation is taking place in a particular manufacturing process, collection of data is subject to certain process conditions being satisfied, for example, certain process *variables* (or *factors*) such as temperature, pressure etc. being set at specific combinations of values (*factor levels*). These factor combinations are by no means random. They are decided according to certain statistical experimental designs, which provide the proper structure for efficient experimentation. In this way, the effect of the process factors on process variation (and hence on process performance) can be easily evaluated so that the process is optimized. (The subject of *experimental design* is very important, and will be examined in detail in Chapter 7.)

The parent population is assumed to be stable, in the sense that its pattern of variation will not be changed by the deletion of the sample, and the same will be true if sampling is repeated. Of course, resampling produces a different set of values, and so the sample itself is not stable in this sense. Therefore the measures associated with sampling (the sample statistics) are variable and change with every new sample. Recognizing the pattern of change in the sample statistics over repeated sampling from a process helps significantly in the confident estimation of the (fixed) population parameters, and hence in the efficient characterization and optimization of the process under study.

■ 6.2 Measures of central tendency and dispersion

There are various measures of *central tendency* and *dispersion*, the most commonly used of which are as follows.

Measures of centrality

The *mode* is the most commonly occurring observation. Note that more than one mode may exist in a population.

The *mid-range* is the mid-point between the highest and the lowest observation.

The *median* is the middle observation when all observations are arranged in order of magnitude. In other words, this is the value for which it can be said that half of the observations lie above the value and the other half lie below.

The *mean* is the arithmetic average of all observations. With respect to a sample of sample size n represented by

$$y_1, y_2, ..., y_n$$

the sample mean is given by

$$\bar{y} = \frac{\Sigma \; y_j}{n} \tag{6.1}$$

where Σ is the summation symbol, with Σ representing the total sum of all values in the sample ($j = 1, ..., n$). The sample mean provides an excellent estimate of the population mean (usually denoted by the symbol μ) except when the population is highly *skewed*, that is, highly asymmetric.

CASE STUDY 6.1

The following sample data represent light output (in microamperes – μA) emitted from 11 lamps which were drawn randomly from the production line:

9.1, 9.8, 9.5, 10.4, 10.7, 10.2, 9.8, 10.0, 10.3, 10.1, 9.6

Then:

Sample size = 11
Mode   = 9.8
Mid-range   = $(y_{max} + y_{min})/2 = (10.7 + 9.1)/2 = 9.9$
Median   = 10.0
Mean   = $(9.1 + 9.8 + \cdots + 9.6)/11 = 109.5/11 = 9.95$

Measures of dispersion

The most useful measure of dispersion is the *standard deviation*, whose definition needs the concepts of *degrees of freedom* and *variance*, as follows.

Degrees of freedom (*df*) are the number of observations that can be varied independently of each other. For example, there are 10 degrees of freedom associated with the sample data of case-study 6.1 ($df = n - 1$), because we can vary 10 out of the 11 data values of the sample independently of each other, and still obtain the same sample mean of 9.95, provided that the 11th value is an appropriate function of the other 10. When the sample is being used to estimate a functional relationship (a *model*) involving many (unknown) parameters, 1 degree of freedom is lost with every parameter estimated.

The *variance* is the sum of squared deviations from the mean, divided by the degrees of freedom. For the case of a sample,

$$\text{sample variance} = \text{Var}(Y) = s^2 = \frac{\Sigma(y_j - \bar{y})^2}{n - 1} \tag{6.2}$$

The sample variance s^2 provides an excellent estimate for the population variance, usually denoted by σ^2. The numerator of (6.2) can be easily calculated using the formula

$$\Sigma(y_j - \bar{y})^2 = \Sigma y_j^2 - n(\bar{y})^2 \tag{6.3}$$

or

$$\Sigma(y_j - \bar{y})^2 = \Sigma y_j^2 - \frac{(\Sigma y_j)^2}{n} \tag{6.4}$$

We are now able to define the *standard deviation* (*SD*) as the square root of the variance. Therefore:

$$\text{sample } SD = s = \sqrt{\frac{\Sigma(y_j - \bar{y})^2}{n - 1}} \tag{6.5}$$

Formulae (6.1), (6.3) or (6.4) can be used for the calculation of *s*. For example, using (6.5) and (6.3) on the data of case-study 6.1 we have (using the more exact value $\bar{y} = 9.95455$)

$$s = \sqrt{\frac{(9.1^2 + 9.8^2 + \cdots + 9.6^2) - 11(9.95)^2}{10}} = 0.455$$

Another name for standard deviation is *standard error* (*SE*). It is common to talk about the standard error of an estimate. Indeed, every estimate, such as the sample statistics $\bar{y}$ and s (used respectively as estimates of the population parameters μ and σ), are also subject to variation and hence subject to error.

For example, it can be shown that the standard deviation of the sample mean $\bar{y}$ is given by

$$SE(\bar{y}) = s/\sqrt{n} \tag{6.6}$$

where n is the sample size and s is the sample standard deviation. This is obtained using the following property of the variance, applicable for any n independent variables y_i, each with standard deviation s:

$$\text{Var}(k_1 y_1 + \cdots + k_n y_n) = k_1^2 \, \text{Var}(y_1) + \cdots + k_n^2 \, \text{Var}(y_n)$$

where k_i, $i = 1, \ldots, n$, are constants.

Another useful measure of dispersion is the *range*, which is the difference between the highest and the lowest observation. (This measure will be used extensively in Chapter 9.) For example, for the data of case-study 6.1

range = $10.7 - 9.1 = 1.6$

Depending on the degree of prior knowledge one has about a population, certain sample statistics might be preferred to others. For example, if it is suspected that the population is highly skewed (asymmetric), the median or the mode might be more appropriate for estimating the population's central tendency. In addition, the median is not affected by abnormal values (*outliers*) as is the mid-range or, to a lesser degree, the mean. On the other hand, the median and mid-range make strong use of the order property and very little use of the magnitude of the data values or the distance between them. In this sense, the measures of the mean and standard deviation are much more informative; they utilize all numerical information incorporated in the data. But their main attraction is their usefulness in conjunction with the idea of *confidence intervals* and the related concept of *hypothesis testing*, examined below.

■ 6.3 Confidence intervals

As already stated, *sample statistics* can be used to estimate the population parameters. But the fact remains that these statistics are only point estimators, in that they provide a single numerical estimate but no measure of its probable accuracy. However, some idea of probable accuracy can be obtained by calculating interval estimators associated with a certain prespecified degree of confidence – the *confidence intervals* (*CI*). Confidence intervals can be constructed for any individual population parameter (such as μ or σ^2), or even any combination of parameters from more than one population, such as $\mu_1 - \mu_2$, σ_1/σ_2 etc.

We will concentrate on interval estimators for the mean. In these cases, if Θ represents a population parameter (or a combination of parameters) and

θ represents an estimate for Θ, then a $(100 - \alpha)\%$ confidence interval for (the real) Θ generally has the form

$$CI(\Theta): \quad [\theta \pm t(df; \alpha)SE(\theta)] \tag{6.7}$$

where $SE(\theta)$ is the standard error (standard deviation) of the estimate θ and $t(df; \alpha)$ is a value (t-value) obtained from t-tables (see Appendix A, Table A1). The t-values depend on the degrees of freedom associated with the sample, and on the *level of significance*, α, which is a predetermined constant associated with the degree of confidence required (or of the allowable risk); typical values for α are 1%, 5% or 10%.

We must be careful not to misinterpret (6.7). In the course of calculating (6.7), the population parameter Θ will not change its character. It will not become a variable; it always remains a population constant. However, the interval (6.7) is a variable interval; it varies with every new sample, and hence with every new sample statistic θ and $SE(\theta)$. With every new sample, the interval calculated using the formula (6.7) may or may not include the real parameter Θ. But the important point to recognize is that we are using a method with $(100 - \alpha)\%$ of success: there is a $(100 - \alpha)\%$ chance that the real Θ will fall within the range determined by (6.7). In other words, if we continue constructing intervals in this way, $(100 - \alpha)\%$ of them will bracket the population parameter Θ. So, if for example $\alpha = 5\%$, whenever we assert that Θ belongs to $CI(\Theta)$, then 95% of the time we will be correct; this is often referred to as being 95% confident that Θ belongs to $CI(\Theta)$.

Clearly (6.7) represents a two-sided interval, with the minus being used for the calculation of the lower confidence limit and the plus for the calculation of the upper confidence limit. If only one-sided intervals are required (with only one of the limits in need of calculation, the other generally being $-\infty$ or $+\infty$, then (6.7) again applies but the value of $t(df; \alpha)$ is not the same as for the two-sided case (see, for example, Appendix A, Table A1).

In some statistical books the t-tables are presented without a distinction between a one-sided and two-sided interval (or test – see Section 6.4). In such cases, the entries are headed either by the significance level α or by $P = 100 - \alpha$, known as the percentile point (representing the confidence level for the interval). In either case, if the t-value for a two-sided interval (or test) is required, one should look for $t(df; \alpha/2)$ rather than $t(df; \alpha)$ which is now applicable only for one-sided confidence limits (or one-sided tests – see Section 6.4).

6.3.1 One-sample confidence intervals

As an example, we can use the sample data of case-study 6.1 to construct a 95% confidence interval ($\alpha = 5\%$) for the population mean μ. We already know that $n = 11$, $\bar{y} = 9.95$, $s = 0.455$, and by using (6.6) we find

$$SE(\bar{y}) = s/\sqrt{n} = 0.455/\sqrt{11} = 0.137$$

Also

$$t(df; \alpha) = t(10; 5\%) = 2.23$$

found from the *t*-tables (see Appendix A, Table A1), with reference to a two-sided (interval) with $df = 10$ and $\alpha = 5\%$ (or 0.05). Then, as in (6.7)

$$CI(\mu): \quad [\bar{y} \pm t(df; \alpha)s/\sqrt{n}] \tag{6.8}$$

and so

$$CI(\mu): \quad [9.95 \pm 2.23 \times 0.137] = [9.95 \pm 0.306]$$

Therefore, we are 95% confident that the real mean light output μ of all the lamps in the production line (from which the sample was drawn) will belong to the interval {9.64µA, 10.26µA}.

Reducing the width of a *CI*

Obviously, the smaller the confidence interval, the more accurate our estimate for μ, that is, the more reliable it is. From (6.8) it is clear that, for a given sample size, a reliable estimate for the mean can be expected only when the sample standard deviation is reasonably small. The reliability of an estimate improves as the sample size n increases; note that this reliability depends on the size of the sample, not on the size of the population.

The standard deviation can only be reduced by improving the production process, and usually this is a difficult task; the methods described in Parts III and IV of this book provide some means for achieving this. On the other hand, the sample size n can easily be changed, assuming availability of time and money. Having had some idea of the variability in the values of the light output of the lamps produced from the sample statistics ($s = 0.455$), we can calculate the sample size that would be needed in a future investigation to give a sufficiently narrow *CI*. It can be shown that the approximate sample size needed to estimate the population mean to within $\pm k$, using a confidence interval, is given by

$$n = [t(df; \alpha)s/k]^2$$

For example, for our case-study, if we want to reduce the present width of our *CI* to within $\pm 0.2\mu A$, we would need a sample size of

$$n = (2.23 \times 0.455/0.2)^2 = 25.7$$

that is, around 26 lamps (rather than just 11). Note that the $t(df; \alpha)$ has the same value as before, namely, the one obtained using 10 degrees of freedom – the df associated with the estimated s of 0.455. Of course, if we now examine a new sample of 26 lamps, new values for s and t ($= t(25; \alpha)$) will have to be used for the construction of the new confidence interval.

We finally note that the confidence level can also affect the width of a *CI*. Clearly, if we need a greater confidence, we should be prepared to accept a larger width. For example, if we wish to construct a 99% *CI* for the mean light output, by applying (6.8) we have

$$[9.95 \pm t(10; 1\%) \times 0.455/\sqrt{11}] = [9.95 \pm 3.17 \times 0.137]$$

which yields the interval

$$\{9.52\mu A, \ 10.38\mu A\}$$

This 99% confidence interval is (not surprisingly) greater in length than the previously calculated 95% *CI*. But, of course, there is now only a 1% risk that we are wrong, in supposing that the real mean light output will be between $9.52\mu A$ and $10.38\mu A$. So the confidence level must be determined by the risk that we consider acceptable for the problem under review.

6.3.2 Two-sample confidence intervals

It has already been stated that confidence intervals can be constructed even for combinations of parameters associated with different populations. We will now refer to the construction of a confidence interval for the difference between the means of two different populations. This can be very useful for purposes, say, of comparing the performances of two different processes.

Suppose $(y_1, ..., y_n)$ and $(x_1, ..., x_m)$ are two samples drawn from two independent populations, with (respectively) sample means $\bar{y}$, $\bar{x}$ and sample standard deviations s_y, s_x. Let μ_y and μ_x respectively be the (unknown) population means. We are interested in constructing a confidence interval for the difference $\mu_y - \mu_x$. This can be done by utilizing the available sample statistics.

According to (6.7) we need an estimate of the (unknown) difference and the standard error of that estimate. The best estimate of the difference in the population means is given by the difference of the sample means, that is, $\bar{y} - \bar{x}$. It can be shown that the standard error of this estimate is given by

$$SE(\bar{y} - \bar{x}) = s_p\sqrt{\frac{1}{n} + \frac{1}{m}} \tag{6.9}$$

where s_p, the pooled standard deviation, is some kind of an average of the two sample standard deviations s_y and s_x, and is given by

$$s_p = \sqrt{\frac{\Sigma(df)s^2}{\Sigma(df)}} = \sqrt{\frac{(n-1)s_y^2 + (m-1)s_x^2}{(n-1) + (m-1)}} \tag{6.10}$$

So, according to (6.7)

$$CI(\mu_y - \mu_x): \ \left[(\bar{y} - \bar{x}) \pm t(df; \alpha)s_p\sqrt{\frac{1}{n} + \frac{1}{m}}\right] \tag{6.11}$$

where in this case, $df = (n-1) + (m-1) = n + m - 2$.

The relationship between the formulae corresponding to the two-sample case and the one-sample case is obvious. In fact, formulae (6.9) and (6.11) are the direct generalizations of formulae (6.6) and (6.8) respectively.

CASE STUDY 6.2

After some modification in the production process of light bulbs, the chief engineer was interested to know whether the modifications had resulted in a significant change in the mean light output of the produced lamps. A sample of 10 lamps randomly selected from the new process yielded the following results (in μA):

9.4, 9.3, 9.8, 10.3, 9.9, 10.5, 10.7, 10.4, 9.7, 10.6

On the basis of the above sample results and the sample results of case-study 6.1, the engineer had to ascertain whether there was any evidence to suggest that the process modification had affected the mean process performance as far as light output for the lamps was concerned.

Remember that the sample statistics associated with the sample data of case-study 6.1 were as follows:

$n = 11$, $\bar{y} = 9.95$, $s_y = 0.455$

The sample statistics of the sample data from the modified process can be easily found to be

$m = 10$, $\bar{x} = 10.06$, $s_x = 0.506$

At first glance, the process modification seems to have resulted in the lamps producing a higher light output on average. However, comparisons should not be based only on sample means; the sample measures about dispersion should also be taken into consideration. In fact, the variability in the lamps' performance seems also to have been increased, something that should give rise to doubts about the usefulness of the process modification.

A more systematic and statistically-based approach would be to calculate a (statistical) confidence interval for the difference in the unknown population means; this can provide a more reliable way of ascertaining whether the mean process performances are statistically different. If, for example, the 95% confidence interval for the difference (of the means) includes the value of zero, this will indicate (with 95% confidence) that $\mu_y - \mu_x$ is not significantly different from zero, and therefore, in the long run, that the means μ_y and μ_x are not significantly different from each other.

For the present case, following (6.10), we obtain

$$s_p = \sqrt{\frac{10 \times (0.455)^2 + 9 \times (0.506)^2}{11 + 10 - 2}} = 0.48$$

Then, by (6.11),

$$CI(\mu_y - \mu_x): \left[(9.95 - 10.06) \pm t(19; 5\%) \times 0.48 \times \sqrt{\frac{1}{11} + \frac{1}{10}} \right]$$

or

$$[-0.11 \pm 2.09 \times 0.48 \times 0.437] = [-0.11 \pm 0.438]$$

Therefore, a 95% confidence interval for the difference in the mean performance between the original and the modified process is given by

$$CI(\mu_y - \mu_x): \{-0.548, 0.328\}$$

Since the value of zero is included in the above interval, there is no evidence, at the 5% level of significance, to suggest that the variation in the process performances (between before and after the modification) is significantly different from zero. In other words, there is no statistical evidence to suggest that the process modification has had any effect in substantially altering the process performance (in the long run) as far as light output from the lamps is concerned.

The above case-studies demonstrate that confidence intervals are not only useful in providing a measure of probable accuracy for the point estimators (as shown in Section 6.3.1), but they are also valuable tools for the related subject of *hypothesis testing*, to be examined in detail in the next section. Indeed, as in the last example, having established that the confidence interval of the difference (of the means) does not include the value of zero, we have indirectly established that there is no evidence to suggest that the hypothesis of equal mean performances can be rejected.

■ 6.4 Hypothesis testing

Making hypotheses and testing them for validity is a basic scientific process. We might erroneously reject a true hypothesis (*Type I error*) or we might erroneously accept a false one (*Type II error*). These errors are due to the presence (yet again) of the great nuisance called variability. Statistical theory takes this into account and tells us how to perform hypothesis testing in the presence of random fluctuations.

The statistical process of hypothesis testing can be divided into three stages.

Stage 1: Statement of the hypotheses to be tested

There are two hypotheses of interest. The *null hypothesis* (H_0) is a statement about a single population characteristic usually having a specific value, for example

$$H_0: \mu = k \ (k \text{ being any real number})$$

or

$$H_0: \sigma^2 = m \ (m > 0)$$

etc. The null hypothesis can also be a statement concerning two or more population parameters, usually specifying 'no change' or 'no difference' between them (hence the word 'null'). For example, in the case of two populations

H_0: $\mu_1 = \mu_2$ (i.e. $\mu_1 - \mu_2 = 0$) or even $\mu_1 - \mu_2 = k$ $(k \neq 0)$

or

H_0: $\sigma_1^2 = \sigma_2^2$

etc.

The *alternative hypothesis* (H_1) is a statement about a population characteristic usually being larger (or smaller) than a specific value (one-sided test) or, more generally, different from a specific value (two-sided test): for example,

H_1: $\mu > k$ or $\mu < k$ (one-sided)

or

H_1: $\mu \neq k$ or $\sigma^2 \neq m$ (two-sided)

etc., or a statement about two or more population parameters, usually specifying that a change or difference has taken place in the populations:

H_1: $\mu_1 > \mu_2$ or $\mu_1 < \mu_2$ (one-sided test)

or

H_1: $\mu_1 \neq \mu_2$ or $\sigma_1^2 \neq \sigma_2^2$ (two-sided test)

etc. Note that when testing whether there is simply an increase or simply a decrease, we are dealing with a one-sided test rather than a two-sided test, which is more generally associated with a test for difference.

Stage 2: Calculation of the test statistic (*TS*)

The *TS* is a measure calculated on the basis of sample characteristics (such as the sample mean, sample standard deviation and the sample size), on the assumption that H_0 is *true*; this means that the *TS* will include a specific value of the (unknown) population parameter, which (value) is *assumed* to hold under H_0. For example, if we test (under H_0) that $\mu = k$ (k being any real number, not necessarily zero), then the value k will be involved in the appropriate *TS* along with the values of the associated sample statistics.

The choice of which *TS* to use depends on the hypothesis under consideration. For example, if the hypothesis testing deals with population means, the general form of *TS* (the t-ratio) is

$$TS = \frac{|\theta - \Theta|}{SE(\theta)} \tag{6.12}$$

In the above the vertical lines indicate absolute values, for example $|z|$ is the part of z without the sign. The entries of (6.12) are the same as the corresponding entries of (6.7). Note that (6.12) always yields a positive value because the numerator is taken absolutely (the denominator represents a standard deviation and hence is *always* positive). If we test assumptions about dispersion, the *TS* usually has the form of a ratio between variances; the *TS* will therefore always be positive, as in the means case. The value of *TS* will indicate whether to accept or reject the null hypothesis: the larger (the more significant) the value of *TS*, the less the chance of being able to accept H_0.

Stage 3: Decision making

The calculated value of *TS* is compared with a critical value (*cv*) found from appropriate statistical tables (Appendix A). The choice of which statistical table to use depends on the hypothesis under consideration. For example, if the hypothesis is concerned with means, the *t*-table (Appendix A, Table A1) is usually consulted; if we are dealing with variances, the *F*-tables (Appendix A, Tables A2) are used.

Whatever the statistical table, the *cv*'s depend upon the degrees of freedom associated with the sample, and upon a prespecified level of significance (α), already mentioned in Section 6.3.

The value of *TS* is significant if it is larger than the critical value $cv = cv(df; \alpha)$. In such a case we say that we cannot accept the null hypothesis at the α-level of significance, running an $\alpha\%$ chance of being wrong by doing so. Conversely, if *TS* is less than $cv(df; \alpha)$, we say that we cannot reject the null hypothesis at the $\alpha\%$ level. Note that the level of significance α, when expressed in decimals, is the probability of being wrong if we reject the null hypothesis. This is sometimes called the probability of Type I error as opposed to the probability of Type II error, which is the probability of being wrong when we do not reject the null hypothesis.

The above three-stage procedure will be demonstrated below in testing various hypotheses concerning population means and population variances.

6.4.1 The one-sample *t*-test

With reference to the sample data of case-study 6.1 (page 109), suppose we wanted to test the hypothesis that, in the long run, the mean light output of the lamps in the (original) process will be 10 μA. Following the three stages for hypothesis testing we obtain the following results.

(Stage 1) Null hypothesis (H_0) $\mu = 10$ μA, that is, the average process performance is the production of lamps with light output of 10 μA. Alternative hypothesis (H_1): $\mu < 10$ μA, that is, the long-run average of light output in the produced lamps is significantly less than 10 μA. This is a one-sided test. The decision on whether we should have tested for H_1: $\mu < 10$ rather than H_1: $\mu > 10$, was taken intuitively by examining the value of the sample mean ($\bar{y} = 9.95$), which is less than 10 μA.

(Stage 2) Applying formula (6.12) and using (6.6) we have

$$TS = \frac{|\bar{y} - \mu|}{SE(\bar{y})} = \frac{|\bar{y} - \mu|}{(s/\sqrt{n})} \qquad (6.13)$$

Now, under the null hypothesis (which assumes that $\mu = 10 \ \mu A$) we have

$$TS = \frac{|9.95 - 10.0|}{(0.455/\sqrt{11})} = 0.36$$

(Stage 3) To make a decision on whether to accept or reject H_0, we need to assess whether TS is small enough or large enough (significant) in comparison to a critical value. The critical value is a t-value to be found in Table A1 (Appendix A) depending on $n - 1$ ($= 10$) degrees of freedom and on a level of significance which, for this case, is chosen to be at 5%. Then using the one-sided column of Table A1 (we are dealing with a one-sided test) we find

$$cv = cv(df; \alpha) = t(10; 5\%) = 1.81$$

Since $TS < cv$ we cannot reject the null hypothesis that $\mu = 10\mu A$ at the 5% level of significance.

It should be noted that testing against $H_1: \mu < 10$ (one-sided test) is an almost identical procedure to testing against $H_1: \mu \neq 10$ (two-sided test). The only difference is reflected in the value of cv; in the latter case we would have $cv = 2.23$ ($= t(10; 5\%)$ for the two-sided test: see Table A1). Again we would not be able to reject the null hypothesis. In fact, if we cannot reject H_0 for the one-sided test, we cannot reject it for the two-sided test either (the converse is not true). Likewise, if we cannot reject H_0 at the 5% level, we cannot reject it at the 1% level, because $cv(df; 5\%) < cv(df; 1\%)$.

Note that we usually say 'we cannot reject H_0' rather than 'we accept H_0'. In fact, there are many values for μ that we cannot reject, for example $\mu = 9.9$ (for this case $TS = 0.73$). An indication of how many values for μ we cannot reject at the 5% level can be given by a 95% confidence interval for μ (see Section 6.3.1). A two-sided interval would correspond to a two-sided test. For example, recall that a (two-sided) confidence interval for μ was found for our case-study to be (see Section 6.3.1)

$$\{9.64 \ \mu A, \ 10.26 \ \mu A\}$$

This indicates that we cannot reject at the 5% level any null hypothesis that $H_0: \mu = k$ against $H_1: \mu \neq k$ (two-sided test), with k being any value between 9.64 and 10.26 μA.

The above demonstrates the relationship between confidence intervals and hypothesis testing.

6.4.2 The two-sample t-test

The two-sample confidence interval (see Section 6.3.2) was presented as a very useful tool for comparing the performances of two different processes. The procedure would be to construct, say, a 95% *CI* for the difference in the means and observe whether this interval covered the value zero; if it did, we would ascertain (with 95% confidence) that the population means were not significantly different from each other.

A more formal approach would be to carry out a significance test for comparison, the two-sample *t*-test. This is one of the most popular (and most powerful) statistical tools and, although it is equivalent to the two-sample confidence interval, it is worthwhile examining in detail.

We shall again utilize data from case-studies 6.1 and 6.2, which are reproduced below along with the associated sample statistics.

Light output of lamps (in μA)											Mean	SD	Size
Y	9.1	9.8	9.5	10.4	10.7	10.2	9.8	10.0	10.3	10.1	9.6	9.95	0.455	11
X	9.4	9.3	9.8	10.3	9.9	10.5	10.7	10.4	9.7	10.6		10.06	0.506	10

The *Y*-data values signify the results obtained prior to a process modification, and the *X*-data values correspond to results after the modification. In order to establish whether the process modification has influenced the light output of the produced lamps, we can test the following hypothesis:

H_0: $\mu_y - \mu_x = 0$

against

H_1: $\mu_y - \mu_x \neq 0$ (two-sided test)

Following (6.12) and using (6.9) we have

$$TS = \frac{|(\bar{y} - \bar{x}) - (\mu_y - \mu_x)|}{s_p\sqrt{\dfrac{1}{n} + \dfrac{1}{m}}} \tag{6.14}$$

with s_p defined as in (6.10).

As in Section 6.3.2 we can find $s_p = 0.48$, and so, under H_0,

$$TS = \frac{|(9.95 - 10.06) - 0|}{0.48\sqrt{\dfrac{1}{11} + \dfrac{1}{10}}} = 0.52$$

Intuitively, it seems obvious that there is no evidence to reject the null hypothesis, because the value of *TS* is very small (a rule of thumb for *t*-tests with small sample sizes would be to accept H_0 if $TS < 2$ and reject it if $TS > 2$). Nevertheless, a proper test treatment requires a comparison of *TS* with a critical value, which in this case depends on $n + m - 2$ degrees of freedom and on a level of significance α, which is the risk we are prepared to take of being wrong if we eventually decide to reject H_0. Assuming $\alpha = 5\%$, from Table A1 in Appendix A (two-sided) we find

$$cv = t(df; \alpha) = t(19; 5\%) = 2.09$$

Since $TS < cv$ we cannot reject the null hypothesis of equal population means at the 5% level of significance. In other words, there is no evidence to suggest that the process modifications have had any effect on the light output performance of the produced lamps.

What becomes clear (yet again) is the relationship that exists between the concepts of confidence intervals and hypothesis testing. Indeed, the same conclusions as above were reached in Section 6.3.2 when a 95% *CI* for $\mu_y - \mu_x$ was constructed, using exactly the same sample statistics and the same *t*-value from the *t*-tables. In general, the relationship between the two concepts can be demonstrated by relating formulae (6.7) and (6.12). Indeed, starting from (6.7) we can see that there is a $(100 - \alpha)\%$ chance that the true (but unknown) parameter Θ is given by

$$\{\theta - t(df; \alpha) \times SE(\theta) < \Theta < \theta + t(df; \alpha) \times SE(\theta)\}$$

This is equivalent to

$$\{-t(df; \alpha) \times SE(\theta) < \Theta - \theta < +t(df; \alpha) \times SE(\theta)\}$$

or

$$\left\{ -t(df; \alpha) < \frac{\Theta - \theta}{SE(\theta)} < +t(df; \alpha) \right\}$$

or

$$\frac{|\theta - \Theta|}{SE(\theta)} < t(df; \alpha) \qquad \text{i.e. } TS < cv$$

which leads us to the condition for not rejecting a null hypothesis. For example, as in Section 6.4.1, we can say that the null hypothesis

$$H_0: \mu_y - \mu_x = k$$

cannot be rejected at the 5% level for any k in the interval

$$\{-0.548, +0.328\}$$

which is the 95% confidence interval for $\mu_y - \mu_x$ found in Section 6.3.2.

We conclude the subject of the two-sample *t*-test by providing a formula useful for determining the sample size required in order to detect a significant change in the population means. Assuming a pooled standard deviation s_p, the sample size required for each of the two samples to detect a significant change in k using the two-sample *t*-test is given by

$$n = m = 2[2t(df; \alpha)s_p/k]^2$$

For example, for our case-study, assuming a variability level of $s_p = 0.48$, in order to detect that an average change of 0.5 μA (between the original and modified process) is significant, we would need sample sizes of at least

$$n = m = 2 \times (2 \times 2.09 \times 0.48/0.5)^2 = 32.2$$

that is, 32 lamps should be tested from each process.

6.4.3 Paired-comparison tests

Suppose that we deal with two samples for which some sort of one-to-one correspondence exists between their sample units, so that the members used in the first sample might be required to be used again for the second sample; their new response is then paired with (or matched against) the response already obtained. For example, a drug is tested on a group of people; their health before and after the drug treatment is recorded pairwise, and on the basis of the paired results the effectiveness of the drug is to be assessed. We are again dealing with two samples (before and after) but, if the sample data are paired, the results are not independent. This means that, for comparison purposes, (6.14) or (6.11), which require unrelated (independent) samples, are no longer applicable. Note that if the results were not paired (if, for example, the results after the drug treatment were randomly allocated next to the results before the treatment without any regard to the identity of the patient), the samples would be rendered independent, despite the fact that the same people were used for both samples.

For paired comparisons, the appropriate formulae to use are those usually reserved for a single sample. This is because we create a single sample out of the original two samples, by calculating the differences in the scores for each pair. This requires that the sample sizes for both in the original samples be the same. So, instead of dealing with the two samples

$$(y_1, ..., y_n) \text{ and } (x_1, ..., x_n)$$

we deal with a single sample

$$(d_1, ..., d_n)$$

where

$$d_i = y_i - x_i \qquad i = 1, ..., n$$

Then, to compare population means, instead of testing

$$H_0: \mu_y - \mu_x = 0$$

we test

$$H_0: \mu_d = 0$$

recognizing μ_d as the difference in the means of the two related populations. Everything said about single samples applies here. The formula for the test statistic to be used for hypothesis testing is the same as (6.13), that is,

$$TS = \frac{|\bar{d} - \mu_d|}{SE(\bar{d})}$$

utilizing formulae (6.1), (6.5) and (6.6). In the drug-treatment case (assuming the results for each patient were paired), if the above null hypothesis were not rejected, it would show that there was no evidence to support the supposition that the drug had had any effect.

It is desirable to design the pairing (matching) of observations into the sampling experiment whenever possible. This is because, when we deal with a single sample $(d_i, i = 1, ..., n)$ rather than two (y_i and x_i), the sampling fluctuation is radically reduced. This can easily be demonstrated by constructing a 95% confidence interval for μ_d, first using formula (6.8) for the sample d_i, and then using formula (6.11), assuming independence in the two original samples y_i and x_i, $i = 1, ..., n$. The pairing of two samples (assuming the sampling structure makes this possible) substantially simplifies matters because it allows us to keep other things equal (so that the patients are the same and the drug-treatment effects are not obscured by the second sample of patients being entirely different).

The theory behind all *t*-tests examined so far and behind the construction of any confidence interval using *t*-values, is applicable only when certain statistical assumptions underlying the calculations are reasonably upheld. These assumptions are as follows:

1. The samples have been selected at random. This has already been mentioned earlier in this chapter.
2. The parent populations form a *normal distribution*. We will revert to the subject of normality in Section 6.6.
3. When comparing populations (for example, via the two-sample *t*-test) the variability of items is the same in all populations. The easiest way of checking this is to carry out a significance test for *homogeneity of variance*, called the *F*-test, described below.

6.4.4 Comparing variances

Prior to performing a two-sample *t*-test, as in Section 6.4.2, we might be interested in assessing the validity of assumption 3, that is, whether $\sigma_y = \sigma_x$. The following procedure might be followed:

H_0: $\sigma_y^2 = \sigma_x^2$

that is, the variability in the light output is, in the long run, the same despite the process modifications. The alternative hypothesis is

H_1: $\sigma_y^2 \neq \sigma_x^2$ (two-sided)

The test statistic for these cases is a ratio of the sample variances, as follows:

$$TS = \frac{\text{larger sample variance}}{\text{smaller sample variance}} = \frac{s_x^2}{s_y^2} = \frac{(0.506)^2}{(0.455)^2} = 1.24$$

The critical value for variance tests is found from the F-tables (see Tables A2, Appendix A). For the present case we look at Table A2.1 (two-sided) at the 5% level, for the entry corresponding to $m - 1 = 9 df$ for the larger sample variance (numerator) and $n - 1 = 10 df$ for the smaller sample variance (denominator). We find $cv = F(df_1, df_2; 5\%) = 3.78$.

Since $TS < cv$, we cannot reject the null hypothesis of equal population variances at the 5% level. Therefore assumption 3 of homogeneity of variance between the considered populations is satisfied.

■ 6.5 Frequency distributions and histograms

In order to assess the quality of individual items, it might be necessary to collect samples much larger than those used, for example, in the previous sections when we made inferences about the population mean. One such large sample is depicted in Table 6.1, concerning the handling times (in seconds) of telephone directory enquiry calls.

Clearly, it is rather difficult to draw any conclusions from the raw data of Table 6.1 by visual examination only. Some means of summarizing the information is required. Often the first step in reducing a mass of raw data to a more comprehensible form is to define a number of distinct and exhaustive categories or groups into which observations may be divided. We then replace the raw data by a listing of the groups (categories), and of the number of data points lying in each – called frequency. Such a listing is called a *frequency distribution*. The frequency distribution of the raw data of Table 6.1 is shown in Table 6.2.

Obviously, the reduction of the raw data of Table 6.1 to the data contained in Table 6.2 results in a loss of information – we have lost sight of the detailed handling time for each individual enquiry – but we are gaining a greater appreciation of the main properties of the available data. For example, it is clear that there is a concentration of values around the 5th group (50–60). But, we may also be losing information in another way: in the example above,

Table 6.1   Directory enquiry-handling times

46	56	37	71	72	61	81	60	54	50	56	80	60	80	64	68	46	46
42	55	52	62	90	56	67	44	72	42	34	60	89	72	58	19	36	76
52	50	55	70	76	75	73	52	80	46	70	46	26	66	58	64	46	86
44	102	52	30	64	66	70	44	64	56	50	58	32	66	52	68	36	69
52	55	44	52	80	38	54	35	71	42	90	46	21	91	50	80	32	62
58	92	52	38	86	62	66	44	76	45	58	44	97	78	60	61	46	78

Table 6.2 Frequency distribution of enquiry-handling times

Groups for handling times (seconds)	Mid-point (label)	Group frequency
1 [10– 19.9]	15	1
2 [20– 29.9]	25	2
3 [30– 39.9]	34	10
4 [40– 49.9]	45	18
5 [50– 59.9]	55	26
6 [60– 69.9]	65	21
7 [70– 79.9]	75	15
8 [80– 89.9]	85	9
9 [90– 99.9]	95	5
10 [100–109.9]	105	1
		108

the 108 data values of Table 6.1 might represent consecutive average weekly figures for enquiry-handling times; in such a case, much valuable information about seasonal fluctuations is lost by the formulation depicted by Table 6.2. Nevertheless, we may still use a frequency distribution to gain an appreciation of the measures of central tendency and dispersion, but if we wanted to invest-igate the question of seasonal patterns we would have to refer back to the raw data.

The important features of a set of data can be seen even more clearly in a graphic representation of the frequency distribution, known as a histogram (or bar chart). The histogram corresponding to the frequency distribution of Table 6.2 is shown in Figure 6.1. The baseline of the diagram is divided according to the group lengths, and a bar (rectangle) is drawn on each division

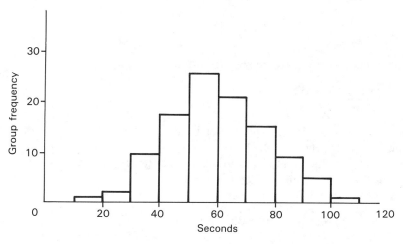

Figure 6.1 Histogram for call-handling times

125

so that the areas of the bars formed for each group are proportional to the corresponding group frequencies. With equal group lengths the heights of the bars will also be proportional to the corresponding group frequencies. With unequal group lengths, the height of each bar should be chosen so that the area of the bar is proportional to the corresponding frequency; this can be achieved by defining the height as proportional to the ratio

$$\frac{\text{group frequency}}{\text{group length}}$$

This ratio gives the density of data values in the group – that is, the number of data values per unit of group length. The limiting value of this ratio, if the sample size keeps increasing and the group lengths keep decreasing, is called the *probability density* function.

Equal-length groups are easier to work with but not essential. On certain occasions, the amount of data available might require different lengths. For example, if the number of individual observations in some groups is too small, the shape of the histogram is likely to be erratic, and hence some group merging may be necessary.

The histogram in Figure 6.1 indicates that the distribution of the enquiry-handling times is nearly symmetrical, with a peak around 60 seconds. However, there is also an obvious spread around the central point, ranging from 10 to 110 seconds. The calculation of measures for central tendency and dispersion using the formulae outlined in Section 6.2 might be a laborious exercise, although the availability of modern calculators can greatly minimize the effort involved. Nevertheless, simple calculations of the sample mean and sample standard deviation for a frequency distribution can easily be carried out using the following formulae:

Sample mean for frequency distribution

$$\bar{X} = \frac{\Sigma f_i X_i}{\Sigma f_i} \tag{6.15}$$

Sample variance for frequency distribution

$$S^2 = \frac{\Sigma f_i (X_i - \bar{X})^2}{\Sigma f_i} \tag{6.16}$$

where the X_i's are the mid-points (or labels) of the groups, f_i's are the corresponding frequencies, and the sums range over all the groups (not over all the individual values as in, for example, (6.1) or (6.2)), that is, $i = 1, \ldots, k$, with k being the total number of groups.

For the data of Table 6.2, applying (6.15) we have

$$\bar{X} = \frac{\begin{array}{c}1 \times 15 + 2 \times 25 + 10 \times 35 + 18 \times 45 + 26 \times 55 \\ + 21 \times 65 + 15 \times 75 + 9 \times 85 + 5 \times 95 + 1 \times 105\end{array}}{1 + 2 + 10 + 18 + 26 + 21 + 15 + 9 + 5 + 1} = 60.1$$

If we apply (6.1) to the raw data of Table 6.1 (sample size $n = 108$) we find

$$\bar{x} = \frac{\sum\limits_{j=1}^{n} x_j}{n} = \frac{46 + 56 + \cdots + 78}{108} = \frac{6364}{108} = 58.9$$

Note that the accuracy achieved by formula (6.15) makes it worthwhile applying it (instead of formula (6.1)) to data sets of large sample size.

Applying (6.16) to the data of Table 6.2 we have

$$S^2 = \frac{1 \times (15 - 60.1)^2 + 2 \times (25 - 60.1)^2 + 10 \times (35 - 60.1)^2 \\ + \cdots + 1 \times (105 - 60.1)^2}{1 + 2 + 10 + \cdots + 1} = 17.5^2$$

from which we obtain

$$S = 17.5$$

The equivalent formula (6.5) for the standard deviation of the raw data of Table 6.1 would give $s = 17$, which is reasonably close to S.

■ 6.6 Probability distributions

As Figure 6.2 indicates, a smooth curve can be superimposed on the original histogram (Figure 6.1) of the frequency data of Table 6.2. We can then suggest that, if the histogram represents the distribution of the enquiry-handling times for the 108 values of the sample, then the curve might represent the

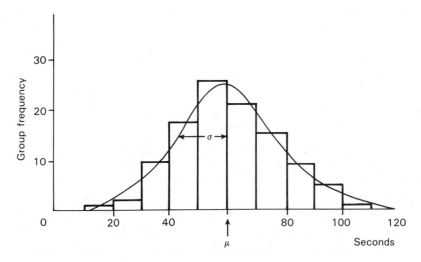

Figure 6.2 Histogram (call-handling times) and normal curve

distribution of the handling times of the population of all enquiry calls. Clearly, the curve and the histogram are similar but not identical. But if we consider smaller and smaller group lengths by using larger and larger sample sizes, the resulting histograms will tend to approach the smooth curve: see, for example, Figure 6.3. Thus, the curve can be considered as the limiting value of a histogram when the lengths of the intervals (on its base) approach zero, and when the sample size approaches infinity. This curve is then called the *probability distribution*, describing the population of items from which the samples originate.

6.6.1 The normal distribution

There are many different families of probability distributions. A family of distributions found to be of great use is that of the *normal* (or *Gaussian*) distribution, a frequently occurring symmetric distribution with a characteristic bell shape. This distribution and those associated with it dominate both statistical theory and method, by virtue of their many attractive mathematical properties. Many other probability distributions can often be approximated by the normal curve. The methods based on this distribution are the most useful of all statistical methods.

The normal distribution describes the randomness of measurement errors and it occurs in the study of many physical phenomena such as heat flow, diameters of machined parts, lengths of tobacco leaves, and also in the study of many natural measurements such as the heights and weights of human beings, IQ scores etc. The distribution can be completely described once its mean and standard deviation are known. For example, Figure 6.4 shows

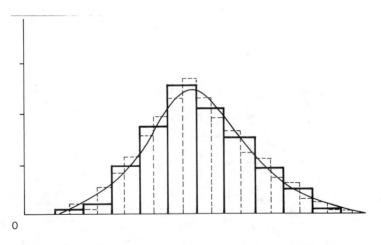

Figure 6.3 Histogram approaching normal curve as sample size increases

some normal curves with varying standard deviation (σ) and mean (μ) of zero; the formula for the normal probability density function $f(x; \mu, \sigma)$ is also shown (perhaps one of the less attractive features of the normal distribution!).

The shapes of the distributions depicted in Figure 6.4 depend on the value of the standard deviation. Note that the narrower of the distributions is also the taller. This must be so because the areas under the curves are equal. The total area under the curve corresponds to a probability of 1, the highest value a probability can have. Any subsection of the total area corresponds to a probability value of less than 1. The main usefulness of the normal distribution arises from the existence of readily available normal tables (see Table A3, Appendix A) which make the calculation of these probabilities extremely easy. The tables available are in fact those for the standard normal distribution which is simply the normal distribution with parameter values $\mu = 0$ and $\sigma = 1$.

Knowledge of the standard deviation of a normal distribution is sufficient to enable various assertions to be made concerning the spread of values in the population. For example:

1. Approximately 68% of the values lie within 1 standard deviation on either side of the mean of the distribution.

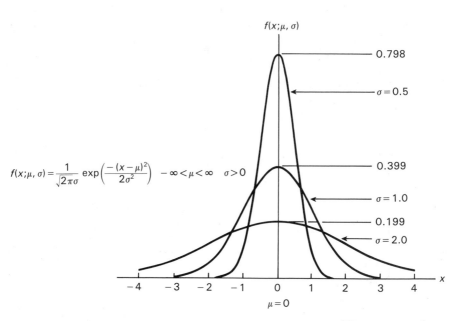

$$f(x; \mu, \sigma) = \frac{1}{\sqrt{2\pi}\sigma} \exp\left(\frac{-(x-\mu)^2}{2\sigma^2}\right) \quad -\infty < \mu < \infty \quad \sigma > 0$$

Note: If $\mu = 0$ and $\sigma = 1$, the standard normal distribution $N(0, 1) = (1/\sqrt{2\pi}) \exp(-(1/2)x^2)$, is obtained.

Figure 6.4 Normal (or Gaussian) distributions

2. 95% of the values lie within 1.96 standard deviations on either side of the mean.
3. 99% (or 99.73%) of all values lie within 2.58 (or 3) standard deviations on either side of the mean.

Figure 6.5 illustrates this point.

On the basis of Figure 6.2 it is reasonable to expect that the distribution of call-handling times will peak near the single value of 60 seconds, but that perturbations in the process will lead to symmetrical departures on each side of the peak, indicating that the population of call-handling times (for enquiries) could be described by a normal distribution. Note that the standard deviation σ is simply the distance of the central vertical line (at the value of μ) from the points of inflection of the curve (that is, the points where the curve changes from convex to concave — see Figure 6.5).

Central limit theorem

One of the most powerful theorems in statistics associated with the normal distribution is called the central limit theorem (CLT). According to the CLT, for sufficiently large sample sizes, the distribution of the sample mean (which is a variable in its own right) is normal; hence, when one works with sample means, all the nice properties of the normal distribution apply, irrespective of the fact that the parent population (from which the sample is drawn) is not normally distributed. Moreover, the distribution of the sample mean retains the mean of the parent population, but has a smaller variance: in fact, the nth of the parent population-variance, with n being the sample size.

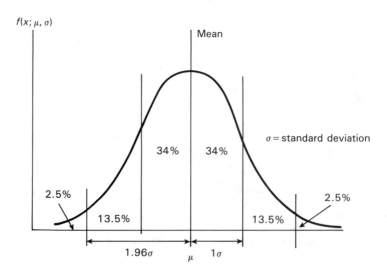

Figure 6.5 Spread of values in a normal distribution

The CLT is formally expressed as follows: If $X_1, ..., X_n$ are independent identically distributed random variables with means μ and variances σ^2, then for large enough n, approximately

$$\bar{X} \sim N(\mu, \sigma^2/n) \qquad \text{(normal)}$$

or equivalently

$$\frac{\bar{X} - \mu}{\sigma/n} \sim N(0, 1) \qquad \text{(standard normal)}$$

As we shall see in Part III, the CLT provides the theoretical support for the important SPC tool of the control chart. We will there be establishing charts for sample means rather than for individual observations; in this way, thanks to the CLT, the procedure for calculating (statistical) control limits becomes much more flexible and statistically valid.

Checking for normality

We have already stated that certain statistical methods, such as t-tests and confidence intervals, are based on the assumption that the samples under consideration originate from a normal population. Although it is impossible to prove this assumption, we can follow the method of *median ranks*, described below, to check that it is reasonable.

In Table 6.3 the 108 call-handling times (CHT) from Table 6.1 have been ranked in order of magnitude. Alongside each value is a *median rank* (*MR*) which is a crude estimate of the cumulative percentage of all the directory enquiries needing a call-handling time up to the value under consideration. For example, based purely on the median rank of 37 seconds, it is estimated that 9.87% of the directory enquiries need up to 37 seconds' handling time. The median rank is calculated by

$$MR = \frac{\text{rank} - 0.3}{n + 0.4} \times 100$$

For example, the 17th highest rank in the sample of $n = 108$ handling times has a median rank calculated as

$$MR = \frac{17 - 0.3}{108 + 0.4} \times 100 = 15.41\%$$

The median ranks are then plotted against the corresponding values of handling times on normal probability paper (see figure D.2, Appendix D), as shown in Figure 6.6.

The scale on normal probability paper has been chosen so that, if the data formed a normal distribution, the points would lie on a straight line. Of course, due to variation that always exists, sample data will never lie exactly on a straight line; however, it is evident in Figure 6.6 that a straight line provides a reasonable fit and so we can safely conclude that the normal

Table 6.3 Median ranks (*MR*) for call-handling times (CHT)

Rank	CHT	*MR*	Rank	CHT	*MR*
1	19	0.65	55	58	50.46
2	21	1.57	56	58	51.38
3	26	2.49	57	58	52.31
4	30	3.41	58	60	53.23
5	32	4.34	59	60	54.15
6	32	5.26	60	60	55.07
7	34	6.18	61	60	56.00
8	35	7.10	62	61	56.92
9	36	8.03	63	61	57.84
10	36	8.95	64	62	58.76
11	37	9.87	65	62	59.69
12	38	10.79	66	62	60.61
13	38	11.72	67	64	61.53
14	42	12.64	68	64	62.45
15	42	13.56	69	64	63.38
16	42	14.48	70	64	64.30
17	44	15.41	71	66	65.22
18	44	16.33	72	66	66.14
19	44	17.25	73	66	67.07
20	44	18.17	74	66	67.99
21	44	19.10	75	67	68.91
22	44	20.02	76	68	69.83
23	45	20.94	77	68	70.76
24	46	21.86	78	69	71.68
25	46	22.79	79	70	72.60
26	46	23.71	80	70	73.52
27	46	24.63	81	70	74.45
28	46	25.55	82	71	75.37
29	46	26.48	83	71	76.29
30	46	27.40	84	72	77.21
31	46	28.32	85	72	78.14
32	50	29.24	86	72	79.06
33	50	30.17	87	73	79.98
34	50	31.09	88	75	80.90
35	50	32.01	89	76	81.83
36	52	32.93	90	76	82.75
37	52	33.86	91	76	83.67
38	52	34.78	92	78	84.59
39	52	35.70	93	78	85.52
40	52	36.62	94	80	86.44
41	52	37.55	95	80	87.36
42	52	38.47	96	80	88.28
43	52	39.39	97	80	89.21
44	54	40.31	98	80	90.13
45	54	41.24	99	81	91.05
46	55	42.16	100	86	91.97
47	55	43.08	101	86	92.90
48	55	44.00	102	89	93.82
49	56	44.93	103	90	94.74
50	56	45.85	104	90	95.66
51	56	46.77	105	91	96.59
52	56	47.69	106	92	97.51
53	58	48.62	107	97	98.43
54	58	49.54	108	102	99.35

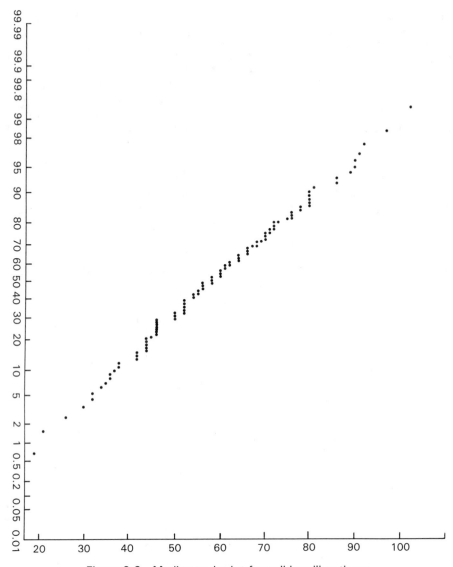

Figure 6.6 Median rank plot for call-handling times

distribution reasonably describes the variability in the directory enquiry handling times.

It is worthwhile mentioning here another two important distributions which, perhaps indirectly, we have already made use of in Sections 6.3 and 6.4.

6.6.2 The *t*-distribution

One might characterize the *t*-distribution (or *Student's t-distribution*) as being the distribution nearest to the normal for small sample sizes. It is symmetrical about zero and has a shape very similar to that of the standard normal curve except that the 'tails' are somewhat thicker (see, for example, Figure 6.7). It depends on a parameter m, which signifies the associated degrees of freedom. In fact, the limiting value of the $t(m)$-distribution as m approaches infinity is the standard normal $N(0, 1)$ distribution.

We find the t-distribution very useful when we want to make inferences about the population mean μ, on the basis of sample statistics only (population variance unknown). Recall from (6.6) that

$$SE(\bar{y}) = s/\sqrt{n}$$

Then it can be shown that the ratio $(\bar{y} - \mu)/SE(\bar{y})$, which is a variable in its own right, has the t-distribution with $n - 1$ degrees of freedom. In other words

$$\frac{(\bar{y} - \mu)}{s/\sqrt{n}} \sim t(n - 1) \tag{6.17}$$

Note the relationship of (6.17) to the CLT of Section 6.6.1. One could also relate (6.17) to any statement involving t-values – the $t(df; \alpha)$ values – in Sections 6.3 and 6.4.

6.6.3 The F-distribution

The importance of the F-distribution in statistical theory derives mainly from its applicability to the distribution of ratios of independent estimators of

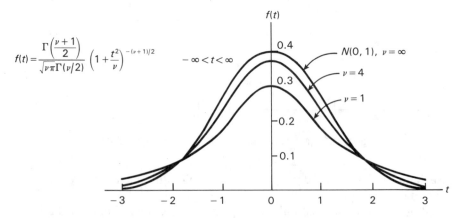

$$f(t) = \frac{\Gamma\left(\frac{\nu + 1}{2}\right)}{\sqrt{\nu\pi}\,\Gamma(\nu/2)} \left(1 + \frac{t^2}{\nu}\right)^{-(\nu + 1)/2} \quad -\infty < t < \infty$$

Note: $\Gamma(n + 1) = n\Gamma(n) = n!$

$\Gamma(1/2) = \sqrt{\pi}$

Figure 6.7 Student's t-distribution ($\partial = 4$ and 1) with the standard normal distribution N (0, 1) for comparison

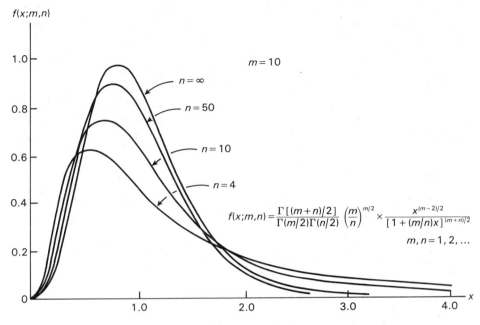

Figure 6.8 *F*-distributions

$$f(x;m,n) = \frac{\Gamma[(m+n)/2]}{\Gamma(m/2)\Gamma(n/2)} \left(\frac{m}{n}\right)^{m/2} \times \frac{x^{(m-2)/2}}{[1+(m/n)x]^{(m+n)/2}}$$

$$m, n = 1, 2, \ldots$$

variance. The commonest application is in testing the equality of the variances of two normal populations. We have already made use of such a test and of the associated *F*-tables (Tables A2, Appendix A) in Section 6.4.4, when we looked at the ratio of estimated variances from two different samples.

The *F*-distribution depends on two parameters *m* and *n* which, in the *F*-tables (Tables A2), are specified respectively as the degrees of freedom for the numerator (*m*) and the degrees of freedom for the denominator (*n*). Note that the order of writing these parameters is important. Figure 6.8 shows some *F*-distributions for a fixed *m* and various values of *n*.

As in the case of all important distributions mentioned so far, the least attractive feature of the *F*-distribution is the analytic expression of its probability density function $f(x; m, n)$ which is also shown in Figure 6.8. However, the reader should note that the density functions have been shown here only for the sake of completeness, and are not expected to be used for any numerical evaluations.

■ 6.7 Measuring linear association

There is often a need to measure the strength of the relationship between two variables. On many occasions we find ourselves drifting towards measuring the extent to which the relationship can be described as being of a particular form, that is, a linear relationship. This is because linear relationships, fitting straight lines to data, are particularly simple (mathematically) and can provide a reliable tool for forecasting purposes (statistically). In practice, many relationships between variables can be described as approximately linear, either within a certain range, or after some suitable transformation of the variables has taken place. For example, from transistor theory, it is expected that the value of the voltage (V) applied to the gate of a MOSFE (metal oxide silicon field effect) transistor operating in the subthreshold mode, is related to the resulting drain current (C) in the following way:

$$\log(C) = a + bV$$

where a and b are constants that can be estimated on the basis of some available data. We can see here that V is linearly related to the log-transformed variable C.

We will now describe, through a case study, some simple methods for measuring the strength of a linear association.

CASE STUDY 6.3

For testing the strength of some large castings, a small test-piece was produced at the same time as each casting. In order to demonstrate that the test-piece gave a reliable indication of the strength of the whole casting, 11 castings were chosen at random, and they, together with their associated test-pieces, were deliberately broken and their breaking stress was measured. The following results were obtained:

Breaking stress (tons per square inch)

Casting (Y)	45	67	61	77	71	51	45	58	48	62	36
Test-piece (X)	39	86	97	102	74	53	62	69	80	53	48

A high level of linear association between the two variables Y and X would demonstrate that the test-pieces could be utilized (instead of the large castings) in life-testing exercises (through destructive testing) to obtain information about the strength of the whole casting, which it would be prohibitively expensive to test to destruction.

It would be natural to start the investigation of any relationship between two variables by plotting the available data on a *scatter diagram* such as Figure 6.9. Examination of Figure 6.9 reveals that, overall, the breaking strength of the castings (Y) seems to be linearly related to the breaking strength of the test-pieces: a high value of the breaking stress needed to break the test-piece seems to correspond to a high value for the breaking stress needed to break the associated casting.

Although scatter diagrams are very convenient tools for asserting two-way relationships, they do not provide formal measures of these relationships, nor

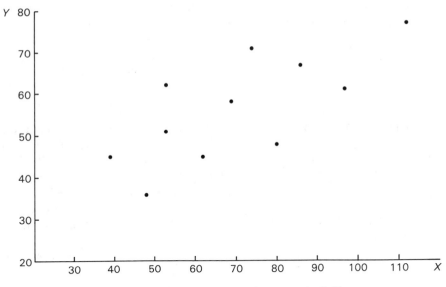

Figure 6.9   Scatter diagram (case-study 6.3)

do they provide any means of establishing whether any apparent associations are actually due to chance or not. In this section, using the sample data from case-study 6.3, we shall provide some statistical methods for measuring linear relationships and for testing for their statistical significance.

6.7.1 Correlation coefficient

A useful measure for calculating the degree of linear association between two variables is the *correlation coefficient* (or product–moment correlation coefficient) usually symbolized by ρ. This can be estimated by

$$r(Y, X) = r = \frac{\mathrm{Cov}(Y, X)}{SD(Y)SD(X)} \tag{6.18}$$

where $\mathrm{Cov}(Y, X)$ is the covariance between Y and X, which for the case of a sample with sample size n (n = number of pairs of observations) is given by

$$\mathrm{Cov}(Y, X) = \sum_{j=1}^{n} (y_j - \bar{y})(x_j - \bar{x})/(n - 1) \tag{6.19}$$

For calculation purposes we can use the relationship

$$\sum (y_j - \bar{y})(x_j - \bar{x}) = \sum y_j x_j - n\bar{y}\bar{x} \tag{6.20}$$

Using formulae (6.19) and (6.5) we can obtain a formula for r (the estimate for ρ) as

$$r = \frac{\Sigma(y_j - \bar{y})(x_j - \bar{x})}{\sqrt{\Sigma(y_j - \bar{y})^2 \Sigma(x_j - \bar{x})^2}} \tag{6.21}$$

Formulae (6.20) and (6.3) can be utilized to facilitate calculation of (6.21).

It can be shown that a correlation coefficient will always have a value between -1 and $+1$ (inclusive). A value of -1 corresponds to a perfect negative linear relationship, whereas a value of $+1$ corresponds to a perfect positive linear relationship: see, for example, Figures 6.10(a) and 6.10(b). A correlation of 0 is an indication of the absence of a linear association between two variables (see Figure 6.10(c)), but this does not imply the absence of any association – see, for example, Figure 6.10(d) which depicts a relationship which, although not linear ($r = 0$), is actually a very strong curvilinear relationship.

It is, in fact, very dangerous to conclude that a high correlation coefficient indicates a strong association, as this could be the result of an *outlier* (abnormal or freak value): see, for example, Figure 6.10(e). An examination of the scatter diagram can reveal such an irregularity. One should also be

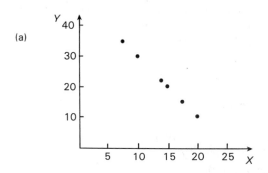

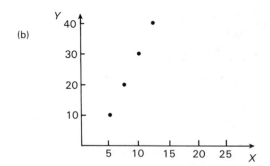

Figure 6.10 (a) Perfect negative linear relationship ($r = -1$);
(b) perfect positive linear relationship ($r = +1$);

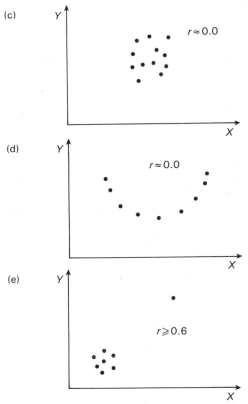

Figure 6.10 (*continued*) (c) no linear association; (d) strong curvilinear association (although $r \approx 0$); (e) no relationship although r is high.

aware of the fact that high correlations do not always indicate strong cause and effect relationships; for example, a high positive r between the salaries of Methodist ministers and whisky sales, does not suggest that a reduction in ministers' salaries will result in a drop in the sales of whisky!

Returning to our case-study 6.3, we can calculate the correlation coefficient between castings (Y) and test-pieces (X) by making use of Table 6.4. From Table 6.4 we can see that

$$\bar{y} = 621/11 = 56.5, \quad \bar{x} = 763/11 = 69.4$$

and, making use of (6.21), (6.20) and (6.3), we have

$$r = \frac{44891 - 11 \times 56.5 \times 69.4}{\sqrt{(36639 - 11 \times 56.5^2)(57133 - 11 \times 69.4^2)}} = 0.699$$

(Actually, if we use an accuracy to 3 decimal places for $\bar{y}$ and $\bar{x}$, we find $r = 0.704$).

Table 6.4 Calculations for case-study 6.3

	y_j	x_j	$y_j x_j$	y_j^2	x_j^2
	45	39	1755	2025	1521
	67	86	5762	4489	7396
	61	97	5917	3721	9409
	77	102	7854	5929	10404
	71	74	5254	5041	5476
	51	53	2703	2601	2809
	45	62	2790	2025	3844
	58	69	4002	3364	4761
	48	80	3840	2304	6400
	62	53	3286	3844	2809
	36	48	1728	1296	2304
Total	621	763	44891	36639	57133

Testing for significance

The sample correlation coefficient r is an estimate of the population correlation coefficient ρ. To test whether any existing correlation between the breaking strengths of the castings and those of the test-pieces is due to chance (that is, whether the value of $r = 0.699$ is statistically significant), we can apply a simple significance test (see Section 6.4) as follows.

- Null hypothesis (H_0): $\rho = 0$: there is no linear relationship between the breaking strength of the whole castings and the test-pieces.
- Alternative hypothesis (H_1): $\rho > 0$: there is a positive linear relationship (one-sided test) between the breaking strength of the whole castings and that of the test-pieces.
- Test statistic (TS): $r = 0.699$.
- Critical value (cv): from Table A4 (Appendix A), for a one-sided test with 9 degrees of freedom ($df = 11 - 2$; bivariate case) at 1% level of significance:

$$cv(df; \alpha) = cv(9; 1\%) = 0.685$$

- Decision: since $TS > cv$, we reject H_0 at the 1% level, in favour of H_1 (running a 1% risk of being wrong by doing so).

6.7.2 Linear regression analysis

There are many occasions when we have an *independent* variable (or regressor) X that we can control, and a *dependent* variable (or response) Y that we can observe at different levels of X. On the basis of some sample observations, we may wish to estimate a functional relationship between Y and X, in the best possible way. If the estimation of this relationship is successful, we may even be able to use it to predict values of Y, having observed the related values of X. For example, if we had a model accurately describing the relationship between the breaking strength of the castings (Y) and the associated test-pieces (X), we would be able to utilize it to predict the breaking strength of a particular casting on the basis of the breaking strength of its associated test-piece (which could be tested to destruction for this purpose).

There is a simple method, known as *regression analysis*, by which we can investigate the relationship between Y and X through a *linear model* which can be estimated on the basis of only a limited amount of sample data. Inferences can then be made as to how close this relationship is, and on the predictive capability or uncertainty of the model. The method can be generalized to situations involving more than one independent variable (*multiple regression analysis*).

The general form of the model for the case of *simple regression* (with a single independent variable X) is that of a straight-line equation:

$$Y = \alpha + \beta X + e$$

or, in terms of the data (of sample size n),

$$y_j = \alpha + \beta x_j + e_j \qquad j = 1, \dots, n$$

where x_j is the value of the independent variable X on the jth observation, y_j is the corresponding response (value of the dependent variable Y at the jth observation), α and β are, respectively, the intercept and the gradient, and e_j are random error terms, assumed to be independent and normally distributed with mean zero and variance σ^2. Note that the linear form of the model might be the result of an appropriate transformation of the available data, for example the log-transformation.

We need to calculate the sample intercept a (estimate of the real α) and the sample regression coefficient b or slope (estimate of the real gradient β) so that the line

$$\hat{Y} = a + bX \tag{6.22}$$

has the best possible fit, in the sense that the errors e_j are minimal; a and b are then the best (unbiased) estimators for α and β. Gauss formalized the fitting of straight lines by adopting the principle of least squares. This principle suggests that we should choose the line which passes closest to all the points in the following sense. The vertical distance of the point from the fitted line is measured (see, for example, Figure 6.11) and this, from (6.22), is

$$e_j = y_j - \hat{y}_j = y_j - a - bx_j$$

This distance is squared (to avoid spurious cancellation of large positive with large negative discrepancies); the total of these squared distances is then calculated to provide a measure of how well the suggested line fits; we then choose our line to minimize this measure of closeness.

141

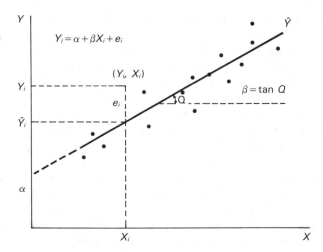

Figure 6.11   Graph for regression analysis

Mathematically speaking, we need to minimize the *residual sum of squares* (*RSS*) given by

$$RSS = \sum (Y - \hat{Y})^2 = \sum_{j=1}^{n} e_j^2 = \sum_{j=1}^{n} (y_j - a - bx_j)^2$$

Differentiating *RSS* with respect to a and b, and setting the results equal to zero, we obtain two equations from which expressions for the estimates a and b can be found to be given by

$$b = \frac{\Sigma (y_j - \bar{y})(x_j - \bar{x})}{\Sigma (x_j - \bar{x})^2} \tag{6.23}$$

and

$$a = \bar{y} - b\bar{x} \tag{6.24}$$

Note that, from (6.2), (6.3), (6.19) and (6.20), the formula (6.23) is equivalent to

$$b = \frac{\text{Cov}(Y, X)}{\text{Var}(X)} \tag{6.25}$$

or

$$b = \frac{\Sigma \; y_j x_j - n\bar{y}\bar{x}}{\Sigma x_j^2 - n\bar{x}^2} \tag{6.26}$$

There is an obvious connection between the regression coefficient and the correlation coefficient. Indeed, combining (6.18) and (6.25) we obtain

$$b = r \, \frac{SD(Y)}{SD(X)} \tag{6.27}$$

Formula (6.27) is easier to apply for the calculation of b (or r) when r (or b) is known.

With reference to case-study 6.3, an examination of Figure 6.9 reveals that, although there is not a perfect relationship between Y and X, the data do appear to scatter around a straight line. In order to fit the best straight line possible to the data, we shall make use of formulae (6.24) and (6.26) to estimate the intercept and the slope (regression coefficient) for this line. Thus, also making use of Table 6.4, we have:

$$b = \frac{44891 - 11 \times 56.5 \times 69.4}{57133 - 11 \times (69.4)^2} = 0.424$$

and

$$a = 56.5 - 0.424 \times 69.4 = 27.1$$

(Actually, if accuracy to 3 decimal places is used for $\bar{y}$ and $\bar{x}$, we find $\beta = 0.432$ and $\alpha = 26.521$). There is an easy way of drawing a regression line. We need only two points that we know to fall on the line. One point is where the line intercepts the vertical axis (the Y axis); in terms of coordinates, this point is $(Y, X) = (a, 0)$. It can also be shown that the regression line goes through the point $(Y, X) = (\bar{y}, \bar{x})$. So, in our case, we can graphically draw the line by simply joining the points

$$(a, 0) = (27.1, 0) \quad \text{and} \quad (\bar{y}, \bar{x}) = (56.5, 69.4)$$

The regression line is shown in Figure 6.12.

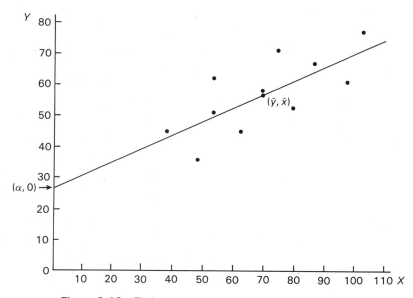

Figure 6.12 Fitting a regression line (case-study 6.3)

Regression rationale

The total variability in the response of interest, Y, can be represented by the *total sum of squares* (*TSS*) of the deviations of each y_j from the mean $\bar{y}$, that is, in general,

$$TSS = \Sigma(Y - \bar{Y})^2$$

or, in terms of the observations,

$$TSS = \sum_{j=1}^{n} (y_j - \bar{y})^2$$

In terms of area, these squared deviations from the mean are shown in Figure 6.13.

By fitting the best straight line $\hat{Y}$ using regression, we try to find a straight line other than $\bar{Y}$, which will reduce the area of the squared deviations from the line. Comparing Figure 6.13 with Figure 6.14, we can observe a significant reduction in the area (of the squared residuals) achieved by fitting the regression line $\bar{y}$. The relative reduction in area can be utilized to obtain an important measure called the *coefficient of determination* (or R^2), which is given by

$$R^2 = \frac{TSS - RSS}{TSS} = \frac{\Sigma(Y - \bar{Y})^2 - \Sigma(Y - \hat{Y})^2}{\Sigma(Y - \bar{Y})^2} \qquad (6.28)$$

This measure gives an indication of how successful we have been in fitting a straight line to the data. It always has a value between 0 and 1, and in

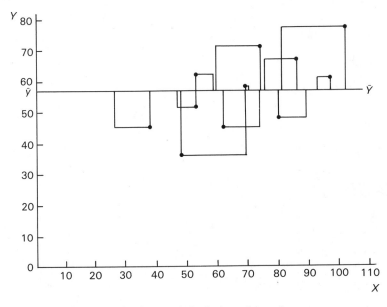

Figure 6.13 Squared deviations from the mean

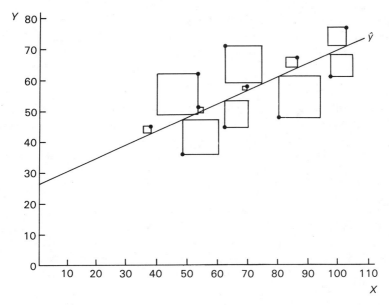

Figure 6.14 Squared deviations from the regression line

percentage terms, it indicates the amount of variation (from the total) in Y that has been explained by the independent variable X or, in more general cases, by all the independent variables (or regressors) involved in the regression model.

For the case of simple regression (one independent variable), the numerator of (6.28) – which is called the *regression sum of squares* – is given by

$$RegSS = TSS - RSS = b^2 \, \Sigma(X - \bar{X})^2$$

Therefore, from (6.28),

$$R^2 = b^2 \, \frac{\Sigma(X - \bar{X})^2}{\Sigma(Y - \bar{Y})^2}$$

or

$$R^2 = b^2 \, \frac{\text{Var}(X)}{\text{Var}(Y)} \tag{6.29}$$

Combining (6.29) with (6.27) we note that, in the case of simple regression, the coefficient of determination is simply the square of the correlation coefficient. For our case-study, since $r = 0.699$ we have $R^2 = (0.699)^2 = 0.489$. So we can say that 48.9% of the variability in the dependent variable Y can be explained by the independent variable X. This means, of course, that over 51% of the variability in Y is still unexplained; this accounts for the squared areas depicted in Figure 6.14.

It should be noted that in the case of multiple regression the general formula (6.28) still applies, although the *RegSS* is more difficult to calculate. On the whole, although the general principles of least squares apply in the same way, fitting a model of the form

$$Y = a + b_1 X_1 + b_2 X_2 + \cdots + b_k X_k$$

without a computer is an extremely laborious exercise. However, the availability of a wide range of statistical packages has made the task of performing regression analysis (multiple or not) an easy one.

Significance testing

There are various ways for testing for goodness of fit of the regression line. One of these was used in Section 6.7.1, when we tested for the significance of the correlation coefficient between Y and X. A more formal method is to test for the significance of the regression coefficient. For this we need the standard error of the estimate b; in a case of simple regression this is given by

$$SE(b) = S\sqrt{\frac{1}{\Sigma(X - \bar{X})^2}} \qquad (6.30)$$

where S is an estimate of σ (the residual standard deviation) obtained from

$$S^2 = \frac{RSS}{n-2} = \frac{\Sigma(Y - \hat{Y})^2}{(n-2)} = \frac{1}{(n-2)} \{\Sigma(Y - \bar{Y})^2 - b^2 \Sigma(X - \bar{X})^2\} \qquad (6.31)$$

S provides a measure of the average deviation from the regression line. Clearly, the smaller the S the better the fit. Note that the degrees of freedom associated with S (the residual degrees of freedom) are $n - 2$, two less than the number of pairs of observations. We are restricted twice because two parameters (α and β) have been estimated from the available data.

We can now test the hypothesis H_0: $\beta = 0$ (X has no significant effect on Y), against the alternative H_1: $\beta \neq 0$, by applying the usual t-test which makes use of the following test statistic:

$$TS = \frac{|b - \beta|}{SE(b)}$$

which follows the general formula (6.12), with $SE(b)$ being the standard error of the estimate of b given by (6.30). TS is calculated under H_0 and compared to a critical value from the t-tables (Table A1, Appendix A) depending on $n - 2$ degrees of freedom. We can also obtain a confidence interval for the real β, following the general formula (6.7).

For case-study 6.3, using (6.31) we obtain $S = 9.4$, and from (6.30)

$$SE(b) = 0.145$$

Then, under H_0,

$$TS = \frac{|b|}{SE(b)} = \frac{0.424}{0.145} = 2.9$$

From the t-tables for a two-sided test at the 5% level and 9 ($= 11 - 2$) degrees of freedom we find

$$cv = cv(n - 2; 5\%) = t(9; 5\%) = 2.26$$

Since $TS > cv$ we reject the null hypothesis (running a risk of 5% by doing so) of a non-significant linear relationship between Y and X.

On the basis of b and $SE(b)$, a 95% confidence interval for the real regression coefficient β can easily be constructed using the general formula (6.7). We have

$$CI(\beta): \quad [b \pm t(n - 2; 5\%)SE(b)]$$

or

$$[0.424 \pm 2.26 \times 0.145]$$

that is,

$$\{0.096, 0.752\}$$

The above principles apply in a similar way in the multiple regression case.

Prediction using regression

A simple regression relationship is frequently estimated so that the values of the (dependent) variable Y may be predicted from a knowledge of the value of the (independent) variable X. The average value $\hat{Y}_0$ of observations of Y corresponding to a particular (known) value X_0 of X could be predicted by

$$\hat{Y}_0 = a + bX_0$$

Of course, $\hat{Y}_0$ is only a point estimate of the real Y_0 and we usually need to calculate a confidence interval for Y_0. We can again apply the general formula (6.7) to obtain

$$CI(Y_0): \quad [\hat{Y}_0 \pm t(n - 2; 5\%)SE(\hat{Y}_0)]$$

where the $SE(\hat{Y}_0)$, the standard error of the estimate $\hat{Y}_0$, is given by

$$SE(\hat{Y}_0) = S\sqrt{\left\{\frac{1}{n} + \frac{(X_0 - \bar{X})^2}{\Sigma(X - \bar{X})^2}\right\}} \tag{6.32}$$

with S being defined by (6.31).

Note that it is safer to interpolate (predict unknown values of Y within the range of the available sample data) than to extrapolate (predict Y beyond the range of the sample data). This is demonstrated by Figure 6.15, where the

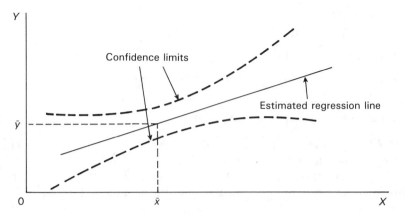

Figure 6.15   Confidence about a regression line

dotted lines represent the confidence limits which are the closest to each other at the point $(\bar{y}, \bar{x})$ − known as the *centroid*.

With reference to case-study 6.3, the test-piece of a further casting had a breaking strength of 58 tons per square inch. We wish to give limits within which we would be willing to state with 95% confidence that the average strength of the whole casting lies. We have

$$X_0 = 58, \ b = 0.424, \ a = 27.1$$

and so

$$\hat{Y}_0 = 27.1 + 0.424 \times 58 = 51.7$$

Using (6.31) we obtain $S = 9.4$, and using (6.32) we obtain

$$SE(\hat{Y}_0) = 3.28$$

Then

$$CI(Y_0): \ [\hat{Y}_0 \pm t(n-2; 5\%)SE(\hat{Y}_0)]$$

or

$$[51.7 \pm 2.26 \times 3.28]$$

that is,

$$\{44.3, 59.1\}$$

Therefore we can say, with 95% confidence, that, on the basis of the breaking stress associated with the test-piece, the average breaking strength of the corresponding casting could be anything from 44.3 to 59.1 tons per square inch.

The multiple regression case

The general form of a multiple regression equation is as follows:

$$Y = \alpha + \beta_1 X_1 + \beta_2 X_2 + \cdots + \beta_k X_k \qquad (6.33)$$

where $X_1, \ldots, X_k$ are k independent variables (regressors) of interest which may (or may not) affect the response Y, α is the regression constant, and $\beta_1, \ldots, \beta_k$ are the associated regression coefficients which can be estimated using again the principle of least squares. Each regression coefficient (say β_1) can be seen as being the amount of change in the value of Y, when the value of the associated regressor (say X_1) changes by one unit (in X_1 units) while everything else remains constant.

We have already stated that when the number of the regressors is more than one, manual calculation of the regression equation and its associated statistics is rather tedious and should be performed with the help of a statistical computer package. However, although the calculations can be done by computer, the decision about what to calculate lies with the researcher. A multiple regression equation, no matter how complex, can be useless unless an informed decision has been taken in advance about which variables it should include.

A major problem in multiple regression is that of *multicollinearity*: this is when the independent variables are not precisely independent of each other, in the sense that, during the collection of the sample data, they did not vary independently from each other. This situation is also known as *confounding* and will be mentioned again in Chapter 7. If collection of additional data is not possible, an easy way of avoiding the pitfalls of multicollinearity is to examine the correlation coefficients r (see Section 6.7.1) for every pair of regressors available. Every statistical package provides the facility for the calculation of a *correlation matrix* which, in the case of, say, four regressors, has the following form:

Correlation matrix

	X_1	X_2	X_3	X_4
X_1	1			
X_2	$r(X_2, X_1)$	1		
X_3	$r(X_3, X_1)$	$r(X_3, X_2)$	1	
X_4	$r(X_4, X_1)$	$r(X_4, X_2)$	$r(X_4, X_3)$	1

If, for example, the correlation between X_1 and X_3 is significantly large (see Section 6.7.1 for significance testing of r), only one of the regressors X_1 and X_3 should be allowed in the regression model. This is realistic because, when two regressors are highly correlated, each explains the same amount of variation in Y and so one of them is sufficient for model estimation purposes; if both of them are (wrongly) allowed in the model, the large correlation between them will bias the calculations and will contaminate the estimates of the regression coefficients, the coefficient of determination etc.

When the multicollinearity problem has been taken care of, a decision should be taken on which of the uncorrelated regressors to use in the regression model. There is a lot to be said for model simplicity; there is not much point in allowing a regressor that does not contribute, in the sense that it does not explain much of the variation in Y after the contribution of all the other independent variables has been accounted for.

One way of deciding whether a regressor makes a significant contribution is to test the associated regression coefficient for significance. Every statistical package provides the t-ratios for all the regression coefficients; these are simply the test statistics to be compared to the appropriate t-values from the t-tables. In such cases, one should be careful to allow for only $n - 1 - k$ degrees of freedom, assuming a model of the form (6.33): $k + 1$ parameters are estimated from n sample data.

Some packages even carry out the hypothesis testing themselves: they provide a probability value, P, which is the probability that the null hypothesis of, say,

$$H_0: \beta_k = 0$$

is true. The lower this probability value, the higher the significance of the regression coefficient (and hence the higher the importance of the associated regressor). Generally, one can accept significance if $P < 0.05$. If a regressor is found to be unimportant (that is, found not to explain a significant amount of variation in Y), it is better to exclude it from the regression model. This means that a new regression model will have to be estimated, without the unimportant regressor.

A popular method for finding the best model possible is to make use of the value of the coefficient of determination (R^2) in a stepwise manner. For example, we can start with a simple regression equation by selecting the regressor that contributes the most (a correlation matrix involving the response variable Y, or simple data plots between Y and each regressor can help here). We can then proceed by selecting the next regressor whose inclusion in the model will produce a significant increase in the value of R^2 (clearly, we will be dealing with a newly estimated model and a new R^2). Whether such an increase is significant or not, can be verified by a simple t-test which makes use of the following test statistic:

$$TS = \sqrt{\frac{(\text{new } R^2 - \text{old } R^2)(n - p - 1)}{(1 - \text{new } R^2)}}$$

The value of the TS is compared for significance with a critical value from the t-tables (Appendix A, Table A1) which will depend on $n - p - 1$ degrees of freedom, where p is the number of the regressors involved in the model so far. If $TS > cv$, the newly selected regressor is important and is kept in the model;

Table 6.5 Data for multiple regression example

Call number	Y	X_1	Type	X_2
1	97	7	C	0
2	57	4	S	1
3	78	5	C	0
4	10	1	C	0
5	75	5	C	0
6	62	4	S	1
7	101	7	S	1
8	27	2	C	0
9	53	4	C	0
10	33	2	C	0
11	118	8	C	0
12	65	5	S	1
13	25	2	S	1
14	71	5	C	0
15	105	7	S	1
16	17	1	C	0
17	49	4	C	0
18	68	5	C	0

Table 6.6 MINITAB calculations for multiple regression model

```
? SET C1
? 97,57,78,10,75,62,101,27,53,33,118,65,25,71,105,17,49,68
? SET C2
? 7,4,5,1,5,4,7,2,4,2,8,5,2,5,7,1,4,5
? SET C3
? 0,1,0,0,0,1,1,0,0,0,0,1,1,0,1,0,0,0

? REGR C1,2,C2,C3

THE REGRESSION EQUATION IS
Y=-1.97+14.7 X1+.151 X2


                                           ST. DEV.     T-RATIO=
            COLUMN      COEFFICIENT        OF COEF.     COEF/S.D.
            -             -1.972            2.538         -0.78
X1          C2           14.6870            0.5314        27.64
X2          C3            0.151             2.316          0.07

THE ST. DEV. OF Y ABOUT REGRESSION LINE IS
S=4.563
WITH (18-3)=15 DEGREES OF FREEDOM

R-SQUARED=98.1 PERCENT
R-SQUARED=97.9 PERCENT, ADJUSTED FOR D.F.

ANALYSIS OF VARIANCE

DUE TO       DF         SS     MS=SS/DF
REGRESSION    2    16407.25     8203.63
RESIDUAL     15      312.36       20.82
TOTAL        17    16719.61

FURTHER ANALYSIS OF VARIANCE
SS EXPLAINED BY EACH VARIABLE WHEN ENTERED IN THE ORDER GIVEN

DUE TO       DF         SS
REGRESSION    2    16407.25
C2            1    16407.16
C3            1        0.09
```

Table 6.7 MINITAB calculations for simple regression model

```
? REGR C1,1,C2

THE REGRESSION EQUATION IS
Y=-1.95+14.7 X1
```

	COLUMN	COEFFICIENT	ST. DEV. OF COEF.	T-RATIO= COEF/S.D.
	–	-1.947	2.431	-0.80
X1	C2	14.6930	0.5069	28.99

```
THE ST. DEV. OF Y ABOUT REGRESSION LINE IS
S=4.419
WITH (18-2)=16 DEGREES OF FREEDOM

R-SQUARED=98.1 PERCENT
R-SQUARED=98.0 PERCENT, ADJUSTED FOR D.F.
```

ANALYSIS OF VARIANCE

DUE TO	DF	SS	MS=SS/DF
REGRESSION	1	16407.16	16407.16
RESIDUAL	16	312.45	19.53
TOTAL	17	16719.61	

ROW	X1 C2	Y C1	PRED. Y VALUE	ST. DEV. PRED. Y	RESIDUAL	ST. RES.
1	7.00	97.00	100.90	1.71	-3.90	-0.96
2	4.00	57.00	56.82	1.06	0.18	0.04
3	5.00	78.00	71.52	1.10	6.48	1.51
4	1.00	10.00	12.75	1.98	-2.75	-0.70
5	5.00	75.00	71.52	1.10	3.48	0.81
6	4.00	62.00	56.82	1.06	5.18	1.21
7	7.00	101.00	100.90	1.71	0.10	0.02
8	2.00	27.00	27.44	1.58	-0.44	-0.11
9	4.00	53.00	56.82	1.06	-3.82	-0.89
10	2.00	33.00	27.44	1.58	5.56	1.35
11	8.00	118.00	115.60	2.13	2.40	0.62
12	5.00	65.00	71.52	1.10	-6.52	-1.52
13	2.00	25.00	27.44	1.58	-2.44	-0.59
14	5.00	71.00	71.52	1.10	-0.52	-0.12
15	7.00	105.00	100.90	1.71	4.10	1.00
16	1.00	17.00	12.75	1.98	4.25	1.08
17	4.00	49.00	56.82	1.06	-7.82	-1.82
18	5.00	68.00	71.52	1.10	-3.52	-0.82

```
X DENOTES AN OBS. WHOSE X VALUE GIVES IT LARGE INFLUENCE.
DURBIN-WATSON STATISTIC=1.93
```

otherwise the previously estimated model is preferred (excluding the last regressor).

A multiple regression model is declared the best model possible on statistical grounds, if no subsequent inclusion of any other variable can provide a significant increase in the value of R^2. Note that if an independent variable is found to be unimportant, it could still be the case that a transformation of this variable (for example, taking its square – a case of curvilinearity) might still be important.

We will conclude the subject of regression with an example which involves the estimation (through the statistical package MINITAB) of a regression model involving two independent variables, one of which is a *dummy* variable. Dummy (or indicator) variables are introduced to allow for the effect of important explanatory variables that do not take a range of values (qualitative variables). For example, gender is such a variable, but we can artificially code it by (say) 0 for men and 1 for women.

We will now consider an example (from J. Neter and W. Wasserman: *Applied Linear Statistical Models*). An office equipment firm supplies desk calculators to commercial companies and services them regularly. The data in Table 6.5 show the time, Y, spent by the service man on 18 recent calls. X_1 is the number of machines serviced, and C or S indicates whether the customer's machines were the commercial or student type. The machine type is a dummy variable which we appropriately code by the value of 0 for the commercial type and the value of 1 for the student type. Using the MINITAB package on the data of Table 6.5 we obtain the results outlined in Table 6.6. The estimated regression equation is

$$Y = -1.972 + 14.687X_1 + 0.151X_2$$

The value of R^2 indicates a very good fit. However, X_1 is the only significant variable. This can be seen from the column of the t-ratios for the regression coefficients, and also by the amount of the sum of squares (SS) explained by each variable when entered in the model. These show that we can simplify the model by deleting the variable X_2. A new simplified model (keeping only X_1) is estimated and the calculations are shown in Table 6.7. Note that the achieved R^2 is still very high. This simplified model is therefore preferable.

Design and Analysis
of Experiments

*Nothing is good or bad
but by comparison.*
Thomas Fuller

■ 7.1 Introduction

The greatest consumer of time and expense in research and development is not the new idea itself, but the construction of prototypes and the calculation or testing of the prototype, through some sort of experimentation, to evaluate whether the new idea is of any value. To promote efficiency in R&D, rationalization of this evaluation by proper experimental methods is of paramount importance; generation of valuable technical information can only be achieved by efficient experimental research.

The idea that science needs careful experimentation goes back at least as far as Francis Bacon and his *crucial experiment* (*experimentum crucis*), which proposes that if an experiment in which all conditions are the same except A produces an effect, then A is the cause of that effect. This proposition essentially describes the *change one factor at a time* method of experimentation, by which the engineer observes the results of an experimental trial, having changed the setting (level) of only one *factor* (a factor being a process variable or any controllable source of variation, either quantitative or qualitative) while keeping every other factor fixed (see Table 7.1). The popularity of this method is mainly due to its simplicity: assignment of the controllable factors according to one of the designs of Table 7.1 allows the experimenter to get by with changing only the level (setting) of one factor (from $A, B, ..., G$) in each run (trial) of the experiment. The apparent simplicity of this method is, however, misleading and it can lead to unreliable results and wrong conclusions.

For example, the difference in the results between the first two experimental runs of the designs in Table 7.1 provides an estimate of the effect of A (the contribution of A to the total variability), using data obtained by holding all other factors $B, ..., G$ constant, in this case at their level 1. No matter how precisely this effect has been estimated, it is still possible that it will be produced only when all other factors are at levels $B(1), ..., G(1)$;

Table 7.1 Versions of the one factor at a time method

Trial	A	B	C	D	E	F	G
Version 1							
1	1	1	1	1	1	1	1
2	2	1	1	1	1	1	1
3	1	2	1	1	1	1	1
4	1	1	2	1	1	1	1
5	1	1	1	2	1	1	1
6	1	1	1	1	2	1	1
7	1	1	1	1	1	2	1
8	1	1	1	1	1	1	2
Version 2							
1	1	1	1	1	1	1	1
2	2	1	1	1	1	1	1
3	2	2	1	1	1	1	1
4	2	2	2	1	1	1	1
5	2	2	2	2	1	1	1
6	2	2	2	2	2	1	1
7	2	2	2	2	2	2	1
8	2	2	2	2	2	2	2

there is no guarantee whatsoever that A will have the same effect when the conditions of the other factors change.

One should start the experimental process with the understanding that real life rarely allows the manipulation of only a single factor; this premise is particularly true in today's dynamic manufacturing environment, where the relationship between a large number of variables, with different levels, is always in need of systematic study for reliable effects to be obtained. A factorial effect is reliable only if it has a high degree of *reproducibility*, that is, only when its influence on experimental values holds consistently even when other factors change. A reliable experiment, therefore, is an experiment which allows the determination of factorial effects when everything else varies, not when everything else is kept constant.

For a one factor at a time experiment to be reliable, all possible combinations of level settings should be incorporated. But, the effort and experimental cost required for such an experiment, termed a *full factorial*, could be prohibitively large and unrealistic (unless only a few factors are under study). For example, in the case of the 7 two-level factors $A, ..., G$ of Table 7.1, a full factorial would require 128 trial runs.

A far better alternative than any of the designs of Table 7.1, which does not require any additional experimental effort and expense, is the experimental set up outlined in Table 7.2. In Table 7.2, some factors are changed simultaneously in a systematic way (to be explained later in this chapter), providing the best method possible for determining the average effects occurring as other conditions change; note that in this design, every level of each factor occurs with every level of all other factors the same number of times. In this way,

Table 7.2 A better alternative to the one factor at a time design

Trial	A	B	C	D	E	F	G
1	1	1	1	1	1	1	1
2	1	1	1	2	2	2	2
3	1	2	2	1	1	2	2
4	1	2	2	2	2	1	1
5	2	1	2	1	2	1	2
6	2	1	2	2	1	2	1
7	2	2	1	1	2	2	1
8	2	2	1	2	1	1	2

more reliable and statistically valid conclusions can be drawn at minimum experimental cost.

Having laid out some simple prescriptions for the one factor at a time method, scientists then largely ignored a more detailed theory of experimentation. The breakthrough came with R.A. Fisher in the 1920s working at the Agricultural Field Station at Rothamstead in the United Kingdom. Fisher was concerned with arranging trials of fertilizers (treatments) on plots to guard against the effects of the fertilizers. The idea was to randomize the allocation of the treatments or arrange them in a pseudo-random matrix layout, with rows and columns, like the layout of a Latin square: see, for example, Table 7.3.

Later, a full theory of factorial experimentation was developed, with the treatments, and also the rows and columns themselves, being thought of as factors; this also permitted combinatorial experiments in more general factorial settings. Fisher himself has successfully compared the quality of plant varieties by first dividing the land into several blocks of homogeneous fertility conditions, and then randomly planting the plant varieties within each of these blocks; this allowed comparisons to be made, not only between plant varieties, but also between fertility conditions.

Fisher's clear awareness of the need for block construction and randomization formed the basis of all subsequent developments of *experimental design* and led to the development of the concept of factorial analysis. In fact, it is possible to consider a very large part of recent work in experimental design as a continuation of Fisher's work on agricultural experimentation.

In the 1930s and 1940s a range of combinatorial structures was discovered, with interesting links to algebra: orthogonal arrays, balanced incomplete

Table 7.3 A 3 × 3 Latin square

Rows	Columns		
	1	2	3
1	a	b	c
2	b	c	a
3	c	a	b

blocks, Greco-Latin squares, Youden squares, screening designs and so on. Most of these structures are *factorial fractions* (that is, subsets of full factorials) possessing the following properties:

- *Balance*: the different levels of each factor occur the same number of times.
- *Estimability*: every factor effect must be capable of being estimated.
- *Orthogonality*: the ability to extract and separate out the effects of different factors. This property is satisfied if, for example, for each pair of factors, every combination of factor levels exists and occurs equally often.

Japanese industry was first to realize the potential of the *fractional factorial experiment*, as opposed to the costly and unreliable (but still very popular in the West) method of one factor at a time experimentation. Fractional experimentation advocates changing many factors at the same time, in a systematic way (adhering, for example, to the requirements of balance and orthogonality), which ensures the reliable and independent study of the factors' effects at a cost much less than that required for full factorial experimentation.

Once the factor effects have been adequately characterized, steps can then be taken to control them appropriately during production, so that variability (the cause of bad quality) in the product's performance is minimized. This can significantly contribute to the accurate characterization and optimization of industrial processes, to the quality improvement of products, and to the reduction of costs and waste. In this chapter we will discuss the most commonly used experimental designs, outline simple ways of constructing them, and describe a powerful statistical method for analysing the experimental results, known as *analysis of variance*.

In fact, different designs exist (and are readily available) to suit any experimental capability:

- Full factorials (designs studying every possible combination of factor setting) are utilized when experimentation is easy or when the number of factors under study is small (3 or 4).
- Fractional factorials are designs consisting of only a certain number of combinations of factor settings out of all possible; these are the most useful designs as they provide a statistically valid and cost-effective way of studying many factors in a single experiment.

One of the great advances in the science of experimentation during this century has been the final demise of the unreliable one factor at a time method (although it should be said that there are still organizations which have never heard – or do not want to hear – of factorial experimentation, and waste many working hours wandering a crooked path).

■ 7.2 Factorial experiments

If we reconsider case-studies 6.1 (page 109) and 6.2 (page 115), we can see them as the result of a single factorial experiment. The factor of interest is the process modification, which has two levels: the first level is the absence of modification, corresponding to the data in case-study 6.1, and the second level is the presence of modification, corresponding to the data of case-study 6.2. This can be defined as a small-scale experiment, in which two samples are collected and compared, usually through the two-sample *t*-test, as explained in Section 6.3.2.

In practice, there are many situations which cannot (or should not) be reduced to these simple terms. A simple expansion of the above case would be to deal with a factor with more than two levels, or with more than one factor. But, the more complex the situation, the greater the need for properly planning the experiment in advance. There are many occasions when much effort is wasted in obtaining massive amounts of data with very little informative value. Requests are frequently made for statisticians to carry out a post-mortem analysis on results from a large-scale experiment incorporating many factors; unfortunately, lack of proper experimental design (before the experiment took place) often means that no clear-cut results can be obtained. The usual reason for this is *confounding*. This means that the factors under consideration have been combined in such a way that their individual effects on the response of interest cannot be determined. This confusion usually arises when the levels of every factor change simultaneously.

For example, if in case-studies 6.1 and 6.2 the process operator was another factor of interest, with operator Op1 being responsible for the original process (case-study 6.1) and operator Op2 being responsible for the modified process (case-study 6.2), then the 2 two-level factors process modification and process operator are confounded: they change from the first level to the second level at the same time. The experiment, although *balanced* (the levels for each factor occur equally often) is not *orthogonal*. There is no way of distinguishing between the two factor effects unless further data are collected with Op2 being responsible for the original process and Op1 for the modified process. The experimental set up will then have the form outlined in Table 7.4. The set up of Table 7.4 clearly satisfies the properties of balance and orthogonality as defined in Section 7.1. Although this two-dimensional set up is clear enough when one is dealing with two factors (irrespective of the number of factor levels), it can be rather confusing if more than two factors are involved.

Table 7.4 A two-dimensional experimental set up

	Op1	Op2
Original process	Data(1, 1)	Data(1, 2)
Modified process	Data(2, 1)	Data(2, 2)

A simple way of understanding the structure of more complicated experiments with several factors, is to look at a standard tableau such as Table 7.5. In Table 7.5, the letters A, B and C represent 3 factors of interest, and the entries -1 and $+1$ represent respectively their first and second levels (or their low and high levels). There are 8 combinations of levels (*trials*) involved, and they are, in fact, all the possible level combinations that 3 two-level factors can take; so, for this particular case, we are dealing with a full factorial design. For every trial, the entries in the tableau direct the experimenter as to how to perform the experiment. For example, for the fourth trial, the experimenter has to keep factor A at its low level and factors B and C at their high level. The order in which the trials are performed should ideally be randomized. During each trial, more than one observation may be taken; these are then called *replications* or *replicates*.

A full factorial design would also result if we expressed the set up of Table 7.4 in tableau form, as Table 7.6 shows. In Table 7.6, A represents the factor process modification with -1 being the absence of modification and $+1$ being the presence of modification; B represents the factor operator with -1 being operator Op1 and $+1$ being operator Op2. The reason for representing the factor levels with -1 and $+1$ (rather than with 1 and 2) will become clear later in this section.

The full factorial designs of Tables 7.5 and 7.6 clearly satisfy the properties of balance and orthogonality. But a design does not have to be a full factorial to possess these properties. For example, the tableau of Table 7.5 can be extended to accommodate a 4th two-level factor D and still be balanced and orthogonal, as Table 7.7 shows. The design of Table 7.7 is a fractional design;

Table 7.5 A standard tableau for a factorial experiment involving 3 two-level factors

Trial	A	B	C	Data
1	-1	-1	-1	...
2	-1	-1	$+1$	...
3	-1	$+1$	-1	...
4	-1	$+1$	$+1$	...
5	$+1$	-1	-1	...
6	$+1$	-1	$+1$	...
7	$+1$	$+1$	-1	...
8	$+1$	$+1$	$+1$	...

Table 7.6 A standard tableau for an experiment with 2 two-level factors

Trial	A	B	Data
1	-1	-1	Data(1, 1)
2	-1	$+1$	Data(1, 2)
3	$+1$	-1	Data(2, 1)
4	$+1$	$+1$	Data(2, 2)

Table 7.7 A balanced and orthogonal fractional design for the study of 4 two-level factors

Trial	A	B	C	D
1	− 1	− 1	− 1	− 1
2	− 1	− 1	+ 1	+ 1
3	− 1	+ 1	− 1	+ 1
4	− 1	+ 1	+ 1	− 1
5	+ 1	− 1	− 1	+ 1
6	+ 1	− 1	+ 1	− 1
7	+ 1	+ 1	− 1	− 1
8	+ 1	+ 1	+ 1	+ 1

only 8 out of the possible 16 ($= 2^4$) factor-level combinations are used. We say here that we use a

$$\frac{1}{2} \text{ fraction of a } 2^4 \text{ full factorial}$$

In general, for k two-level factors, there are 2^k possible level combinations (trials) that can be experimented upon, and so a full factorial requires 2^k trials; usually, because of restrictions in the experimental capability, only a

$$\frac{1}{2^p} \text{ fraction of the full factorial}$$

is utilized ($1 < p < k$), thus leading to experiments requiring only

$$\frac{1}{2^p} \times 2^k = 2^{k-p} \text{ trials}$$

Such designs are called 2^{k-p} factorial designs. For example, the design of Table 7.7 is a

$$2^{4-1} \text{ factorial design}$$

In general, we can talk about m^{k-p} factorial designs: these are

$$\frac{1}{m^p} \text{ fractions of full } m^k \text{ factorial designs}$$

which can study up to k factors with m levels each.

7.2.1 Main and interaction effects

The columns of all the designs examined so far can be utilized to numerically determine the main effects (on the response of interest) of the associated factors; by *main* (factor) *effect* we mean the individual contribution of the factor to the total variability inherent in the experimental results.

However, apart from main effects we might be required to study the measure of the extent to which the value of the response associated with changes in the level of one factor depends on the value (the level) of one or more other factors. This is commonly known as an *interaction effect*. In other words, factor A interacts with factor B if the effect of A (on the response of interest) differs significantly according to the levels of B. In regression analysis (see Section 6.7.2), if A and B are two independent quantitative variables, their interaction can be introduced into the regression model by simply creating another variable which is the product $A \times B$. In factorial experiments, the numerical determination of main and interaction effects can be done using the technique of *analysis of variance*, to be outlined later in this chapter.

Interaction is better explained by considering a chemical experiment. Imagine four similar plots of farmland, one of which has been treated with potash fertilizer, one with nitrate fertilizer, one with neither and one with both. The same crop is sown on all the plots and the resulting crop yields (in tons per acre) are given in the following two-way table:

	No potash	Potash
No nitrate	2	3
Nitrate	3	8

It might be reasonably expected that, since nitrate alone increases the yield by one unit and potash alone also increases it by the same amount, the combination of nitrate and potash would (at most) increase the yield to 4 (twice as much as in the untreated ground), whereas in fact the yield from the combined fertilizer increases the yield to 8 (four times that of the untreated ground). The reason for the unexpected result is that the two separate treatment effects are not strictly additive; the two chemicals acting together result in a yield disproportionally better than expected, an effect which has been given the name interaction. Note that the value of the crop yield (response) associated with changes in the levels of the nitrate factor (from absence of nitrite to presence of nitrate) very much depends on the absence (low level) or presence (high level) of the potash factor, and vice versa.

Table 7.8 A 2^{4-1} factorial design with an interaction column

Trial	A	B	C	D	$A \times B$
1	-1	-1	-1	-1	$+1$
2	-1	-1	$+1$	$+1$	$+1$
3	-1	$+1$	-1	$+1$	-1
4	-1	$+1$	$+1$	-1	-1
5	$+1$	-1	-1	$+1$	-1
6	$+1$	-1	$+1$	-1	-1
7	$+1$	$+1$	-1	-1	$+1$
8	$+1$	$+1$	$+1$	$+1$	$+1$

The experimental designs studied so far can easily be extended to accommodate columns corresponding to interaction effects; see, for example, Table 7.8 where the design of Table 7.7 is reproduced together with an additional column corresponding to the interaction between factors A and B, headed '$A \times B$'. The entries in the last column of the design in Table 7.8, the interaction column for $A \times B$, can easily be found by literally multiplying, term by term, the corresponding entries for the columns associated with the factors involved in the interaction, that is, the columns for A and B, as below:

$$
\begin{array}{ccc}
A & B & A \times B \\
(-1) \times (-1) = +1 \\
(-1) \times (-1) = +1 \\
(-1) \times (+1) = -1 \\
(-1) \times (+1) = -1 \\
(+1) \times (-1) = -1 \\
(+1) \times (-1) = -1 \\
(+1) \times (+1) = +1 \\
(+1) \times (+1) = +1
\end{array}
$$

This is the main reason for representing the levels of a two-level factor by -1 and $+1$. Note that when we make use of the design of Table 7.8 in order to perform an experiment, during experimentation the last column (for the interaction) is ignored – only the first four columns are used to indicate the specific factor settings to be tried. All interaction columns are left unassigned to any factor, so that the interaction effect can be studied independently during the analysis of the experimental results. We will revert to the subject of analysis of (main and interaction) effects later in this chapter.

■ 7.3 Aliasing

The design of Table 7.8 has kept the properties of balance and orthogonality of the original design of Table 7.7. In fact, we can add another two interaction columns and these properties will still hold: see, for example, Table 7.9.

Table 7.9   A 2^{4-1} factorial design with three interaction columns

Trial	A	B	C	D	$A \times B$	$A \times C$	$B \times C$
1	-1	-1	-1	-1	$+1$	$+1$	$+1$
2	-1	-1	$+1$	$+1$	$+1$	-1	-1
3	-1	$+1$	-1	$+1$	-1	$+1$	-1
4	-1	$+1$	$+1$	-1	-1	-1	$+1$
5	$+1$	-1	-1	$+1$	-1	-1	$+1$
6	$+1$	-1	$+1$	-1	-1	$+1$	-1
7	$+1$	$+1$	-1	-1	$+1$	-1	-1
8	$+1$	$+1$	$+1$	$+1$	$+1$	$+1$	$+1$

However, if we attempt to introduce the column corresponding to the interaction $A \times D$ we will discover that it is identical to the $B \times C$ column. This phenomenon is called *aliasing* and causes confounding of effects. It is the consequence of working with fractional factorials rather than with full factorials; the fewer the trials, the greater the aliasing.

So if we use the design of Table 7.9, the effects of the $B \times C$ and $A \times D$ interactions cannot be distinguished. We then say that the effects $A \times D$ and $B \times C$ belong to the same *alias group*. The experimental design should be chosen in such a way that no two effects of interest belong to the same alias group. Of course, if from past experience and/or engineering judgment it is believed that, say, the $A \times D$ interaction effect is not likely to be significant, then we can proceed with the design of Table 7.9 and attribute any effect to $B \times C$ and not to $A \times D$. Unfortunately, the only way of avoiding aliasing is to use full factorials. If we want to use fractional (and hence more economical) experimental designs, aliasing of some of the effects is the price we have to pay.

However, past experience, or just common sense, can help to make a fractional experiment successful. For example, the design of Table 7.9 can be utilized to study 4 main effects and all the two-way interactions between 3 (out of 4) factors; and this might be enough. The price we pay is that we lose information about the two-way interactions involving the fourth factor and all the higher order interactions (such as $A \times B \times C$). But if the experimental capability allows no more than 8 experimental trials, there is no better alternative (a full factorial would require 16 trials).

Except, perhaps, in the case of chemical experiments, there is little justification for using full factorials on the remote possibility that some high-order interactions (third-order or higher) may be significant. This may involve greater expenditure than is warranted for the job; in any case, the organization required to keep a large experiment on the rails is considerable, and experience suggests that an experiment with many trials is rarely completed wholly satisfactorily. A full factorial can be a highly expensive exercise, especially if more than two levels need to be studied. For example, 4 factors at three levels would require 81 ($= 3^4$) experimental trials. The experimental design of Table 7.9 is very flexible, allowing many choices of experiments. Indeed, if we reorganize and recode this design as in Table 7.10, it is clear that we can use it to study:

1. Either the main effects of 3 factors (assigned to columns A, B and D) and all possible interactions between them – a 2^3 factorial.
2. Or the main effects of 4 factors (A, B, D, G) and three interactions $(A \times B, A \times D, B \times D)$ – a 2^{4-1} factorial.
3. Or the main effects of 5 factors (A, B, D, F, G) and the two-way interactions of one of the factors and each of two others $(A \times B, A \times D)$ – a 2^{5-2} factorial.
4. Or the main effects of 6 factors (A, B, D, E, F, G) and one two-factor interaction $(A \times B)$ – a 2^{6-3} factorial.

Table 7.10 Orthogonal design dealing with 3, 4 or 7 main effects

Trial	A	B	C $A \times B$	D	E $A \times D$	F $B \times D$	G $A \times B \times D$
1	1	1	1	1	1	1	1
2	1	1	1	2	2	2	2
3	1	2	2	1	1	2	2
4	1	2	2	2	2	1	1
5	2	1	2	1	2	1	2
6	2	1	2	2	1	2	1
7	2	2	1	1	2	2	1
8	2	2	1	2	1	1	2

5. Or the main effects of 7 factors (A, B, C, D, E, F, G) and no interactions (thus resulting in a completely saturated design) – a 2^{7-4} factorial.

Case 1 corresponds to a full factorial whereas cases 2–5 are fractional factorials confounding main effects with certain interactions.

■ 7.4 Constructing fractional designs

Experimental designs exist to suit any experimental capability or any assumptions the researcher cares to make concerning the main or interaction effects under study. Many ready-made designs, adequate for the majority of experimental requirements, are readily available; but even when a needed design is not available, there are some simple rules that can be followed in order to construct it.

Clearly, there is no difficulty in constructing a full factorial, provided the number of factors under study is small, or assuming that time is not an issue: all one has to do is to write down every possible combination of the factor levels. However, when it comes to fractional designs (the most likely to be needed) some systematic construction procedures are needed. In this section we will outline some of the simplest procedures available.

7.4.1 Starting from a full factorial

Assuming only a small number of factors is under study, a fractional design can be constructed by first constructing the associated full factorial and then dividing it appropriately into two or more (equivalent) subdesigns. Any of those subdesigns can then be used as the fractional factorial. We will demonstrate this for the case when we need to study 3 two-level factors (A, B, C) but there is only an experimental capability of 4 trials (rather than the 8 required for the full factorial).

We first construct the 2^3 (full) factorial design by writing down all possible combinations of the factor levels (8) – thus creating the columns A, B and C – and then adding the interaction columns $A \times B$, $A \times C$, $B \times C$ and $A \times B \times C$, by simply multiplying term by term the columns involved in the interaction (for this purpose we use the codes -1 and $+1$ for the factor levels). Table 7.11 shows the resulting orthogonal and balanced full factorial design. Note that the associated tableau is equivalent to that shown in Table 7.9 or in Tables 7.2 and 7.10.

Since there is an experimental capacity of only 4 trials, we seek a half-fraction of the full factorial with which to estimate the effects of A, B and C. The design should be such that at least the main effects of A, B and C are not aliased. A simple way of achieving this is to use the third-order interaction $A \times B \times C$ as a 'knife' to do surgery on the full factorial. Indeed, we can split the full factorial into two parts:

Part 1. All those trials with $A \times B \times C$ at low level (-1); this means the trials 1, 4, 6 and 7.

Part 2. All those trials with $A \times B \times C$ at top level $(+1)$; that is, trials 2, 3, 5 and 8.

The two parts are presented in Table 7.12. Note that each part represents a 2^{3-1} (fractional) factorial. A glance at the subdesigns of Table 7.12 reveals the following:

1. There is no way of studying the effect of the three-way interaction $A \times B \times C$ within any of the two parts (the levels do not change sign).
2. For each part, every two-way interaction column is identical to a main factor column (except, perhaps, for a sign change in Part 1). This means that if one uses the (fractional) design of Part 1 or of Part 2, every two-way interaction effect is aliased with a main effect. In fact A is aliased with $B \times C$, B is aliased with $A \times C$ and C is aliased with $A \times B$.

We cannot therefore simultaneously study aliased terms (such as A and $B \times C$). If we are interested in all three factors A, B and C (whose effects are not aliased with each other), we must assume that all interaction effects are insignificant.

Table 7.11 The 2^3 factorial design

Trial	A	B	C	$A \times B$	$A \times C$	$B \times C$	$A \times B \times C$
1	-1	-1	-1	$+1$	$+1$	$+1$	-1
2	-1	-1	$+1$	$+1$	-1	-1	$+1$
3	-1	$+1$	-1	-1	$+1$	-1	$+1$
4	-1	$+1$	$+1$	-1	-1	$+1$	-1
5	$+1$	-1	-1	-1	-1	$+1$	$+1$
6	$+1$	-1	$+1$	-1	$+1$	-1	-1
7	$+1$	$+1$	-1	$+1$	-1	-1	-1
8	$+1$	$+1$	$+1$	$+1$	$+1$	$+1$	$+1$

Table 7.12 Two parts of the 2^3 factorial

Trial	A	B	C	$A \times B$	$A \times C$	$B \times C$	$A \times B \times C$
Part 1							
1	-1	-1	-1	$+1$	$+1$	$+1$	-1
4	-1	$+1$	$+1$	-1	-1	$+1$	-1
6	$+1$	-1	$+1$	-1	$+1$	-1	-1
7	$+1$	$+1$	-1	$+1$	-1	-1	-1
Part 2							
2	-1	-1	$+1$	$+1$	-1	-1	$+1$
3	-1	$+1$	-1	-1	$+1$	-1	$+1$
5	$+1$	-1	-1	-1	-1	$+1$	$+1$
8	$+1$	$+1$	$+1$	$+1$	$+1$	$+1$	$+1$

Each part of Table 7.12 is called a block. Of course, we can still perform the whole experiment of 8 trials, by carrying out, say, block 1 on the first day and block 2 on the second day. However, if there is a hidden day effect, then this will be aliased with the $A \times B \times C$ interaction. This leads to a piece of terminology: 'the interaction $A \times B \times C$ is confounded with blocks'. So, in general for the two-level case, we can split a full factorial into half-fractions by using a high-order interaction as a 'knife'. Furthermore, we can split a design into quarter-fractions by using two high-order interactions (one after the other), and so on. Generally, using p interactions, we can eventually obtain a

$$\frac{1}{2^p} \times 2^k = 2^{k-p} \text{ fractional design}$$

A high-order interaction used in such a way is sometimes called a *defining contrast*.

Looking at Table 7.12 it is fairly easy to determine the aliased groups resulting from the surgery on the original full factorial. With more complicated designs, this may not be so obvious. However, there is an algebraic method that can be applied, making use of the defining contrast. We can demonstrate this by looking again at the case of 3 two-level factors. This method can be similarly applied to any number of two-level factors.

Let us define I to represent a constant term or an identity factor in the algebraic sense, that is, as having the property:

$$A \times I = A, \ B \times I = B \text{ and } C \times I = C \tag{7.1}$$

and assume the additional property that

$$I = A \times A = B \times B = C \times C \text{ or } I = A^2 = B^2 = C^2 \tag{7.2}$$

Then, we can set up the following aliasing rule. Assume that I is identical to the defining contrast, that is, for our case

$$I = A \times B \times C \tag{7.3}$$

Now, generate alias groups by multiplying both sides of (7.3) by each effect, making use of the properties (7.1) or (7.2). For example, if we multiply both sides of (7.3) by the effect A we have

$$A \times I = A \times (A \times B \times C) \sim A = (A \times A) \times B \times C \sim A = B \times C$$

This indicates that the interaction $B \times C$ is aliased with the main effect A; in other words, $\{A, B \times C\}$ is an alias group. We can similarly find that $\{B, A \times C\}$ and $\{C, A \times B\}$ are also alias groups.

The above simple method for recognizing aliasing can easily be generalized to m^k factorials, that is, to experiments involving k factors with m levels each. In such cases, properties (7.1) and (7.3) will still hold, with property (7.2) being generalized to

$$I = A^m = B^m = \ldots$$

For experiments involving a combination of multilevel factors, constructing highly fractionated designs and recognizing all alias groups using the methods described so far is a more complicated task. However, many ready-made designs are readily available or can be constructed using other simple methods to be described below.

7.4.2 Using Latin squares

Generally speaking, a *Latin square design* is a three-factor experimental design in which each level of each factor is combined only once with each level of the two other factors. It was originally used in particular for the study of one special factor of interest using a square-format layout, on which there was blocking column-wise as well as row-wise; see for example Table 7.3 for a 3×3 Latin square or Table 7.13 for a 4×4 Latin square. Note that in both tables, the letters a, b etc. represent factor levels. Note in Table 7.13 the level a appears once in every column and in every row; similarly for levels b, c and d. Interest might be centred on one four-level factor (with levels a, b, c and d), but its levels have not been allocated in a completely random manner; two restrictions are placed on the randomization, one column-wise and one row-wise. Such a design is only possible if the number of levels of both restrictions (block factors) equals the number of the levels of the factor of interest.

Table 7.13 A 4×4 Latin square

Rows	Columns			
	1	2	3	4
1	a	b	c	d
2	b	c	d	a
3	c	d	a	b
4	d	a	b	c

All randomization is not lost in this design, as the particular Latin square to be used may be chosen at random from many possible Latin squares of the required size. For example, for the above 4×4 standard square, another $4!3! - 1 = 143$ Latin squares, all different, may be generated by permuting all the rows, except the first, and all the columns; one of these Latin squares may be chosen at random. (For an integer k, $k! = k(k-1)(k-2)\ldots 1$).

The Latin square can be generalized to the *Greco-Latin square*; this is a design in which four factors are arranged in such a way that each level of each factor is combined once and only once with each level of the other three factors. For example, assuming 2 block factors, and 2 four-level factors, one with levels x, y, z and w, and the other with X, Y, Z and W, we can have the design of Table 7.14. This is an extended Latin square where a third restriction on randomization is imposed. Every level from x, y, z or w appears once and only once in each row, in each column and with each level X, Y, Z or W of the other factor. A Greco-Latin square can be considered as the result of superimposing on each other two Latin squares, one with upper case letters and the other with lower case letters (its name has arisen because Greek letters are normally used for the lower case symbols). These Latin squares are orthogonal to each other, because when they are superimposed, every letter of one square occurs once and only once with every letter of the other.

If we consider the block factors (the row factor and the column factor) as factors in their own right, then the Latin square can be viewed as a 3-factor design and the Greco-Latin square as a 4-factor design. We can then represent the designs of Tables 7.13 and 7.14 in the usual tableau form, as in Tables 7.15 and 7.16. Note that both the designs of Tables 7.15 and 7.16 are balanced and orthogonal fractional designs and they both deal with four-level factors. In fact, Table 7.15 represents a (fractional) 4^{3-1} factorial or a 1/4 fraction of the (full) 4^3 factorial, and Table 7.16 represents a (fractional) 4^{4-2} factorial or a 1/16 fraction of the (full) 4^4 factorial.

So, it is clear that a simple way of constructing (fractional) orthogonal designs is by superimposing orthogonal Latin squares on each other. The question, of course, arises as to when such orthogonal Latin squares exist. For example, it can be shown that there does not exist even one pair of orthogonal 6×6 Latin squares. The general question of whether a complete orthogonal system of Latin squares of order q (that is, a set of $q-1$ pairwise orthogonal $q \times q$ Latin squares) exists, is, in fact, one of the famous unresolved problems

Table 7.14   A 4×4 Greco-Latin square

Rows	Columns 1	2	3	4
1	X, x	Y, y	Z, z	W, w
2	Y, z	X, w	W, x	Z, y
3	Z, w	W, z	X, y	Y, x
4	W, y	Z, x	Y, w	X, z

Table 7.15 A Latin square design in a tableau form

Trial	Column factor	Row factor	3rd factor
1	1	1	a
2	1	2	b
3	1	3	c
4	1	4	d
5	2	1	b
6	2	2	c
7	2	3	d
8	2	4	a
9	3	1	c
10	3	2	d
11	3	3	a
12	3	4	b
13	4	1	d
14	4	2	a
15	4	3	b
16	4	4	c

Table 7.16 A Greco-Latin square design in a tableau form

Trial	Column factor	Row factor	Greek factor	Latin factor
1	1	1	x	X
2	1	2	z	Y
3	1	3	w	Z
4	1	4	y	W
5	2	1	y	Y
6	2	2	w	X
7	2	3	z	W
8	2	4	x	Z
9	3	1	z	Z
10	3	2	x	W
11	3	3	y	X
12	3	4	w	Y
13	4	1	w	W
14	4	2	y	Z
15	4	3	x	Y
16	4	4	z	X

of discrete mathematics (such a system is also known as a *hyper-Greco-Latin square*). For example, this problem is still unresolved for $q = 10$. However, if q is a prime power, such a system exists; ways of constructing such a system can be found in Dey (1985).

It should be noted that when we want to convey information about the maximum number of factors (say, k) that can be studied with a specific design, the number of factor levels (say, m), and the number of trials required (say, n), we can symbolize orthogonal designs by

$$OA_n(m^k)$$

where OA stands for orthogonal array. For example, the designs of Tables 7.15 and 7.16 are respectively

$$OA_{16}(4^3) \text{ and } OA_{16}(4^4)$$

whereas that of Table 7.11 is an $OA_8(2^7)$.

Using Latin squares, let us now construct the most economic design for dealing with 5 four-level factors. The required fractional design can be obtained by superimposing the three orthogonal 4×4 Latin squares of Table 7.17 on each other. The resulting 4^{5-3} factorial design is shown in Table 7.18.

7.4.3 Plackett and Burman designs

The Plackett and Burman designs are designs suitable for studying up to $k = (N-1)/(L-1)$ factors each with L levels with the expense of N trials,

Table 7.17 Three 4×4 Latin squares

$$L_1 = \begin{matrix} 1 & 2 & 3 & 4 \\ 2 & 1 & 4 & 3 \\ 3 & 4 & 1 & 2 \\ 4 & 3 & 2 & 1 \end{matrix} \qquad L_2 = \begin{matrix} 1 & 2 & 3 & 4 \\ 3 & 4 & 1 & 2 \\ 4 & 3 & 2 & 1 \\ 2 & 1 & 4 & 3 \end{matrix} \qquad L_3 = \begin{matrix} 1 & 2 & 3 & 4 \\ 4 & 3 & 2 & 1 \\ 2 & 1 & 4 & 3 \\ 3 & 4 & 1 & 2 \end{matrix}$$

Table 7.18 A 4^{4-2} factorial

(Row)	(Column)			
1	1	1	1	1
1	2	2	2	2
1	3	3	3	3
1	4	4	4	4
2	1	2	3	4
2	2	1	4	3
2	3	4	1	2
2	4	3	2	1
3	1	3	4	2
3	2	4	3	1
3	3	1	2	4
3	4	2	1	3
4	1	4	2	3
4	2	3	1	4
4	3	2	4	1
4	4	1	3	2

$$= OA_{16}(4^5)$$

that is, orthogonal arrays of the form

$$OA_N(L^k)$$

They were first introduced by Plackett and Burman (1946) and are most useful for *screening* experiments, that is, for experiments where the experimental capability is limited and designs for studying main effects only are required.

The designs are constructed with the help of a *generating vector*, or a number of *generating square blocks*. When a generating vector is provided, this is first written down as a column. A second column is obtained by moving down the elements of the previous column once, and placing the last element in the first position. This procedure is repeated until $(N-1)/(L-1)$ columns are obtained. Finally a row of elements, all representing the first factor level, is added to complete the design. For example, an $OA_8(2^7)$ can be constructed by first considering that $L = 2$, $N = 8$ and so

$$k = (8-1)/(2-1) = 7$$

and by using the generating vector

(2 2 2 1 2 1 1)

which can be found in Table B1, Appendix B, for the case corresponding to $L = 2$ and $N = 8$. Arranging this vector as the first column and offsetting (altogether $(N-2)$ times) by one vector element for each new column, we first obtain a $(N-1) \times (N-1)$ matrix which is finally completed by a row of ones (1 represents the first level in this case). The resulting array is shown in Table 7.19. Note that, by a simple readjustment of the rows or columns of the design of Table 7.19, we obtain the design shown in Table 7.2, or Table 7.10 or even that of Table 7.11 (after also recoding the levels).

If generating square blocks are provided (as in the cases when $L = 2$ and $N = 28$, 52, 76 or 100 – see Appendix B), the designs can be constructed by permuting the blocks cyclically among themselves. For example, for $L = 2$ and $N = 28$, if X, Y and Z are the three supplied 9×9 square blocks (see Appendix B), these are written down cyclically as

$$
\begin{array}{ccc}
X & Y & Z \\
Y & Z & X \\
Z & X & Y
\end{array}
$$

and the resulting 27 rows are followed by a row of ones. Note that in the cases of $N = 52$, 76 and 100, the first row and first column are also given; these have alternatively 1 and 2 throughout, apart from the corner element (which is a 2). Appendix B provides the generating vectors and blocks for $L = 2$ and, with N

Table 7.19 A Plackett–Burman design equivalent to $OA_8(2^7)$

2	1	1	2	1	2	2
2	2	1	1	2	1	2
2	2	2	1	1	2	1
1	2	2	2	1	1	2
2	1	2	2	2	1	1
1	2	1	2	2	2	1
1	1	2	1	2	2	2
1	1	1	1	1	1	1

being a multiple of 4, from $N = 4$ to 100; it also provides the vectors for:

$L = 3$ and $N = 9$, 27 or 81

$L = 5$ and $N = 25$ or 125

and

$L = 7$ and $N = 49$

Note that the Plackett–Burman designs are not just for studying main factor effects. When N is a power of 2, these designs can also study interactions; this is, for example, the case for the design of Table 7.19 (equivalent to that of Table 7.10) which allows the study of a wide choice of interactions. Of course, in these cases, the number of factors for study needs to be less than $N - 1$.

When N is not a power of 2, these designs do not generally allow the study of interactions. As an example we can refer to the

$OA_{12}(2^{11})$

which is generated by the vector ($L = 2$, $N = 12$):

(2 2 1 2 2 2 1 1 1 2 1)

as shown in Table 7.20. Note that, if we replace 1 and 2 by -1 and $+1$

Table 7.20 The $OA_{12}(2^{11})$

2	1	2	1	1	1	2	2	2	1	2
2	2	1	2	1	1	1	2	2	2	1
1	2	2	1	2	1	1	1	2	2	2
2	1	2	2	1	2	1	1	1	2	2
2	2	1	2	2	1	2	1	1	1	2
2	2	2	1	2	2	1	2	1	1	1
1	2	2	2	1	2	2	1	2	1	1
1	1	2	2	2	1	2	2	1	2	1
1	1	1	2	2	2	1	2	2	1	2
2	1	1	1	2	2	2	1	2	2	1
1	2	1	1	1	2	2	2	1	2	2
1	1	1	1	1	1	1	1	1	1	1

respectively, it can be shown that no column in the array of Table 7.20 can be considered as the product of two other columns in the same array. So the array of Table 7.20 cannot be used to analyse interactions.

7.4.4 Recognizing interaction columns

For those arrays that allow the study of interactions, Taguchi (see also Part IV) has devised an easy way of recognizing the two-way interaction columns. For this, we make use of certain triangular interaction matrices such as the one shown in Table 7.21 corresponding to the design $OA_8(2^7)$ as presented in Table 7.10. The entries indicate the columns corresponding to the two-way interaction between the factors assigned to the columns whose position is also indicated by the column number. For example, entry 5 in the first row of the triangular matrix of Table 7.21 means that the interaction between the factors assigned in columns 1 and 4 can be assigned to column 5. Also, entry 7 in the second row means that, if we choose to assign two factors on columns 2 and 5, their two-way interaction can be represented by column 7.

Interaction matrices for more complicated designs can be found in Appendix C, where the orthogonal arrays recommended by Taguchi are also presented; these arrays are identical or equivalent to Plackett and Burman designs.

The novelty of Taguchi's orthogonal arrays lies in the straightforward manner in which they are presented, which allows the utilization of the associated interaction matrices. The reader should therefore be aware of the fact that these interaction matrices can only be used if the corresponding experimental designs have the particular format shown in Appendix C. For example, although the triangular matrix of Table 7.21 corresponds to $OA_8(2^7)$, it can only be used if the array has the format depicted in Table 7.10, not that in Table 7.11.

It is worthwhile completing the discussion of interaction matrices with another example concerning three-level designs. The array of Table 7.22 can be used for an experiment involving up to 4 three-level factors, that is, it is an $OA_9(3^4)$ or a 3^{4-2} (fractional) factorial, or it can be used as a 3^2 (full)

Table 7.21 Interaction matrix corresponding to $OA_8(2^7)$ (Table 7.10)

Column no.	Column no.						
	1	2	3	4	5	6	7
1	—	3	2	5	4	7	6
2		—	1	6	7	4	5
3			—	7	6	5	4
4				—	1	2	3
5					—	3	2
6						—	1

Table 7.22 The $OA_9(3^4)$

Trial	Column 1	2	3	4
1	1	1	1	1
2	1	2	2	2
3	1	3	3	3
4	2	1	2	3
5	2	2	3	1
6	2	3	1	2
7	3	1	3	2
8	3	2	1	3
9	3	3	2	1

Table 7.23 Interaction matrix for $OA_9(3^4)$

Column no.	1	Column no. 2	3	4
1	–	3	2	2
	–	4	4	3
2		–	1	1
		–	4	3
3			–	1
			–	2

factorial. The interaction matrix corresponding to the $OA_9(3^4)$ is shown in Table 7.23.

Note that for studying two-way interactions between 2 three-level factors, two columns in the design need to be assigned to the interaction (that is, left unassigned of factors); the reason for this will become clear later in this chapter. This is demonstrated in Table 7.23 which shows two columns corresponding to each two-factor interaction. For example, if two factors are assigned to columns 1 and 2, their interaction corresponds to the two columns 3 and 4; or, the interaction between the factors on the columns 2 and 4 is assigned to the two columns 1 and 3. This means that the design of Table 7.22 is capable of studying only one (two-way) interaction between only 2 three-level factors.

This completes our discussion of simple methods for constructing basic experimental designs and for allocating main and interaction effects within them. When the need arises, these basic designs can be used to construct more complicated designs, in order to study factors on the levels of which certain restrictions have been imposed. We will cover some of these methods in Part IV.

■ 7.5 Analysis of variance

Having properly designed an experiment and having obtained the experimental results, a formal method for statistically analysing them is needed. This differs from the usual practice associated with a one factor at a time experiment, where conclusions are reached after a simple comparison of the observed results from one trial run with the results from a previous trial run. With properly designed experiments, the researcher normally has to wait until all the experimental trials are complete (except in obvious situations where further experimentation is rendered unnecessary); after the completion of the trials, statistical analysis of the experimental data has to take place.

One of the most powerful statistical methods for data analysis is the method of *analysis of variance* (*ANOVA*). The method can be considered as a generalization of the two-sample *t*-test (see Chapter 6). Indeed, if the two-sample *t*-test can be used to compare the levels of a two-level factor, ANOVA can be utilized to compare the levels of a multilevel factor and the levels of many factors.

The basic idea behind ANOVA is to break down the total variability (of the experimental results) into components of variance, and then assess their significance. The variation components will be those associated with factor effects (main or interaction effects) and that associated with random variation, commonly referred to as *residual* (*res*); the residual can be seen as the amount of variance we would expect if none of the factors had any effect. This can be expressed by:

$$\text{total variation} = \text{variation due to factor effects} + \text{residual} \qquad (7.4)$$

The significance of the variation components associated with factor effects is assessed by comparison with the residual. The usual *F*-test for comparing variances (see Section 6.4.4) is utilized for this purpose.

We will now demonstrate the ANOVA technique through a case study.

CASE STUDY 7.1

Two telephone companies are providing services in a particular area. There are two classes of service: residential and business. A TV advertising campaign was undertaken by both companies, and a study was made to assess whether customer phone usage had increased as a result. Three telephone lines were randomly chosen for each company and each class of service, and the number of phone calls made on these lines within a certain time-period before and after the campaign was recorded.

There are 3 factors of interest, each with two levels, as follows:

Factors	Levels	
	1	2
A Advertising	Before	After
B Telephone company	Company 1	Company 2
C Class of service	Residential	Business

175

Table 7.24 Telephone usage data (case-study 7.1)

Trial	A	B	C	Data (phone calls in thousands)
1	1	1	1	1, 3, 4
2	1	1	2	4, 4, 8
3	1	2	1	3, 4, 7
4	1	2	2	3, 5, 6
5	2	1	1	2, 1, 2
6	2	1	2	5, 7, 7
7	2	2	1	4, 5, 4
8	2	2	2	3, 5, 5

Every combination of the levels of these factors has been considered in the study; we are therefore dealing with a full factorial design which is shown, along with the recorded data (number of phone calls), in Table 7.24.

We will apply the ANOVA technique to analyse the data in the standardized form in which they appear in Table 7.24, not in thousands. This is allowed, provided the standardization (in this case a division by 1000) is applied to all available data points. The conclusions of the analysis will be exactly the same as if we had analysed the actual results, that is, put three zeros after each digit appearing in Table 7.24. Recall that every measure of variability is associated with the sum of squares of the deviations of the observations from a central value (see Section 6.2). On this basis, it can be shown that statement (7.4) is equivalent to the following:

total sum of squares (TSS) = sum of squares for factor effects (SS_F)
+ sum of squares for residual (RSS)   (7.5)

There is an analogous relationship between the degrees of freedom associated with each of the terms of (7.5):

total df = (sum of df for effects) + (df for residual)

Easy formulae exist to calculate the various terms of (7.5); it is common to calculate every term, except RSS, which is then found by subtraction. The procedure that follows is applicable to most of the cases.

7.5.1 ANOVA formula for total sum of squares (TSS)

We first calculate the *correction factor* (CF) as follows:

$$CF = \frac{(\text{sum total of all observations})^2}{\text{total number of all observations}} = \frac{(\Sigma \ y_j)^2}{n} \qquad (7.6)$$

CF is used to correct (hence the name correction factor) the sum of all squared observations

$$\Sigma \ y_j^2$$

in order to obtain the (corrected) total sum of squares, TSS, as

$$TSS = \Sigma \ y_j^2 - CF \qquad (7.7)$$

Note that from (7.6), formula (7.7) is equivalent to formula (6.4) (see Section 6.2) which represents the numerator for the sample variance. It is self-evident, therefore, that the degrees of freedom associated with *TSS* are $df_{tot} = n - 1$, and the ratio TSS/df_{tot} provides an estimate for the total variability inherent in the experimental results.

For our case-study we have

$$CF = \frac{(102)^2}{24} = 433.5$$

and so

$$TSS = (1^2 + 3^2 + 4^2 + \cdots + 5^2) - 433.5 = 80.5$$

In addition,

Total $df = 24 - 1 = 23$

7.5.2 ANOVA formula for main effects

For the sum of squares of the main effect of a k-level factor A, with m observations corresponding to each level $A(i)$, $i = 1, \ldots, k$, we have

$$SS_A = \frac{(A_1)^2 + \cdots + (A_k)^2}{m} - CF \tag{7.8}$$

where A_i is the sum total of the observations in level $A(i)$, $i = 1, \ldots, k$. If the number of observations per level is different, m_i, say, then

$$SS_A = \frac{(A_1)^2}{m_1} + \cdots + \frac{(A_k)^2}{m_k} - CF \tag{7.9}$$

The degrees of freedom corresponding to a k-level factor (or k-level column in a balanced design) are equal to $k - 1$.

For our case-study we have $n = 24$ and $k = 2$; we also note that level one of A corresponds to the 12 observations associated with the first 4 trials, and level two to the 12 observations associated with the last 4 trials (see Table 7.24). So,

$$SS_A = \frac{(A_1)^2 + (A_2)^2}{12} - CF$$

$$= \frac{(1 + 3 + \cdots + 5 + 6)^2 + (2 + 1 + \cdots + 5 + 5)^2}{12} - 433.5$$

$$= \frac{(52)^2 + (50)^2}{12} - 433.5 = 0.17 \qquad \text{with } df_A = k - 1 = 2 - 1 = 1$$

The ratio SS_A/df_A, called the *mean sum of squares* for factor $A\,(MSS_A)$ provides an estimate of the amount of variability in the experimental results

177

which is due to factor A. So

$$MSS_A = 0.17/1 = 0.17$$

We similarly have

$$SS_B = \frac{(B_1)^2 + (B_2)^2}{12} - CF$$

$$= \frac{(1 + \cdots + 8 + 2 + \cdots + 7)^2 + (3 + \cdots + 6 + 4 + \cdots + 5)^2}{12} - 433.5$$

$$= \frac{(48)^2 + (54)^2}{12} = 1.5 \qquad (df_B) = 1)$$

and

$$SS_C = \frac{(40)^2 + (62)^2}{12} - 433.5 = 20.17 \qquad (df_C = 1)$$

7.5.3 ANOVA formulae for interactions

In the previous sections of this chapter we have seen how we can construct interaction columns or how to recognize them through the interaction matrices. For example, the design of Table 7.24, complete with interaction columns, is shown again in Table 7.25.

For calculating the sum of squares for interaction effects, similar formulae to (7.8) or (7.9) can be applied, by viewing the interaction column as a factor column in its own right, with levels as indicated by the column. For example, to calculate the sum of squares for the interaction $A \times B$ we use the fourth column of Table 7.25 and we apply formula (7.8) as though we had another factor assigned to this column:

$$SS_{A \times B} = \frac{([A \times B]_1)^2 + ([A \times B]_2)^2}{12} - CF$$

$$= \frac{(1 + 3 + \cdots + 5 + 5)^2 + (3 + 4 + \cdots + 7 + 7)^2}{12} - 433.5 = 0.17$$

Table 7.25 Complete design for telephone usage data (case-study 7.1)

Trial	A	B	C	$A \times B$	$A \times C$	$B \times C$	$A \times B \times C$	Data (phone calls in thousands)
1	1	1	1	1	1	1	1	1, 3, 4
2	1	1	2	1	2	2	2	4, 4, 8
3	1	2	1	2	1	2	2	3, 4, 7
4	1	2	2	2	2	1	1	3, 5, 6
5	2	1	1	2	2	1	2	2, 1, 2
6	2	1	2	2	1	2	1	5, 7, 7
7	2	2	1	1	2	2	1	4, 5, 4
8	2	2	2	1	1	1	2	3, 5, 5

It is important to note that if this method is used to calculate the sum of squares of interactions between three-level factors, formula (7.8) has to be applied for both columns involved in the interaction (as in Table 7.23), and the two results are then added. In general, every column involved in a multi-level interaction needs to be evaluated separately through (7.8), and then the individual results need to be added to obtain the sum of squares for that interaction.

In order to avoid the separate calculation of the sum of squares of all the columns involved in the interaction, there is a general formula which can be applied for any non-aliased interaction sum of squares. For example, if A is an a-level factor and B is a b-level factor then, assuming $A \times B$ is not aliased with another effect,

$$SS_{A \times B} = \frac{(A_1B_1)^2 + (A_1B_2)^2 + (A_2B_1)^2 + \cdots + (A_aB_b)^2}{m} - SS_A - SS_B - CF$$

$$(7.10)$$

where A_iB_j is the sum total of the observations corresponding to the level-combination $A(i)B(j)$, $i = 1, \ldots, a$; $j = 1, \ldots, b$ (that is, of the data values obtained when both levels $A(i)$ and $B(j)$ were used) and m is now the number of observations in each level-combination, assumed to be the same for all combinations. If m is not the same and there are, say, m_{ij}-values in the level-combination $A(i)B(j)$, then

$$SS_{A \times B} = \frac{(A_1B_1)^2}{m_{11}} + \frac{(A_1B_2)^2}{m_{12}} + \frac{(A_2B_1)^2}{m_{21}} + \cdots + \frac{(A_aB_b)^2}{m_{ab}} - SS_A - SS_B - CF$$

The degrees of freedom associated with an interaction effect are the product of the degrees of freedom of the factors involved in the interaction, so that $df_{A \times B} = (a - 1)(b - 1)$. For example, if $a = b = 3$, then $df_{A \times B} = 2 \times 2 = 4$.

In other words, 4 degrees of freedom need to be allocated to the interaction between 2 three-level factors; consequently, 2 three-level columns (each associated with $2df$) need to be left unassigned in an orthogonal design capable of studying three-level factors. This explains why the interaction matrices for three-level designs (see Appendix C) indicate two columns for the study of any interaction between 2 three-level factors.

Obvious generalizations can be obtained for higher-order interactions. For example, for a non-aliased three-way interaction (involving a 3rd factor C with c levels),

$$SS_{A \times B \times C} = \frac{(A_1B_1C_1)^2}{m_{111}} + \cdots + \frac{(A_aB_bC_c)^2}{m_{abc}}$$

$$- SS_A - SS_B - SS_C - SS_{A \times B} - SS_{A \times C} - SS_{B \times C} - CF \quad (7.11)$$

with

$$df_{A \times B \times C} = (a - 1)(b - 1)(c - 1)$$

where $A_iB_jC_k$ is the sum total of the observations when A, B and C are respectively at levels i, j and k.

Returning to our case-study, using (7.10) with $a = 2$, $b = 2$, $SS_A = 0.17$ and $SS_B = 1.5$, we have (see Table 7.24),

$$S_{A \times B} = \frac{(1 + \cdots + 8)^2 + (3 + \cdots + 6)^2 + (2 + \cdots + 7)^2 + (4 + \cdots + 5)^2}{6}$$

$$- 0.17 - 1.5 - 433.5$$

$$= \frac{(24)^2 + (28)^2 + (24)^2 + (26)^2}{6} - 435.17 = 0.17 \quad (df_{A \times B} = 1 \times 1 = 1)$$

Similarly

$$S_{A \times C} = \frac{(22)^2 + (30)^2 + (18)^2 + (32)^2}{6}$$

$$- 0.17 - 20.17 - 433.5 = 1.5 \qquad (df_{A \times C} = 1)$$

$$S_{B \times C} = \frac{(13)^2 + (35)^2 + (27)^2 + (27)^2}{6}$$

$$- 1.5 - 20.17 - 433.5 = 20.17 \qquad (df_{B \times C} = 1)$$

Since we are dealing with a 2^3 full factorial, we can calculate a three-way interaction. Using (7.11) with $a = 2$, $b = 2$ and $c = 2$, we have

$$S_{A \times B \times C} = \frac{8^2 + 16^2 + 14^2 + 14^2 + 5^2 + 19^2 + 13^2 + 13^2}{3}$$

$$- 0.17 - 1.5 - 20.17 - 0.17 - 1.5 - 20.17 - 433.5$$

$$= 1.5 \qquad (df_{A \times B \times C} = 1 \times 1 \times 1 = 1)$$

The mean sum of squares (estimate of the variation component) for each main effect or any interaction effect is simply the ratio of the effect's sum of squares to the associated degrees of freedom.

7.5.4 Residual

Having evaluated the sum of squares of all non-aliased effects, we can easily calculate the residual sum of squares (or error sum of squares $-$ SS_e), by subtraction from the TSS. We have

error sum of squares = $TSS -$ (total of the SS of all non-aliased effects)

So, for our case-study,

$$SS_e = TSS - SS_A - SS_B - SS_C - SS_{A \times B} - SS_{A \times C} - SS_{B \times C} - SS_{A \times B \times C}$$

with

$$df_e = df_{tot} - df_A - df_B - df_C - df_{A \times B} - df_{A \times C} - df_{B \times C} - df_{A \times B \times C}$$

Therefore

$$SS_e = 80.5 - 0.17 - 1.5 - 20.17 - 0.17 - 1.5 - 20.17 - 1.5 = 35.3$$

with

$$df_e = 23 - 1 - 1 - 1 - 1 - 1 - 1 - 1 = 16$$

The ratio SS_e/df_e, the residual mean sum of squares (MSS_e) represents the amount of variability that remains after the components of variance due to main and interaction effects have been accounted for. It actually corresponds to the variance between the replicates within each experimental trial. Numerically, the residual variance is the square of the difference between each replicate and its trial average, summed over all trials. Therefore, the SS_e can be calculated using a general formula like

$$SS_e = \sum_{i=1}^{n} TSS_i$$

where n is the number of experimental trials and TSS_i is the total (corrected) sum of squares of the observations within the ith trial. For example, if in the ith trial there are r replications

$$y_{i1}, y_{i2}, \ldots, y_{ir}$$

then, utilizing formula (6.4) again,

$$SS_e = \sum_{i=1}^{n} \left\{ \sum_{j=1}^{r} y_{ij}^2 - \frac{(\sum_{j=1}^{r} y_{ij})^2}{r} \right\} \tag{7.12}$$

(Note the similarity between formula (7.7) — associated with the TSS over all the experimental trials — and the section of (7.12) in brackets associated with the TSS within the ith experimental trial.)

For our case-study, since $n = 8$ and $r = 3$, applying (7.12) we have

$$SS_e = \left\{ 1^2 + 3^2 + 4^2 - \frac{8^2}{3} \right\} + \cdots + \left\{ 3^2 + 5^2 + 5^2 - \frac{13^2}{3} \right\}$$

$$= 4.67 + \cdots + 2.67 = 35.3$$

This agrees with the result found following the simple method of subtraction of the sum of squares of the non-aliased effects from the total sum of squares TSS.

Note that when there is only one observation per trial, formula (7.12) cannot be applied. This means that a residual component of variance is not retrievable. In such cases, a high-order interaction is usually considered to be non-existent, and its sum of squares is attributed to the error sum of squares. It is also common to pool together the sum of squares of the smallest magnitude. The purpose of pooling is to obtain a more accurate estimate of the error variance against which comparatively large components of variance can be tested through the usual *F*-test. The sum of squares of a particular source can be considered small if it constitutes less than 4% of the total (corrected) sum of squares (*TSS*); it can then be pooled with the error, by adding it to any existing error sum of squares. The source's degrees of freedom are also added to any existing residual degrees of freedom.

7.5.5 ANOVA table

We usually present the results of the sum of squares decomposition in an ANOVA table, in the format of Table 7.26. The last column of the ANOVA table is the column of the *F*-ratios. These are the ratios we first encountered in Chapter 6 for comparing variances. In an ANOVA table they have exactly the same purpose: to compare the variance attributed to a particular (main or interaction) factor effect with the variance attributed to randomness (the residual variance). In this way, the significance of the effect can be assessed. If the *F*-ratio is large (rule of thumb: larger than 4) we say that the effect is significant, in other words, the variation it causes cannot be attributed to chance or randomness. Normally, the critical values from the one-sided *F*-tables are utilized (Appendix A, Table A2.2) in the usual way for some prespecified level of significance.

For example, the ANOVA table for our case-study 7.1 is as shown in Table 7.27. It is fairly obvious from the last column of Table 7.27 that the only significant effects are those of C (main effect) and of $B \times C$ (interaction). For confirmation, we need to compare the associated *F*-ratios with the critical value from the *F*-tables (one-sided, Appendix A, Table A2.2). For 1 degree of freedom for the numerator and 16 degrees of freedom for the denominator we have

$$cv(1, 16; 5\%) = 4.49 \text{ and } cv(1, 16; 1\%) = 8.53$$

Since

$$9.13 > cv(1, 16; 1\%)$$

Table 7.26 ANOVA table

Source	df	SS	$MSS = SS/df$	F-ratio
A	df_A	SS_A	$MSS_A = SS_A/df_A$	MSS_A/MSS_e
B	df_B	SS_B	$MSS_B = SS_B/df_B$	MSS_B/MSS_e
$\vdots$	$\vdots$	$\vdots$	$\vdots$	$\vdots$
$A \times B$	$df_{A \times B}$	$SS_{A \times B}$	$MSS_{A \times B} = SS_{A \times B}/df_{A \times B}$	$MSS_{A \times B}/MSS_e$
$\vdots$	$\vdots$	$\vdots$	$\vdots$	$\vdots$
Res	df_e	SS_e	$MSS_e = SS_e/df_e$	
Total	df_{tot}	TSS		

Table 7.27 ANOVA table for case-study 7.1

Source	df	SS	MSS = SS/df	F-ratio	
A	1	0.17	0.17	0.08	
B	1	1.5	1.5	0.68	
C	1	20.17	20.17	9.13	(significant at 1%)
$A \times B$	1	0.17	0.17	0.08	
$A \times C$	1	1.5	1.5	0.68	
$B \times C$	1	20.17	20.17	9.13	(significant at 1%)
$A \times B \times C$	1	1.5	1.5	0.68	
Residual	16	35.3	2.21		
Total	23	80.5			

we can actually accept significance for factor C (class of service) and for the interaction between C and B (telephone company) at the 1% level (running a risk of only 1% of being wrong). So, the obvious conclusion is that the TV advertising campaign (factor A) has not had any effect on the telephone usage, which, in fact, mainly depends on whether the service is residential or business; it also depends on which company provides the service.

For more detailed conclusions, we need to examine the sum totals of the levels of the important effects, which are as follows:

For factor C: $C_1 = 40$, $C_2 = 62$

For the interaction $B \times C$: $B_1C_1 = 13$, $B_1C_2 = 35$, $B_2C_1 = 27$, $B_2C_2 = 27$

For factor B: $B_1 = 48$, $B_2 = 54$

The above can be easily represented graphically: Figure 7.1 shows the behaviour of factors C and B, whereas Figure 7.2 depicts the significance of the interaction effect $B \times C$. It is evident from Figure 7.1, that level two of factor C, the business class of service, accounts for most of the telephone calls, whereas factor B (type of telephone company) does not seem to affect telephone usage. This can be confirmed by the ANOVA table 7.27.

However, looking only at Figure 7.1 we might wrongly conclude that class of service is always an important factor for telephone usage, irrespective of the telephone company. But Figure 7.2 indicates that class of service (factor C) is only important for company 1 (level B (1)) and not for company 2.

In fact, Figure 7.2 is typical of a graph showing a strong interaction effect. If the interaction effect were insignificant, the two lines of Figure 7.2 should be parallel. As they stand, they indicate that the effect of factor class of service (factor C) on the telephone usage depends on which company (factor B) provides the service. This makes factor B a significant factor in its own right, something that contradicts the conclusion that would have been drawn by looking only at the graph for the main effect of B in Figure 7.1.

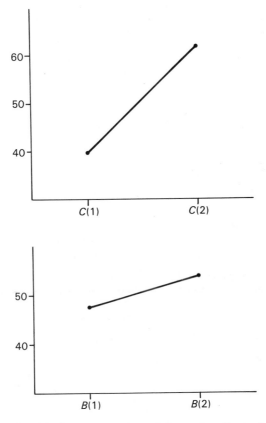

Figure 7.1 Graphical representation of the main effects for factors *B* and *C* (case-study 7.1)

7.5.6 Investigating curvature

For investigating only the linear effects of quantitative factors, 2^k (full or fractional) factorial designs can be used. However, in order to assess curvature (non-linear effects) for a particular factor, it is necessary to study more than two levels for that factor, and appropriate multilevel designs should be employed. For example, linear as well as quadratic effects for a quantitative factor can be extracted by studying this factor at three equispaced levels; if cubic effects need also to be extracted, four levels should be studied, and so on.

To see first how to extract linear and quadratic effects, let us consider a quantitative factor *A* with three equispaced levels $A(1)$, $A(2)$ and $A(3)$. If A_i represents the response total at level A(i), $i = 1, 2, 3$, suppose we find the results presented in Figure 7.3. If factor *A* produces a linear response, the total linear effect from $A(1)$ to $A(2)$ can be estimated by $(A_2 - A_1)$, whereas the

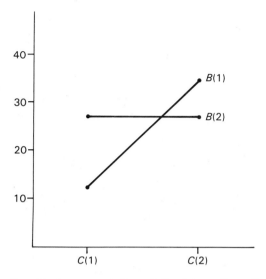

Figure 7.2 Graphical representation of the interaction effect for $B \times C$
(case-study 7.1)

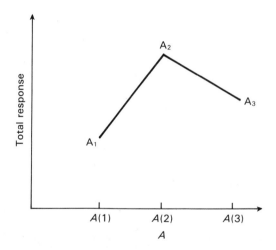

Figure 7.3 Linear and quadratic effects of factor A

total linear effect from $A(2)$ to $A(3)$ is estimated by $(A_3 - A_2)$. Therefore, the total linear effect (linear component) for factor A is estimated by

$$A_L = (A_2 - A_1) + (A_3 - A_2) = A_3 - A_1$$

Now, if the factor A produces a quadratic effect on the response, the slope from $A(1)$ to $A(2)$ will be different from the slope between $A(2)$ and $A(3)$; the difference in slopes will provide an estimate of the quadratic effect for factor A (quadratic component):

$$A_Q = (A_3 - A_2) - (A_2 - A_1) = A_3 - 2A_2 + A_1$$

In order to assess the significance of each component, we need a way of calculating the associated sums of squares; an easy way of obtaining these is by using the following formula which is generally applicable for any k-level factor A:

$$SS\{\text{component}\} = \frac{(W_1 A_1 + \cdots + W_k A_k)^2}{Sr} \tag{7.13}$$

where r is the number of observations corresponding to each factor level,

$$S = \sum_{i=1}^{k} W_i^2$$

and the coefficients W_i, $i = 1, \ldots, k$ for each component (linear, quadratic, cubic etc.) can be found in Table A5 of Appendix A.

For example, if A is a three-level factor ($k = 3$), then

	Linear	Quadratic
W_1	-1	1
W_2	0	-2
W_3	1	1
S	2	6

So

$$SS(A_L) = \frac{(-A_1 + A_3)^2}{2r} \qquad (df = 1)$$

and

$$SS(A_Q) = \frac{(A_1 - 2A_2 + A_3)^2}{6r} \qquad (df = 1)$$

Each of the above sum of squares corresponds to 1 degree of freedom. The total sum of squares for A can thus be obtained by summing up the sum of squares of each component of A. So, for the three-level case,

$$SS_A = SS(A_L) + SS(A_Q) \qquad (df = 1 + 1 = 2)$$

Formula (7.13) can be applied even for slightly unequally spaced levels, provided the deviation from what would be considered equidistant is within about 20% compared with the spacing. If the number of observations per level (r) is not the same for all levels, and is generally r_i for level $A(i)$, provided that each r_i comes within roughly a factor of 2 of the mean number of replications, formula (7.13) can still be applied by using (instead of r) the harmonic mean (the reciprocal of the mean of reciprocals) of the numbers r_i, $i = 1, ..., k$.

7.5.7 Testing without pooling

The pooling of small effects for the creation of an estimate for the error variance has attracted much criticism as a method which can induce extreme bias in a statistical analysis and which can result in spurious conclusions.

A technique which avoids pooling and allows the determination of significant effects even in cases where an estimate of the error variance is not available, is that recommended by Daniel (1959). The technique involves plotting the ordered absolute values of the single degree of freedom components of the effect (when there is a three-level quantitative factor we plot the linear as well as the quadratic component of the effect) against the quantiles of the half-normal distribution using half-normal probability paper, illustrated in Figure D4 in Appendix D. To evaluate the component effects we make use of the orthogonal polynomial coefficients W of Appendix A, Table A5. In general, for a k-level factor A, the component effect is given by

$$A_1 W_1 + \cdots + A_k W_k$$

where A_i for $i = 1, ..., k$, is the sum total of the observations in level $A(i)$, and the W_i's are taken from Table A5.

Half-normal probability paper uses half the scale of ordinary probability paper and can be easily prepared as follows. We fold a normal probability paper in half and delete the printed probability scale P for the range of $P < 50\%$. For the range of $P > 50\%$ we replace P by

$$P' = 2P - 100$$

Having calculated say, n, single degree of freedom effects, we rank them in terms of absolute magnitude, and for each one we calculate a corresponding empirical (probability) rank (ER) given by

$$ER = \frac{(i - 1/2)}{n} \times 100 \qquad i = \text{rank} = 1, 2, ..., n$$

The empirical ranks are then plotted against the ordered absolute values of the component effects on the half-normal probability paper. Effects which are composed only of random variation would lie approximately on a straight line through the origin. Effects which are significant will not conform to this linearity, and will tend to fall independently of the linear configuration determined by the rest of the effects. If a linear pattern does not go through the origin, this is an indication of the possible presence of abnormal values. Plots showing two distinct lines rather than just one indicate, perhaps, that proper randomization procedures have not been adhered to.

The half-normal plots approach is a significant step towards greater objectivity in deciding what is random and what is systematic; it is strongly recommended, especially in situations where an estimate of error variance is not retrievable.

8 Supporting the Quality Improvement Process

Life is the art of drawing sufficient conclusions from insufficient premises.

Samuel Butler

There are certain simple tools and techniques which can naturally be positioned within the TQM philosophy. Many of these tools can easily be utilized for everyday problem solving or for realizing opportunities, and can thus be effectively used to support the implementation of the methodology for quality management and improvement.

This chapter contains a list of such tools, which, although by no means exhaustive, includes the most popular and commonly used techniques; these are briefly described and arranged in alphabetical order for ease of access.

In the process of describing each technique, other tools will be referred to, and can be found elsewhere within this book. Most of the techniques are common-sense techniques, apparently simple and outright obvious. But the most useful ideas are often the simple ones!

■ 8.1 Affinity diagram

This is an organizing tool, useful, for example, in sorting out ideas generated through a *brainstorming* session (see Section 8.4). It is particularly necessary when a large amount of information, ideas, opinions or issues have been collected in situations when a process needs defining, or customer requirements need identifying, or when a problem needs solving.

The technique organizes the collected pieces of information into groupings based on the natural relationships that exist among them. The number of groupings is limited to a maximum of 10. A single piece of information can constitute an independent group in its own right. A heading is created for each group, capturing its meaning.

The technique is useful in reducing an otherwise unmanageable amount of information into a smaller number of homogeneous groups which are much easier to handle independently, prioritize in order of significance (*Pareto principle* – see Section 8.13), or allocate to specific projects for further study or investigation.

Table 8.1 is the basis for constructing an affinity diagram related to the different practices of a consultancy firm. The first part of the table shows a plethora of activities that the firm can be involved with. The second part shows how these activities can be organized into homogeneous and independently managed consultancy units.

Table 8.1 Affinity diagram (in tabular form) for a consultancy firm

1. *Consultancy activities*

Data presentation and interpretation;	Process mapping and analysis;	TQM principles and tools;
Risk analysis;	Survey design;	Econometrics;
Market research;	Target setting;	Time series analysis;
SPC;	Taguchi methods;	Simulation;
Cost analysis;	Optimization methods	Project management;
Quality function deployment;	Statistical estimation;	Questionnaire setting;
Networking;	Systems modelling;	Operational research;
Systems design;	Forecasting;	Data analysis

2. *Consultancy units*

Measurement and information

Survey design;	Sampling;	Data presentation and interpretation;
Market research;	Questionnaire design	

Resource utilization

Simulation; Networking	Optimization methods;	Cost analysis;

Quality

Taguchi methods;	SPC;	Quality function deployment;
TQM principles and tools		

Organization, systems and processes

Process mapping and analysis;	Risk analysis;	Systems modelling;
Operational research	System design;	Project management;

Statistical techniques

Statistical estimation;	Data analysis;	Forecasting;
Time series analysis;	Econometrics	

■ 8.2 Bar chart

A bar chart is a graphical representation of discrete groups or categories of data, shown in such a way that clear comparisons can easily be made.

A bar chart is frequently used to emphasize a point; this will dictate the way in which the chart is drawn. The chart is normally used to emphasize the variation and unevenness in data. Using this information, further investigation could follow to determine why the variation was occurring. The items are usually ranked from high to low, with the lengths of the bars indicating the value or frequency that a bar represents. For example, Figure 8.1 shows a bar chart comparing groups of companies which are categorized according to the level of company-wide utilization of quality cost figures (Section 8.14). Note that, within the category of those companies that use a quality costing system, there is a further breakdown into groups according to the length of time they have used the system.

A special version of the bar chart is the 100% bar chart which has all its bars of equal lengths; each bar (representing 100% of the item) is subdivided according to the size of its components. For example, the 100% bar chart in Figure 8.2 represents the views of a number of managers from within a particular company (internal views) in relation to the views of managers from other companies (external views) on the subject of the various benefits of quality costing.

When the data are spread across a continuous range of values, a bar chart is equivalent to a *histogram*, considered in detail in Section 6.5.

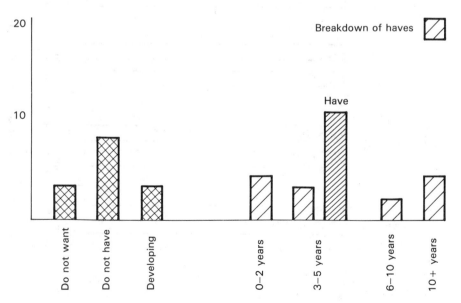

Figure 8.1 Existence of company-wide quality costing system (financial accounting system) for external companies

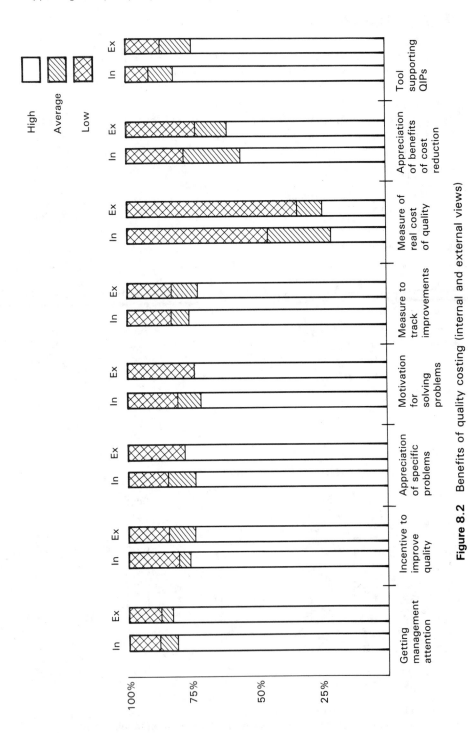

Figure 8.2 Benefits of quality costing (internal and external views)

■ 8.3 Block diagram

If every activity which is part of a process is represented by a block (box), and all blocks are connected by lines representing the interfaces between activities, a macrolevel view of the process is obtained; this is called a block diagram. The diagram traces the paths that any information, necessary actions or materials can take between the original input and the final output of the

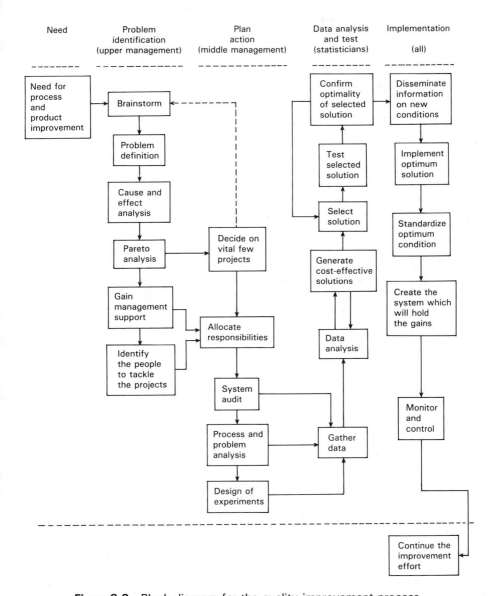

Figure 8.3 Block diagram for the quality improvement process

process. For each activity in the process, there is a determination of the output it produces, what other activities it feeds into, and, through the identification of special groups for particular work activities, there is also a determination of who performs the activity. Figure 8.3 shows a block diagram representing the (continuous) effort of quality improvement for processes and products.

■ 8.4 Brainstorming

Brainstorming is an activity which promotes group participation and teamwork, encourages creative thinking and stimulates the generation of as many ideas as possible in a short period of time.

The participants in a brainstorming meeting are invited on the basis of their particular knowledge and experience, and are expected to contribute to the topic under discussion. An atmosphere is created where everybody feels free to express themselves. The production of random 'off the top of the head' ideas is encouraged; the emphasis is on quantity rather than quality. No criticism, expression of doubt or hasty judgment of the ideas is allowed until after the brainstorming session; this is crucial if the barriers to creative thinking (such as the fear of seeming foolish or impractical) are to be overcome.

All ideas, without exception, are recorded and made visible to all the participants. Each input and contribution is recognized as important, and the output of the whole session is seen in context. The continuing involvement of each participant is assured and the group's future is reinforced by mapping out the exact follow up actions (analysis and evaluation of the ideas) and the future progress of the project.

■ 8.5 Cause and effect analysis

This is a technique for identifying the most probable causes affecting a problem, a condition or a project. It can help in the analysis of cause and effect relationships, and it can be used iteratively in conjunction with brainstorming (Section 8.4) and *Pareto analysis* (Section 8.13).

The tool that is being used, the cause and effect diagram, is a visually effective way of recording the possible causes of a particular effect (see Figure 8.4). The effect is placed in a box on the right and a long process line is drawn pointing to the box. After deciding the major categories of causes, these are recorded on either side of the process line within other boxes connected with the main process line through other lines. In this way, each main cause can be viewed as an effect in its own right with its own process line, around which other (associated) causes can be clustered.

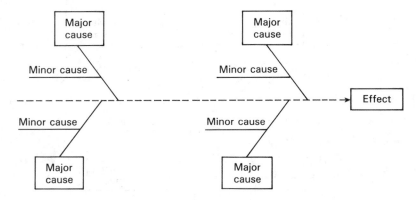

Figure 8.4 Principles of the cause and effect diagram

Examples of major categories of causes are methods, machines, manpower and materials. If a category of causes begins to dominate the diagram, it may be necessary to isolate that group on a separate diagram. The most likely causes can be circled to signify that they should be tackled first.

The cause and effect diagram is also known as the fishbone diagram, because of its appearance, or as the Ishikawa diagram after Professor K. Ishikawa who introduced it to Japan; it has since become an indispensable tool for Japanese management. Figure 8.5 provides a self-explanatory example.

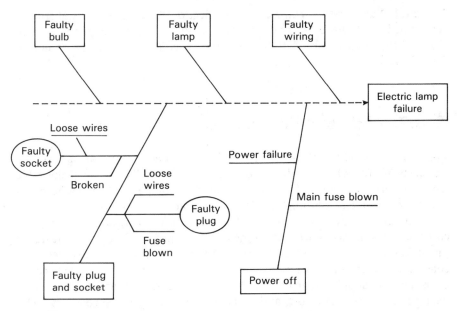

Figure 8.5 Cause and effect diagram investigating failures of electric lamps

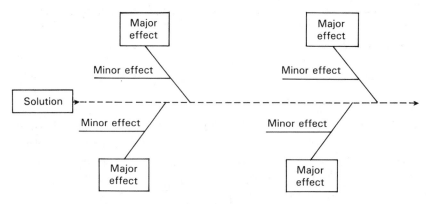

Figure 8.6 Principles of the solution-effect diagram

The cause and effect diagram is the mirror image of the solution–effect diagram which helps to identify the probable effect of a proposed solution on a project or problem. The procedure is similar to that used in cause and effect analysis. The resulting diagram in its general form is shown in Figure 8.6.

■ 8.6 Control charts

A control chart is a *line (run) chart* (see Section 8.12) to which statistically determined limits have been added. An extended description of the control chart – the main tool of statistical process control – can be found in Chapter 9.

■ 8.7 Cost–benefit analysis

This is a technique for assessing the viability of an action in monetary terms. The costs of taking a particular action are compared to the benefits achievable from the future outcome. It can also be used to compare, in money terms, a number of problem solutions or plans of action.

A necessary first step should be to decide on the period over which the cost–benefit analysis will be performed. All the potential costs in setting up the action or solution should be considered at this stage. The next step is to consider all the factors involved which will either incur costs or provide benefits. Consideration should be given to hidden cost factors such as training, maintenance costs and so on. Costs and benefits should be estimated conservatively.

The final analysis should be based on the calculation of the benefit to cost ratio, and the net benefit, perhaps in conjunction with non-financial aspects.

Table 8.2   Cost–benefit analysis on the purchase of a company van

| Costs (£) | Year | | | | | Total |
	1	2	3	4	5	
Purchase	20000					20000
Less trade in	3000					3000
Net cost	17000					17000
Maintenance		1000	1000	1500	1500	5000
Running costs	3000	3000	3000	3500	3500	16000
Depreciation		1000	1500	1500	2000	6000
Total costs	20000	5000	5500	6500	7000	44000
Benefits (£)						
Staff savings	30000	30000	32000	35000	35000	162000
Time savings	1000	1000	1000	1200	1200	5400
Total benefits	31000	31000	33000	36200	36200	167400

Analysis

$$\text{benefit to cost ratio} = \frac{\text{total benefits}}{\text{total costs}} = \frac{167400}{44000} = 3.8:1$$

net annual benefit for first year
$$= \text{first year benefit} - \text{first year cost} = 31000 - 20000 = £11000$$

net annual benefit averaged over all years
$$= \frac{\text{total benefits} - \text{total costs}}{5} = \frac{167400 - 44000}{5} = £24680$$

The results can be used to evaluate a number of options. Table 8.2 shows a cost–benefit analysis on the purchase of a company van. The results of the analysis support the decision to purchase the van.

■ 8.8   Customer – supplier relationship checklist

This type of checklist can be used to help in the assessment of the relationship between the supplier and the (external or internal) customer. It can help in the identification of customer requirements, in the better definition of the process, and in the unbiased assessment of the process performance and of customer satisfaction or dissatisfaction. The checklist should attempt to answer the following questions, which can be allocated to three main groups:

Group 1. Questions about issues concerning relationships with the customer:
1.1. What are your primary inputs – in terms of product or service?

1.2. Who are your customers – internal and external recipients of your output?

1.3. What are your customer's requirements? What are the methods you use to determine these requirements?

1.4. How satisfied are your customers with your product or service? How do you measure their satisfaction?

Group 2. Questions about issues concerning the process performance:

2.1. What are the characteristics of your process output that can be measured to determine whether it meets your customer's requirements?

2.2. What major quality problems prevent you from meeting your customer's requirements?

2.3. What are the obstacles standing in the way of resolving these quality problems, and what would it take to remove these obstacles?

Group 3. Questions about issues concerning the relationship with the supplier:

3.1. Which suppliers or subcontractors affect your capability to meet your customer's requirements? How do you select them?

3.2. What are your primary supplies and what are your requirements for these supplies?

3.3. How do you communicate your requirements to your suppliers and subcontractors? Do you help them to meet these requirements?

3.4. How satisfied are you with your suppliers or subcontractors? Do you provide feedback to them about their performance?

■ 8.9 Decision analysis

Decision analysis is a technique assisting in the choice of an action and its course in view of the objectives, other alternatives and the risks involved. The technique provides a structured route towards a less biased and more balanced decision by considering the potential drawbacks of each option, all aspects for and against each option, and all factors vital to its success.

The starting point of the technique is a statement which clearly defines the decision required. The statement should clarify the objectives of the decision, that is, what the decision is meant to accomplish; this is called the action component of the decision. The statement should also clarify the scope of the objective, that is, the supporting requirements which tailor the decision to the specific needs; this is called the boundary component of the decision. For example, if we are faced with the decision to buy a portable microcomputer which is compatible with the computing network of the company, the action component of the decision is 'buy a microcomputer', and the boundary components are 'portable' and 'compatible with the company's network'.

The next stage of the technique is to clarify the decision criteria, which are divided into:

1. The *musts* criteria, which are mandatory for any solution to be effective.
2. The *wants* criteria, which are non-mandatory for the solution but which we would like to include in order to judge between the relative merits of the available alternatives.

In our example, the musts might include:

- The micro must be IBM compatible.
- It must operate with 5.25 inch floppy disks.
- It must have a minimum 10 Kbyte hard disk memory.
- It must be able to use internally supported software.

The wants might include:

- Available in the UK.
- Repair and maintenance available within 24 hrs.
- To weigh less than 12 kg.
- Compatible with existing printer equipment.

The options which do not satisfy all the musts should be excluded from any further consideration. Those remaining should be rated, taking the wants into consideration. This can be done using a weighted rating sheet. In this, we make use of the weight factor which is a value allocated to each want reflecting its importance. For example, the highest weighting can be 10 and this will be allocated to the most important want. To each option, we also assign a rating, an option score, again in the range 1 to 10, reflecting the way the option satisfies the wants criteria.

For our example, Table 8.3 is a weighted rating sheet referring to the wants listed above.

The table shows the weight factor, the option scores (*A*, *B* and *C*), and also the weighted option scores reflecting how the weight factor for each want affects the option ratings; these are the values obtained after multiplying the weight factor for each want by its associated option rating. The total score for

Table 8.3 Weighted rating table

Wants criteria	Weight factor	Option scores			Weighted option scores		
		A	*B*	*C*	*A*	*B*	*C*
Availability	8	6	10	9	48	80	72
24 hrs repair/maintenance	10	8	7	6	80	70	60
Weight less than 12 kg	5	2	8	8	10	40	40
Printer compatible	7	7	6	7	49	42	49
Total scores					187	232	221

Table 8.4 Solution-effect analysis

Adverse consequences	Probability			Seriousness		
	A	*B*	*C*	*A*	*B*	*C*
Hardware faults	High	Medium	Medium	Medium	High	High
Product discontinuity	Medium	High	Low	High	High	High
Price rise of 10%	Low	Medium	High	Low	Low	Low

each option is the sum of the products associated with it. On the basis of the total scores, option *B* seems to be the most advantageous.

Before a final decision is taken any adverse consequences of the selected option should be considered. For example, if there is to be a product discontinuity for option *B* within 12 months, there might be a difficulty in finding spare parts in the future. The probability of any adverse consequence occurring should be estimated, together with the seriousness of the situation if it were to take place. For our example, Table 8.4 should also be consulted (in conjunction with Table 8.3) before the final decision. In this case, one might opt for option *C*.

■ 8.10 Flow charts

A flow chart is a pictorial representation of the stages in a process. A series of symbols, connected to each other in a logical series, portrays activities,

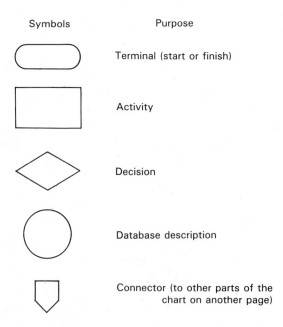

Symbols	Purpose
	Terminal (start or finish)
	Activity
	Decision
	Database description
	Connector (to other parts of the chart on another page)

Figure 8.7 Main symbols for flow-charting

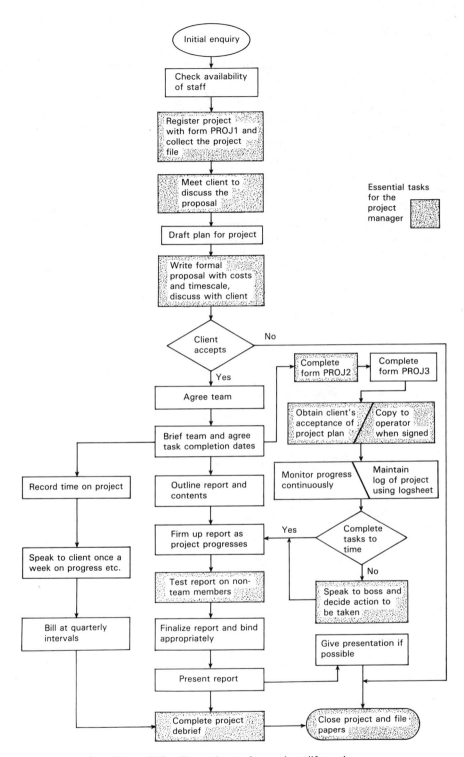

Figure 8.8 Flow chart of a project lifecycle

decisions and databases, thus determining how the process actually works. This allows complex procedures to be broken down into manageable parts for examination, better understanding and, if necessary, redesigning. Potential sources of trouble and wastage can be uncovered, thus making flow-charting a cost-saver in many diverse fields such as processing orders, faulting procedures, corporate planning, product realization, operations methodology etc. The main symbols used and their purpose are shown in Figure 8.7.

In order to flow-chart a particular process we must first identify the inputs and the activities involved. For each input we must determine who receives the input and what is the first thing to be done with it. For each activity we must determine its output, who receives this output and what happens next. Using the appropriate flow-chart symbols, we should connect all inputs, activities and outputs.

The chart should be reviewed as many times as necessary in order to answer questions such as:

- Do any activities require inputs not already shown?
- Do all activities map properly to process inputs and outputs?
- Does the chart show all potential paths that the process can take?
- Does the chart accurately capture what *really* happens?

Figure 8.8 shows a flow chart depicting the lifecycle of a project.

■ 8.11 Force field analysis

This is a technique for identifying the forces that help or obstruct a change or an important effort. In this way, the difficulty in implementing a change can be assessed, and plans for overcoming barriers to change can be developed. Through this type of analysis, an overall picture can be developed which can help in the identification of all assets as well as inhibitors.

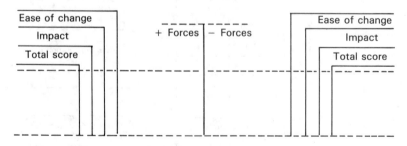

Figure 8.9 Force field table

Having clearly defined the problem to be tackled and the objectives to be reached, the positive and negative forces are identified through *brainstorming* (Section 8.4). An evaluation of the forces is then taking place in terms of ease of change and impact. Ease of change indicates how far it is possible to influence or change the force, whereas impact indicates how significant the consequences would be if the force were changed. A score should be assigned to each force on a rating scale which, for ease of change and impact respectively, is defined according to:

- Cannot be influenced/changed – no impact.
- Could be influenced/changed – small impact.
- Can be influenced/changed – major impact.

The forces and their ratings can now be recorded in a force field table as shown in Figure 8.9. The scores are totalled in the appropriate column so that the forces which score highest can be highlighted. In this way, a clear indication is obtained of which forces need to be acted upon in order to achieve the objectives.

An alternative way of representing the results of a force field analysis is shown in Figure 8.10, with an example in Figure 8.11 referring to the forces which tend to increase and decrease defects.

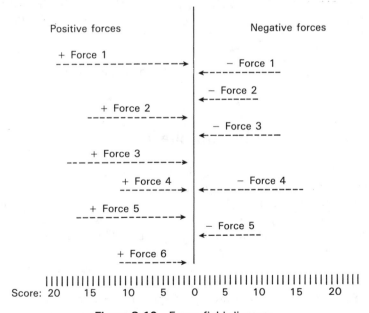

Figure 8.10 Force field diagram

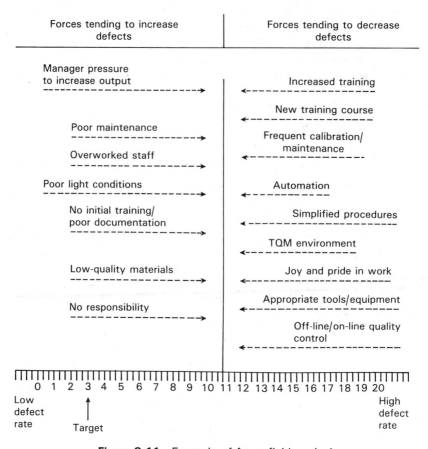

Forces tending to increase defects	Forces tending to decrease defects
Manager pressure to increase output	Increased training
Poor maintenance	New training course
Overworked staff	Frequent calibration/ maintenance
Poor light conditions	Automation
No initial training/ poor documentation	Simplified procedures
	TQM environment
Low-quality materials	Joy and pride in work
No responsibility	Appropriate tools/equipment
	Off-line/on-line quality control

0 1 2 3 4 5 6 7 8 9 10 11 12 13 14 15 16 17 18 19 20

Low defect rate

Target

High defect rate

Figure 8.11 Example of force field analysis

■ 8.12 Line graphs/run charts

A line graph is a simple way of graphically representing data. Direct relationships between two quantities can be shown easily without looking at the actual data. They can be used not only to determine the existence of linear or nonlinear relationships, but they can also serve as a useful guide of what is expected in the future for a particular variable. They can also be used to summarize complex information, to point out trends, fluctuations and relationships, and generally to effectively organize data and communicate important results.

Line graphs are usually drawn to display the relationship between two variables set up as a two-dimensional system of coordinates. When the horizontal axis represents time, then the *time series* graph, or run chart, is obtained,

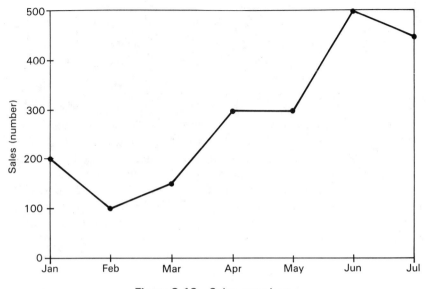

Figure 8.12 Sales run chart

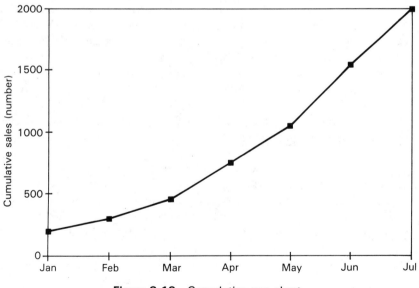

Figure 8.13 Cumulative run chart

Table 8.5 Sales data

Month	Sales	Cumulative sales
Jan	200	200
Feb	100	300
Mar	150	450
Apr	300	750
May	300	1050
Jun	500	1550
Jul	450	2000

useful in monitoring trends (runs) of a variable of interest. An example of a run chart is shown in Figure 8.12 where sales volume is plotted against time in monthly intervals. The data are taken from the second column of Table 8.5.

A related run chart is the cumulative run chart, where the data are added together sequentially to give cumulative totals which are plotted against time. An example is shown in Figure 8.13, the data for which are taken from the last column of Table 8.5.

■ 8.13 Pareto analysis

Pareto analysis is a technique for ordering causes or problems from the most to the least significant. In this way, the most significant aspects are identified (what Juran calls 'the vital few') and the efforts can be concentrated on those, thus getting the maximum benefit with the least effort. The analysis makes use of the Pareto diagram, which is a special case of the *bar chart* (Section 8.2), and is used in conjunction with *brainstorming* (Section 8.4), *cause and effect analysis* (section 8.5) and *cumulative line charts* (Section 8.12). The diagram displays, in decreasing order, the relative contribution of each cause (or problem) to the total. The relative contribution can be based on the number of occurrences, the quality damage or the cost associated with each cause (or problem).

The Pareto diagram is based on the Pareto principle which states that a few causes account for most of the effect. This common concept was first noted in the nineteenth century by the Italian economist Vilfredo Pareto, who noticed that a large proportion of the national wealth was controlled by a relatively small number of people, roughly according to the ratio 80:20. This fact has also been referred to by Juran in his concept of the 'vital few and the trivial many'. The Pareto principle can also be applied to quality improvement: solving a few key quality problems can lead to major improvements.

Figure 8.14 provides an example of Pareto analysis with reference to the number of defects in the manufacturing process of printed circuit boards (PCBs). The diagram indicates that the improvement effort should first focus

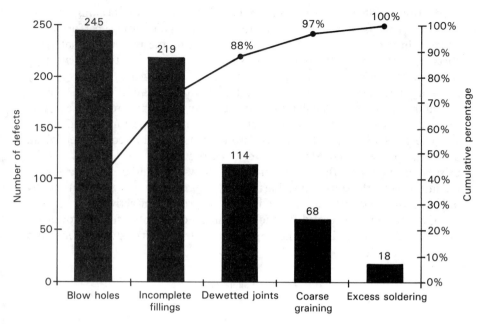

Figure 8.14 Pareto analysis for printed circuit board products

on the elimination of blow holes and incomplete fillings, which account for 71% of the defects in the PCB soldering process (vital few). Obviously, the rest of the defects (dewetted joints, coarse graining, excess soldering) should not be ignored.

■ 8.14 Quality costing

Quality costing is normally used to provide a measure of the cost of quality-related activities. All costs can be classified into one of the following activities:

1. Basic work costs: value-added; unnecessary.
2. Failure costs: external (off site); internal (on site).
3. Appraisal costs.
4. Prevention costs.

Basic work refers to the essential and unavoidable activities required to do a job. Failure refers to any activities taking place as a result of not meeting requirements first time. These cover the correction, disposal or rework of incorrect work, duplication of work, dealing with complaints from (external and internal) customers, service under guarantee, reinspection, fire-fighting, penalty costs, recalls, scrap disposal, system or manpower failure, lost production or idle time. Appraisal refers to the activities of checking whether the requirements have been met; these include measuring performance, product inspection, testing, verification, inspecting the purchased materials, checking procedures, audits and assessing customer satisfaction. Prevention refers to any activity aimed at preventing things going wrong, such as quality planning, preventive maintenance, vendor appraisal, calibration, QIP teams, planning experiments, analysing data for improvement projects, contract review, field trials, setting up procedures and, most importantly, training.

The costs under (2), (3) and (4) are known as quality costs. Ideally, all costs, except the value-added basic work and prevention costs, should be non-existent or minimal. But, as Figure 8.15 shows, an initial classification of quality costs (at the start of a serious quality improvement programme) usually indicates that very little effort is allocated to prevention activities.

Quality costing is useful for the recognition of the need for improvement and for the identification of the opportunities for quality advancement, in a

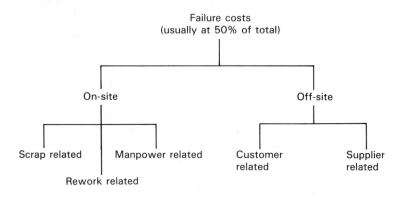

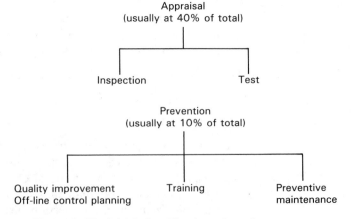

Figure 8.15 Initial classification of quality costs

Table 8.6 Classification of visible quality costs

	R&D	Engineering and maintenance	Quality	Logistics	Manufacturing	Assembly and packing	Sales	Finance	Administration	£ thousand
Prevention costs										
Audits	5	10	55	10	25	15	—	—	—	120
Training	10	10	35	5	80	50	75	25	10	300
Quality planning	300	200	220	30	45	10	—	—	—	805
Process capability	10	10	10	—	10	—	—	—	—	40
Calibration	—	—	10	—	5	—	—	—	—	15
Vendor assessment	—	—	40	30	—	—	—	—	—	70
QIP teams	25	20	20	5	50	10	10	5	5	150
Prevention total	350	250	390	80	215	85	85	30	15	1500
Appraisal costs										
Inspection of product	200	—	700	—	400	200	—	—	—	1500
Supplier monitoring	—	—	140	60	—	—	—	—	—	200
Product audits	—	—	80	25	—	5	110	—	—	220
Test materials	10	—	100	—	—	40	—	—	—	150
Checking procedures	40	10	30	10	30	20	—	60	30	230
Appraisal total	250	10	1050	95	430	265	110	60	30	2300
Failure costs										
Isolation of causes	60	10	80	20	20	10	—	—	—	200
Reinspection	—	—	50	—	30	—	—	—	—	80
Customer returns	—	—	70	—	—	—	340	—	—	410
Concessions and downgrading	20	—	30	—	—	—	10	—	—	60
Scrap disposal	10	—	70	—	270	150	—	—	—	500
System failure	—	—	20	20	40	30	30	80	—	220
Material supply	40	—	—	170	30	—	—	—	—	240
Manufacturing losses	—	—	—	—	2100	310	—	—	20	2430
Manpower failure	—	—	—	—	80	60	—	—	—	140
Process equipment	—	610	—	—	230	80	—	—	—	920
Failure total	130	620	320	210	2800	640	380	80	20	5200

language that everybody understands – money. By focusing on the cost of poor quality, managers are made aware of the benefits to be obtained by reducing this cost. Especially during the initial stages of a quality improvement programme, awareness of quality costs promotes a proper appreciation of specific quality problems and provides the motivation to solve them. This can also prove to be a useful tool, on a project-by-project basis, for demonstrating the effectiveness of individual efforts and illustrating the benefits of doing things right first time.

Of course, quality costing is meaningless unless it is combined with action to eliminate root causes of costs. We should always be aware of the fact that, usually, the process of quality costing accounts for costs only where they fall, not where they are caused and that, sometimes, it fails to take into account important costs that are not visible, such as customer dissatisfaction, loss of goodwill, loss of pride in work for the workforce, opportunity costs etc. Table 8.6 shows a real example of classification of the visible quality costs.

Experience shows that it is very much cheaper to prevent trouble in the first place than recognize it (through quality costing) and cure it once it is occurring. It therefore follows that the return on investment on money spent in prevention will certainly be significant.

■ 8.15 Quality function deployment (QFD)

Quality function deployment (QFD) is a process which brings together the essential elements and crucial characteristics of the various phases in the lifecycle of a product, from its conception through design, development, manufacture, distribution and use. It focuses and coordinates skills within an organization, and encourages teamwork between marketing people, design engineers and manufacturing staff. By recognizing the interrelationships between the engineering properties of the product and the customer's requirements, appropriate actions can be taken at every stage of the product's development, so that the customer needs are anticipated, prioritized and effectively incorporated into the product.

The basic QFD procedure to follow is the pictorial construction of the *house of quality*. One such house is represented in Figure 8.16 and relates to the production of telephones.

1. The construction of the house of quality starts with the identification of the customer's requirements, known as *customer attributes* (CA), which are listed on the left-hand side of the house. These describe product characteristics or represent areas of concern. Next to each CA, its relative importance (in numerical terms), as perceived by the customer, is added. This information can be obtained through market research surveys.

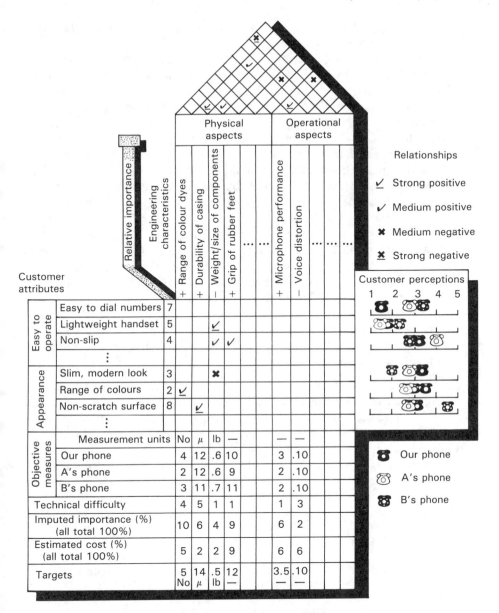

Figure 8.16 Quality house
(reproduced by permission of British Telecommunications plc)

2. On the right-hand side of the house a list is constructed of customer evaluations of how the product stands relative to the competition. In this way, opportunities for improvement will be identified, so that the competitive advantage is gained. This representation is also known as a *perceptual map* and provides a comparative assessment in relation to the products of

other competitors; this information will be enhanced if warranty claims or specific customer complaints are known.

3.   The product is then described in terms of its engineering characteristics (EC) which are listed along the top of the house of quality. Each EC is likely to affect one or more CAs. At this stage, further rows could be added below the initial CA rows describing, for example, the engineer's estimates as to the degree of technical difficulty in making changes to the specific ECs, or even regulatory, cost and company control items. If possible, the ECs should be described in measurable terms which directly affect customer perceptions. Each EC should be preceded by a ' + ' or a ' − ' sign according to whether the EC contributes or counts against the product's target value. The roof of the house is filled in to show the correlations between ECs.

4.   The main body of the house is now filled in, providing a relationship matrix linking ECs to CAs. Based on experience or previous statistical studies, a completed relationship matrix shows how much engineers affect customer-perceived qualities. What is seen as better in the CA rating (relative importance) should correlate with technically better. It is possible to use numerical scales or symbols to relate the two. When the relationship matrix has been completed, objective measures are added at the foot of the house, which will eventually be moved to form target values for a new or redesigned product.

On the whole, QFD is very effective for determining opportunities that can be developed effectively to achieve total customer satisfaction. The house of quality is a useful summary of data that can serve as a permanent and complete record of all the relevant available information, thus providing a solid and valuable starting point for any future work. For example, having decided the targets for the ECs in the initial house, these can be used as customer attributes in their own right for the construction of a second house concerned with detailed product design. This process can continue further through parts deployment, process planning and production; see, for example, Figure 8.17.

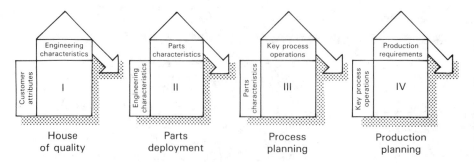

Figure 8.17 A continuous process for QFD

But the greatest advantage of the QFD technique is that it encourages disciplined and detailed thinking, as well as discussion among the various groups of engineers, marketing and production staff, thus providing an implicit link from the customer's voice through to manufacturing.

■ 8.16 Quality project approach and the problem-solving process

The process for solving quality problems is likely to be successful only if it is managed properly, through quality improvement projects. A well-managed improvement project is based on clear understanding of the problem and of the requirements, on facts and scientific analyses, on open channels of communication, and on the full commitment of all involved.

The quality project approach consists of five stages:

Stage 1. Quality improvement proposal: this is a thorough project proposal revealing the project owner, identifying the problem and its symptoms, stating the requirements and project objectives, determining the measurement process, milestones and targets, and defining the quality improvement team.

Stage 2. Problem analysis and planning: at this stage, relevant data are collected and analysed so that the root causes can be identified. A range of possible solutions is generated and a selection is made of the solution which best meets the objectives. The solution's associated costs, benefits and other implications are estimated, and plans for action are developed.

Stage 3. Education and communication: the people involved in, or affected by, the action plans, are identified and appropriately educated in order to ensure their cooperation and agreement to the planned solution.

Stage 4. Implementation plans: detailed implementation plans are drawn up for all involved, making absolutely clear who does what, by when, and with what measurements, to ensure that everything is ready for implementation.

Stage 5. Implementation: at this stage, the selected solution is implemented, and the results are measured and assessed. Implementation may have to be phased, and tests might have to take place to confirm the success of the solution. In the case of a successful outcome, an effort should be made to hold the gains and to maintain the improvement, to communicate the lessons learned, and to apply the solution wherever else is relevant.

The relationship between the five-stage project approach and the problem-solving process is illustrated in Figure 8.18.

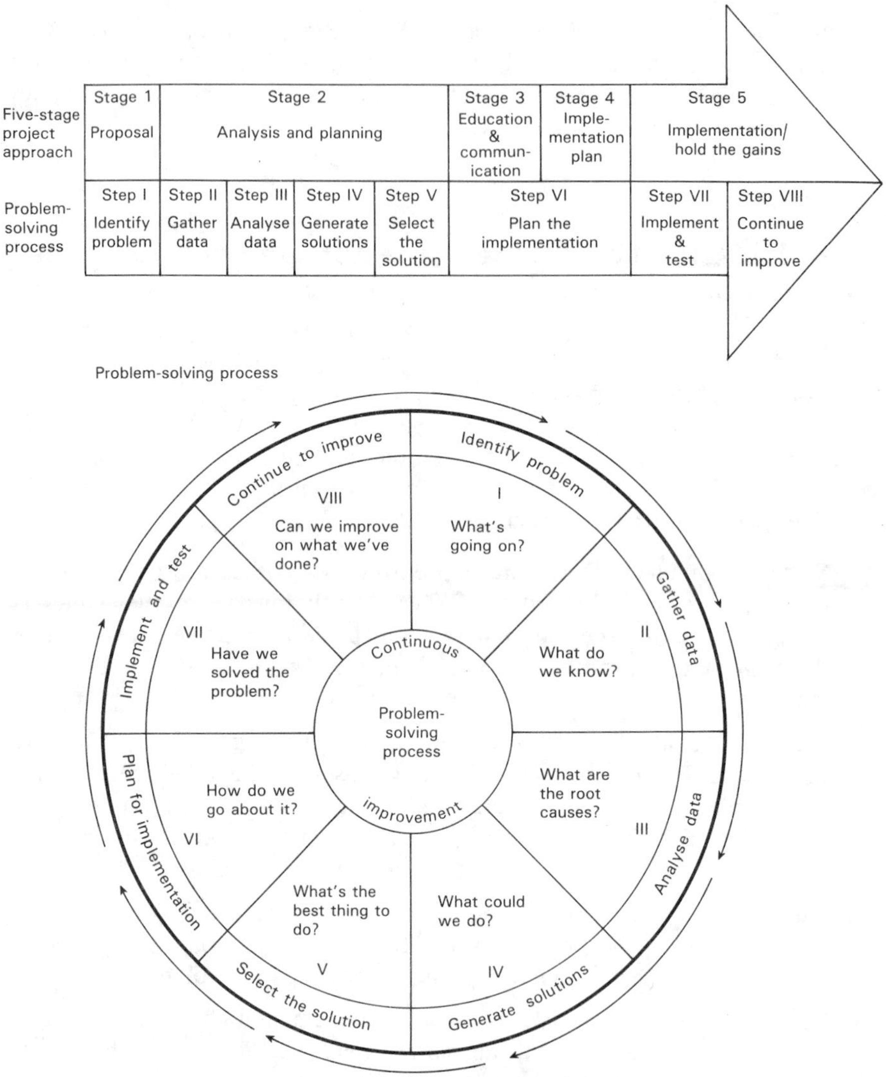

Five-stage project approach	Stage 1	Stage 2				Stage 3	Stage 4	Stage 5
	Proposal	Analysis and planning				Education & commun-ication	Imple-mentation plan	Implementation/ hold the gains
Problem-solving process	Step I	Step II	Step III	Step IV	Step V	Step VI	Step VII	Step VIII
	Identify problem	Gather data	Analyse data	Generate solutions	Select the solution	Plan the implementation	Implement & test	Continue to improve

Problem-solving process

Figure 8.18 Relationship of a five-stage project approach and
problem-solving process
(reproduced by permission of British Telecommunications plc)

■ 8.17 Risk analysis

The purpose of risk analysis is to identify and quantify all risks which could jeopardise the successful completion of a project or a quality improvement effort. Appropriate risk management can control and possibly eliminate each risk. Risk analysis in conjunction with risk management can reduce costs and effort, can assess potentially damaging circumstances and control any slippage in the project plan.

The main tasks of risk analysis are as follows:

1. Identify and list potential areas of risk. Potential risk areas can be many and varied. There may be technical problems in design, low quality or late delivery of supplies, insufficient and inexperienced staff, problems with the existing equipment or budget overspend. The risk manager should establish whether or not certain circumstances constitute a risk likely to affect a particular project or related areas.

2. Quantify the risks. The likelihood and the impact of each risk should be assessed and estimated on the basis of past experience, of the dependencies between activities, and of the complexity of the situation. Risks should be quantified according to the implications of the situation if it occurred and according to the probability that it will occur. The categories of risk can be represented in a two-dimensional grid as shown in Table 8.7. Risks in category 1 in Table 8.7 require extra careful assessment and quantification of cost, loss of benefits, time and resources involved. Risks classified in categories 2 and 3 require a proportionally lower level of analysis.

3. Develop contingency plans and associated trigger criteria. This applies especially to risks in category 1. Contingency plans should be defined in order to contain the potential damage. It may be possible to modify the planned activity in order to eliminate or reduce the risk. Trigger criteria should be determined, to be used to raise the alarm when the risk starts to materialize, and finally a trigger point should be defined, at which the contingency action should be initiated.

4. Monitor and review the risks. The activities at risk should be monitored closely and reviewed as often as necessary by the *risk owner*. In the event of a significant change in the planned activities, an updated risk report should be issued and the appropriate action should be taken. Periodically, on the basis of recent information, all risks should be reassessed and new contingency plans should be drawn up.

Table 8.8 shows a risk report referring to the risk of not obtaining in time a particular machine component from a subcontractor. The report format is representative of the one to be used for all types of risks, in advance of a major project.

Table 8.7 Categories of risk

Likelihood	Impact		
	Severe	Intermediate	Minor
Large	1	1	2
Average	1	2	2
Small	2	2	3

Table 8.8   Risk report pro forma

Wire Ltd	Ref: STD 19
	Issue: 1.1
	Date: 25/09/90
	Page: 16

Project title: Assembly of a wire-bending/cutting/straightening machine.
Owner of risk: Project manager
Project status: Urgent order
Date raised: 20/09/90
Description of risk: Delay in obtaining straightening unit from sub-contractor A
Duration of risk: Over 2 months from order
Impact: Severe
Likelihood: Average
Risk category: 1 (*high risk*)
Other areas affected: Delay in delivery and installation
Trigger date/event: 1 month from order

Actions required
Monitoring: Product manager to be responsible for monitoring sub-contractor A; keep in touch and communicate once every 10 days.
Corrective (contingency plan):   At trigger date, order of straightening unit from supplier B. Ask for delivery at 20 days from trigger date.

Prepared by: J. Smith

■ 8.18 Scatter diagrams

A scatter diagram is used to determine if a relationship exists between two variables. It can highlight possible relationships and can give a useful guide as to what can be expected in the future. For an example the reader is referred to case-study 6.3 (Figure 6.9) in Section 6.7 (page 136).

■ 8.19 Weibull analysis

Weibull analysis is a technique used to assess the reliability of failure data. The basic steps to follow will be demonstrated by analysing certain sets of electric-lamp life data. A distinction will be made between complete and censored failure data. We start by defining the notions of *reliability* and *hazard rate*.

8.19.1 Reliability

Reliability is a measure of the ability of a product to function successfully, when required, for the period required, under specified operating conditions. It is usually expressed as a mathematical probability, and so can lie between 0 or 0% (complete unreliability) and 1 or 100% (perfect reliability). For example, if a light bulb is said to be 70% reliable at 200 hours, this means that 70% of light bulbs will last at least 200 hours without failing. The failure percentage is $(100 - R)$ where R is the percentage reliability.

If we consider failures in a population of items, the time to failure will have some distribution. We can then quantify the reliability of failure percentage at any desired age by estimating this failure distribution using data from a sample.

8.19.2 Hazard rate and failure distributions

The failure distribution is characterized by a measure called the hazard rate, defined by

HR = rate at which remaining items fail

$$= \frac{\text{number of units failing in a time interval}}{(\text{number of survivors at start of interval}) \times (\text{length of time interval})}$$

There are three types of hazard rate:

1. Decreasing – infant mortality: early failures resulting from construction errors.
2. Constant – useful life/prime of life: random failures resulting from misuse by customer, occasional operating stress exceeding designed strength etc.
3. Increasing – wearout failures due to wear, fatigue, chemical ageing such as corrosion etc.

Items can experience one, two or all three of the above types. The Weibull distribution (see Figure 8.19) can be used to model failure modes from any of the three types of HR. In its simplest form it involves two parameters:

β – the slope or shape parameter

α – the scale parameter

The value $\eta = 1/\alpha$ is usually called the *characteristic life*. Mathematically, this value represents the age by which 63.8% of the items under consideration fail. Variation of the shape parameter allows the modelling of the life distribution of items which follow any of the three types of HR. In fact we have:

Phase	HR	Shape (β)
Early life	Decreasing	<1
Useful life	Constant	$=1$
Wear out	Increasing	>1

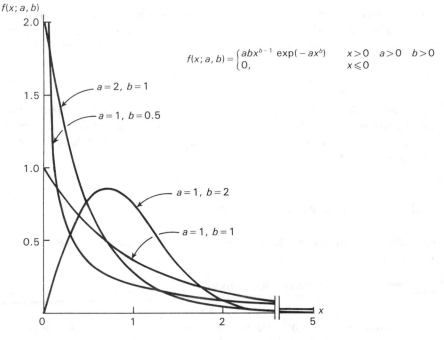

$$f(x; a, b) = \begin{cases} abx^{b-1} \exp(-ax^b) & x>0 \quad a>0 \quad b>0 \\ 0, & x \leqslant 0 \end{cases}$$

Figure 8.19   Weibull distributions

When $\beta = 1$, we obtain the exponential distribution, a special case of the Weibull distribution. So the exponential distribution is characteristic of a constant hazard rate. It is useful for describing the life of certain electrical and electronic equipment, and also for describing failures (due to any mode) of complex assemblies which are repaired, in which case, the characteristic life (η) represents the (constant) mean time between failures for repairable systems, and mean time to failure for non-repairable systems.

When $\beta > 5$, the Weibull distribution is characterized by an increasing *HR* and is useful for certain wear out processes (such as corrosion) and for describing in general the breaking strength of materials (in building codes, aircraft loads etc.).

Life testing

In general, testing to failure is the most powerful way of estimating reliability. When all the test items have failed, we obtain what is termed a 'complete' set of data. But, as can be seen from Figure 8.19, common failure distributions have quite long right-hand tails – an indication that some items from the sample data have lives considerably in excess of the mean life. In such cases, as it may be too costly to continue the test until all the sample items have failed, it could be better to terminate (or censor) the test for a particular item

218

at some convenient time. Clearly, such suspensions must be included in the analysis, because they convey information regarding reliability. We shall first demonstrate the basic steps to follow for the analysis of complete data, followed by the more general approach for the case when the failure data include suspensions (censored data).

8.19.3 Weibull analysis of complete data

The method of analysis will be demonstrated by a case study.

CASE STUDY 8.1

In order to check the durability of a particular type of filament lamp, 17 lamps were selected at random from the production line and tested to failure in a machine which simulated typical operating conditions. The failure lives of the lamps were as shown in Table 8.9. The first column of Table 8.9 shows the life of the lamps in hours, ordered from the lowest to the highest lifetime. In the second column, the order of the failures is listed (called the rank order number). Against each order number we assign a median rank (*MR*), shown in the third column of Table 8.9 and calculated by

$$MR = \frac{(ON - 0.3)}{N + 0.4} \times 100\%$$

where *ON* is the rank order number for the failure, and *N* is the sample size (in our case *N* = 17). The median rank for a particular failure life is a crude estimate of the

Table 8.9 Lamp-lives and median ranks

Life (hours)	Rank order number	Median rank (%)
32	1	4.0
34	2	9.8
90	3	15.5
103	4	21.3
170	5	27.0
179	6	32.8
232	7	38.5
360	8	44.3
360	9	50.0
360	10	55.8
360	11	61.5
415	12	67.3
603	13	73.0
603	14	78.8
717	15	84.5
718	16	90.3
1009	17	96.0

cumulative percentage of items failing by that value. For example, it is estimated that 4% of lamps fail by 32 hours, based purely on the median rank for that life.

The data can now be plotted on Weibull probability paper – see Figure 8.20. The scales of this paper are constructed so that, when median ranks are plotted against the failure lives, the result will be a straight line if the data are Weibull distributed. Figure 8.20 indicates the result. We note that, as a straight line can be drawn through the points, the Weibull distribution fits the data very well. The

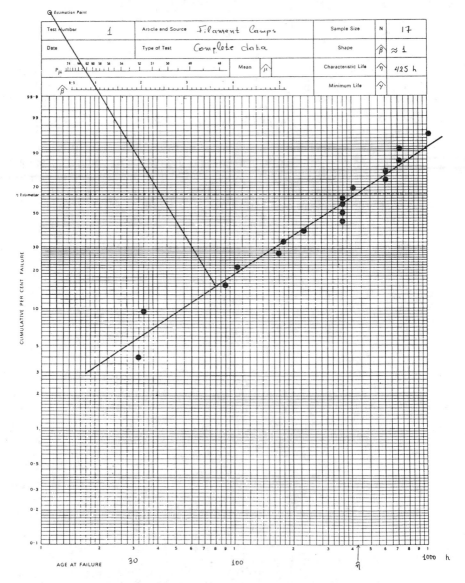

Figure 8.20 Weibull analysis of complete data (case-study 8.1)

median rank line represents the best estimate of the Weibull distribution, and we may read off any points we require. Using the straight line fitted, we can obtain estimates of failure percentages at different ages, and also estimated lives at different percentages.

For example, if we are interested in a particular age, say 700 hours (represented on the horizontal scale), then we can read off (on the vertical axis) the corresponding estimate of the percentage failed, in this case 82%. Similarly, the estimated percentage failed by 100 hours is 19%. We may go in the opposite direction; for example, 36% of the lamps are estimated to fail by 200 hours; this is equivalent to saying that a lamp is 64% reliable at 200 hours.

The estimated values of the shape β and characteristic life η, which characterize the Weibull distribution, can easily be found. The estimate of β is found by drawing a line at right angles to the best fit line which passes through the estimation point in the top left-hand corner (see Figure 8.20). The estimate of β is then read off at the point where this new line intersects the β scale. This produces a value very near to 1, suggesting that the lamps are failing with a constant hazard rate. This in turn suggests that the exponential distribution (a special case of the Weibull when $\beta = 1$) fits the present data.

The exponential fit indicates that this type of lamp is characterized by the fact that, at least in their early life (up to at least 1000 hours), the rate by which remaining items fail is constant. In other words, the lamps do not age from this point of view: if we are given a working lamp and we are considering when it might fail, its present age would be immaterial; it would make no difference whether the lamp was 1 or 100 hours old. Of course, it might make a difference if the lamp were over 1000 hours old. In our particular limited sample, all lamps failed by 1010 hours; there is no way of making inferences about the hazard rate of lamps lasting beyond 1000 hours.

The estimate of η (characteristic life) is obtained by using the mathematical property that η is the age by which 63.8% fail. A dotted horizontal line indicates the 63.8% point which, for this batch of lamps, corresponds to an age of about 425 hours. Since we are dealing with an exponential distribution, this is also the expected life (mean time to failure) of the lamps.

8.19.4 Weibull analysis of censored data

Although testing to failure is the best way of estimating reliability, cost considerations sometimes lead to the termination (censoring) of the test at some convenient time. The most general type of censoring is multiple censoring (also called arbitrary or progressive censoring), which happens when the suspensions occur at any age and are spread throughout the ordered failure lives. When, for example, a lamp's life test is terminated without failure at, say, 100 hours, this clearly means that the eventual failure life of the lamp will exceed 100 hours. Obviously this indicates something about the reliability of this type of lamp. Consequently, suspensions should be included in the reliability analysis. We will now look at this with another case study.

CASE STUDY 8.2

A set of 70 telephone lamps had to be analysed after testing which included suspensions. The results are shown in Table 8.10.

Table 8.10 has been ordered as far as possible on the basis of what is known so far. For example, we know that the failure at 4 hours must be the first failure out of the sample of 70 lamps, hence the order of 1. But there is no way of knowing the order of the failure at 230 hours, since there were 10 suspensions at 95 hours. If these suspensions were to last for more than 230 hours, the failure at 230 hours would be the second failure; if not, it could be the third or fourth etc. depending on how many of the 10 suspended lamps were to last beyond 230 hours.

Evidently, some compromise formula is needed in order to assign an order number and a median rank to all the failures when suspensions are present. Once this is achieved, the failures can be plotted, as in the case of complete data. Note that only failures are plotted on the Weibull probability plots. The method employed is to calculate a new increment (NI) in failure order number whenever any suspension is encountered. This NI is added to the previous order number (of the last failure) to give the (expected) order number of the failure following the suspension. The new increment is given by the formula

$$NI = \frac{(N+1) - OP}{1 + RS}$$

where N is the total sample size (including suspensions), OP is the order number of the previous failure, and RS is the remaining sample size, that is, the number of failed and suspended items with ages at, or higher than, the failure being considered (including the failure itself). Note that, if there were no suspensions in the sample, the above formula would always yield the value of 1.

Table 8.10 Censored data

Burning hours	Order	Result
4	1	Failure (F)
95		The test was suspended for 10 lamps (S × 10)
230	?	F
256		S × 10
266	?	F
461		S × 8
483		S × 10
486	?	F
666	?	F
713	?	F
784		S × 9
881		S × 8
1091		S × 9

Table 8.11 Censored data and median ranks

Life (hours)	Order number (increment)		Median rank (%)
4	1.0		0.99
230	2.17	(1.17)	2.66
266	3.58	(1.41)	4.65
486	5.83	(2.25)	7.85
666	8.08	(2.25)	11.10
713	10.33	(2.25)	14.30

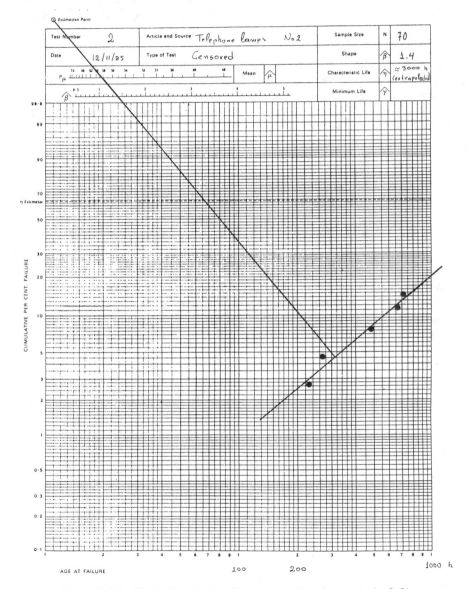

Figure 8.21 Weibull analysis of censored data (case-study 8.2)

For example, for our case study, for the failure at 230 hours we have $N = 70$, $OP = 1$ (the order number of the failure at 4 hours), and $RS = 59$ (the number of lamps with ages greater than or equal to 230 hours). Therefore

$$NI = \frac{(70 + 1) - 1}{1 + 59} = 1.17$$

This NI can now be added to the order number of the last failure (at 4 hours) to give the (expected) order number for the failure at 230 hours which will be

$$1 + 1.17 = 2.17$$

We keep on adding this increment to the previous order number for any failure that follows, until new suspensions are encountered, in which case the increment changes (the formula for NI is used again).

Now the median rank for each of the failures may be found using the same formula as for the case of complete data:

$$MR = \frac{(ON - 0.3)}{N + 0.4} \times 100\%$$

where ON is the (real or expected) order number for that failure. For example, for the failure at 230 hours

$$MR = \frac{(2.17 - 0.3)}{70 + 0.4} \times 100\% = 2.66\%$$

Using the formulae for NI and MR, we can now construct Table 8.11. We can now plot the results of Table 8.11 on Weibull probability paper (as before) to obtain the Weibull plot of Figure 8.21. Note that despite the small amount of failure data, a reasonably straight line is obtained, with $\beta = 1.4$. This value of β indicates that the lamps are failing with a slightly increasing hazard rate.

Sources of Further Information (Part II)

Adair, J. (1984), *Effective Leadership*, Gower: Aldershot.

Adair, J. (1986), *Action Centred Leadership*, Gower: Aldershot.

AT & T (1987), *Process Quality Management and Improvement Guidelines*, AT & T Laboratories: Short Hills, NJ.

Box, G.E.P., Hunter, W.G. and Hunter, J.S. (1978), *Statistics for Experimenters*, Wiley: New York.

Caulcutt, R. (1982), *Statistics for Research and Development*, Chapman and Hall: London.

Cullen, J. and Hollingum, J. (1987), *Implementing Total Quality*, IFS Publications: Kempston.

Dale, B. (1989), *Tools and Techniques for TQM*, IFS Publications: Kempston.

Daniel, C. (1959), 'Use of half-normal plots in interpreting factorial two-level experiments', *Technometrics*, **1**, pp. 311–41.

Davies, O.L. and Goldsmith, P.L. (1972), *Statistical Methods for Research Production*, Oliver and Boyd: Edinburgh.

Dey, A. (1985), *Orthogonal Fractional Factorial Designs*, Wiley Eastern: New Delhi.

Duncan, D.B. (1956), 'Multiple range and multiple F-tests', *Biometrics*, **11**.

Edosomwan, J.A. (1988), *Productivity and Quality Improvement*, IFS Publications: Kempston.

Fisher, R.A. (1935), *The Design of Experiments*, Oliver and Boyd: Edinburgh.

Fordyce, J.K. (1986), *Managing with People*, Raymond Weil, Addison-Wesley: Reading, MA.

Garvin, D.A. (1988), *Managing Quality*, Free Press: New York.

Hicks, C.R. (1982), *Fundamental Concepts of Design of Experiments*, 3rd edn, Holt, Rinehart and Winston: New York.

Juran, J.M. (1984), *Managerial Breakthrough*, McGraw-Hill: New York.

Juran, J.M. and Gryna, F.M. (1988) (eds), *Juran's Quality Control Handbook*, 3rd edn, McGraw-Hill: New York.

Noon, J. (1987), *'A' Time*, Van Nostrand Reinhold: London.

Plackett, R.L. and Burman, J.P. (1946), The design of optimum multifactorial experiments, *Biometrica*, **33**, pp. 305–25.

Rothschild, V. and Logothetis, N. (1986), *Probability Distributions*, Wiley: New York.

Snedecor, G.W. and Cochran, W.G. (1980), *Statistical Methods*, 7th edn, Iowa State University Press: Ames, IA.

Wonnacott, T.H. and Wonnacott, R.J. (1977), *Introductory Statistics*, 3rd edn, Wiley: New York.

PART III
Technical Tools
for Quality
Techniques for On-Line
Quality Control

A state of Statistical Control is not a natural state for a process; it is an achievement.

W.E. Deming

In this part of the book (Chapters 9–10) we present the technique of statistical process control (SPC), representative of on-line quality control methods. The technique is equally applicable in manufacturing (during production) as well as in service industries.

Supporting tools as well as alternatives to SPC are also outlined and assessed.

Statistical Process
Control

You have to be able to mathematically compute Quality.

Frederick W. Smith, Federal Express Corporation

■ 9.1 Introduction

The traditional methods of quality control in a manufacturing process have been those of 100% inspection and sampling inspection. Both methods concentrate on the final output of the process. When the products were safety critical, or when the production was carried out in small quantities, 100% inspection of the final output was the type of quality control usually preferred. However, even 100% inspection is not 100% reliable and, on some occasions, full inspection was carried out twice or more.

When the production consisted of large consignments for which full inspection was prohibitive in terms of cost and time, sampling inspection was the preferred quality control method. The method involves the inspection of only a sample from the whole batch, and from the quality of the sample an estimate is made of the quality of the whole batch. There are various refinements to sampling plans; one of these is when samples are taken until there is a sufficient amount of confidence to accept or reject the batch. But, always, there is an uncertainty involved, and this has two aspects:

1. There is a chance that a batch may be rejected although it is not as bad as it appears from the sample.
2. There is a chance that a batch is accepted although it is worse than originally thought on the basis of the sample.

The risk involved in (1) is equivalent to the probability of Type I error (wrong rejection), and the risk involved in (2) is equivalent to the probability of Type II error (wrong acceptance). Recall that these types of risk were first encountered in Section 6.4 when the topic of hypothesis testing was discussed.

Whatever the sampling plan, the fact remains that the producer has to accept a certain amount of risk that some defective products will slip through the quality control net. This contradicts the principle of total quality, and many companies committed to TQM ideas are increasing their efforts to discover and use alternative methods of quality control which will give their products a high degree of precision and reliability.

A valuable alternative is provided by the technique of statistical process control (SPC), whose aim is to prevent defective work being produced by focusing on the producing process rather than on the final product. This is definitely superior to sampling inspection plans whose only aim is to trap the defects after they have been produced, a feature which makes this type of quality control an appraisal procedure rather than a quality improvement effort.

Nevertheless, sampling plans and SPC have a common characteristic. As in the case of sampling plans, SPC attempts to utilize the connection between the properties of a sample and the properties of the parent population. The difference lies in the fact that SPC provides the operator with an opportunity of correcting or appropriately tuning the production process in time to avoid whole batches being rejected later. It also encourages continual process improvement, with this improvement being reflected in the product as well as in the production equipment. SPC is a step forward in the evolution of quality control systems but, in terms of effort concentration, it is actually a step backwards from full inspection of the final product to the production process. Although the technicalities of SPC have been known for a long time (Shewhart, 1931), it was not until Japanese industry proved the usefulness of SPC in practice (stimulated by Deming's teachings) that interest in SPC revived in the West. Deming's involvement in the teaching of the subject has enhanced the reputation of SPC as an extremely important technical tool for quality management.

In Section 1.5.2, the idea of the control chart, the main tool of SPC, was briefly discussed. A distinction was made between special or assignable causes and common or unassignable causes. Violations of the limits in a control chart (see, for example, Figure 9.1), or the presence of specific patterns within the control limits, are indicative of special causes of variations which require local action, normally (but not exclusively) by the operator. Common causes of variation behave like a constant system of random causes requiring action on the system, and are normally a management responsibility.

The ability of the control chart to distinguish between special and common causes, is what makes SPC a necessary and fair tool for the management of any process. It helps to avoid unnecessary blame and recrimination by assigning the appropriate responsibilities to the appropriate people. Deming has been known to say that the first control charts to be drawn in any organization should not be on shop-floor processes but on the data which land on the chief executive's desk, such as figures on budgets, forecasts, absenteeism and accidents. Are these processes in control? If so, are they being improved, or are they merely being tampered with, possibly with much worse results?

Although the achievement of statistical control is an important requirement of SPC, it is not the only one. As specification limits cannot be ignored, it is a requirement to have capable processes – satisfying the customer's

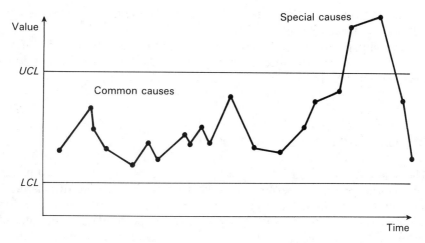

Figure 9.1 SPC control charts

requirements (see Figure 9.2) – as well as processes which are under control. Even though capability and control are quite distinct, there it a close association between the two in their relevance to the principle of continuous improvement. There is also a definite priority order: first ensure consistency and stability (statistical control), then take care of the capability issue (meeting the specification).

There are two types of control charts: charts for variables and charts for attributes. These two types will be examined in Sections 9.3 and 9.4 respectively. Whatever the type, the rules for recognizing the existence of special

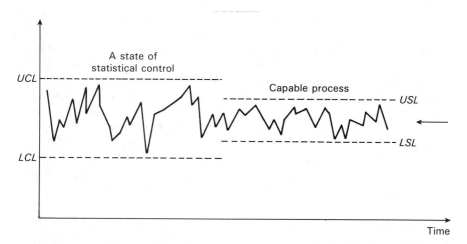

Figure 9.2 A process in control as well as capable

causes of variation are the same; these will be noted in the examples used and will be summarized in Section 9.5.

We will start (Section 9.2) with the most important prerequisite of any control chart: the data collection plan. This needs to be carefully developed for the gathering, recording and plotting of the data.

■ 9.2 Data collection plan

The objective of the control chart is to obtain a reliable and unbiased picture of how the process is performing. The success of this objective naturally depends on the reliability and lack of bias of the collected data. It is therefore important that, before any SPC study is carried out, careful plans for data collection, adequate education of the operating personnel and well-maintained/calibrated measuring equipment are available. The importance of the collection of clean data can never be overstated, because this is the only way in which an accurate reflection of process performance can be achieved.

The factors to be taken into consideration for the plan are as follows:

1. **The quality characteristic:** This will have to be easily measurable and representative of a key operation which has a significant impact on factory and business performance.

2. **The type of data to be collected:** The data will either be expressed quantitatively and measured on a continuous scale (variable data) or expressed in a yes/no format, that is, in the form go/no go, pass/fail, conforming/non-conforming etc. (attribute data). Depending on the data type, a different type of control chart will have to be used.

3. **The sample or subgroup size, and the frequency of sample collection:** These depend on the type of data, practical experience and past knowledge of the process. Some initial experimentation and consideration of statistical criteria may be required. There are no strict guidelines to be followed and there is no need to always keep to the same number for sample size and sampling frequency. The only guideline to be followed is that these numbers should reflect the inherent variability in the process. It is therefore natural that numbers should be higher at the beginning of the SPC effort, when little information is available about the process variability. When further process data become available and confidence is built up, these numbers can decrease. Nevertheless, for variable data, frequent SPC applications in the automotive-related industry have led to widespread acceptance of a sample size of 5 and a one-hourly sampling frequency. For attribute data, a much larger sample size is necessary, large enough to allow several items per subgroup to appear on average. For example, in a process running with a 2% defective level, a sample size of at least 200

is required to allow a mean of at least 2 defectives per sample. The sampling frequency will then depend on the ability to collect such a sample.

4. **The number of subgroups to be used in the chart**: For the purpose of initially obtaining an adequate idea of the variability inherent in the process for the construction of the original control limits, there is a widespread acceptance that at least 20 subgroups need to be collected. Subsequently, in order for the control chart to reflect the most recent process performance, the control limits should be recalculated for the latest 20 subgroups. There is nothing sacrosanct about the number 20 or the number 5 in the subgroup size. It so happens that, in various relevant statistical analyses of case-studies in the past, it has been found that these numbers are appropriate enough to indicate important changes in the process yet, at the same time, to smooth out smaller or irrelevant changes.

5. **Costs**: Every improvement effort should be cost-effective. Before embarking on any SPC programme, an estimate should be made of the cost of taking samples, the cost of analysis and investigation, and the cost of correction of special causes of variation. This can avoid unpleasant surprises later and can ensure the continuation of the effort.

■ 9.3 Variables charts

The guidelines for control charts for variables (scalar measurements that are continuously variable, such as temperature, thickness, amount of leakage, weights, sales etc.) are based on the properties of the normal distribution, for which over 99% of the values fall within a band of 6 standard deviations –

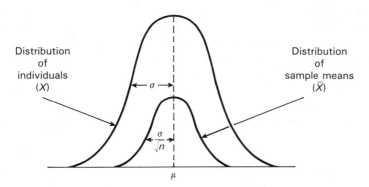

Figure 9.3 Principles of the central limit theorem

plus or minus 3 standard deviations from the central line. If one deals with subgroup/sample averages, the algorithms of the normal distribution can be applied. This follows from the principle of the central limit theorem (see Section 6.6.1) which states the following: 'Irrespective of the distribution of the individual readings, the sample means are normally distributed with the same mean but narrower standard deviation than that of the individual readings' (see Figure 9.3). Thus, some nice properties of the normal distribution hold for the population of the sample means. In particular, we can say that 99.73% of the sample means fall within plus or minus 3 standard deviations (*SD*) measured outwards from the central value (the grand mean of the sample means). These ±3 *SD* lines (see Figure 9.4) define the control limits in the control chart. The probability of a point (a sample mean) falling outside the control limits is equal to 0.0027, roughly 3 in a 1000 and is so slight that, if it does occur, it can be assumed that it has occurred not by chance, but because a special cause of variation is present.

The recognition that an event has a very slight probability of occurring by chance, forms the basis for the determination of the presence of a special cause of variation. So in taking action, one looks for unlikely events. The presence of a sample mean outside the control limits *is* an unlikely event, providing there is sufficient statistical evidence that a special cause (or causes) of variation is present.

The principles of the normal distribution provide the basis for most of the SPC rules for taking action. For example, action should be taken when there is a concentration of points near the control lines of the chart, rather than near the central line. This is based on a property of the normal distribution according to which 68.3% (approximately two-thirds) of the readings should lie within ±1 *SD* from the mean (approximately the middle third of the total range of 6 *SD*).

Many SPC practitioners prefer to also utilize the *warning limits*: these are lines drawn at ±2 *SD* from the mean, in addition to the control limits (at ±3 *SD* from the mean) which are now called action limits. The warning lines can easily be drawn at two-thirds of the distance (outwards) between the central line and each control limit. The guideline (not a universally accepted rule) associated with the warning limits is that action should be taken when at least two consecutive points fall outside the warning lines. Other unlikely events include the presence of non-random patterns or trends on the chart, such as a cyclic pattern, a number of consecutive points (rule of thumb: 7 points – hence the name *rule of seven*) all falling on one side of the central line, or all increasing or all decreasing.

All the above are associated with a very low probability of occurrence and should therefore prompt some kind of action. An action may not necessarily mean action for elimination (of the special cause). It could mean a preventive action, or simply investigation; the latter applies particularly to situations where a special cause is a cause that contributes positively to the improvement effort and should be emulated in the future.

From this

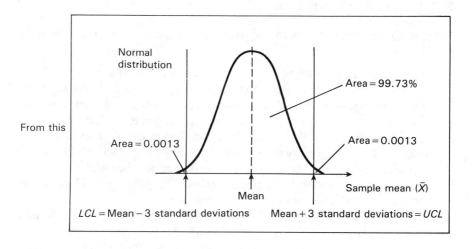

to this

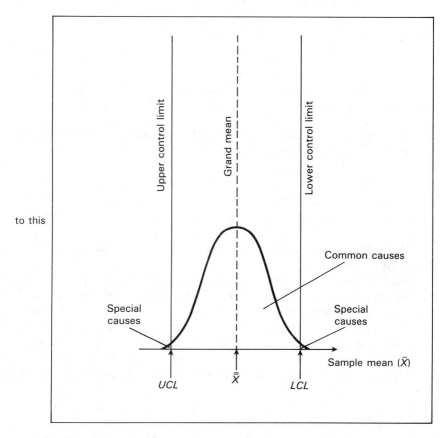

Figure 9.4 Principles of the control chart

9.3.1 The *X*-bar and *R*-charts

For generating control charts for variable data, the following procedure could be applied.

1. During normal production, record the measurements of k samples of size n. Typical values for k and n are respectively 20 and 5. These numbers reflect the guideline that, for an initial process study with variable data, at least 20 samples of size 5 are required to adequately reflect the natural variability inherent in the process. The sampling frequency depends on the volume of production. A typical frequency would be 1 sample per hour, although engineering common-sense and past experience with the process should indicate what the time period between sampling should be to allow the inherent process variability to express itself.

2. For each of the k samples, record the mean (arithmetic average) $\bar{X}_i$ and the range (largest minus smallest value) R_i, $i = 1, \ldots, k$.

3. Compute the overall average $\bar{\bar{X}}$ and the average range R as:

$$\bar{\bar{X}} = \frac{\sum\limits_{i=1}^{k} \bar{X}_i}{k}$$

$$\bar{R} = \frac{\sum\limits_{i=1}^{k} R_i}{k}$$

4. Calculate the upper control limits (UCL) and lower control limits (LCL) for the $\bar{X}$-chart (or X-bar-chart) and the R-chart as

	$\bar{X}$-chart	R-chart
UCL	$\bar{\bar{X}} + A_2\bar{R}$	$D_4\bar{R}$
LCL	$\bar{\bar{X}} - A_2\bar{R}$	$D_3\bar{R}$

The coefficients A_2, D_3 and D_4 depend on the sample size n and are given in Table 9.1.

The band width of values covered by the control limits in the $\bar{X}$-chart is the approximation to a band width of 6 standard deviations in the normal population of sample averages. The distribution of the sample ranges is not normal but skewed, especially for small sample sizes. But, although it is not statistically valid to think in terms of the 'mean $\pm SD$', it is still statistically possible to determine constants (such as D_3 and D_4) which will enable the limits to be fixed at probability levels of approximately 3 in a 1000.

5. Plot the $\bar{X}$-chart and R-chart. If all $\bar{X}_i$ and R_i values (for each sample) fall randomly within their respective control limits, the process is considered to be in statistical control. Otherwise, special causes of variability are present and have to be investigated and eliminated.

Table 9.1   Coefficients for variables charts ($\bar{X}$- and R-charts)

Sample size n	Control limit coefficients			Divisors for estimation of σ
	Average chart A_2	Range chart D_3	D_4	d_2
2	1.880	0	3.267	1.128
3	1.023	0	2.574	1.693
4	0.729	0	2.282	2.059
5	0.577	0	2.114	2.326
6	0.483	0	2.004	2.534
7	0.419	0.076	1.924	2.704
8	0.373	0.136	1.864	2.847
9	0.337	0.184	1.816	2.970
10	0.308	0.223	1.777	3.078
11	0.285	0.256	1.744	3.173
12	0.266	0.283	1.717	3.258
13	0.249	0.307	1.693	3.336
14	0.235	0.328	1.672	3.407
15	0.223	0.347	1.653	3.472
16	0.212	0.363	1.637	3.532
17	0.203	0.378	1.622	3.588
18	0.194	0.391	1.608	3.640
19	0.187	0.403	1.597	3.689
20	0.180	0.415	1.585	3.735
21	0.173	0.425	1.575	3.778
22	0.167	0.434	1.566	3.819
23	0.162	0.443	1.557	3.858
24	0.157	0.451	1.548	3.895
25	0.153	0.459	1.541	3.931

Control chart rationale

In an $\bar{X}$-chart, the distance of the control limits from the grand mean $\bar{\bar{X}}$ is a measure of the inherent variability of the process at a particular period of time. Consequently, the control limits reflect the performance of the process at the time when the data are collected. Our conclusions from using the control chart are associated with a certain amount of confidence; to be exact, with 99.73% confidence. It is fairly obvious, therefore, how the principles of confidence intervals (see Section 6.3) apply here. Indeed, as we have already seen, the formula for the control limits for the mean

$$\bar{\bar{X}} \pm A_2\bar{R} \tag{9.1}$$

is equivalent to 'mean $\pm$ 3 SD', with the 3 SD being approximated by $A_2\bar{R}$. This is a reminder of the general formula (6.7) for confidence intervals (Section 6.3):

$$CI(\Theta): [\theta \pm t(df; \alpha)SE(\theta)]$$

which was used to obtain formula (6.8):

$$CI(\mu): [\bar{y} \pm t(df; \alpha)s/\sqrt{n}]$$

For the case of the control limits, $\bar{y}$ (or θ) represents the mean of the sample means $\bar{\bar{X}}$, $s/\sqrt{n}$ (or $SE(\theta)$) represents the standard deviation of $\bar{X}$, and $t(df; \alpha)$ assumes the value of the normal percentage point ($=3$) corresponding to 99.73% confidence (see Appendix A, Table A3).

From the above, it is clear that an alternative to formula (9.1) is given by

$$\bar{\bar{X}} \pm 3\hat{\sigma}/\sqrt{n} \tag{9.2}$$

where n is the sample size and $\hat{\sigma}$ is an estimate of the population standard deviation σ (of the individual X's). Now σ can be approximated by $\bar{R}/d_2$, where d_2 depends on the sample size n and can be obtained from the last column of Table 9.1.

CASE STUDY 9.1

A quality characteristic for a manufacturing process making plastic insulated cables was the breakdown voltage, which had to be over 2.2 kV. In order to monitor and control this characteristic at satisfactory levels, an SPC study was undertaken. Five cables from each daily batch were measured for their breakdown voltage (sample size = 5). The results from the samples for the first 20 batches (over 20 working days) are shown in Table 9.2. The sample mean, sample range and sample standard deviation for each of the 20 samples are also shown. The

Table 9.2 Breakdown voltage data (case-study 9.1)

Sample no.	Data (kV)					Mean ($\bar{X}$)	Range (R)	Standard deviation (s)
1	2.70	2.80	2.45	2.62	2.90	2.694	0.45	0.172
2	3.01	2.90	3.20	3.13	2.77	3.002	0.43	0.173
3	2.72	3.05	2.68	3.11	2.78	2.868	0.43	0.198
4	2.50	2.68	3.13	2.40	2.92	2.726	0.73	0.300
5	2.30	2.80	2.93	2.69	3.16	2.776	0.86	0.318
6	2.94	2.75	3.15	3.22	3.30	3.072	0.55	0.224
7	3.32	3.25	2.95	2.85	3.02	3.078	0.47	0.200
8	2.86	2.65	3.09	2.94	2.96	2.900	0.44	0.162
9	2.55	2.73	2.96	2.75	2.87	2.772	0.41	0.155
10	2.98	3.28	3.17	3.40	3.50	3.266	0.52	0.202
11	3.05	2.90	2.75	3.30	3.05	3.010	0.55	0.204
12	2.75	2.95	2.65	3.10	3.08	2.906	0.45	0.200
13	2.50	2.78	2.45	2.33	2.45	2.502	0.45	0.168
14	2.80	2.75	2.30	2.55	2.25	2.530	0.55	0.251
15	3.30	3.05	3.15	2.98	2.75	3.046	0.55	0.205
16	3.15	2.92	3.05	2.72	2.45	2.858	0.70	0.279
17	2.95	2.82	2.55	2.34	2.22	2.576	0.73	0.309
18	2.90	3.35	3.20	2.85	2.95	3.050	0.50	0.215
19	2.85	2.78	2.94	2.63	2.56	2.752	0.38	0.156
20	2.73	2.66	2.52	2.65	2.47	2.606	0.26	0.107

sample data of Table 9.2, along with the associated sample means and ranges, are shown at the lower part of the control chart for variables of Figure 9.5.

We can now plot the sample means, $\bar{X}$, and the sample ranges, R, on the corresponding chart. Note that, at this point, two separate run charts (see Section 8.12) have been obtained. These are useful for determining performance trends within a certain period of time, but they are not capable of showing whether and when action needs to be taken for process improvement. For this, we need statistically-based limits superimposed on the run chart. These limits, the control limits, are now easy to obtain on the basis of the available data and the associated sample statistics. Indeed, we can obtain $\bar{\bar{X}}$ as the average of the 20 sample means $\bar{X}$ by

$$\bar{\bar{X}} = \frac{2.694 + 3.002 + \cdots + 2.606}{20} = 2.8495$$

We can also obtain $\bar{R}$ as the average of the 20 sample ranges R by

$$\bar{R} = \frac{0.45 + 0.43 + \cdots + 0.26}{20} = 0.5205$$

Since the sample size is 5, from Table 9.1 we obtain

$$A_2 = 0.577, D_3 = 0, D_4 = 2.115$$

We are now in a position to calculate the upper and lower control limits for the mean and the range as

$$UCL(\text{mean}) = \bar{\bar{X}} + A_2\bar{R} = 2.8495 + 0.577 \times 0.5205 = 3.1498$$
$$LCL(\text{mean}) = \bar{\bar{X}} - A_2\bar{R} = 2.5492$$

Also,

$$UCL(\text{range}) = D_4\bar{R} = 2.115 \times 0.5205 = 1.1009$$
$$LCL(\text{range}) = D_3\bar{R} = 0 \times 0.5205 = 0.0$$

The control charts for the mean and the range can now be completed by superimposing the relevant control limits.

The control chart for the range (bottom chart) indicates that the process is in statistical control as far as variability is concerned. If anything, recent results show that the performance is improving in terms of within batch variation. However, the control chart for the mean (top chart) indicates an out of control situation for average performance. There is a better than normal performance on the 10th day, and a worse than normal performance on the 13th and 14th day. Following a materials investigation it was found that the insulation material used for the cables during the last 10 days of the monitoring was supplied by a different supplier from the one used for the first 10 days.

A cyclic behaviour is also apparent on the mean chart. This was connected with the use of certain measuring equipment at particular times within each week, something that prompted further investigation. As a result of the SPC study, a decision was taken to revert to the original supplier of the insulation material, and also to put more effort into the calibration and maintenance of the measuring equipment.

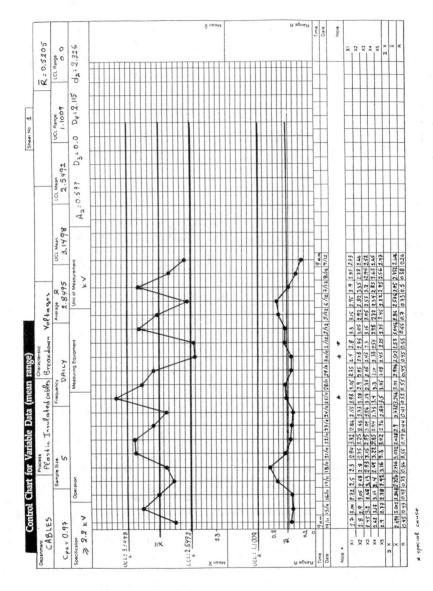

Figure 9.5 SPC study for breakdown voltages (mean/range)

Finding and eliminating a special cause of variation might not be easy. If it cannot be tracked down, it must be assumed that the cause is due to the system, and the problem has to be accepted as a short-term approach to get the control chart operating. During subsequent monitoring, one should always try to identify the circumstances which influence the process for the better, or to take action immediately when another out of control point is observed.

9.3.2 The X-bar and s-charts

The main advantage of using the range as a measure of within sample variability is the fact that it is very easy to calculate. However, assuming the existence of some computing capability, the use of standard deviation is a preferable alternative. The procedure is exactly the same as for the case of the X-bar and R-chart except that different coefficients are used for the calculation of the control limits. This will be demonstrated using the data from case-study 9.1 (Section 9.3.1).

For each of the 20 available samples we calculate the sample standard deviation using the formula (see Section 6.2, page 110):

$$s = \sqrt{\frac{\Sigma(X - \bar{X})^2}{n - 1}}$$

The results are shown in the last column of Table 9.2. As in the case of $\bar{R}$, a central value for s is needed. This is obtained by the following formula:

$$\bar{s} = \frac{\Sigma s}{k}$$

where k is the number of samples, in this case 20. Using the values from Table 9.2 we have

$$\bar{s} = \frac{(0.172 + 0.173 + \cdots + 0.107)}{20} = 0.2099$$

The control limits for the $\bar{X}$-chart are given by

$$UCL(\bar{X}) = \bar{\bar{X}} + A_3\bar{s}$$
$$LCL(\bar{X}) = \bar{\bar{X}} - A_3\bar{s}$$

whereas the control limits for the s-chart are given by

$$UCL(s) = B_4\bar{s}$$
$$LCL(s) = B_3\bar{s}$$

where the coefficients A_3, B_3 and B_4 depend on the sample size n and can be found in Table 9.3. For our example, since $n = 5$, we have

$$A_3 = 1.427, \ B_3 = 0, \ B_4 = 2.089$$

Table 9.3 Coefficients for variables charts ($\bar{X}$- and s-charts)

Sample size n	Control limit coefficients Average chart A_3	s-chart B_3	B_4	Divisors for estimation of σ c_4
2	2.659	0	3.267	0.7979
3	1.954	0	2.568	0.8862
4	1.628	0	2.266	0.9213
5	1.427	0	2.089	0.9400
6	1.287	0.030	1.970	0.9515
7	1.182	0.118	1.882	0.9594
8	1.099	0.185	1.815	0.9650
9	1.032	0.239	1.761	0.9693
10	0.975	0.284	1.716	0.9727
11	0.927	0.321	1.679	0.9754
12	0.886	0.354	1.646	0.9776
13	0.850	0.382	1.618	0.9794
14	0.817	0.406	1.594	0.9810
15	0.789	0.428	1.572	0.9823
16	0.763	0.448	1.552	0.9835
17	0.739	0.466	1.534	0.9845
18	0.718	0.482	1.518	0.9854
19	0.698	0.497	1.503	0.9862
20	0.680	0.510	1.490	0.9869
21	0.663	0.523	1.477	0.9876
22	0.647	0.534	1.466	0.9882
23	0.633	0.545	1.455	0.9887
24	0.619	0.555	1.445	0.9892
25	0.606	0.565	1.435	0.9896

and so

$$UCL(\bar{X}) = \bar{\bar{X}} + A_3\bar{s} = 2.8495 + 1.427 \times 0.2099 = 3.1490$$
$$LCL(\bar{X}) = \bar{\bar{X}} - A_3\bar{s} = 2.5499$$

and

$$UCL(s) = B_4\bar{s} = 2.089 \times 0.2099 = 0.4385$$
$$LCL(s) = B_3\bar{s} = 0.0$$

The results are depicted in Figure 9.6.

Note that the control limits for the mean on the basis of s are almost identical to the control limits calculated on the basis of the range (see Figure 9.5). In addition, the control chart for the standard deviation, although numerically different from that for the range, provides conclusions identical to those of the range chart in Figure 9.5.

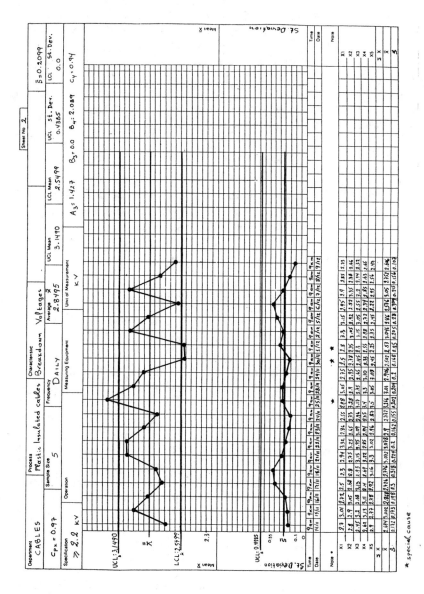

Figure 9.6 SPC study for breakdown voltages (mean/standard deviation)

9.3.3 Capability

Once the process is brought under statistical control by detecting and eliminating special causes of variation, its performance is predictable; its capability to meet customers' expectations can now be assessed. For this, we need measures which express the relationship between the specified *tolerance* (allowed deviation from the nominal) and the *process variability*.

Let $\hat{\sigma}$ be an estimate of the process standard deviation which can be approximated by $\bar{R}/d_2$, where d_2 can be found in Table 9.1. In particular, when $n = 5$, then approximately $6\hat{\sigma} = 2.58\bar{R}$. Note that $\hat{\sigma}$ estimates the standard deviation of the distribution of the individual X's.

The *capability index*, C_p, is defined as

$$C_p = \frac{\text{tolerance}}{6\hat{\sigma}} = \frac{USL - LSL}{6\hat{\sigma}}$$

where USL and LSL are respectively the upper and lower specification limits. The equation above provides an indication of how capable the process is, despite its inherent variability, of meeting the specifications expected by the customer.

Another useful capability index is defined by

$$C_{pk} = \begin{cases} \dfrac{USL - \bar{\bar{X}}}{3\hat{\sigma}} & \text{when } \bar{\bar{X}} \text{ is above nominal} \\[2ex] \dfrac{\bar{\bar{X}} - LSL}{3\hat{\sigma}} & \text{when } \bar{\bar{X}} \text{ is below nominal} \end{cases}$$

Note that when the process is running on nominal, then $C_{pk} = C_p$. For the process to be capable, the values of both the above measures have to be larger than 1.

If sample standard deviations are being used instead of sample ranges, then an estimate of the process standard deviation is given by $\hat{\sigma} = s/c_4$, where c_4 depends on n and can be found in Table 9.3. The same formulae for C_p and C_{pk} apply.

We can deduce that the process in case-study 9.1 is not only out of statistical control but also incapable. Indeed, if the range is used, from Table 9.1, $d_2 = 2.326$, and so

$$\hat{\sigma} = \frac{\bar{R}}{d_2} = \frac{0.5205}{2.326} = 0.2238$$

The specification demands a breakdown voltage of at least 2.2 kV. Therefore $LSL = 2.2$, and so

$$C_{pk} = \frac{\bar{\bar{X}} - LSL}{3\hat{\sigma}} = \frac{2.8495 - 2.2}{3 \times 0.2238} = 0.97$$

Since $C_{pk} < 1$, the process is incapable, that is, not capable of always meeting the specification. A similar result is obtained when s (and c_4) is used.

9.3.4 Moving mean/range chart

There are continuous processes whose quality characteristics provide only one value for analysis. For example, the production processes of chemicals, oils, paint or coils of aluminium, steel etc. do not provide the circumstances of proper sampling required in a typical X-bar- and R-chart. In these cases, use is made of a moving mean/range chart.

In such a chart, a pseudo-sample is created, making use of the new as well as the most recent values. A typical sample size is 3, where the sample consists of the new and the two previous values of the quality characteristic. From there on, the usual guidelines for an SPC study apply. For example, the sample means and sampling ranges will need to be calculated; these will be moving averages and moving ranges, and Tables 9.1 and 9.3 will have to be utilized for the calculation of the control limits.

The only consequence of the creation of the pseudo-samples is that the resulting sample statistics are not independent of each other. Therefore, certain action rules are less applicable to this type of chart. In particular the rule of seven should not be applied rigidly, unless it is modified to signify seven *independent* consecutive points, for which a minimum of $7n$ data values is required, with n being the sample size. For example, if the 5th point on the moving mean chart is the average of the 7th, the 6th and the 5th observation ($n = 3$), then the next *independent* point on the chart is the 8th point which is the average of the 10th, the 9th and the 8th observation.

A sample size of 3, although typical for a moving mean/range chart, does not have to be followed rigidly. The determining factor for the sample size is the time between sample readings, which can be as large as the related requirements allow: it can be as small as 2 or as large as 20. If high sensitivity is required, or if there is a long delay between readings, individual values may have to be plotted on the mean chart, although sample statistics will still have to be utilized for the determination of the control limits. The larger the sample size, the smoother the effect on the chart.

CASE STUDY 9.2

The management of a mechanical engineering department wanted to monitor the weekly performance of the department's workforce. The total time taken to complete the weekly projects was compared to an estimated time for particular projects. The estimation was based on past experience and was considered reliable and unbiased. The performance was viewed as satisfactory if, consistently, the weekly difference between the estimated and the actual working time was not less than − 10 hours.

An SPC study was undertaken with the purpose of monitoring and analysing the deviation from the expected working time, the deviation being considered as the quality characteristic. The performance was monitored for 20 weeks. Only a single value for each week (estimated weekly time − actual weekly time) was available, and a moving mean/range chart was therefore utilized. A sample size of 3 was chosen; consequently there were only 18 pseudo-subgroups available for the calculation of the control limits. Note that, since $n = 3$, from Table 9.1

$$A_3 = 1.023, \ D_3 = 0, \ D_4 = 2.575 \text{ and } d_2 = 1.693$$

Figure 9.7 shows the data, the associated sample statistics, and the resulting (moving mean/range) charts. We note that the weekly performance of the work-force is in statistical control: all points fall randomly within the control limits for both charts. However, the capability index C_{pk} is equal to 0.51. This indicates that the process 'working time of the workforce', although in control, is incapable. The process is in control, therefore predictable, but in need of further improvement. The SPC results indicate that improvement in the working time performance is possible, but can only materialize through action on the system, being a management responsibility.

For example, the first thing that has to be checked is the possibility of underestimating the complexity of the weekly projects. If there is no doubt of the reliability of the estimation procedure, the management has to improve the working conditions, the training procedures, and performance of the equipment through better maintenance etc. The satisfactory individual results could also be studied. For example, the performance of the 8th week, viewed as a single point, lies beyond the upper control limit. So one could study the working conditions in the 8th week and try to emulate them in the future.

9.3.5 SPC for large samples

There are occasions when the collection of data is easy and is achievable in a short period of time and in large quantities. In these cases, Tables 9.1 and 9.3, which deal with small sample sizes ($n < 26$), cannot be utilized. Nevertheless, we can still calculate control limits for the mean based on the general formula 'mean $\pm$ 3 *SD*' approximated by (9.2):

$$\bar{\bar{X}} \pm 3\sigma/\sqrt{\bar{n}}$$

which, in the general case of large k and different sample sizes $n_1, \ldots, n_k$ will have the form

$$\bar{\bar{X}} \pm 3S_p/\sqrt{\bar{n}} \tag{9.3}$$

where $\bar{n}$ is the average of all sample sizes:

$$\bar{n} = \frac{n_1 + \cdots + n_k}{k}$$

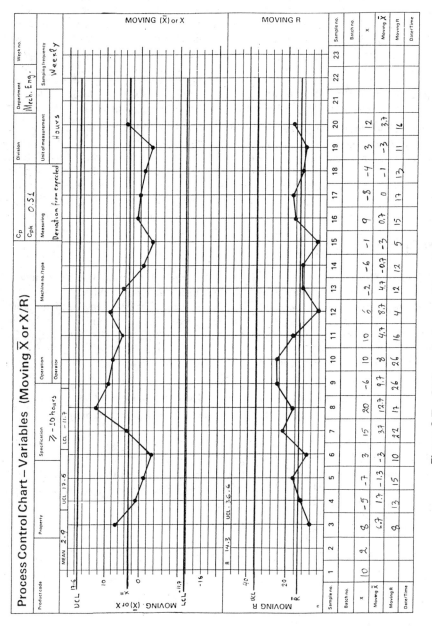

Figure 9.7 SPC study for working-time performance

$\bar{\bar{X}}$ is the usual grand average of all sample means, and S_p is an estimate of the pooled standard deviation of the process; this can be approximated on the basis of all standard deviations $s_1, \ldots, s_k$ of the k samples as follows:

$$S_p = \sqrt{\frac{(n_1 - 1)s_1^2 + \cdots + (n_k - 1)s_k^2}{(n_1 - 1) + \cdots + (n_k - 1)}}$$

Note that the above is a generalization of formula (6.10) from Section 6.3.2, and represents a pooled estimate of the within sample variability.

We can also calculate control limits for the process variability. Assuming a normal distribution, these limits can be approximated by

$$S_p \times \frac{\sqrt{2\bar{n} - 3} \pm 3}{\sqrt{2n - 2}} \tag{9.4}$$

CASE STUDY 9.3

A self-regulating monitoring system for detecting and timing the clearance of certain types of faults on telephone lines has provided large-size monthly samples of the time taken to clear the faults. The sample sizes, sample means and standard deviations are shown in Table 9.4. The data are expressed in hours and decimals; for example, '1.60' means 1 hour and 60% of the hour, that is, 1 hour and 36 minutes.

Table 9.4 Monthly statistics for fault-clearing times

Month	Sample size	Sample mean	Sample standard deviation
Oct 88	321	2.31	3.26
Nov 88	358	1.61	2.82
Dec 88	275	2.17	3.22
Jan 89	346	1.91	3.03
Feb 89	318	1.92	3.97
Mar 89	376	1.79	2.89
Apr 89	386	1.71	3.06
May 89	442	1.80	3.03
Jun 89	464	1.51	2.82
Jul 89	410	1.95	2.93
Aug 89	388	1.56	2.89
Sep 89	409	1.63	3.20
Oct 89	329	1.61	2.96
Nov 89	449	1.54	2.87
Dec 89	367	2.87	3.19
Jan 90	373	1.61	3.23
Feb 90	373	1.79	3.00
Mar 90	459	1.67	3.16

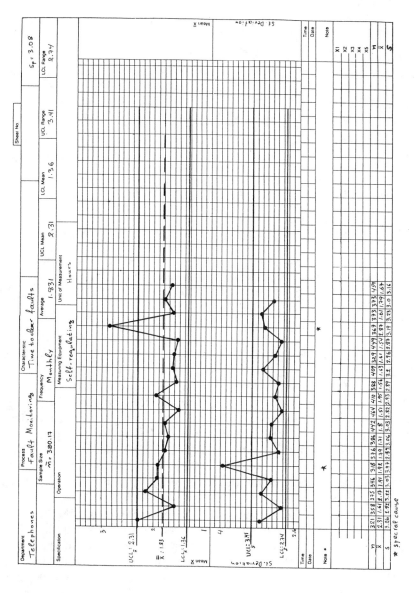

Figure 9.8 SPC study for fault-clear times

We find that

$$\bar{n} = \frac{321 + 358 + \cdots + 459}{18} = 380.17$$

$$\bar{\bar{X}} = \frac{2.31 + 1.61 + \cdots + 1.67}{18} = 1.831$$

and

$$S_p = \sqrt{\frac{320 \times (3.26)^2 + \cdots + 458 \times (3.16)^2}{(321 - 1) + \cdots + (459 - 1)}} = 3.08$$

Then from (9.3) and (9.4)

$$UCL(\bar{X}) = \bar{\bar{X}} + 3S_p/\sqrt{\bar{n}} = 1.831 + 3 \times 3.08/\sqrt{380.17} = 2.31$$
$$LCL(\bar{X}) = \bar{\bar{X}} - 3S_p/\sqrt{\bar{n}} = 1.36$$

and

$$UCL(s) = S_p \times \frac{\sqrt{2\bar{n} - 3} + 3}{\sqrt{2\bar{n} - 2}} = 3.08 \times \frac{\sqrt{2 \times 380.17 - 3} + 3}{\sqrt{2 \times 380.17 - 2}} = 3.41$$

$$LCL(s) = S_p \times \frac{\sqrt{2\bar{n} - 3} - 3}{\sqrt{2\bar{n} - 2}} = 2.74$$

The associated control charts for $\bar{X}$ and s are shown in Figure 9.8. There is a special cause for concern for the mean in December 1989, and a special cause for concern for the variability in February 1989.

■ 9.4 Attribute charts

When the data do not relate to measurable items but to quantities satisfying a yes/no definition (defective items, incorrect invoices, defects on a product etc.), attribute charting is necessary. The main difference from variable charting lies in the sampling procedure and in the calculation of the control limits. In many situations it is not uncommon to record all the attributes in an output, such as all calls unanswered in a day, all orders not completed by a certain date etc. In such a case it is as though the entire output is being checked, and so no sampling is necessary.

If for a certain period of time it is not the entire output that is being checked (for defects, for example), then the sample chosen should be representative of the current defect rate. For example, in a process running with a 2% defect rate, a mean of 2 defects per sample requires a sample size of at least 100 for recording purposes. The calculation of the control limits depends on whether *numbers* (for constant sample size) or *proportions* (for varying sample size) are being plotted, and on whether *defective* items or *defects* are being considered – an item can possess a certain number of defects before being classified as defective.

Two types of questions will need to be answered before the type of chart is chosen:

1. Is the sample size constant or dose it vary from sample to sample?
2. Is the quality characteristic viewed as a defective (completely failed) or a defect (one of many in the item)?

Depending on the answers to the above two questions there are four types of attribute charts:

1. The p-chart (varied sample size – defective)
2. The np-chart (constant sample size – defective)
3. The u-chart (varied sample size – defects)
4. The c-chart (constant sample size – defects)

These are outlined in Figure 9.9.

For setting up the upper and lower control limits, the idea of 'mean ± 3 *SD*' still applies (as in the variable charts), irrespective of the type of the attribute chart. But as we cannot talk about negative proportions or a negative

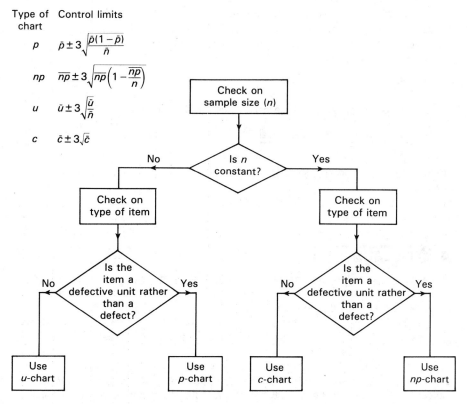

Figure 9.9 SPC study for attribute charting

number of defects, whenever calculations of the *LCL* result in a negative value, it is treated as zero.

A particularly useful chart associated with attribute charting is the *multiple characteristics chart*, which enables the simultaneous monitoring of more than one characteristic for the same purpose. Examples of such charts will be given in the next subsection.

9.4.1 Attribute charts for defective items

Defectives are items that fail to meet a required standard due to the presence of defects. Such items could be faulty telephones, wrong bills or advice notes, calls not answered within a predetermined time etc. There are two types of attribute charts for defectives, depending on whether the sample size n is varied (*p*-chart) or constant (*np*-chart).

The *p*-chart

The *p*-chart is used for process control of defectives when it is not possible to take a sample of a constant sample size. The data plotted on the chart is the fraction or proportion, p, of defectives per sample. The control limits are given by

$$\bar{p} \pm 3 \sqrt{\frac{\bar{p}(1 - \bar{p})}{\bar{n}}} \tag{9.5}$$

where $\bar{n}$ is the average of all sample sizes and $\bar{p}$ is defined as

$$\bar{p} = \frac{\text{total number of defectives}}{\text{total number of items inspected}} \tag{9.6}$$

If the calculation of the lower limit results in a negative quantity the value is treated as zero.

CASE STUDY 9.4

The special delivery section of the mail service guarantees packet delivery within 24 hours anywhere in the world. Depending on the destination, target times are agreed in advance with the customer.

An SPC study was undertaken to determine whether the special delivery process was in statistical control. During a period of 25 weeks, the weekly number of deliveries not meeting the target time was monitored. The data are shown in Table 9.5. Note that the sample size is not constant from week to week and the quality characteristic can be classified as defective/non-defective (a delivery either meets the target time or it does not); hence a *p*-chart is the appropriate chart to use.

Table 9.5 Special-deliveries data for case-study 9.4

Week no.	Total deliveries	Deliveries not meeting target	Proportion of failed deliveries
Week 1	800	96	0.120
Week 2	845	106	0.125
Week 3	830	99	0.119
Week 4	780	79	0.101
Week 5	770	76	0.099
Week 6	880	66	0.075
Week 7	875	61	0.070
Week 8	780	77	0.099
Week 9	700	56	0.080
Week 10	920	110	0.120
Week 11	900	121	0.134
Week 12	830	133	0.160
Week 13	850	153	0.180
Week 14	750	131	0.175
Week 15	780	109	0.140
Week 16	730	88	0.121
Week 17	800	80	0.100
Week 18	815	57	0.070
Week 19	830	25	0.030
Week 20	900	99	0.110
Week 21	910	77	0.085
Week 22	875	87	0.099
Week 23	830	62	0.075
Week 24	850	93	0.109
Week 25	750	90	0.120
Total	20580	2231	

The data value to be plotted is the proportion of deliveries not completed within the target time every week. These values are shown in the last column of Table 9.5. We have

$$\bar{n} = \frac{20580}{25} = 823.2$$

and, using (9.5) and (9.6),

$$\bar{p} = \frac{2231}{20580} = 0.108$$

and

$$UCL = 0.108 + 3\sqrt{\frac{0.108(1 - 0.108)}{823.2}} = 0.141$$

$$LCL = 0.108 - 3\sqrt{\frac{0.108(1 - 0.108)}{823.2}} = 0.076$$

The associated *p*-chart is shown in Figure 9.10.

The process of the special mail delivery was obviously not in statistical control. Before any attempts were made to improve the service overall, an effort was made to determine the reasons why the process went badly out of control during the 12th, 13th and 14th weeks. Weeks 7, 18 and 19 were also looked at,

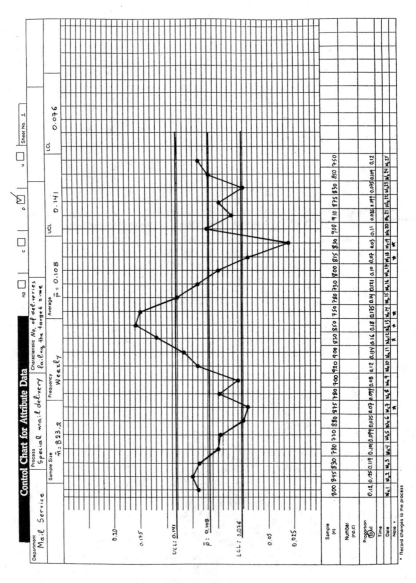

Figure 9.10 SPC study for special-delivery process

to determine the special causes of the relatively good performance. The bad performance of the 12th to 14th week was eventually traced to a fault in the newly installed order-sorting equipment which, due to bad calibration at the middle of the 11th week, was assigning some of the orders to wrong destinations. The fault was spotted during routine maintenance at the end of the 15th week, which explains the improvement in the performance from the 16th week onwards. Bearing in mind that this fault was not likely to reappear in the future, a recalculation of the control limits took place, excluding the data for weeks 11–15. The resulting chart is shown in Figure 9.11. Note that the average proportion of defective deliveries has fallen to $p = 0.096$ and the control limits have been improved accordingly (inwards).

One of the arguments against SPC targets its requirement of frequent recalculation of the control limits. But if the system is already in place, recalculation needs no more than a small change on a spreadsheet or the pressing of a button on a pocket calculator. But even more importantly, this continuous inwards readjustment of the control limits is what makes SPC a dynamic, continuously evolving system for quality control, rewarding the efforts by showing the progress achieved, in agreement with the principle of continuous improvement.

The *np*-chart

The *np*-chart is similar to a *p*-chart, the main difference being that the sample size is constant. The data values plotted are the actual number of defective items per sample represented by np rather than the proportion p. The control limits are given by

$$\overline{np} \pm 3\sqrt{\overline{np}\,[1 - (\overline{np}/n)]} \qquad (9.7)$$

where $\overline{np}$ is the grand average of all defectives:

$$\overline{np} = \frac{\text{total number of defectives}}{\text{number of samples inspected}} \qquad (9.8)$$

CASE STUDY 9.5

The billing department of the electricity board had been experiencing customer complaints about its quarterly bills. The complaints concerned incorrect amounts, damaged/torn envelopes, wrong bills to the wrong people, no bill in the envelope, duplication of bills, wrong addressing etc. An SPC study was undertaken on the billing process, which is fully automatic and capable of producing up to 5000 ready for despatch bills per hour. Every two hours, samples of 1000 completed bills were examined for damages or incorrectness.

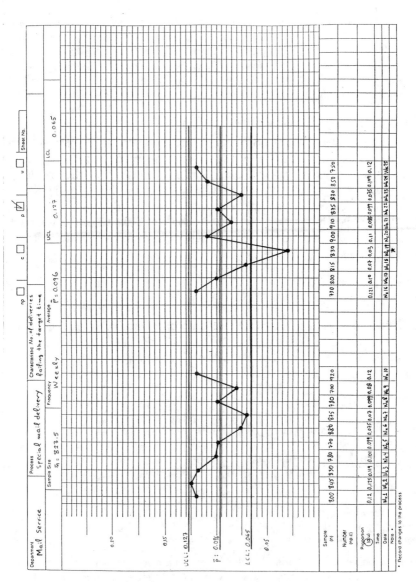

Figure 9.11   Recalculated SPC chart for special-delivery process

As the sample size is constant and the characteristic of interest is 'defective bills', the appropriate control chart to use is the *np*-chart. The data and the associated control chart are shown in Figure 9.12. The control limits were calculated using (9.8) as

$$\overline{np} = \frac{15 + 12 + \cdots + 16}{20} = 14.7$$

and by (9.7) as

$$UCL = 14.7 + 3\sqrt{14.7(1 - 14.7/1000)} = 26.1$$

and

$$LCL = 14.7 - 11.4 = 3.3$$

Figure 9.12 indicates that the billing process is in statistical control. Any improvement in the process can only result from management action on the system; in this case this perhaps means better calibration and maintenance of the automatic billing equipment, allowance for statistical experiments aimed at the optimization and better tuning of the factors associated with the existing machines, or even replacement of the billing equipment.

Of course, replacement should be the last resort. Optimization of the performance of existing equipment should always be attempted first with the help of statistically designed experiments (see also Part IV). But this requires the equipment to be made available for such systematic study. This, in turn, might require the billing process to be stopped until the experiments and data analyses were over and the optimal conditions were statistically determined. Balancing the costs of stopping a process with the possible benefits that a statistical study might bring is a management responsibility. It requires a decision that will eventually affect the system.

9.4.2 Attribute charts for defects

Defects are faults or non-conforming characteristics that cause items to fail to meet the required standard. An item can possess a different number of defects before being classified as defective. There can be a number of defects in one defective item, some more significant than others. It might be necessary to record all defects (in multi-characteristic charts) or just the most important one. Examples include: different types of errors in invoices, imperfection in a product, accident or injuries recorded, various typing mistakes, flaws in a service offered etc.

As in the case of defectives, there are two types of attribute charts for defects depending on whether the sample size *n* is varied (*u*-chart) or constant (*c*-chart). A chart for defects is usually combined with a multiple characteristics chart (see Figure 9.13); apart from clarifying the defect situation, such a chart helps in pinpointing the main causes of trouble.

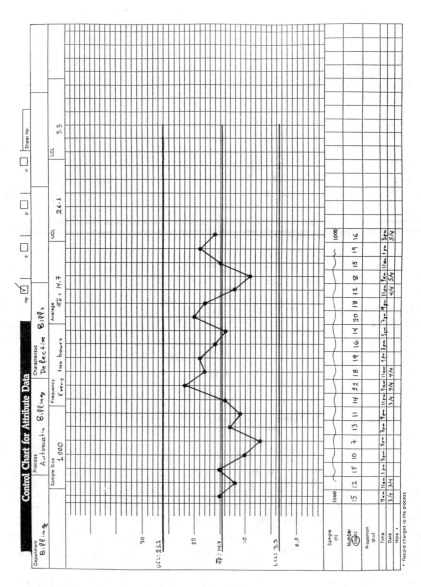

Figure 9.12 SPC study for billing process

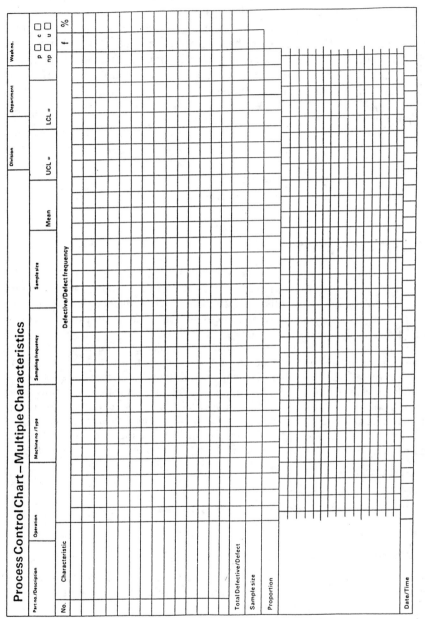

Figure 9.13 General format for multiple characteristics chart

The u-chart

The u-chart is used for process control for defects when it is not possible to take a sample of constant sample size. As in the case of the p-chart, the data values plotted on the chart are the proportion of faults per sample, now symbolized by u. Note that it is the number of non-conformities per item within the sample that is being monitored, and not the number of items per sample which have been rejected; in the latter case a p-chart would have been appropriate. The control limits are given by

$$\bar{u} \pm 3\sqrt{\frac{\bar{u}}{\bar{n}}} \tag{9.9}$$

where $\bar{n}$ is the average of all sample sizes and $\bar{u}$ is defined as

$$\bar{u} = \frac{\text{total number of defects}}{\text{total number of items inspected}} \tag{9.10}$$

CASE STUDY 9.6

A company manufacturing burglar alarm systems provides free on-site service once a year for the first five years from installation of the system. Service records from visits to customers over the past 20 months were collected for the purpose of an SPC study. This was felt to be a necessary part of the effort to improve the product and minimize the service costs.

In order to be able to pinpoint the most troublesome characteristics, a multiple characteristics chart was utilized in combination with a u-chart, which was chosen as the appropriate chart to use on account of the fact that the sample size (monthly service visits) varied from month to month and the study was concerned with defects. Nine types of defect were identified as those contributing most to the service costs. These are outlined on the multiple characteristic chart of Figure 9.14, where the monthly defect frequencies and the associated u-chart are also shown. The control limits are calculated using (9.9) and (9.10) as follows:

$$\bar{n} = 2110/20 = 105.5$$
$$\bar{u} = 592/2110 = 0.28$$
$$UCL = \bar{u} + 3\sqrt{\bar{u}/\bar{n}} = 0.28 + 3\sqrt{0.28/105.5} = 0.44$$

and

$$LCL = \bar{u} - 3\sqrt{\bar{u}/\bar{n}} = 0.13$$

The control chart shows two special causes of concern. To improve the process one should concentrate first on the most frequent type of defect. A Pareto check column on the right-hand side of the characteristics table shows that sticking buttons account for 30% of all the defects. Unless cost considerations indicate otherwise, this type of defect should be the main quality characteristic to be improved as part of a quality improvement programme. A separate u-chart could be utilized for the study of this particular defect; see, for example, Figure 9.15.

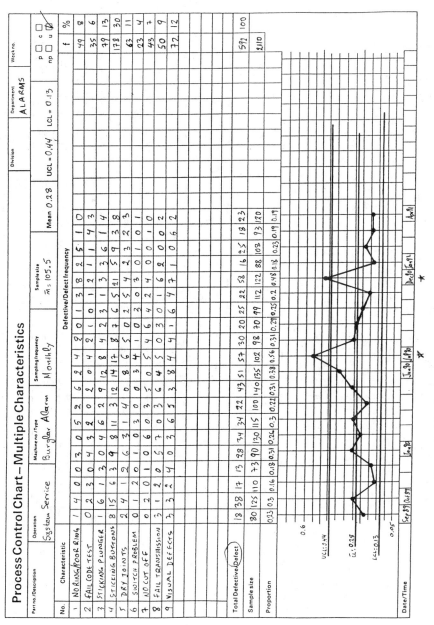

Figure 9.14 SPC study for alarm-systems service records

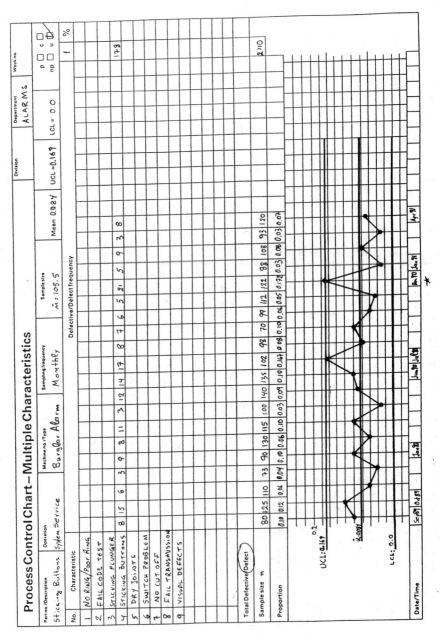

Figure 9.15 SPC analysis for a single defect

The *c*-chart

The *c*-chart is used for process control of defects when it is possible to take samples at a constant sample size. The data plotted on the chart are the number of defects c in each sample. The control limits are given by

$$\bar{c} \pm 3\sqrt{\bar{c}} \qquad (9.11)$$

where $\bar{c}$ is the average number of defects calculated by

$$\bar{c} = \frac{\text{total number of defects}}{\text{number of samples tested}} \qquad (9.12)$$

CASE STUDY 9.7

A telephone company serving a large number of residential and business customers, wishes to improve the quality of its service by testing, on a daily basis, a sample of telephone lines at certain locations in the country. A central automatic system generates calls every 3 minutes throughout the busy period (8 am to 6 pm, Monday to Friday), testing a number of access points at each location. An automatic analysis of failed calls also takes place, providing information on the various reasons for the failure. These types of failure, together with their daily frequencies for a particular location are shown on the multiple characteristics chart of Figure 9.16.

The associated control chart is a *c*-chart because the daily sample size is constant (200) and there are various types of defects; the *c*-chart is also shown in Figure 9.16 with the control limits calculated on the basis of formulae (9.11) and (9.12).

We can note that the limits are not violated; however, there is an obvious cyclic pattern, with most of the plotted points concentrated near the limits, that is, outside the ± 1 *SD* band. These provide enough statistical evidence to indicate that the process is out of control.

The special causes for this case can, perhaps, be easily determined by studying Figure 9.16. Indeed, the chart shows that the peaks of the problem occur at the end and at the beginning of each week (Fridays and Mondays). A glance at the Pareto checklist in the defects table shows that most of the failures are due to the overloading of the system. This clearly indicates an inability in the telephone lines to cope with the increased usage towards the end and at the beginning of each week. An improvement, therefore, in the quality of telephone service for this particular area can certainly be expected if the telephone company provides the means (an adequate number of lines) to avoid overloading the system.

9.4.3 Further notes on attribute charting

Individual control limits

For *p*-charts and *u*-charts, if the sample sizes vary by more than 25%,

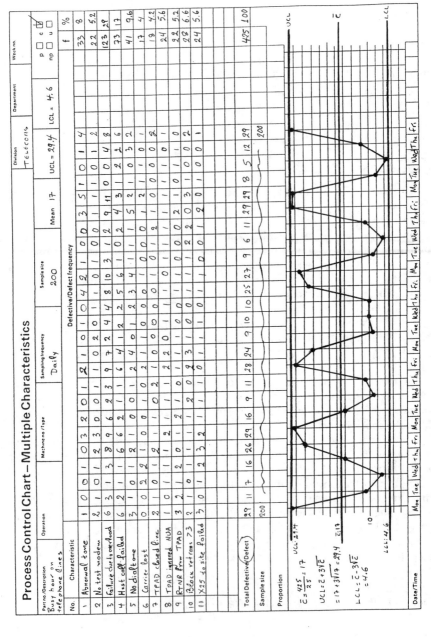

Figure 9.16 SPC study for the telephone service

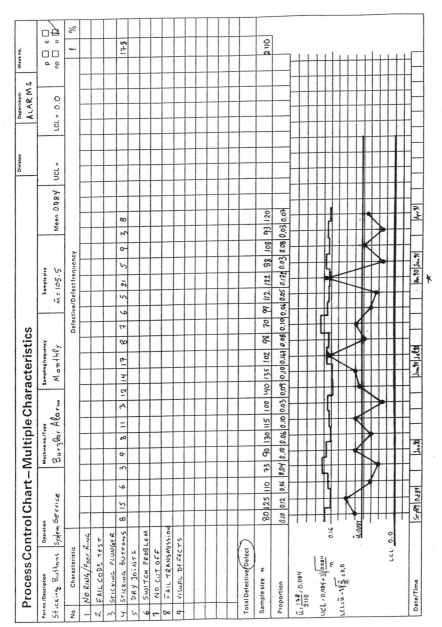

Figure 9.17 SPC analysis for individual control limits (case-study 9.6)

individual control limits (*ICL*) need to be calculated. The *ICL* values are calculated in a similar way to the usual limits for the *p*- and *u*-charts, but by using (in the formulae) the associated (individual) sample size *n* rather than the mean sample size $\bar{n}$. For example, Figure 9.17 shows the *u*-chart of Figure 9.15 with individual upper control limits recalculated.

A generally accepted guideline is to recalculate an individual control limit if the associated sample size is outside the interval $\{\bar{n} \pm 0.25\bar{n}\}$. For the example in Figure 9.17, the sample sizes of 73, 140, 135 and 70 lie outside the range of $\{79, 132\}$. Recalculation of the *ICL*'s is therefore necessary only for those cases.

Capability

With attribute charts there is no tolerance, but only the aim of zero defects or 100% acceptable items. A simplistic measure of capability can therefore be provided by the relevant mean value:

$\bar{p}$ or $\overline{np}$ or $\bar{u}$ or $\bar{c}$

with the aim of making this figure zero.

Recap

The flow chart of Figure 9.9 shows the different choices with regard to the type of attribute chart needed. The basic formulae needed are also shown. Note that for all charts there is a common format for calculating the control limits: each involves the relevant mean ± 3 standard deviations; the standard deviation is denoted by the expression involving the square root. For the *p*- and *u*-charts (varying sample size) the average sample size $\bar{n}$ is used. Theoretical justification of the SPC formulae is beyond the scope of this book. Nevertheless, it is sufficient to know that the formulae for the defectives charts (*p*, *np*) are statistically based on the binomial distribution, whereas the formulae for the defects chart (*u*, *c*) are based on the Poisson distribution. Both distributions are used here as approximations to the normal distribution, providing an adequate and statistically valid approach to attribute charting.

■ 9.5 Interpreting the control charts

A control chart can tell us whether or not a process is in statistical control, in other words, whether or not more than common causes of variation are present. It can also provide clues which can help us to determine and eliminate any special causes of variation present. The chart characteristics of a process operating with only common causes of variation are:

1. All points fall within the control limits.
2. There is an approximately equal number of points on either side of the central line.
3. There is no specific pattern apparent.
4. Most points are near the centre (the middle third region) although a few (about one-third) approach the control lines.

Generally, any chart not satisfying the above characteristics is indicative of the presence of special causes of variation in need of investigation and, if required, elimination. We can therefore define certain action rules applicable to all control charts in general; these rules determine the circumstances when action should be taken.

An action may not necessarily mean an action for elimination (of the special cause); it could mean an action for investigation. For example, a point below the lower control limit of an attribute chart for defects or of a range chart for variables (if such a limit exists that is positive), should prompt an investigation of the circumstances for such a desirable situation, so that it can be repeated (continuously if possible) again in the future.

The basic action rules are as follows:

Action rule 1: Action should be taken when at least one of the plotted points lies outside the (3σ) control limits. If the reason for the special cause is found and permanently taken care of, the out of control reading is removed and new control limits are calculated. If the reason is not found, then it must be accepted that the sample value is part of the system which generated the limits.

Action rule 2: (*rule of seven*). Action should be taken when there are seven consecutive points, either all on one side of the mean, or all increasing, or all decreasing. Since the probability of any of these alternatives occurring by chance is very small, a special cause in need of investigation might be present.

Action rule 3: Action should be taken when non-random patterns are clearly shown in the chart. It should not be difficult to determine the reasons for these patterns. For example, a cyclic pattern might indicate that the material from a specific supplier, or the circumstances of a specific time period, might regularly have an undesired (or beneficial) effect.

Action rule 4: (*middle third rule*). Action should be taken when the number of plotted points in the middle third of the total range between the control lines is much less than two-thirds of the total number of points. Care should be taken when applying this rule in situations when the distribution of the readings is skewed, as in the range chart.

Warning limits

Many SPC practitioners prefer the use of the warning limits; these are lines drawn at ± 2 *SD* from the mean, in addition to the control lines (at ± 3 *SD* from the mean) which are now called action limits. The warning lines can easily be drawn at two-thirds of the distance (outwards) between the central line and each control limit. Again, care should be taken in the case of non-symmetrical distributions, as in the range charts.

The guideline (not a universally accepted rule) associated with the warning limits is that action should be taken when at least two consecutive points fall outside the warning lines.

9.5.1 The service area

It has already been noted that SPC is applicable to both manufacturing and service areas. What needs to be established is an appropriate characteristic which is measurable. Obviously, this is much easier for the manufacturing sector, where the production process is much more clearly measurable. However, it can be said that almost 80 per cent of what is viewed as manufacturing sector is actually service: personnel, administration, procurement, materials handling, design etc. It is important, therefore, to be able to define measurable characteristics, appropriate to the service area which, at the end of the day, are equally applicable to the manufacturing area. Some suggestions are given below.

Administration

- Average number of typing errors per document.
- Typing throughput time
- Proportion of reports delivered to schedule.
- Customer complaint rate.
- Number of debtors or creditors outstanding.
- Number of projects/customer orders completed to schedule.
- Number of telephone rings before answering.
- Improperly directed calls to switchboard.
- Number of customers waiting on line.
- Processing errors.
- Downtime in processing equipment.
- Time spent to locate documents.
- Timeliness of courier deliveries.
- Payment errors.

Personnel

- Recruitment rate.
- Turnover rate.
- Cost per recruitment.
- Time taken to fill vacancies.
- Number of resignations.
- Unfulfilled planned training.
- Absenteeism.

Procurement

- Proportion of purchasing orders completed on time.
- Average order throughput time.
- Average time spent chasing orders.
- Supplier quality performance.
- Number of return to supplier items.
- Number of purchasing errors due to the purchaser.

Materials handling

- Average time of out of stock periods.
- Ratio of stock-out to demand.
- Material throughput time.
- Proportion of internal orders concluded on time.
- Number of stock items not used as planned.
- Response time to customer requests.

Design

- Number of drawing errors.
- Number of checking mistakes.
- Number of void designs.
- Proportion of drawings not completed on schedule.
- Timeliness of design-error resolution.
- Missing or illegible drawings.

9.5.2 A final word on the control chart

The control chart is an economic tool, as it balances the economics of looking for special causes when none exists, and not looking when they do exist. It helps in the fairer assignment of responsibilities (operator for special causes, management for common causes), thus avoiding unjustifiable blame and recrimination. It provides a systematic procedure clearly pointing out where to start, what the next step should be, and when to finish. This make SPC an indispensable tool for the operator as well as for the manager.

The growth of SPC has reinforced the value of other simple, but powerful problem-solving techniques such as brainstorming, flow-charting, cause and effect analysis (through the fishbone diagram), scatter diagrams and Pareto analysis (see Chapter 8). These techniques are even more effective when they are properly incorporated into an SPC programme.

The process of continuous improvement should be a gradual one. First achieve stability (statistical control), then shrink variation. As Deming says: 'A process under statistical control has an identity; its performance is predictable; it has a measurable, communicable capability. Costs are predictable. Productivity, under the present system, is at a maximum'. Once stability has been achieved, management's job of dealing with the common causes becomes easier, because 'the effects of changes in the system (management responsibility) can then be measured with greater speed and reliability'. And this is how the shrinking of variation can actually be achieved. By listening (through the control charts) to what the process tells us, and not focusing on specification demands.

It is clear how SPC charts can help, not only in the avoidance of unnecessary tampering with the process, but also in indicating the proper actions and in assigning responsibilities for further quality improvement.

10

Complements and
Alternatives to SPC

The great thing about History is that it is
adaptable.

Peter Ustinov

Towards the end of the last chapter, we noted the importance of incorporating the supporting techniques of Chapter 8 in any SPC programme. It is clear, therefore, that SPC should not be taken to simply mean 'the control chart'. It should be seen as an overall programme of quality improvement incorporating techniques for efficient defect detection and prevention. In fact, the control chart, although the basic tool of SPC, is not the only chart associated with it. In this chapter, we will briefly outline three other types of process charts which perfectly complement the control chart in the following important aspects:

1. For quickly detecting small changes in the mean level.
2. For dealing with drifting processes.
3. For recognizing certain variability patterns.

We conclude this chapter by providing a perspective on SPC alternatives.

■ 10.1 CUSUM charts

For effectively detecting small but important changes in process level, the cumulative sum (CUSUM) chart can be more effective than the conventional control chart. The CUSUM technique requires a prespecified target value and a sequence of readings. These readings could be anything from individual data values, discrepancies, counts or binary data to sample statistics (mean, range, rate per unit) for variables or attributes. The deviations of the readings from the target are added cumulatively and the sums are plotted sequentially. This provides the CUSUM line which, when the process is running on target, is horizontal. The slope of this line over a certain period of time corresponds to the mean level of performance for that period. Therefore, a change in slope indicates a change in process performance.

The above will be demonstrated by the following case study.

CASE STUDY 10.1

In the production of silicon wafers, it is important to control the line width of a nominally 1 μm wide resist trench on the wafer's surface. Every hour, the line width for one wafer was measured at 5 points on the north, south, east, west and centre site of the wafer, using a Leitz MPV-CD optical instrument. Twenty-five wafers were measured in that way, and the data (in μm) are shown in the data section of Figure 10.1. The associated mean/range charts are also shown.

The mean chart reveals three out of control situations. There is evidence to suggest the existence of three special causes of variation on the 4th, 10th and 25th sample. But apart from the special causes, nothing else alarming is evident from Figure 10.1; if anything, the within wafer variability seems to be improving. However, a glance at the associated CUSUM chart of Figure 10.2 (on the sample means) reveals a sustained change in the process performance after the 15th sample. (Note that T = target = 1 μm). This is indicated by the change in the slope of the CUSUM line (after the 15th reading) which in turn indicates a shift in the mean line width. The superimposed protractor shows that the process level has changed to around 1.04 μm as opposed to the functional target of 1.0 μm.

10.1.1 Construction of the protractor

A comparison of the slope of the CUSUM line with the corresponding slope of the protractor or slope guide, can reveal the associated value of the process level. These values can be calculated, as demonstrated in Figure 10.3. As shown in Figure 10.3(a), each value is the sum of the predetermined target T and the slope of the line. The slope is the ratio of the vertical distance on the CUSUM axis to the horizontal distance (from the origin) of the sample intervals. This ratio could be either positive or negative depending on whether the process is running above or below the target respectively. Two examples are shown in Figure 10.3(b) Using the protractor, the mean performance level over any selected interval can be easily estimated without reverting to the original individual values.

10.1.2 Scaling the CUSUM axis

The scale chosen for the CUSUM axis should be large enough to allow genuine shifts in the process level to be detected, and small enough to smooth out random changes or natural irregularities. A guideline for readings from a normal distribution with a standard deviation s suggests that a CUSUM interval should be equal to one sampling interval and both should be equal to $2s$.

For our case study, the readings are sample means which, according to the central limit theorem (Section 6.6.1), form a normal distribution with standard deviation

$$s_{\bar{x}} = \hat{\sigma}/\sqrt{n}$$

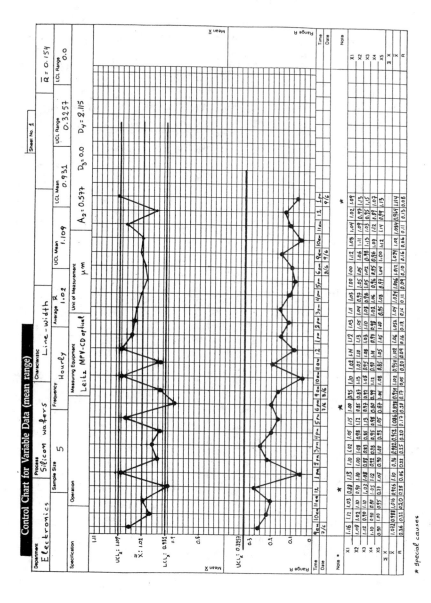

Figure 10.1 SPC study for silicon wafers

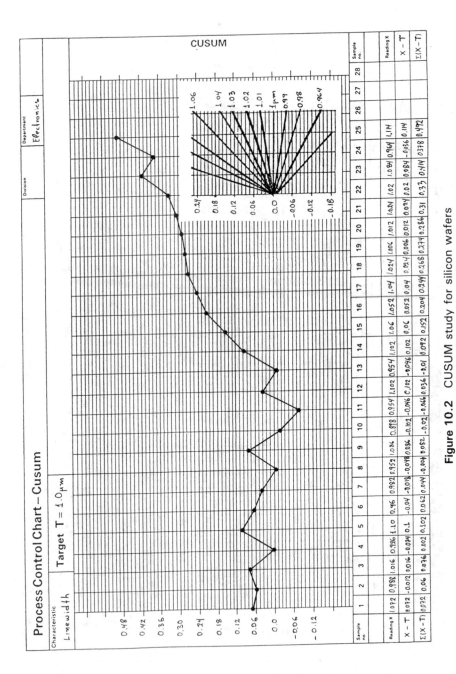

Figure 10.2 CUSUM study for silicon wafers

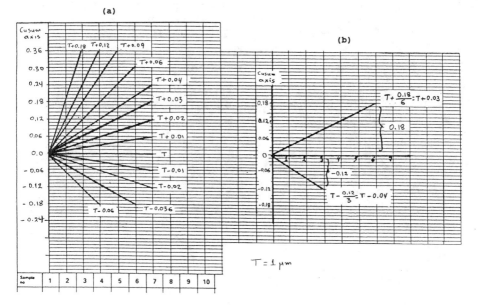

Figure 10.3 Measuring the slope in a CUSUM chart

where $n = 5$ and $\hat{\sigma}$ is an estimate of the standard deviation of the population of the original values (line width) given by (see Section 9.3)

$$\hat{\sigma} = \bar{R}/d_2$$

For our case

$$\bar{R} = 0.154, \quad d_2 = 2.326 \qquad \text{(from Table 9.1)}$$

and so

$$s_{\bar{x}} = \frac{\bar{R}}{(d_2\sqrt{n})} = 0.03$$

Therefore, the CUSUM interval should be equal to $2 \times 0.03 = 0.06$, as can be seen in Figure 10.2.

10.1.3 The V-mask

The V-mask is a template in the shape of a truncated V, as shown in Figure 10.4(a), which enables the determination of significant slopes in a CUSUM line. The arms of the V-mask (called the decision lines) can vary in steepness, as can the width of the nose of the mask. Two parameters that can determine the shape of the V-mask (and hence the sensitivity of the mask in detecting change) are those of the slope of the arms and the half-width of the

275

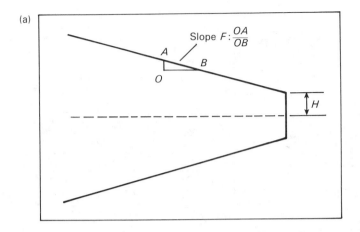

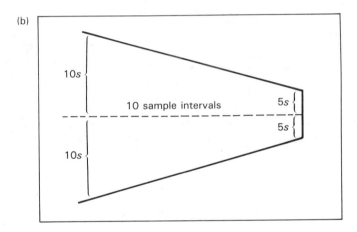

Figure 10.4 (a) V-mask; (b) construction of a general purpose V-mask

nose of the mask (called the decision interval). To follow the notation of the related British Standard BS 5703, the above parameters are symbolized by F and H respectively, as shown in Figure 10.4(a).

The parameters F and H can vary depending on the requirements for the sensitivity of the mask. Obviously, the smaller the values for F and H, the more sensitive the mask will be. The values of F and H are determined on the basis of the number of points required, on average, to detect a change in the process level; this number is called the *average run length* (ARL) and is representative of the degree of sensitivity required. For example, if $ARL = 10$, the sensitivity of the V-mask will be high enough to detect a change in the process level in 10 sample points on average. The values of F and H on the basis of the *ARL* required have already been determined for various values of *ARL* and are available in BS 5703(2).

A useful general purpose V-mask for normally distributed readings can be constructed as shown in Figure 10.4(b), with

$$H = 5s \quad \text{and} \quad F = 0.5s$$

where s is the standard deviation of the distribution ($s = 0.03$ for case-study 10.1). The mask is placed on the CUSUM chart, horizontally, with the notch on the last reading of a time sequence on the CUSUM line. If any of the points in this time sequence fall outside the arms of the V-mask, then a significant shift in the process level has occurred.

For example, for the CUSUM chart of case-study 10.1, placement of the V-mask with the notch on the 13th sample reading shows no evidence of a change in the process level – see Figure 10.5(a). This is because all previous readings fall within the arms of the mask. However, when the notch of the mask is placed on the 21st sample (see Figure 10.5(b)) many of the previous readings fall below the low arm of the mask, which indicates an upward shift in the process level.

10.1.4 CUSUM vs. control chart

A direct comparison between Figures 10.1 and 10.2 reveals the complementary aspects of the control and CUSUM charts. Although the control chart is ideal in providing statistical evidence for the existence of special causes of variation (something that the CUSUM chart does not do), it is rather weak in determining shifts in the process level; this is mainly due to the fact that no allowance is made in the control chart for the numerical values of the previous points.

This weakness of the control chart is compensated for by the CUSUM chart which, through the cumulative sum of the deviations from the target, makes use of all the previous performance values. It is also more sensitive than the control chart in detecting small changes in the process level, thus enabling appropriate decisions to be made at an earlier stage than with the control chart for fine-tuning the process. For detecting large changes in the process level, the conventional control chart is more effective.

The method of CUSUM plotting permits estimation of change points (useful in diagnosis of causes of change) and of local mean levels (mean performance over a selected period of time directly from the chart), useful in prescribing corrective action. Any indication of a change in the mean level is less prone to influences by occasional abnormal (freak) values, and reliable decisions can be based on much less sample information than that required for the conventional control chart.

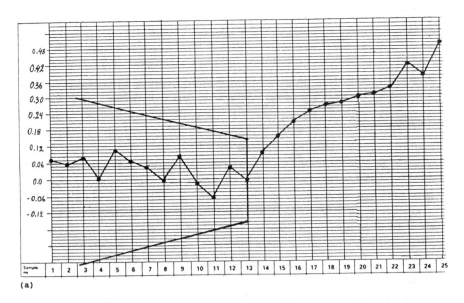

(a)

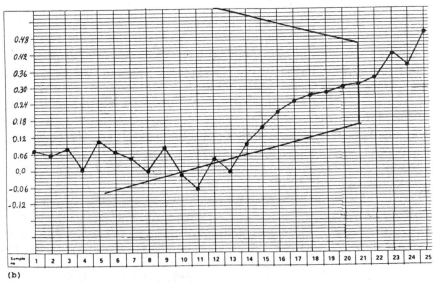

(b)

Figure 10.5 Uses of the V-mask on a CUSUM chart (case-study
10.1); (a) no significant change in process level; (b) significant
upward change in process level

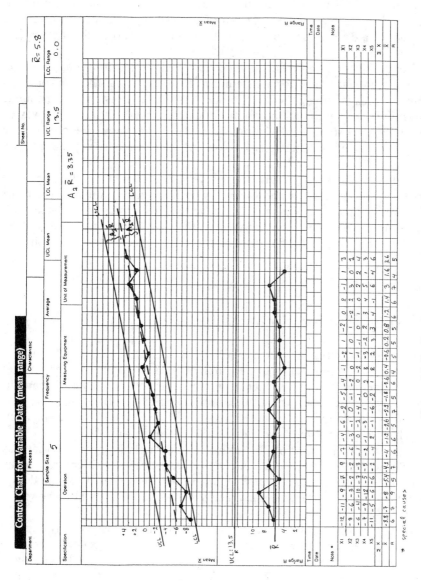

Figure 10.6 Dealing with drifting processes

■ 10.2 Charts for drifting processes

There are processes which, although they do not exhibit any change in their variability level, may be subject to a gradual shift as far as their average performance is concerned. This may be due to tool wear, component deterioration, chemical reaction over time etc. The mean chart will usually reveal the existence of a drift in the process, perhaps evident from the rule of seven (see Section 9.5).

For drifting processes, horizontal control limits are no longer appropriate. To enable special causes to be determined for these cases, the control limits should be inclined along the direction of the drift. The distance of the limits outwards from the line of the drift is calculated in exactly the same way as before, i.e. at 3 standard deviations or at $A_2\bar{R}$. The line of the drift can be visually estimated, although a regression line might be more appropriate (see Section 6.7.2).

A theoretical example is given in Figure 10.6. Note that the drifting in the process is not apparent in the R-chart, whereas a conventional X-bar chart (with horizontal control limits) would have rendered almost half of the readings as out of control points. As it stands, the process is in statistical control, assuming of course that the drifting in the average performance is explicable and expected.

■ 10.3 Multi-vari charts

The multi-vari chart is an extension of the basic control chart, useful in providing a visual representation of the different types of variability. The simplest way of generating a multi-vari chart is to plot on the basic control chart the largest and smallest data value for each sample and join them by a line. The pattern of variability within and between samples will then become apparent. The chart will also show how variability can change with time.

This is a development of SPC which is concerned with processes that may be influenced by several factors in need of identification and control. As an example, we refer to case-study 10.1, where the mean chart is replaced by a multi-vari chart – see Figure 10.7. The associated R-chart is also shown for comparison.

The conventional R-chart deals with the within sample (or within piece) variation; irregularities in this type of variation are statistically determined on the basis of the control limits on the R-chart (or s-chart). The multi-vari chart can complement the R-chart by showing clearly the pattern of variability between samples (between piece variation) and the change of this pattern with time (time to time variation). For example, Figure 10.8(a) shows evidence of a large amount of variability between samples, something that would not be apparent on a conventional R-chart. Moreover, an inability in pattern

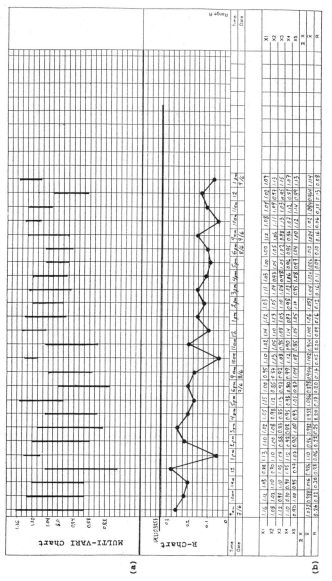

Figure 10.7 Multi-vari analysis for case-study 10.1; (a) multi-vari chart; (b) R-chart

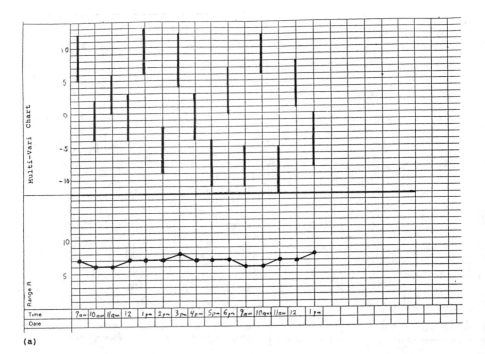

(a)

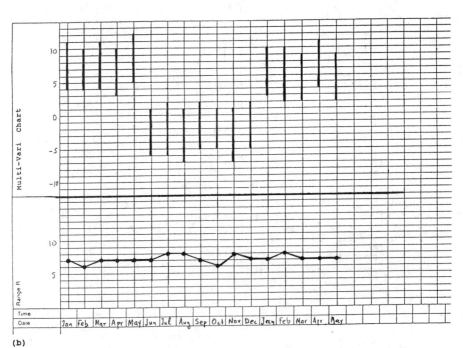

(b)

Figure 10.8 (a) Variability between samples; (b) variability pattern changing with time

detection on the part of the R-chart can be demonstrated in the case of Figure 10.8(b), which shows how variability can change with time. In both the above cases, the within sample variability is fairly constant.

Generally speaking, the multi-vari chart can be a supportive tool to the control chart for purposes of identification of variability patterns, in conjunction with the SPC rules outlined in Section 9.5.

■ 10.4 Alternatives to SPC

It is an ironic fact that, because the SPC techniques for on-line quality control and monitoring were first appreciated and seriously implemented in Japanese industry, they are still wrongly regarded as Japanese inventions. This in turn has prompted efforts in the West to discover something different with the hope of (eventually) doing better than the Japanese. These efforts are, of course, always desirable, and the increasing nature of worldwide competition demands them.

Pre-control, an alternative technique to quality control, can be considered as a product of those efforts. In this section we will provide a perspective on pre-control viewed in relation to SPC.

10.4.1 Pre-control for quality control

The 'colourful world' of pre-control can be adequately revealed by K.R. Bhote's management briefing on *World Class Quality* (1988). Pre-control (originally developed by the US consulting company of Rath & Strong) is heavily tolerance-based, coloured-zone oriented and extremely simple. The basic rules to follow are described below.

Pre-control rules

> **Rule 1:** Divide the specification width by 4. The middle half of the area within the specification limits is then defined as the green zone. The two areas outside the green zone and within the specification limits are called the yellow zones. Finally the two areas beyond the specification limits are called the red zones.

> **Rule 2:** To determine process capability, take a sample of 5 consecutive units from the process. If all 5 fall within the green zone, the process is in control, and full production can commence. If even one of the units falls outside the green zone, a 'serious cause' of variability is present and needs to be investigated and reduced or eliminated before full production starts.

Rule 3: Once full production starts, take a sample of 2 consecutive units from the process periodically. Then:

(a) If even one of the units falls in the red zone or if both units fall in the yellow zones, production must stop. When the cause of variation has been reduced or eliminated, Rule 2 must be reapplied before production can resume.

(b) In any other case continue production.

Rule 4: The sampling frequency is determined by dividing the time period between two stoppages by 6.

Rule 5: In order to deal with attributes, a subjective scale of 10 is utilized: the attribute is converted into an artificial variable by grading it using a numerical scale from (a totally unacceptable) 1 to (a perfect) 10.

10.4.2 Pre-control vs. SPC – a critique

The main advantage of pre-control seems to be the simplicity of the procedures used. The method is also claimed to be much more economical than SPC.

Simplicity

No calculations are necessary, apart from the division of the specification width by 4. Once the tolerance limits have been specified, prerecorded forms can become available with green, yellow and red zones (assuming, of course, the absence of colour-blind staff). No prior statistical training is necessary and no recalculation of control limits is required. Only one type of chart is needed, and this can deal with both variable and attribute data.

Economy

No expensive training is required. The necessary calculations require a minimum of paperwork. Process capability is determined by only 5 units (Rule 2) whereas the sample size in the testing procedures (Rule 3) is just 2.

Simple or simplistic?

Pre-control is a tolerance-based system, not a performance-based system like SPC. As such, it is subject to all the limitations associated with predetermined specification limits. The tolerance value itself is open to question. Unless a systematic approach to tolerance design was followed at the product design stage, or unless the specification limits are reassessed (at regular intervals), accommodating reasonable data-based expectations (which does not usually appear to be the case), the choice of *USL* and *LSL* does not adequately reflect the process capabilities downstream.

There is no way of taking sensible and low-risk decisions until the process performance is known. There is no way of knowing that the product will continue to meet specifications unless the process is in statistical control, that is, until special causes have been identified and eliminated. And as far as SPC is concerned, this is not the end of the story: this is exactly when the serious work of process improvement really starts. To begin with, process capability should be taken care of (see Section 9.3.3). But for proper capability and control, adequate and proper data are required. Pre-control advocates that a single original sample of 5 consecutive units is sufficient to determine process capability (Rule 2). This is just too good to be true! How can 5 consecutive measurements reflect:

1. The inherent variability of the process over time?
2. The existence and amount of random variation as opposed to non-random variation?
3. The distinction between chronic problems (common causes) and sporadic problems (special causes)?
4. The current capability of the process?

Sensible decisions (on important actions such as stopping or readjusting a whole production line) can only be made on the basis of a sensible amount of available data. This is the only way of minimizing the risks associated with such decisions.

The same arguments apply in Rule 3. A sample size of 2 consecutive items could be completely inadequate for revealing stability and capability, especially if the sampling frequency (Rule 4) coincidentally happens to be small. In such cases (which, due to the small amount of initial and subsequent data and information available, could happen frequently by coincidence), a completely incapable process could be allowed to run, with (eventually) disastrous consequences (Rule 4 is also incomplete: there is no indication about when the first sampling should take place after full production commences).

Simplicity in tools and techniques should always be encouraged, but not at the expense of validity. For example, there does not seem to be any justification for converting attributes into variables using the scale of 10 (Rule 5). Grading on a scale of 10 is arbitrary and highly subjective. Moreover, it falls short of explaining what happens in the simple yes/no situation, unless, of course, there is actually a difference (of 10 grades) between 'totally unacceptable scrap' and 'perfectly acceptable scrap'!

In contrast, SPC provides four different types of attribute charts covering a wide range of situations (see Section 9.4), based on the theory of binomial and Poisson distributions (depending on the type). There is a valid theory justifying every SPC practice, something that cannot be said for pre-control. These theories, of course, need not be learned by the operator; but, they exist, validating every SPC action. Whatever is required to be learned is simple enough to be assimilated in a day. To say that SPC is too complicated for the engineer is patronizing and not worth an argument.

One of the complication arguments against SPC, targets the SPC requirement of recalculation of control limits. But if the system is already in place, recalculation needs no more than the pressing of a button on a pocket calculator. But, even more importantly, this continuous inward readjustment of the control limits is what makes SPC a dynamic, continuously evolving system for quality control, rewarding the efforts by showing the progress achieved, completely in agreement with the principle of continuous improvement.

Economy or bankruptcy?

It is claimed that pre-control is economical because it only needs 5 units to initially determine capability, and only 2 units to subsequently keep the process under control. But is this really the total amount of expense required?

In a new and untried process, when (by definition of pre-control) no prior information is available about the natural process variability, or about the existence of special causes of variability, there is no reason to believe that all 5 original units will fall in the green zone (Rule 2). So the chances are that the process will be allowed to run only for 5 units, then stopped, investigated and restarted many times before full production commences. This continuous start/stop/adjust/restart (tampering with), apart from making things worse as far as variability is concerned (Deming, 1986, p. 327) can actually be far more expensive than the initial effort of data collection required in SPC.

The procedure advocated is so sensitive that it would stop the process 99 times out of a 100 samplings. Suprisingly, this sensitivity is hailed as the main achievement of pre-control (Bhote, 1988, p. 40), rather than as its main disadvantage. What is the cost of stopping/investigating/adjusting/restarting a process (maybe for no reason) 99% of the time, even before full production is allowed to start? It is certainly more than the cost required for the investigation of the special causes revealed by the SPC procedures.

Even assuming that full production is eventually allowed to commence, something that will require an extremely capable process, an opposing argument can be brought against Rule 3. It is empirically obvious that Rule 3 cannot be sufficiently sensitive to alert the operator (in good time) when something goes wrong. Indeed, a change from a process which gives 5 inners out of 5 (Rule 2) to one which gives 2 misses out of 2 (Rule 3) clearly needs to be reasonably large; when that happens, the sampling of only 2 consecutive units at probably very wide intervals (because of Rule 4), makes it highly unlikely to alert anybody, until perhaps it is too late.

As far as the expense of training is concerned, obviously SPC is more expensive than pre-control. SPC requires one day of training, whereas pre-control requires almost none. But if one day of training is non-economical, why not scrap training altogether! This could save the company a lot of expense in the short term (assuming it survives until then!).

Pre-control or overcontrol?

It has already been mentioned that one of the main disadvantages of pre-control is its sensitivity to sources of variation, which could lead to an over-reaction which might make things worse. This could lead to numerous erroneous process resettings, in a cycle of endless knob twiddling rather than continuous improvement. These undesirable effects of overadjustment (or overcontrol) can easily be demonstrated by Deming's funnel experiment (Deming, 1986, p. 327). Some pre-control believers accuse the control charts of being too inflexible and insensitive to important variations causing, for example, a shift in the process mean. This, of course, reveals an ignorance of the existence of other simple SPC techniques such as the CUSUM charts or the C_{pk} capability index, which can immediately reveal the problem *if* a problem of this kind really exists.

Pre-control starts with no information, attempting to shrink variation before the amount of variation is known. It attempts to compensate for this lack of information and predictability by tampering with the process through a series of hit and miss actions, which usually makes matters worse.

10.4.3 Demonstration case-studies

K.R. Bhote (1988) has used two case studies to illustrate the weaknesses of the control charts and therefore of SPC (see Bhote, 1988, pp. 31–4). We will use the same studies to demonstrate the usefulness of SPC as a whole and the weaknesses of pre-control.

CASE STUDY 10.2

In a machine shop operation, a bushing had to be made to a length of 0.500 ± 0.002 inches. Table 10.1 shows the data of 12 samples of 5 units each, drawn from the process every hour. The necessary calculations (using the formulae of Section 9.3.1) are also shown. The associated control charts are shown in Figure 10.9.

At a first glance at the control charts of Figure 10.9(a) and (b) the process seems to be in statistical control. Bhote (1988) notes that the upper control limit and the upper specification limit are too close for comfort, and that the upper process limit is over the *USL* which is unsatisfactory; the control chart is then criticized for 'indicating (wrongly) that all is well'.

But SPC is not just control charts and nothing else! A simple glance at C_{pk} (= 0.58) would indicate that all is not well. But all is not disastrous; there is no need to panic! In fact, there is evidence that there has been a upward shift in the process average (this would also have been indicated by utilizing a CUSUM chart using as a target the specified value of 0.500 inches). The process is in

Table 10.1 Data and calculation for case-study 10.2

Bushing length (inches)
Specification 0.500" ± 0.002"

Sample no.	8 am	9	10	11	12 pm	1	2	3	4	5	6	7 pm
1	0.501	0.501	0.502	0.501	0.501	0.500	0.500	0.500	0.501	0.502	0.501	0.500
2	0.501	0.501	0.501	0.502	0.501	0.500	0.501	0.501	0.501	0.502	0.502	0.500
3	0.500	0.501	0.502	0.501	0.501	0.502	0.501	0.501	0.501	0.501	0.501	0.501
4	0.501	0.501	0.501	0.500	0.501	0.502	0.501	0.501	0.501	0.502	0.501	0.502
5	0.502	0.502	0.501	0.500	0.501	0.502	0.500	0.500	0.501	0.501	0.501	0.501
Sum of X's	2.505	2.506	2.507	2.504	2.505	2.506	2.505	2.503	2.505	2.508	2.506	2.504
$\bar{X}_i$	0.501	0.5012	0.5014	0.500	0.501	0.5012	0.501	0.5006	0.5006	0.5012	0.5012	0.5008
R_i	0.002	0.001	0.001	0.002	0.000	0.002	0.002	0.001	0.000	0.001	0.001	0.002

Notes:
Sum of $\bar{X}_i = 6.0128$; sum of $R_i = 0.015$.
$\bar{\bar{X}} = \Sigma \bar{X}_i/N = 6.0128/12 = 0.50107$; $\bar{R} = \Sigma R_i/N = 0.015/12 = 0.00125$.
Control limits: for sample averages: $\bar{\bar{X}} \pm A_2\bar{R} = 0.50107 \pm (0.58)(0.00125)$; $UCL = 0.50180$; $LCL = 0.50034$.
For range: $UCL = D_4\bar{R} = (2.11)(0.00125) = 0.00264$; $LCL = D_3\bar{R} = (0)(0.00125) = 0$.

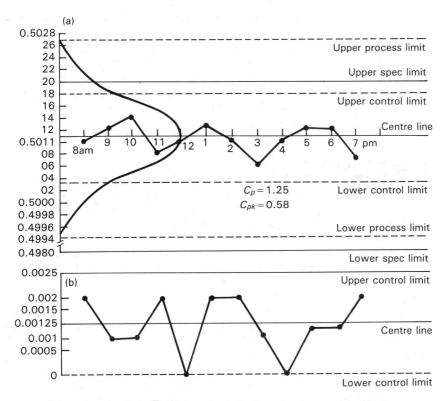

Figure 10.9 (a) $\bar{X}$-chart and (b) R-chart for case-study 10.2

statistical control and should not be interfered with. The shift in the mean can usually be adjusted easily, not by stopping the process, but by manipulating a process parameter known to affect only the process mean and not the process variability. Taguchi calls such a parameter a signal factor (see Part IV). So, SPC has clearly revealed exactly what is wrong with the process and exactly what the next step should be, unlike pre-control which would have stopped the process at the very first sample, without giving any idea of what was wrong and what the next step should be.

In fact, apart from a shift in the mean, the process is stable and predictable. Special causes of variation are not present and there is no need to stop the process (unless the manipulation of the signal factor requires it). The only causes of variability present are common causes, and management action on the system is required. The first of these actions is to look again at the control charts and, in particular, the *R*-chart. In our case, this would immediately indicate a very satisfactory performance of the process at 12 pm and 4 pm. An investigation of the circumstances related to this time period might reveal something which could make all the difference. This simultaneous monitoring of variability (along with the mean) in SPC is an advantage that pre-control does not possess.

It is clear, therefore, how SPC can help, not only in the avoidance of unnecessary tampering with the process, but also in indicating the proper actions and in assigning responsibility for further quality improvement. This is something that can never be said for pre-control.

From our case study, Rule 2 would not be satisfied for 8 out of 12 samples (green zone: from 0.499 to 0.501). Therefore, the process would probably have to stop and be investigated many times for no reason, even before full production had begun. Bearing in mind the usual consequences of unnecessarily readjusting a process, we may wonder whether full production would ever be allowed to start.

CASE STUDY 10.3

The capacitance requirement for an electronic element, for sensing atmospheric pressure in a car, ranges from 31 to 45 picofarads. Table 10.2 shows the data from 24 samples of 10 readings each, along with the necessary calculations. The associated control charts are shown in Figure 10.10.

At a first glance at the control charts in Figure 10.10 the process seems to be hopelessly out of control. But, on considering the capability indices C_p ($= 2$) and C_{pk} ($= 1.92$), it appears nonsensical to stop and reset the process. It has to be a matter of judgment, based on economics, as to how far down the road of improvement one should go with SPC. A stage will eventually be reached when the cost involved in further reducing variability is not justified. The sensor process has obviously reached this stage, and efforts for further improvement would be unnecessary.

One could argue that this was the type of situation where pre-control would be most applicable, as it would allow the process to continue without the smallest doubt that something was wrong. But such situations do not arise very often, unless a serious effort for quality improvement has already been put in at the design stage of the product *and* process. And, when such fortunate situations have been reached, pre-control does not offer anything more than SPC. In fact, as in the sensor case, pre-control is more likely (than SPC) to unnecessarily stop the process – see the 10th sample values in Table 10.2 which are uncomfortably close to the upper limit of the green zone (this zone ranges from 34.5 to 41.5).

Moreover, the SPC study in this case has shown evidence of overcapability, that is, the possibility that some tight control conditions (such as tight tolerances in the components of the sensor) might be allowed to be relaxed (see Part IV), thus saving costs even further.

10.4.4 Conclusion

Pre-control, despite its simplicity, cannot be considered a serious alternative to SPC. With pre-control, there is a constant risk of having to unjustifiably tamper with the process, something that usually leads to a worse situation. On the contrary, SPC – a group of valid statistical techniques including, but also going beyond, the control chart – provides a systematic way of monitoring variability and recognizing poor quality, is able to indicate the proper time to act by showing clearly the current level of process performance and what the

Table 10.2 Data and calculations for case-study 10.3

	Subgroup																							
	1	2	3	4	5	6	7	8	9	10	11	12	13	14	15	16	17	18	19	20	21	22	23	24
1	40.5	37.5	36.5	38.5	38	39	37	36	38	41.5	36	37	35.5	35	39	36.5	37	39	39.5	37.5	38	40.5	39.5	38
2	40	36.5	38.5	39	37	38	36	37	39	40.5	34	36	36	34.5	38	35	38	38	39	37.5	37	40.5	37.5	37
3	39.5	38.5	37.5	36	37.5	36.5	35	35.5	38.5	41	38.5	36.5	35	34.5	37	34.5	35	38	38.5	36	36.5	40.5	37.5	36.5
4	40	38.5	36	39	35	38	35.5	35	38	41.5	38	37	35	35	35	35	34.5	39	37.5	36	36.5	40	37.5	36.5
5	39.5	38.5	34.5	34.5	35	35	36.5	36.5	39	40.5	37	36	36	34.5	36	35.5	35	39.5	37	35.5	37	41	38	37
6	40.5	38.5	36.5	34.5	35	35.5	35	35	36.5	41	37.5	36.5	36	34.5	36.5	35	36	38	37	35.5	36.5	41	38	38
7	40	37.5	37	36.5	35.5	35.5	37	37.5	39	41	36.5	36.5	35	35	37.5	36.5	37	39	38	36	37.5	41	38.5	37
8	40	38.5	37	38	37.5	37	36	36	39	41.5	36	37	35.5	35	38	34.5	35	38	37.5	37.5	37.5	40	38.5	38
9	40.5	38	36	36.5	37.5	37.5	35	36	39	41	36	36	35.5	34.5	36	36.5	36	38	38	37.5	37.5	40	37.5	37
10	39.5	38	35	37.5	36	36	36	35	37	40.5	37	36.5	35.5	35	37	35.5	36.5	38.5	37	36.5	37	40	37.5	37
$\bar{X}$	40	38	36.5	37	36.5	36.5	36	36	38.5	41	36.5	36.5	35.5	34.5	37	35.5	36	38.5	38	36.5	37	40	38	37
R	1	2	4	4.5	3	5	2	2	2.5	1	4.5	1	1	0.5	4.0	2	3.5	1.5	2.5	2	1.5	1	2	1.5

Notes:
Spec: 31 to 45 pF.
$\bar{X} = 37.2$ pF; $\bar{R} = 22$. $UCL_{\bar{X}} = 37.88$; $LCL_{\bar{X}} = 36.52$. $UCL_R = 3.95$. $LCL_R = 0$.
Upper process limit = 39.5; lower process limit = 35.0.
$C_p = 2.0$; $C_{pk} = 1.92$.

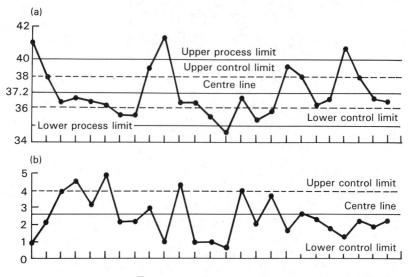

Figure 10.10   (a) $\bar{X}$-chart and (b) R-chart for case-study 10.3

next step should be, and assigns the right responsibilities to the right people (management for common causes, operator for special causes).

Obsessed with the idea of discovering brand new quality tools, in the hope of leapfrogging the Japanese, one is always in danger, not only of reinventing the wheel, but of inventing the square wheel! The only way to leapfrog the Japanese is not by inventing simplistic colourful naiveties but by better appreciating our Western intellectual wealth which Japan borrowed in the first place, and by building on it.

Sources of Further Information (Part III)

Anon (1986), *Statistical Process Control: Instruction guide*, Ford Motor Company: Brentwood.

Bhote, K.R. (1988), *World Class Quality*, AMA Management Briefing, AMA Membership Publications Division: New York.

Bissell, A.F., *An Introduction to CUSUM Charts*, 3rd edn, The Institute of Statisticians: Preston.

BS 5700, *Guide to Process Control using Quality Control: Chart methods and Cusum techniques*.

BS 5701, *Guide to Number-Defective Charts for Quality Control*.

BS 5702, *Guide to Quality Control Charts for Measured Variables*.

BS 5703, *Guide to Data Analysis and Quality Control using Cusum Techniques* (Parts 1, 2, 3 and 4).

Cullen, J. and Hollingum, J. (1987), *Implementing Total Quality*, IFS Publications: Kempston.

Deming, W.E. (1982), *Quality, Productivity and Competitive Position*, MIT Center of Advanced Engineering Study: Cambridge, MA.

Deming, W.E. (1986), *Out of the Crisis*, MIT Center of Advanced Engineering Study: Cambridge, MA.

Edosomwan, J.A. (1988), *Productivity and Quality Improvement*, IFS Publications/Springer-Verlag: Kempston.

Ishikawa, K. (1982), *Guide to Quality Control*, Asian Productivity Organisation: Tokyo.

Juran, J.M. and Gryna, F.M. (1988) (eds), *Juran's Quality Control Handbook*, 3rd edn, McGraw-Hill: New York.

Montgomery, D.C. (1985), *Introduction to Statistical Quality Control*, Wiley: New York.

Mortimer, J. (1988) (ed.), *SPC: An IFS executive briefing*, IFS Publications/Springer-Verlag: Kempston.

Oakland, J.S. (1986), *Statistical Process Control: A practical guide*, Heinemann: London.

Owen, M. (1989), *SPC and Continuous Improvement*, IFS Publications: Kempston and Springer-Verlag: New York, Tokyo.

Shewhart, W.A. (1931), *Economic Control of Quality of Manufactured Product*, Van Nostrand: reprinted American Society for Quality Control, 1980. Milwaukee, WI.

Wheeler, D.J. and Chambers, D.S. (1986), *Understanding Statistical Process Control*, SPC Press: Knoxville, TN.

PART IV
Technical Tools
for Quality
Techniques for Off-Line
Quality Control

The most universal quality is diversity.
Montaigne

In this part of the book (Chapters 11–15) the most important of the techniques advocated by G. Taguchi are presented. Alternatives are also outlined and assessed.

Taguchi's Approach to Experimental Design and Off-Line Quality Control

There is only one thing worse than being talked about, and that is not being talked about.

Oscar Wilde

■ 11.1 Introduction

There is, at last, a worldwide recognition of the fact that pre-production experiments, properly designed and analysed, can significantly contribute to efforts towards the accurate characterization and optimization of industrial processes, quality improvement of products, and reduction of costs and waste.

Japanese industry, however, was the first to realize the potential of the statistical design of experiments (SDE) – originally due to R. Fisher of Britain – as opposed to the costly and unreliable (but still very popular in the West) method of one factor at a time experimentation, in which the engineer observes the results of an experimental trial, having changed the setting of only one factor (a factor being a parameter, variable or any controllable source of variation) while keeping every other factor fixed. In contrast, SDE advocates the changing of many factors at the same time in a systematic way, ensuring the reliable and independent study of the factors' main and interaction effects. Once the factor effects have been adequately characterized, steps can then be taken towards their appropriate control during production, so that variability (the cause of poor quality) in the product's performance is minimized.

Different designs exist (and are readily available) to suit the experimental capability (see Chapter 7). *Full factorials* (designs studying every possible combination of factor settings) are utilized when experimentation is easy or when the number of factors under study is small (3 or 4). *Fractional factorials* (designs consisting of only a certain number of combinations of factor settings out of all possible) are the most commonly used design as they provide a cost-effective way of studying many factors in one experiment, at the expense of ignoring some high-order interactions, which is considered a low-risk strategy since high-order interactions are usually insignificant and in any case difficult to interpret.

One area of current development in manufacturing industry involves statistical experimentation as its main tool; in general terms, it is concerned with the application of modern off-line quality control techniques (pre-production or independent of production experimentation and analysis) to product and process engineering. Much of the work derives from the management principles propounded by W.E. Deming (see Chapter 2), in particular Point 3: 'Cease dependence on inspection to achieve quality'. In other words, eliminate the need for mass inspection by building quality into the product and process at the design stage.

This idea was taken up by Professor Genichi Taguchi, director of the Japanese Academy of Quality and four-times recipient of the Deming Prize. He devised a quality improvement technique that uses experimental design methods for efficient characterization of a product or process, combined with a statistical analysis of its variability. This approach allows quality considerations to be included at an early stage of any new venture: in the design and prototype phase for a product; during routine maintenance; or during installation and commissioning of a manufacturing process.

■ 11.2 Background to the method

In this section we will outline the main components of Taguchi's philosophy. In subsequent sections and chapters, more detailed information on certain important aspects of the method will be provided.

11.2.1 Quality and the loss function

Taguchi defines quality in a negative way as 'the loss imparted to society from the time the product is shipped'. This loss would include the cost of customer dissatisfaction which may lead to a loss of reputation and goodwill for the company. Indeed, apart from the direct loss to the company arising from warranty and service costs, there is an indirect loss due to market-share loss and the increased marketing efforts needed to overcome lack of competitiveness.

Taguchi uses his loss-function approach to establish a value base for the development of quality products. The function recognizes the need for average performance to match customer requirements, and the fact that variability in this performance should be as small as possible. According to Taguchi, a product does not cause a loss only when it is outside specification but whenever it deviates from its target value. Any quality improvement programme should have as its main objective the minimization of the variation of product performance about its target value. The smaller the performance variation, the better the quality. The larger the deviation from the target, the larger society's (producer's and consumer's) loss. This loss can be approximately evaluated by Taguchi's loss function, which unites the financial loss with the function specification through a quadratic relationship.

In general, this loss is proportional to the square of the deviation from the target. Figure 11.1 provides the basic formula for the loss function $L(Y)$ and a graphical representation of the loss to society when the performance (Y) of a product deviates from the desired target, t. In the formula, M is the producer's loss (in monetary terms) when the customer's tolerance D is exceeded.

11.2.2 Objective

The objective of Taguchi's efforts is process and product-design improvement through the identification of easily controllable factors and their settings, which minimize the variation in product response while keeping the mean response on target. By setting those factors at their optimal levels, the product can be made robust to changes in operating and environmental conditions. Thus, more stable and higher-quality products can be obtained, and this is achieved during Taguchi' *parameter-design* stage by removing the bad effect of the cause rather than the cause of the bad effect. Furthermore, since the method is applied in a systematic way at a pre-production stage (off line), it can greatly reduce the number of time-consuming tests needed to determine cost-effective process conditions, thus saving in costs and wasted products.

Division of factors

There are two main aspects to the Taguchi technique. First, the behaviour of

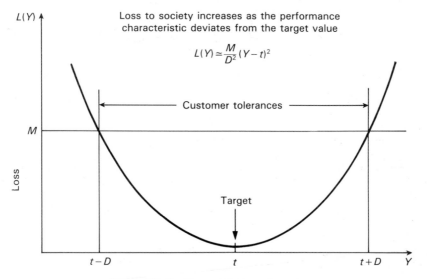

Figure 11.1 Taguchi's loss function

a product or process is characterized in terms of factors (parameters) that are separated into two types:

1. Controllable (or design) factors – those whose values may be set or easily adjusted by the designer or process engineer.
2. Uncontrollable (or noise) factors, which are sources of variation often associated with the production or operational environment; overall performance should, ideally, be insensitive to their variation (see Figure 11.2).

Second are the controllable factors, which are divided into (see Figure 11.3):

1. Those which affect the average levels of the response of interest, referred to as *target control factors* (*TCF*), sometimes called *signal factors*.
2. Those which affect the variability in the response, the *variability control factors* (*VCF*); and

Noise   The variables/factors causing variation and which are impossible or difficult to control.

        Outer noise: Operating conditions
                    Environment
        Inner noise: Deterioration
                    Manufacturing imperfections

Purpose Make product/process *robust* against noise factors (*NF*)

Figure 11.2 Taguchi's definitions of noise

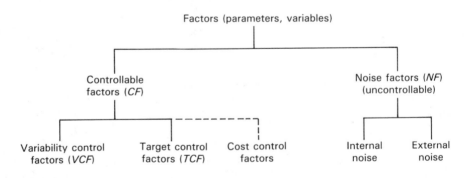

Purpose: To make the process/product insensitive to the effect of *NF*'s

Procedure
(i) Find *VCF*'s and their settings which minimize variability
(ii) Find *TCF*'s and their settings which bring the mean response on to target

Figure 11.3 Division of factors

3. Those which affect neither the mean response nor the variability, and can thus be adjusted to fit economic requirements, called the cost factors.

It is this concentration on variability which distinguishes the Taguchi approach from traditional tolerance methods or inspection-based quality control. The idea is to reduce variability by changing the variability control factors, while maintaining the required average performance through adjustments to the target control factors.

Parameter design

This is the part of the technique which identifies those settings of the controllable factors that reduce performance variation (caused by the noise factors) while keeping the response of interest on target. At this stage one attempts to reduce or remove the effect of the noise factors rather than the noise factors themselves. This effect (variation) is simulated during the experiment, by systematically varying the noise factors at each of the various settings of the controllable factors under study.

The controllable factor settings which are studied are those suggested by the rows of an experimental design (inner array), usually a fractional orthogonal array; in such a design, every level (setting) of a factor occurs with every level of all other factors the same number of times (Taguchi is not the inventor of the orthogonal array; these designs are due to Plackett and Burman – see Section 7.4.3).

At every level-combination of the controllable factors, some observations should be obtained while changing the settings of the noise factors (assuming, of course, that the noise factors can be controlled and changed, at least for the purposes of the experiment). A fractional orthogonal array can then be utilized to determine the level-combinations of the noise factors (outer array). In such a case, the experimenter can simulate the variability (effect) of the noise factors on each controllable-factor setting and determine the setting which minimizes this variability.

This can be expressed in diagrammatic form, as in Figure 11.4. For each of the m rows of the inner array, the n rows of the outer array will provide (at least) n observations on the response of interest (for the whole experiment, there will be at least nm data values). These observations will then be used to compute certain performance measures for each of the m inner rows; these will be described in the next section. The outer array is a selective rather than a random subset of the noise space. The test levels of the noise factors should be appropriately chosen so that the noise space is adequately covered. If the distribution of a noise factor N_i is known, with mean m_i and standard deviation s_i, Taguchi recommends the following. If N_i is assumed to have a linear effect, this factor is tested at the following two levels:

$$(m_i - s_i) \quad \text{and} \quad (m_i + s_i)$$

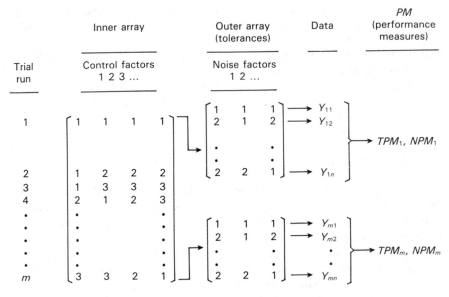

Figure 11.4 Experimental set up

whereas if N_i is assumed to have a curvilinear effect, then it is tested at the following three levels:

$$(m_i - s_i\sqrt{3/2}), \quad m_i, \quad (m_i + s_i\sqrt{3/2})$$

These choices of the test levels are apparently based on the assumption that the noise factors have approximately symmetrical distributions.

A parameter-design experiment can be conducted either through physical trials, or through computer simulation trials, assuming that the response can be numerically evaluated through a *response-model*. This model should relate the product-performance characteristics to the controllable and noise factors. In such cases, assuming some computing capability, more informed analyses can be performed in the presence of both internal and external noise factors.

When physical experiments are used, it is sometimes impossible or very expensive to carry out an experiment according to the set up shown in Figure 11.4. This is when screening or highly fractional experimental designs (studying the factors at two or at most three levels) should be used, as Taguchi strongly recommends.

When the noise factors cannot be controlled for study, Taguchi recommends that some random observations (as many as the economics allow) are taken at each level-combination of the controllable factors (trial). This resembles the classical approach of statistical experimentation. The difference lies in the fact that Taguchi uses the repetitions at each trial for the determination of a variability measure which reflects the effects of the noise factors on this trial, whereas in the classical case, the repetitions are used to determine the overall experimental error and only the mean response is studied.

Performance measures

The observations at each setting of the controllable factors provide the means for the calculation of two performance measures:

1. The noise performance measure (*NPM*), reflecting the variation in the response at each setting; its analysis will determine the controllable factors which can affect (and thus control) this variation (the variability control factors); the optimal combined setting of these factors to minimize the variability (and so the effect of the noise factors) will also be determined.
2. The target performance measure (*TPM*), reflecting the process average performance at each setting; analysis of this will reveal those controllable factors, which are not variability control factors, but have a large effect on the mean response (the target control factors). These can be manipulated to bring the mean response to the required target

Note that the classical pre-Taguchi approach was to concentrate on the statistical analysis of only the *TPM*, something that used to result in unjustified tampering with factors which, although significant for the mean, also affected the variability. As a *TPM* one can use the sample mean $\bar{X}$ of the observations in each trial.

Many measures for the *NPM* have been suggested. When there is a target value to be achieved for the response, Taguchi recommends the use of the *signal to noise ratio* (*SNR*) which estimates the inverse of the coefficient of variation, that is, estimates the ratio μ/σ, with μ being the process mean and σ the process standard deviation. For practical purposes we compute for each experimental trial the measure

$$SNR = 10 \log_{10}(\bar{y}^2/s^2)$$

where $\bar{y}$ and s are respectively the sample mean and sample standard deviation of the (n) observations in each trial.

When the desired characteristic for the response is the smaller the better (as, for example, in the case of leakages, power losses, defective items etc.) Taguchi recommends the use of

$$\eta = -10 \log_{10}\left\{\frac{1}{n} \sum y^2\right\}$$

whereas when the response is the larger the better, Taguchi recommends

$$\theta = -10 \log_{10}\left\{\frac{1}{n} \sum y^{-2}\right\}$$

for the n observations y in each trial. Note that the minus sign in η and θ is used by convention so that the *NPM* is always maximized.

When the performance characteristic is measured on a binary scale (good or bad, success or failure) Taguchi suggests

$$z = 10 \log_{10}\{p/(1 - p)\}$$

where p is the proportion of good.

In fact, the measures that Taguchi recommends should be used with care. For example, in many cases, the simple logarithm of the sample variance s^2 of the observations in each trial can suffice, unless there is a functional relationship between mean and variance. For example, if there is a linear relationship, only then can the signal to noise ratio (SNR) be used. The idea is to obtain a variability measure independent of the mean, so that there is no 'cross-talk' between VCF's and TCF's; in the linear relationship case this independence is achieved by the use of SNR which is (a function of) the ratio of the mean over the variance.

We will return to the problem of choosing the appropriate performance measures in Chapter 13.

Interactions

When the effect of one factor A (on the response) depends on the settings (levels) of another factor B, then an interaction effect (between A and B) is present (usually symbolized by $A \times B$). Depending on the number of factors, orthogonal arrays exist which can also study interactions. For example, the array in Table 11.1 can study:

1. Either the main effects of three factors (assigned on columns A, B and D) and all possible interactions between them.
2. Or the main effects of four factors (A, B, D, G) and three interactions ($A \times B$, $A \times D$, $B \times D$).
3. Or the main effects of seven factors (A, B, C, D, E, F, G) and no interactions.

Case 1 corresponds to a full factorial whereas cases 2 and 3 are fractional factorials confounding main effects with certain interactions.

Table 11.1 Orthogonal array dealing with 3, 4 or 7 main effects

Trial	A	B	C $A \times B$	D	E $A \times D$	F $B \times D$	G $A \times B \times D$
1	1	1	1	1	1	1	1
2	1	1	1	2	2	2	2
3	1	2	2	1	1	2	2
4	1	2	2	2	2	1	1
5	2	1	2	1	2	1	2
6	2	1	2	2	1	2	1
7	2	2	1	1	2	2	1
8	2	2	1	2	1	1	2

Taguchi does not ignore interactions; in fact he suggests that 'a man who does not believe in the existence of non-linear effects is a man removed from reality!' He believes, however, in the ability of engineers to decide on the levels of the factors under study in such a way that some (or all) interaction effects for that particular experiment become insignificant (it is, of course, naive to expect the interactions to disappear in real terms). In such a case, a more economical (fractional) design can be chosen, appropriate to the specific experiment in question. As a safeguard, Taguchi strongly recommends a confirmatory experiment, once an optimal setting for the factors involved has been determined during the statistical analysis of the experimental results.

Allowance or tolerance design

If parameter design fails to remove the effects of the (outer or inner) noise factors, Taguchi recommends *allowance design*, whereby the same steps as before can be followed but additional factors are considered which were previously excluded because of the cost or difficulty of the necessary experimentation. If that also fails, the tolerances of the product's components are considered and *tolerance (re-)design* is advocated. This would mean retaining the optimum nominal levels for the factors (as identified by parameter design), but reducing the tolerances of certain crucial factors (components) in an optimal and cost-effective way so that the overall variability in the response is reduced to acceptable levels. A trade off can be involved by relaxing the tolerances of certain non-crucial components. This approach can be considered as a reassignment of tolerances through scientific method rather than by convention, which was the common practice in industry up to now.

Generally speaking, tolerance design is a systematic procedure which identifies the most crucial noise factors (for example, the tolerances of the most crucial components) and suggests the most cost-effective way of controlling them. In other words, this is the stage when the decision is taken on how best to remove the noise factors, having failed to remove their effect. Therefore the requirement for tolerance design is that it should take place as the last resort, only after the parameter-design stage.

11.2.3 The main points of the Taguchi philosophy

1. Change the timing of the application of quality control from on line to off line, so that you can cease to rely on inspection, can build quality into the product and the process and thus 'do it right first time'.
2. Change the experimental procedures from varying one factor at a time to varying many factors at a time, through statistical experimental design techniques.

3. Change the objectives of the experiments and the definition of quality from 'achieving conformance to specification' to 'achieving the target and minimizing the variability'.

4. Change the attitude for dealing with uncontrollable factors: remove the effect not the cause, by appropriately tuning the controllable factors.

11.2.4 Taguchi's suggested steps

There are certain steps which Taguchi suggests to be taken in carrying out experimental studies; these steps, which should always be followed in the parameter-design stage, are outlined below:

1. **Define the problem:** Provide a clear statement of the problem to be solved. It is important to establish just what the experiment is aiming to solve.

2. **Determine the objective:** Identify the output characteristics (responses) to be studied and eventually optimized (preferably measurable and with good additivity), and determine the method of measurement. To establish measurement reliability, a separate experiment may be required.

3. **Conduct a brainstorming session:** This is a very important stage in performing an experimental study. Managers and operators closely related to the production process or the product under consideration should get together in order to determine the controllable and uncontrollable factors, and to define the experimental range and the appropriate factor levels. Taguchi believes that it is generally preferable to consider as many factors (rather than many interactions) as is economically feasible for the initial screening.

4. **Design the experiment:** Select the appropriate experimental designs assigning the controllable factors and their interactions to the columns of the inner array, and the noise factors to the columns of the outer array (see Figure 11.4).

5. **Conduct the experiment:** Perform the experimental trials and collect the experimental data.

6. **Analyse the data:** Evaluate the performance measures (*TPM* and *NPM*) for each trial run of the inner array and analyse them using the appropriate statistical analysis techniques.

7. **Interpret the results:** Identify the variability control factors (*VCF*) and target control factors (*TCF*) and select their optimal levels. For the *VCF*'s the optimal levels are those which maximize the *NPM* (minimize variability in the response), and for the *TCF*'s they are those which bring the mean response nearest to the target value. Predict the process performance under the optimal conditions.

8. **Run a confirmatory experiment:** It is necessary to confirm, by some follow up experimental trials, that the new parameter settings improve the performance measures over their value at the initial settings. Always run a confirmatory experiment to verify predicted results. A successful confirmation experiment will alleviate concerns about the possibilities of a wrong choice for factor levels and experimental design, wrong assumptions of no interactions or improper assumptions underlying the response model.

If the predicted results (from (7)) are not confirmed, or the results are otherwise unsatisfactory, additional experiments may be required, and a reiteration of (3) to (8) may be necessary.

11.2.5 The new ideas

The principal idea in the Taguchi philosophy is that statistical testing of a product should be carried out *at the design stage* in order to make the product and the process *robust* to variations in the manufacturing and use environment. Hence the widely used term 'off-line quality control', with off line meaning a pre-production or an independent of production phase. This is different from on-line methods such as the analytical process sampling/inspection techniques which fall under the broad heading of statistical process control (see Part III).

Taguchi prefers to measure quality by *statistical reliability* such as standard deviation or mean square error (such as the loss function) rather than percentage defects or other more traditional tolerance-based criteria. The main criterion is keeping the performance at a target value while minimizing variability so that the output is optimized in every aspect. In fact, this criterion is not new, already being the basis for on-line control engineering (such as *quadratic control*). But its use for *static control* of engineering seems to be very new.

Taguchi draws a distinction between controllable factors or design variables, over which the designer has control, and noise factors. The idea of varying the controllable factors as inputs to achieve the target is not new. The important contribution is the systematic inclusion in the experimental design of noise factors, that is, variables over which the designer has no control but which can be controlled in an experiment. A distinction is also made between internal noise, such as component wear and material variability, and external noise such as environmental conditions.

Taguchi also divides the controllable factors (where possible) into those which affect the mean response and those which affect the variability, with cost considerations playing a role in the handling of the variables which affect neither the mean nor the variability (cost factors). Tolerance design is an additional part of the philosophy, providing the means of analysing the effect of internal noise and tolerance on performance.

One of Deming's main contributions, and one recognized in Japan forty years ago, is the necessity of moving quality control backwards from inspection to proper process control (through SPC): control the process and inspection becomes unnecessary. We can see Taguchi's contribution as a shift still further back to the design stage. The principles, however, are similar and control is the best word for summarizing them.

11.2.6 A synthesis

Taguchi's recommended technique is a straightforward, well-integrated system for implementing statistical experimental designs. It has already been proved capable of improving both simple and complex processes and products with the minimum of experiment at an off-line stage. It encourages proper experimentation and closer association between statisticians and engineers, and increases statistical awareness in industry. Most importantly, it completes the *total quality loop*: Taguchi for off-line quality improvement, SPC for on-line quality improvement and, as an umbrella covering both, Deming for management quality improvement.

SPC can assist the operator in the elimination of the special causes of defects, thus bringing the process under control. Its ability to act or react before the process goes out of control also makes it an ideal tool for preventive maintenance. From there on, improving a process which is in control is a management responsibility. This is where Deming's principles come in. According to Deming, management needs to act on the system itself, the system being the current company-wide activities of training, communication and cooperation, purchasing of materials, design, R&D, maintenance and availability of equipment and personnel.

But, something else is still needed: the continuous improvement of manufacturing processes so that the production of robust products can be assured. And this is where Taguchi comes in. He starts where SPC (temporarily) finishes. He can help with the identification of common causes of variation, the most difficult to determine and eliminate in a process. He attempts to go even further: he tries to make the process and the product robust against their effect (elimination of the effect rather than the cause) at the design stage; indeed, in dealing with uncontrollable (noise) factors, there is no alternative. Even if the removal of the effect is impossible, he provides a systematic procedure for controlling the noise (through tolerance design) at the minimum cost.

This cost-effective handling of the common causes of noise is what makes the Taguchi technique an indispensable tool for managers, complementing perfectly SPC and Deming's philosophy. But it cannot succeed without the other two elements of the total quality loop.

Indeed, without the transformation in the current management practices that Deming demands, a proper application of Taguchi's techniques (which requires proper statistical training, adequate communication between design and manufacturing, time and cost allowance for experiments, and is generally more demanding than SPC) will never be established on a routine basis.

A Taguchi success in a process which is not in statistical control will be short lived. Process-predictability is needed before any Taguchi experimentation and analysis takes place; there is little point in attempting to determine optimum process parameter settings, if those parameters cannot be controlled adequately in the future, which brings us back to the need for SPC.

■ 11.3 Taguchi's recommended design techniques

The two-level and three-level orthogonal arrays (OA) recommended by Taguchi are identical or equivalent to two-level or three-level *Plackett–Burman* designs (see Section 7.4.3) and can be found in Appendix C where the corresponding interaction (triangular) matrices for those designs which allow the study of interactions (OA_8, OA_{16}, OA_{27} etc.) can also be found. With a minimum of readjustment, these standard two-level/three-level designs can be utilized for the study of multilevel factors, and are capable of dealing with any required combination of factor levels. In this way the special peculiarities of factors under study can be handled and specific experimental demands can be met, simply by following certain factor assignment and analysis techniques strongly recommended by Taguchi. Some of these techniques will be outlined in this section.

11.3.1 Multilevel-column creation

We can study multilevel factors by first creating the appropriate multilevel columns in two-level or three-level arrays. This is generally achieved by sacrificing 2 columns which are replaced by a new column whose levels directly correspond to every level-combination of the original 2 columns. For example, for a two-level array, the following correspondence holds:

Combination		Levels of new column
1, 1	→	1
1, 2	→	2
2, 1	→	3
2, 2	→	4

whereas, for a three-level array

Combination		New levels	Combination		New levels	Combination		New levels
1, 1	→	1	2, 1	→	4	3, 1	→	7
1, 2	→	2	2, 2	→	5	3, 2	→	8
1, 3	→	3	2, 3	→	6	3, 3	→	9

The only requirement for the creation of multilevel columns in this way is that an interaction column must exist for the 2 sacrificed columns; this is also deleted. Consequently, the creation of multilevel columns can only take place in arrays which originally allow the study of interactions, such as OA_8, OA_{16} etc. (see Appendix C).

Let us take the $OA_8(4 \times 2^4)$ formed by $OA_8(2^7)$ as an example. It is known for the $OA_8(2^7)$ that column 3 is the interaction column for the factors associated with columns 1 and 2. The first 3 columns are therefore removed from the orthogonal array, and in their place we create a new column at four levels – see Table 11.2. Note that the four-level column of $OA_8(4 \times 2^4)$ was constructed by defining its levels 1, 2, 3 and 4 to correspond respectively to the four combinations [1, 1], [1, 2], [2, 1] and [2, 2] between the levels of the first 2 columns of $OA_8(2^7)$; the interaction column 3 of $OA_8(2^7)$ was also deleted.

Any 2 columns and their interaction in $OA_8(2^7)$ can be used. Note that, in this particular array, the technique can be used only once. So, 3 columns with 1 degree of freedom each are utilized to create a new column with 3 degrees of freedom. In general, for the creation of a k-level column, we need to sacrifice enough columns to release $k - 1$ degrees of freedom. For example, for the creation of a nine-level column, we need to sacrifice 4 three-level columns, as the example in Table 11.3 shows. To create a nine-level column in a three-level orthogonal array, we need any 2 columns and their (2) interaction columns.

So, if we consider columns 1 and 2 of $OA_{27}(3^{13})$, their interaction columns 3 and 4 (see triangular matrix for this array in Appendix C, Table C14) will also have to be erased from the original array. The nine levels of the new column will correspond to every combination between the levels of

Table 11.2 Formation of $OA_8(4 \times 2^4)$ from $OA_8(2^7)$

Trial	Column								Column				
	1	2	3	4	5	6	7		(1 | 2 | 3)	4	5	6	7
1	1	1	1	1	1	1	1		1			1	1	1	1
2	1	1	1	2	2	2	2		1			2	2	2	2
3	1	2	2	1	1	2	2		2			1	1	2	2
4	1	2	2	2	2	1	1		2			2	2	1	1
5	2	1	2	1	2	1	2	→	3			1	2	1	2
6	2	1	2	2	1	2	1		3			2	1	2	1
7	2	2	1	1	2	2	1		4			1	2	2	1
8	2	2	1	2	1	1	2		4			2	1	1	2

Table 11.3 The $OA_{27}(9 \times 3^9)$ formed from $OA_{27}(3^{13})$

Trial	(1, 2, 3, 4)	5	6	7	8	9	10	11	12	13
1	1	1	1	1	1	1	1	1	1	1
2	1	2	2	2	2	2	2	2	2	2
3	1	3	3	3	3	3	3	3	3	3
4	2	1	1	1	2	2	2	3	3	3
5	2	2	2	2	3	3	3	1	1	1
6	2	3	3	3	1	1	1	2	2	2
7	3	1	1	1	3	3	3	2	2	2
8	3	2	2	2	1	1	1	3	3	3
9	3	3	3	3	2	2	2	1	1	1
10	4	1	2	3	1	2	3	1	2	3
11	4	2	3	1	2	3	1	2	3	1
12	4	3	1	2	3	1	2	3	1	2
13	5	1	2	3	2	3	1	3	1	2
14	5	2	3	1	3	1	2	1	2	3
15	5	3	1	2	1	2	3	2	3	1
16	6	1	2	3	3	1	2	2	3	1
17	6	2	3	1	1	2	3	3	1	2
18	6	3	1	2	2	3	1	1	2	3
19	7	1	3	2	1	3	2	1	3	2
20	7	2	1	3	2	1	3	2	1	3
21	7	3	2	1	3	2	1	3	2	1
22	8	1	3	2	2	1	3	3	2	1
23	8	2	1	3	3	2	1	1	3	2
24	8	3	2	1	1	3	2	2	1	3
25	9	1	3	2	3	2	1	2	1	3
26	9	2	1	3	1	3	2	3	2	1
27	9	3	2	1	2	1	3	1	3	2

columns 1 and 2. In this way, 1 new column with 8 degrees of freedom will be formed at the expense of 4 original columns of 2 degrees of freedom each. The new orthogonal array is shown in Table 11.3.

11.3.2 Dummy-level techniques

A factor with k levels can be assigned to a column which allows for more than k levels, say, m levels where $m > k$. This is achieved by simply repeating one or more of the factor levels as many times as is necessary in place of the excess column levels. Any of the original factor levels can be repeated but the level which is the cheapest or easiest (to experiment with) is usually chosen, or even the most important level for which more information is needed. This is called the dummy-level or pseudo-level technique. For example, we can assign a two-level factor to the first (three-level) column of the $OA_9(3^4)$ by repeating factor level 1 in place of column level 3, as Table 11.4 shows.

Table 11.4 Dummy-level technique on the $OA_9(3^4)$

Trial	Factors			
	A	B	C	D
1	1	1	1	1
2	1	2	2	2
3	1	3	3	3
4	2	1	2	3
5	2	2	3	1
6	2	3	1	2
7	$1'(=3)$	1	3	2
8	$1'(=3)$	2	1	3
9	$1'(=3)$	3	2	1

Statistically speaking, the new design still retains the most desired property of orthogonal arrays, namely that the effect of the factor assigned to a column created this way will remain uncorrelated with all other factor effects. This is because of the proportional frequencies criterion (see Dey, 1985). According to this criterion, a necessary and sufficient condition for the estimates of two main effects (of factors, say, A and B) being uncorrelated is that the levels of one factor occur with each of the levels of the other factor with proportional frequencies, that is to say that the following is true:

$$n_{ij} = \frac{n_{i.} \times n_{.j}}{n} \qquad i = 1, ..., r; \; j = 1, ..., s$$

where n is the total number of experimental trials, $n_{i.}$ is the number of times that the ith level of the r-level factor A occurs, $n_{.j}$ is the number of times that the jth level of the s-level factor B occurs and n_{ij} is the number of times that the ith level of factor A occurs simultaneously with the jth level of factor B.

For example, in the first column of the design of Table 11.4, the factor level 1 appears 6 times (twice as many times as level 2, since it replaces the original column level 3): so $n_{1.} = 6$. In the second column, factor level 2 appears 3 times, so $n_{.2} = 3$. Since $n = 9$ we have

$$\frac{n_{1.} \times n_{.2}}{n} = \frac{6 \times 3}{9} = 2$$

Since $n_{12} = 2$ (the combination [1, 2] appears twice in the first two columns) the proportional frequencies criterion is satisfied. This can be shown to be the case for any of the other levels of factors A and B, and for any pair of columns of the design of Table 11.4.

Staying with the design of Table 11.4, the sum of squares for the effect of the two-level factor A can be calculated, bearing in mind that level 1 is repeated twice as many times as level 2. Recall that in general (see Section 7.5) the sum of squares of factor A is given by

$$SS_A = \frac{(\text{total sum in level 1})^2}{(\text{number of observations in level 1})}$$

$$+ \frac{(\text{total sum in level 2})^2}{(\text{number of observations in level 2})} - CF$$

$$= \frac{(A_1 + A_{1'})^2}{6r} + \frac{(A_2)^2}{3r} - \frac{(A_1 + A_2 + A_{1'})^2}{9r}$$

where r is the number of replications for each trial and A_i represents the sum of data values in level i, $i = 1, 2, 3$.

Recall that

$$CF = \text{correction factor} = \frac{(\text{grand total})^2}{(\text{total number of observations})}$$

$$= \frac{(A_1 + A_2 + A_{1'})^2}{9r}$$

Multilevel-column creation (Section 11.3.1) can be combined with the dummy-level technique to accommodate various experimental requirements. For example, we can assign a three-level factor on a two-level array by first creating a four-level column and then applying the dummy-level technique by repeating one of the three actual levels — see, for example, Table 11.5.

Similarly, we can assign a five-level factor on to the $OA_{16}(2^{15})$ by first creating the $OA_{16}(8 \times 2^8)$ and then applying the dummy-level technique on the eight-level column with three of the five actual factor levels as a dummy; Table 11.6 is an example. Note that the columns from the $OA_{16}(2^{15})$ that have been erased are the main columns 1, 2 and 4, and all their corresponding interaction columns, namely, columns 3 (1×2), 5 (1×4), 6 (2×4) and 7 ($1 \times 2 \times 4$). Using the $OA_{16}(2^{15})$ and following a similar procedure, we can create up to 5 four-level columns resulting in the $OA_{16}(4^5)$ which can be seen

Table 11.5 Multilevel-column creation with dummy levels

Trial	Column				
	(123)	4	5	6	7
1	$A(1)$	1	1	1	1
2	$A(1)$	2	2	2	2
3	$A(2)$	1	1	2	2
4	$A(2)$	2	2	1	1
5	$A(3)$	1	2	1	2
6	$A(3)$	2	1	2	1
7	$A(4) = A(1')$	1	2	2	1
8	$A(4) = A(1')$	2	1	1	2

Table 11.6 $OA_{16}(8 \times 2^8)$ formed from $OA_{16}(2^{15})$

Trial	Column								
	1–7	8	9	10	11	12	13	14	15
1	1	1	1	1	1	1	1	1	1
2	1	2	2	2	2	2	2	2	2
3	2	1	1	1	1	2	2	2	2
4	2	2	2	2	2	1	1	1	1
5	3	1	1	2	2	1	1	2	2
6	3	2	2	1	1	2	2	1	1
7	4	1	1	2	2	2	2	1	1
8	4	2	2	1	1	1	1	2	2
9	5	1	2	1	2	1	2	1	2
10	5	2	1	2	1	2	1	2	1
11	6 = 3′	1	2	1	2	2	1	2	1
12	6 = 3′	2	1	2	1	1	2	1	2
13	7 = 2′	1	2	2	1	1	2	2	1
14	7 = 2′	2	1	1	2	2	1	1	2
15	8 = 1′	1	2	2	1	2	1	1	2
16	8 = 1′	2	1	1	2	1	2	2	1

in Table 11.7. The dummy-level technique can then be applied to any of the 5 four-level columns thus created.

The procedure can be extended to three-level arrays. For example, an eight-level factor can be studied with the $OA_{27}(3^{13})$ design, by first creating a nine-level column (see Table 11.3) and then utilizing the dummy-level technique.

CASE STUDY 11.1

In the production of paper pulp from wheat straw by the oxygen alkali method, an experiment took place to determine the effects of temperature (*TE*), oxygen pressure (*OP*), NaOH concentration (*NC*), time (*TI*) and gas flow rate (*GR*). The factors *TE* and *TI* were set at four levels and the rest of the factors were set at three levels as follows:

Factors		Levels			
		1	2	3	4
TE	Temperature (°C)	50	65	80	95
TI	Time (min)	30	50	70	90
OP	Oxygen pressure (atm)	1	5	9	
NC	NaOH concentration (%)	40	50	60	
GR	Gas flow rate (l/h)	1	1.4	1.8	

The responses of interest were the pulp yield, breaking length, tear strength, folding endurance and whiteness of the paper pulp. In the present study only the whiteness will be analysed.

The experimental design used was the $OA_{16}(4^5)$, which was constructed from $OA_{16}(2^{15})$ combining its columns (through the multilevel-column creation technique – Section 11.3.1) as indicated in the heading of the array shown in Table 11.7. The 5 factors of interest were assigned to the 5 columns of $OA_{16}(4^5)$ using the dummy-level technique, as shown in Table 11.8. Each experimental trial was repeated twice. The response data (whiteness in Elrepho units) are also shown in Table 11.8.

Analysis

Following the formulae provided in Section 7.5, we start by calculating the correction factor:

$$CF = \frac{(\text{sum total})^2}{\text{number of observations}} = \frac{(25.1 + \cdots + 26.9)^2}{32} = \frac{(836.4)^2}{32}$$

$$= 21861.405$$

Then, the total sum of squares:

$$SS_{tot} = \Sigma \, y^2 - CF = (25.1)^2 + \cdots + (26.9)^2 - 21861.405 = 212.215$$

For the sum of squares of factor TE,

$$SS_{TE} = \frac{(\text{sum total in level 1})^2 + \cdots + (\text{sum total in level 4})^2}{8} - CF$$

$$= \frac{(25.1 + \cdots + 28.3)^2 + \cdots + (24.2 + \cdots + 26.9)^2}{8} - 21861.405$$

$$= 82.473$$

Similarly

$$SS_{TI} = \frac{(204.3)^2 + (206.9)^2 + (217.4)^2 + (207.8)^2}{8} - CF = 12.308$$

Table 11.7 Construction of $OA_{16}(4^5)$ combining the columns of $OA_{16}(2^{15})$

Cols of $OA_{16}(2^{15})$				
(1, 2, 3)	(4, 8, 12)	(5, 10, 15)	(7, 9, 14)	(6, 11, 13)
1	1	1	1	1
1	2	2	2	2
1	3	3	3	3
1	4	4	4	4
2	1	2	3	4
2	2	1	4	3
2	3	4	1	2
2	4	3	2	1
3	1	3	4	2
3	2	4	3	1
3	3	1	2	4
3	4	2	1	3
4	1	4	2	3
4	2	3	1	4
4	3	2	4	1
4	4	1	3	2

Table 11.8 Design and data values for case study 11.1

TE	TI	OP	NC	GR	Data
1	1	1	1	1	25.1, 26.8
1	2	2	2	2	25.7, 28.2
1	3	3	3	3	23.0, 26.6
1	4	2'(4)	1'(4)	3'(4)	25.7, 28.3
2	1	2	3	3'(4)	22.5, 25.8
2	2	1	1'(4)	3	25.8, 25.5
2	3	2'(4)	1	2	29.1, 27.3
2	4	3	2	1	20.4, 25.7
3	1	3	1'(4)	2	26.2, 29.6
3	2	2'(4)	3	1	27.5, 27.7
3	3	1	2	3'(4)	30.8, 32.3
3	4	2	1	3	25.2, 30.3
4	1	2'(4)	2	3	24.2, 24.1
4	2	3	1	3'(4)	24.8, 21.7
4	3	2	1'(4)	1	25.0, 23.3
4	4	1	3	2	25.3, 26.9

For the rest of the factors, we apply the principles of the dummy-level technique:

$$SS_{OP} = \frac{(\text{total in level 1})^2}{8} + \frac{(\text{total in levels 2 and 2'})^2}{16} + \frac{(\text{total in level 3})^2}{8}$$

$$- CF$$

$$= \frac{(218.5)^2}{8} + \frac{(206 + 213.9)^2}{16} + \frac{(198)^2}{8} - CF = 26.626$$

Similarly

$$SS_{NC} = \frac{(\text{total in levels 1 and 1'})^2}{16} + \frac{(\text{total in level 2})^2}{8} + \frac{(\text{total in level 3})^2}{8}$$

$$- CF$$

$$= \frac{(210.3 + 209.4)^2}{16} + \frac{(211.4)^2}{8} + \frac{(205.3)^2}{8} - CF = 2.607$$

and

$$SS_{GR} = \frac{(\text{total in level 1})^2}{8} + \frac{(\text{total in level 2})^2}{8} + \frac{(\text{total in levels 3 and 3'})^2}{16}$$

$$- CF$$

$$= \frac{(201.5)^2}{8} + \frac{(218.3)^2}{8} + \frac{(204.7 + 211.9)^2}{16} - CF = 17.96$$

Finally, we obtain the residual sum of squares by subtraction:

$$SS_e = SS_{tot} - SS_{TE} - SS_{TI} - SS_{OP} - SS_{NC} - SS_{GR} = 70.2$$

We can now construct the ANOVA table shown in Table 11.9.

It is clear from the ANOVA table that the temperature and oxygen pressure significantly affect the whiteness of the paper pulp. The optimum levels for these

Table 11.9 ANOVA for case-study 11.1

Source	df	Sum of squares	Mean sum of squares	F-ratio
TE	3	82.473	27.49	7.4 * significant
TI	3	12.308	4.10	1.1
OP	2	26.626	13.31	3.6 * significant
NC	2	2.607	1.30	0.4
GR	2	17.960	8.98	2.4
Res	19	70.241	3.7	
Total	31	212.215		

factors can be found by examining the level averages of the factors. These are as follows:

Factors	Level averages			
	1	2	3	4
TE	26.18	25.26	28.70	24.41
OP	27.31	26.24	24.75	

Evidently, level 3 for temperature (80 °C) and level 1 for oxygen pressure (1 atm) seem to affect the whiteness of the paper pulp positively.

11.3.3 Trans-factor (or pseudo-factor) technique

This technique is applied for the study of distinct classes of factors which correspond to different levels of a certain factor. The designs allowing this are known as nested factorial designs and cover the case when the type of factor to be studied differs according to the levels of a certain factor.

For example, suppose that B is a factor whose type becomes B' when a factor A is at level 1, and B'' when A is at level 2. Suppose that B' and B'' are to be studied at two levels each. Under the assumption that the interaction $A \times B$ is not significant, the factors A and B can be assigned on an orthogonal array, say the $OA_8(2^7)$, as shown in Table 11.10.

Note that the interaction column 3 (for $A \times B$) has been eliminated from the design, and this made possible the following resolution of the degrees of freedom:

Source	df	
A	1	
B'	1	(df for B when A at level 1)
B''	1	(df for B when A at level 2)
Total	3	

The factor B can be viewed as a pseudo-factor (hence the name of the technique) defined to be B' when A is at its first level, and B'' when A is at its second level. Interest is concentrated not on the main effect of B, but on the

Table 11.10 Assignment by the trans-factor technique

Trial	Column					
	1 A	(2, 3) B	4	5	6	7
		B'				
1	1	1	1	1	1	1
2	1	1	2	2	2	2
3	1	2	1	1	2	2
4	1	2	2	2	1	1
		B''				
5	2	1	1	2	1	2
6	2	1	2	1	2	1
7	2	2	1	2	2	1
8	2	2	2	1	1	2

main effects of B' (within $A(1)$) and B'' (within $A(2)$) separately; these are found by separately analysing the data corresponding to level $A(1)$ (for B') and the data corresponding to level $A(2)$ (for B'').

Other factors or even other pseudo-factors can, of course, be assigned to the other available columns of the design of Table 11.10.

CASE STUDY 11.2

An experiment took place in the photo-optics division of the photo-electronics department, in order to determine optimal process conditions in the semi-automatic fabrication of optical fibre couplers, so that low loss of light is experienced.

The main factors of interest were burner width (BW), pulling speed (PS), propane gas (PG) and pre-fuse time (PT). A peculiarity of the pulling speed was that in its absence (pulling speed of zero) an initial tension (IT) was administered, whereas at a pulling speed of 10 mm/s the air pressure (AP) inside the burner was controlled at two levels. Table 11.11 shows the factors under study (at two levels each) and their relationship. The experimental design used and the resulting data (light loss) are shown in Table 11.12.

Table 11.11 Factors of interest for case-study 11.2

BW: Burner width	[$BW(1)$ = 4 mm, $BW(2)$ = 8 mm]
PG : Propane gas	[$PG(1)$ = 14 units, $PG(2)$ = 26 units]
PT : Pre-fuse time	[$PT(1)$ = 5 s, $PT(2)$ = 10 s]
	PS: Pulling speed

$PS(1)$ = 0 mm/s	$PS(2)$ = 10 mm/s
IT: Initial tension	AP: Air pressure
[$IT(1)$ = 3 gr, $IT(2)$ = 5 gr]	[$AP(1)$ = 2 atm, $AP(2)$ = 4 atm]

Table 11.12 Design and data for case-study 11.2

| Trial | Column | | | | | | Data |
| | 1 | (2, 3) | 4 | 5 | 6 | 7 | (Light loss) |
	PS	IT/AP	BW	PG	PT		
		IT					
1	1	1	1	1	1	1	0.50
2	1	1	2	2	2	2	0.10
3	1	2	1	1	2	2	0.31
4	1	2	2	2	1	1	0.25
		AP					
5	2	1	1	2	1	2	0.70
6	2	1	2	1	2	1	0.55
7	2	2	1	2	2	1	0.80
8	2	2	2	1	1	2	0.70

Note that IT/AP can be considered a pseudo-factor becoming IT (initial tension) when PS is at level 1 (in the absence of any pulling) and AP (air pressure) when PS is at level 2 (when the pulling speed is 10 mm/s). The response values represent the light loss experienced under the conditions determined by the experimental design.

Analysis

As usual,

$$CF = \frac{(\text{total})^2}{8} = 1.9208$$

$$SS_{tot} = \Sigma\ y^2 - CF = 0.4266$$

$$SS_{PS} = \frac{(1.16)^2}{4} + \frac{(2.76)^2}{4} - CF = 0.32$$

$$SS_{BW} = \frac{(2.31)^2}{4} + \frac{(1.61)^2}{4} - CF = 0.061$$

$$SS_{PG} = \frac{(2.06)^2}{4} + \frac{(1.86)^2}{4} - CF = 0.005$$

$$SS_{PT} = \frac{(2.15)^2}{4} + \frac{(1.77)^2}{4} - CF = 0.0181$$

The pseudo-factor IT/AP is analysed separately within each level of PS. First, the effect of IT is estimated using the data in level 1 of the PS factor as follows:

$$SS_{IT} = \frac{(IT_1)^2 + (IT_2)^2}{2} - \frac{(IT_1 + IT_2)^2}{4}$$

$$= \frac{(0.6)^2 + (0.56)^2}{2} - \frac{(1.16)^2}{4}$$

$$= 0.0004 \qquad (df = 1)$$

Table 11.13 ANOVA for case-study 11.2

Source	df	SS	MSS	F-ratio
PS	1	0.32	0.32	46.4 * significance
BW	1	0.061	0.061	8.84 * significance
PG	1	0.005 p		
PT	1	0.0181	0.0181	2.62
IT	1	0.0004 p		
AP	1	0.0169 p		
Res (p)	4	0.0276	0.0069	
Total	7	0.4267		

and the effect of AP is estimated using the data in level 2 of the PS factor as follows:

$$SS_{AP} = \frac{(AP_1)^2 + (AP_2)^2}{2} - \frac{(AP_1 + AP_2)^2}{4}$$

$$= \frac{(1.25)^2 + (1.51)^2}{2} - \frac{(2.76)^2}{4}$$

$$= 0.0169 \qquad (df = 1)$$

The residual sum of squares can be found by subtraction to be

$$SS_e = 0.00525$$

and, by pulling together the sum of squares of IT, AP and PG, we have

$$SS_e = 0.02755 \qquad (df = 4)$$

The ANOVA table is shown in Table 11.13.

The analysis indicates that the pulling speed is the most significant factor, with the burner width also being significant at the 5% level. It can easily be shown that the optimal levels for these factors (for lowest light loss) are PS(1) and BW(2).

11.3.4 Idle-column technique

When using the dummy-level technique, at least 1 degree of freedom is wasted. For example, if we assign a three-level factor on the four-level column of the $OA_8(4 \times 2^4)$, we make use of 3 columns of 1 degree of freedom each, that is, we have 3 degrees of freedom for the study of a factor needing only 2 degrees of freedom. Using, say, the $OA_8(2^7)$, only one independent fourth-level column can be created (see Section 11.3.1); so, if we wish to study, say, 3 three-level factors, the $OA_8(2^7)$ cannot be used.

A way of avoiding the above disadvantages (and still starting from a simple two-level orthogonal design) is provided by the idle-column technique. We will demonstrate this technique for the special case of three-level column creation, and indicate its applicability for more general situations.

Creation of three-level columns

We first choose one of the two-level columns of the array as the idle column I, with levels $I(1)$ and $I(2)$. Suppose A is a three-level factor with levels $A(1)$, $A(2)$ and $A(3)$. We can assign A to any two-level column (other than the idle column) of the array in such a way that:

1. Levels $A(1)$ and $A(2)$ are within level $I(1)$.
2. Levels $A(3)$ and (again) $A(2)$ are within $I(2)$.
3. The interaction column between I and A is erased.

Note that, because of the orthogonality and balance of the original design, level $A(2)$ is thus repeated twice as many times as levels $A(1)$ or $A(3)$.

For example, the first three columns of $OA_8(2^7)$ could be used as follows:

Column	I 1	2	3	I 1	A (2, 3)
	1	1	1	1	1
	1	1	1	1	1
	1	2	2	1	2
	1	2	2	1	2
	2	1	2	2	2
	2	1	2	2	2
	2	2	1	2	3
	2	2	1	2	3

It is now possible to estimate the main effect of A through levels $I(1)$ and $I(2)$. This is because from $I(1)$ we can obtain the difference between $A(1)$ and $A(2)$, and from $I(2)$ we can obtain the difference between $A(2)$ and $A(3)$.

This technique is apparently similar to multilevel creation and the dummy-level technique. The difference lies in the fact that the idle column, I, can be used more than once. For example, it can be used up to three times in the $OA_8(2^7)$, thus taking care of 3 three-level factors, as Table 11.14 shows. Note that, in the resulting design, the original interaction columns 3 (1×2),

Table 11.14 Idle-column technique

Trial	1	2	3	Column 4	5	6	7	I 1	A (2, 3)	B (4, 5)	C (6, 7)
1	1	1	1	1	1	1	1	1	1	1	1
2	1	1	1	2	2	2	2	1	1	2	2
3	1	2	2	1	1	2	2	1	2	1	2
4	1	2	2	2	2	1	1	1	2	2	1
5	2	1	2	1	2	1	2	2	2	2	2
6	2	1	2	2	1	2	1	2	2	3	3
7	2	2	1	1	2	2	1	2	3	2	3
8	2	2	1	2	1	1	2	2	3	3	2

5 (1 × 4) and 7 (1 × 6) have been erased. But it is clear that one uses only as many degrees of freedom as are required, thus avoiding the waste of degrees of freedom arising from the dummy-level technique.

Note from Table 11.14 that I (the first column) is associated with columns 2, 4 and 6 through the following level correspondence:

$$[1, 1] \rightarrow 1$$
$$[1, 2] \rightarrow 2$$
$$[2, 1] \rightarrow 2$$
$$[2, 2] \rightarrow 3$$

The above level correspondence can be used for the creation of three-level columns in any two-level orthogonal arrays, such as in $OA_{16}(2^{15})$.

If possible, it is recommended that no factor is assigned to the idle column I (hence the name idle). This is because one-half of the difference between the first and the third level of the newly created three-level column is confounded with the difference between levels $I(1)$ and $I(2)$ which corresponds to the main effect of the factor assigned to the idle column. It is, of course, possible to correct the effect of, say, A from the effect of I since the difference between $A(1)$ and $A(2)$ can be obtained. But this has to be repeated for any three-level column created in this way. In order to avoid tedious correction calculations, it is best to leave column I unassigned, or assign to it a factor of secondary interest, such as a block factor.

Creation of multilevel columns

The idle-column technique can be applied to the study of any k-level factors $(k > 2)$ utilizing any two-level orthogonal array $OA_n(2^{n-1})$ where n is not a multiple of k. The multilevel-column creation technique (Section 11.3.1) can help in the formation of these k-level columns provided that in the final design:

1. The idle column appears.
2. In any newly created column, one of the k levels appears twice as many times as the other levels: half of the times in the part of the column corresponding to level $I(1)$, and half of the times in the part of the column corresponding to level $I(2)$.

For example, 1 seven-level factor A and 2 three-level factors B, C can be studied using the idle-column technique on the first 11 columns of the $OA_{16}(2^{15})$, as shown in Table 11.15.

The repeated level is called the *control level* and helps in the comparison of all the levels. Usually the level considered the most important is selected as the control level. There can only be one control level; for example, when a six-level factor needs to be studied, two of the six levels can be repeated twice as many times as the others: half of these times corresponding to $I(1)$ and the other half corresponding to $I(2)$.

Table 11.15 Idle-column technique for multilevel creation

Trial	Column			
	1 I	(2–7) A	(8, 9) B	(10, 11) C
1	1	1	1	1
2	1	1	2	2
3	1	2	1	1
4	1	2	2	2
5	1	3	1	2
6	1	3	2	1
7	1	4	1	2
8	1	4	2	1
9	2	1	1	1
10	2	1	3	3
11	2	5	1	3
12	2	5	3	3
13	2	6	1	3
14	2	6	3	1
15	2	7	1	3
16	2	7	3	1

Table 11.16 Idle-column technique starting from three-level arrays

Trial	Column				
	1 Idle	(2 3 4) A	(5 6 7) B	(8 9 10) C	(11 12 13) D
1	1	1	1	1	1
2	1	1	2	2	2
3	1	1	3	3	3
4	1	2	1	2	3
5	1	2	2	3	1
6	1	2	3	1	2
7	1	3	1	3	2
8	1	3	2	1	3
9	1	3	3	2	1
10	2	1	1	1	1
11	2	1	4	4	4
12	2	1	5	5	5
13	2	4	1	4	5
14	2	4	4	5	1
15	2	4	5	1	4
16	2	5	1	5	4
17	2	5	4	1	5
18	2	5	5	4	1
19	3	1	1	1	1
20	3	1	6	6	6
21	3	1	7	7	7
22	3	6	1	6	7
23	3	6	6	7	1
24	3	6	7	1	6
25	3	7	1	7	6
26	3	7	6	1	7
27	3	7	7	6	1

So far, the original orthogonal array considered has been two-level. However, using the same principles, the idle-column technique can also be applied for the assignment of multilevel factors on three-level orthogonal arrays. For example, up to 4 seven-level factors can be studied independently utilizing the $OA_{27}(3^{13})$, by using its first column as the idle column and assuming level one to be the control level for all the factors. The control level in this case appears three times as often as the other levels. This is illustrated in Table 11.16.

The idle-column technique can be seen as a method of creating a pseudo-factor which has different levels depending on the levels of the idle column. The levels, therefore, of the pseudo-factor can be considered as being nested within the levels of the idle column, and so their analysis is similar to the analysis of a nested design as demonstrated in the case of the trans-factor technique (Section 11.3.3).

CASE STUDY 11.3

In order to identify the factors affecting the braking performance of a light railway, emergency braking tests took place. The main objective was a comparison between the two types of wheel which the vehicles were to be fitted with: the original wheel and a reprofiled wheel. Another factor of interest was whether the vehicle was loaded or empty. Some of the braking tests were carried out with empty vehicles, and some with lightly loaded and heavily loaded vehicles (with oil drums filled with water).

The vehicles are load-weighed and the braking system automatically compensates for the heavily loaded vehicle by increasing the braking force. However, this increased braking force can sometimes cause increased brake fade, which would render the load compensation less effective. An added complication is that lightly loaded vehicles seem on some railways to achieve a lower adhesion, perhaps because the wheels skip over roughness on the rail more easily.

Evidence was therefore required on whether the braking performance was seriously affected by the rail condition. The condition of the rail was simulated at three levels: wet/soaped, dry/good condition, and scaled/rusted.

The response of interest was the stopping distance margin (*SDM*), which was calculated as follows:

Step 1. The maximum acceptable stopping distance was determined by reading off a curve of maximum acceptable stopping distance versus vehicle speed at brake application – see Figure 11.5.

Step 2. The actual stopping distance was subtracted from the maximum acceptable value found in Step 1 above.

Step 3. To reduce the effect of the initial speed on the test parameter, the result of Step 2 was divided by the square of the initial speed to obtain the *SDM* which can be expressed as follows:

$$SDM = \frac{(\text{maximum acceptable stopping distance at initial speed} - \text{actual stopping distance})}{(\text{initial speed})^2}$$

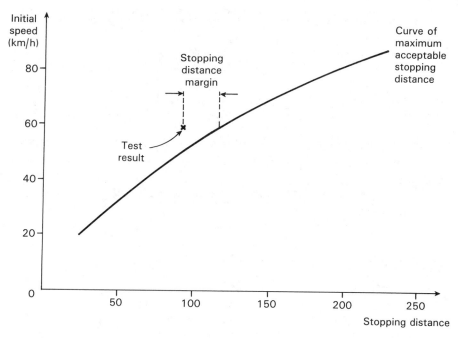

Figure 11.5 Finding the stopping distance margin (case-study 11.3)

The larger the value of the *SDM* the better the test result.
We are dealing here with 1 three-level factor and 2 two-level factors as follows:

Factor	Levels		
	1	2	3
Load condition (*LC*)	Empty	Light	Heavy
Rail condition (*RC*)	Wet/soaped	Dry/good	Scaled/rusted
Type of wheel (*TW*)	Original	Reprofiled	

The appropriate design was constructed using the idle-column technique on the $OA_8(2^7)$, as Table 11.17 shows. Two test results were obtained for each experimental trial and these are also shown in Table 11.17.

Analysis

As usual

$$CF = (\text{sum total})^2/16 = 711.56$$

$$SS_{\text{tot}} = 163.07$$

and

$$SS_{TW} = \frac{(52.1)^2 + (54.6)^2}{8} - CF = 0.39$$

Table 11.17 Experimental design and data for case-study 11.3

Trial	1	(2, 3)	(4, 5)	6	7	Data (SDM)
	I	LC	RC	TW		
1	1	1	1	1	1	3.1, 2.1
2	1	1	2	2	2	7.2, 7.5
3	1	2	1	2	1	7.1, 5.5
4	1	2	2	1	2	9.9, 12.3
5	2	2	2	1	2	11.7, 9.4
6	2	2	3	2	1	5.6, 6.2
7	2	3	2	2	1	8.2, 7.3
8	2	3	3	1	2	2.3, 1.3

Table 11.18 ANOVA table for case-study 11.3

Source	df	SS	MSS	F-ratio
TW	1	0.39	0.39	0.4
LC(1, 2)	1	27.75	27.75	29.7[*]
LC(2, 3)	1	23.81	23.81	25.5[*]
RC(1, 2)	1	45.60	45.60	48.8[*]
RC(2, 3)	1	56.18	56.18	60.1[*]
Res	10	9.34	0.93	
Total	15	163.07		

For the sum of squares of *LC* and *RC* we follow the type of analysis outlined in Section 11.3.3, viewing *LC* and *RC* as pseudo-factors. Indeed, since the levels of *LC* differ according to the levels of the idle column *I*, we perform a different analysis of those levels for each level of column *I*. The sum of squares for *LC* when levels 1 and 2 are used within level *I*(1) is given by

$$SS_{LC(1,2)} = \frac{(LC_1)^2 + (LC_2)^2}{4} - CF_{I(1)} = \frac{(19.9)^2 + (34.8)^2}{4} - \frac{(54.7)^2}{8}$$

$$= 27.75$$

and the sum of squares for *LC* when levels 2 and 3 are used within *L*(2) is given by

$$SS_{LC(2,3)} = \frac{(LC_2)^2 + (LC_3)^2}{4} - CF_{I(2)} = \frac{(32.9)^2 + (19.1)^2}{4} - \frac{(52.0)^2}{8}$$

$$= 23.81$$

Similarly for *RC*:

$$SS_{RC(1,2)} = \frac{(RC_1)^2 + (RC_2)^2}{4} - CF_{I(1)} = \frac{(17.8)^2 + (36.9)^2}{4} - \frac{(54.7)^2}{8}$$

$$= 45.60$$

and

$$SS_{RC(2,3)} = \frac{(RC_2)^2 + (RC_3)^2}{4} - CF_{I(2)} = \frac{(36.6)^2 + (15.4)^2}{4} - \frac{(52.0)^2}{8}$$

$$= 56.18$$

Every sum of squares calculated above is associated with 1 degree of freedom. The ANOVA results are shown in Table 11.18. It is evident from Table 11.18 that load conditions as well as rail conditions significantly affect the braking performance of the light railway. The type of wheel makes no difference to the performance.

11.3.5 Combining technique

We can employ a single three-level column for the study of 2 two-level factors A and B, under the assumption that no significant interaction effect exists between these factors. This is achieved by forming a three-level combination factor $[A, B]$ whose three levels are defined as follows:

$[A, B] (1) = A(1)B(1)$ (= level 1 of A and level 1 of B)
$[A, B] (2) = A(2)B(1)$ (= level 2 of A and level 1 of B)
$[A, B] (3) = A(1)B(2)$ (= level 1 of A and level 2 of B)

By assigning this combination factor $[A, B]$ to a three-level column, we can obtain information about the effects of both A and B. In fact, the main effect of A can be obtained from the difference between $[A, B] (1)$ and $[A, B] (2)$, whereas the main effect of B can be obtained from the difference between $[A, B] (1)$ and $[A, B] (3)$.

For example, suppose a three-level column of $OA_9(3^4)$ is utilized. The total effect of the combination factor $[A, B]$ can be found through the usual formula as:

$$SS_{[A,B]} = \frac{([A,B]_1)^2 + ([A,B]_2)^2 + ([A,B]_3)^2}{3r} - CF$$

where r is the number of replications per trial, with the subscripted terms representing level totals. Now for the main effects of A and B we have

$$SS_A = \frac{([A,B]_1 - [A,B]_2)^2}{\text{number of observations in } [A,B](1) \text{ and } [A,B](2)}$$

$$= \frac{(A_1B_1 - A_2B_1)^2}{6r}$$

and

$$SS_B = \frac{([A,B]_1 - [A,B]_3)^2}{\text{number of observations in } [A,B](1) \text{ and } [A,B](3)}$$

$$= \frac{(A_1B_1 - A_1B_2)^2}{6r}$$

Thus, finding the main effects of 2 two-level factors A and B is the same as comparing the three levels of the combination factor $[A, B]$ which is a combination of A and B. Note that, since A and B are not orthogonal to each other, S_A and S_B do not sum up to $SS_{[A,B]}$.

CASE STUDY 11.4

An experiment took place in the microwave division of the Electronic Devices Department with the aim of determining optimal production conditions in the substrate processing of thin film resistors. The end outcome of this process is the production of a circuit incorporating up to 30 thin film resistors; the objective of these resistors was to satisfy the target of 100 ohms per square inch. Eight controllable process factors were identified: 3 at two levels and 5 at three levels. It was also desirable to achieve robustness of the process against the effect of 3 noise factors which were simulated at two levels each. All factors and their levels are shown in Table 11.19.

The $OA_{18}(2 \times 3^7)$ was used as the inner array, that is, as the design for the assignment of the controllable factors. Factors *BT*, *RT*, *VS*, *PC*, *SP* and *EP* were assigned to columns 1, 2, 3, 4, 6 and 7 respectively (the 8th column was left unassigned). The combining technique was used to create the three-level combination factor [*LP*, *DR*] out of the 2 two-level factors *LP* and *DR*, which was assigned to column 5: see Table 11.20.

The three levels of the combination factor were defined as follows:

$$[LP, DR](1) = LP(1)DR(1)$$
$$[LP, DR](2) = LP(2)DR(1)$$
$$[LP, DR](3) = LP(1)DR(2)$$

Following a Taguchi-type experimental set up (see, for example, Figure 11.4) the three noise factors *S*, *F* and *H* were assigned to the three columns of the $OA_4(2^3)$ which thus represented the outer array. The four trials of the outer array represented four combinations of the noise factors which were simulated at each of the 18 trials of the inner array. Four repetitions thus of each experimental trial

Table 11.19 Controllable and noise factors for case study 11.4

Controllable factors	Levels		
	1	2	3
BT: Bake temperature at plating stage (°C)	340	360	
RT: Rinse time in D.I. water (min)	5	7	9
VS: Voltage during sputtering (V)	900	1000	1100
PC: Plating current (mA/in²)	15	20	25
LP: Laser profile (option)	Yes	No	
DR: Dross removal (method)	Scrape	Scotchbrite	
SP: Spin speed (rpm)	3500	4000	4500
EP: Etch power (kW)	0.8	1.0	1.2
Noise factors			
S: Supplier	MRC	Kohitsu	
F: Furnace	Oven 1	Oven 2	
H: Through hole plating	Yes	No	

Table 11.20 Experimental set-up and data for case-study 11.4

							S	1	1	2	2
			Inner array				F	1	2	1	2
			(control factors)				H	1	2	2	1
Trial	1	2	3	4	5	6	7		Data (ohms)		
	BT	RT	VS	PC	[LP, DR]	SP	EP				
1	1	1	1	1	1	1	1	75	66	69	67
2	1	1	2	2	2	2	2	83	85	88	92
3	1	1	3	3	3	3	3	90	98	110	108
4	1	2	1	1	2	2	3	74	69	83	76
5	1	2	2	2	3	3	1	86	88	99	90
6	1	2	3	3	1	1	1	96	120	113	98
7	1	3	1	2	1	3	2	98	94	99	101
8	1	3	2	3	2	1	3	112	115	118	116
9	1	3	3	1	3	2	1	79	85	88	84
10	2	1	1	3	3	2	2	106	108	114	112
11	2	1	2	1	1	3	3	69	72	71	73
12	2	1	3	2	2	1	1	82	85	88	84
13	2	2	1	2	3	1	3	87	91	93	89
14	2	2	2	3	1	2	1	94	97	95	93
15	2	2	3	1	2	3	2	77	79	83	83
16	2	3	1	3	2	3	1	96	105	98	102
17	2	3	2	1	3	1	2	77	83	79	77
18	2	3	3	2	1	2	3	78	88	82	84

(of the inner array) took place simulating the noise space (see Table 11.20). The response values represent the number of ohms per square inch, and these are also shown in Table 11.20.

Analysis

We will follow a Taguchi-type analysis, by statistically analysing a noise perform-ance measure (*NPM*) and a target performance measure (*TPM*). Since there is a desirable response target to achieve, Taguchi recommends the signal to noise ratio as a *NPM*; for each trial we calculate

$$NPM = 10 \log_{10}(\bar{y}^2/s^2)$$

where $\bar{y}$ and s are respectively the sample mean and sample standard deviation of the (4) observations in each trial.

As a *TPM* we simply use for each trial

$$TMP = \bar{y}$$

Using the data values of Table 11.20 we obtain the 18 values of *NPM* and *TPM* (shown in Table 11.21) that need to be analysed for the determination of the variability control factors and target control factors respectively.

We first analyse the *NPM* in the usual way:

$$CF = \frac{(\text{sum total})^2}{18} = \frac{(498.43)^2}{18} = 13801.804$$

$$SS_{tot} = \Sigma\, y^2 - CF = 312.624 \qquad (df = 17)$$

Table 11.21 *NPM* and *TPM* values for case-study 11.4

Trial	Sample mean	Sample standard deviation	NPM	TPM
1	69.25	4.03	24.70	69.25
2	87.00	3.92	26.93	87.00
3	101.50	9.30	20.76	101.50
4	75.50	5.80	22.29	75.50
5	90.75	5.74	23.98	90.75
6	106.75	11.64	19.25	106.75
7	98.00	2.94	30.46	98.00
8	115.25	2.50	33.27	115.25
9	84.00	3.74	27.03	84.00
10	110.00	3.65	29.58	110.00
11	71.25	1.71	32.40	71.25
12	84.75	2.50	30.60	84.75
13	90.00	2.58	30.85	90.00
14	94.75	1.70	34.92	94.75
15	80.50	3.00	28.57	80.50
16	100.25	4.03	27.92	100.25
17	79.00	2.83	28.92	79.00
18	83.00	4.16	26.00	83.00

$$SS_{BT} = \frac{(BT_1)^2 + (BT_2)^2}{9} - CF = \frac{(228.67)^2 + (269.76)^2}{9} - CF$$

$$= 93.799 \qquad (df = 1)$$

$$SS_{RT} = \frac{(RT_1)^2 + (RT_2)^2 + (RT_3)^2}{6} - CF$$

$$= \frac{(164.97)^2 + (159.86)^2 + (173.6)^2}{6} - CF = 16.076 \qquad (df = 2)$$

Similarly,

$$SS_{VS} = 66.346, \qquad SS_{PC} = 2.058, \qquad SS_{SP} = 1.113$$

and

$$SS_{EP} = 2.548 \qquad (df = 2)$$

The experimental design used allows the determination of the interaction effect between the controllable factors assigned to the first two columns of the array, *BT* and *RT*:

$$SS_{BT \times RT} = \frac{(BT_1 \times RT_1)^2 + (BT_1 \times RT_2)^2 + \cdots + (BT_2 \times RT_3)^2}{3}$$

$$- SS_{BT} - SS_{RT} - CF$$

$$= 123.027 \qquad (df = 2)$$

For the combination factor $[LP, DR]$ we first calculate the sum of squares as usual:

$$SS_{[LP,DR]} = \frac{([LP,DR]_1)^2 + ([LP,DR]_2)^2 + ([LP,DR]_3)^2}{6} - CF$$

$$= \frac{(167.73)^2 + (169.58)^2 + (161.12)^2}{6} - CF = 6.594 \qquad (df = 2)$$

To resolve the effects of LP and DR we calculate the following:

$$SS_{LP} = \frac{([LP,DR]_1 - [LP,DR]_2)^2}{\text{number of observations in } [LP,DR](1) \text{ and } [LP,DR](2)}$$

$$= \frac{(LP_1DR_1 - LP_2DR_1)^2}{12} = \frac{(167.73 - 169.58)^2}{12} = 0.285 \qquad (df = 1)$$

and

$$SS_{DR} = \frac{([LP,DR]_1 - [LP,DR]_3)^2}{\text{number of observations in } [LP,DR](1) \text{ and } [LP,DR](3)}$$

$$= \frac{(LP_1DR_1 - LP_1DR_2)^2}{12} = \frac{(167.73 - 161.12)^2}{12} = 3.641 \qquad (df = 1)$$

Note that, since LP and DR are not orthogonal, $SS_{LP} + SS_{DR} \neq SS_{[LP,DR]}$. Finally, by subtraction we obtain

$$SS_{res} = SS_{tot} - SS_{BT} - SS_{RT} - SS_{BT \times RT} - SS_{VS}$$
$$- SS_{PC} - SS_{SP} - SS_{EP} - SS_{[LP,DR]}$$
$$= 1.063 \qquad (df = 2)$$

and the ANOVA summary is shown in Table 11.22.

The residual variance (MSS_e) cannot be used for elucidation of the separate effects of LP and DR. However, it is clear from the values of SS_{LP} and SS_{DR} that the effect of the combination factor $[LP, DR]$ is due to DR rather than LP. Therefore, although $[LP, DR]$ was assigned to column 5, it can be assumed that the

Table 11.22 ANOVA summary for *NPM* (case-study 11.4)

Source	df	SS	MSS
BT	1	93.799	93.799
RT	2	16.076	8.038
BT × RT	2	123.027	61.514
VS	2	66.346	33.173
PC	2	2.058	1.029
[LP, DR]	2	6.594	3.297
LP	(1)	(0.285)	
DR	(1)	(3.641)	
SP	2	1.113	0.557
EP	2	2.548	1.274
Res	2	1.063	0.532
Total	17	312.624	

factor *DR* alone appeared in column 5 with its first level as a dummy level (repeated twice as many times as level 2).

In this case we can recalculate the sum of squares due to *DR* once again from column 5 on the basis of the dummy level technique:

$$SS'_{DR} = \frac{(DR_1 + DR_{1'})^2}{12} + \frac{(DR_2)^2}{6} - CF = \frac{(167.73 + 169.58)^2}{12} + \frac{(161.12)^2}{6} - CF$$

$$= 6.309 \qquad (df = 1)$$

Note that we now have

$$SS'_{DR} + SS_{PL} = SS_{[PL,DR]}$$

The final ANOVA summary (with a pooled residual) is shown in Table 11.23.

The results of Table 11.23 indicate that factors *BT* and *VS*, and to a lesser degree factors *RT* and *DR*, significantly affect the variation in the response. There is also a significant interaction effect between *BT* and *RT*. So the factors *BT*, *RT*, *VS* and *DR* are variability control factors and should be appropriately tuned in order to minimize the variability in the response.

The optimal levels of these factors are the levels with maximum value of *NPM*. It can be shown that the following combination of levels is the optimal as far as variability is concerned:

$$BT(2) \quad RT(2) \quad VS(2) \quad DR(1)$$

An analysis of the *TPM* in a similar way produced the ANOVA summary of Table 11.24.

After pooling, it can be seen that the only factors which are not variability control factors but do affect the mean response (significant for *TPM*) are factors *PC* and *EP* (to a lesser degree). The average *TPM* on each of their levels is as follows:

	Level		
	1	2	3
PC	87.2	88.9	92.5
EP	87.3	93.5	89.4

It is clear that factor *PC* (plating current) has a linear effect on the mean response; as it is also highly significant, it is the ideal candidate for a target control factor,

Table 11.23   Pooled ANOVA for *NPM* (case-study 11.4)

Source	df	SS	MSS	F-ratio	
BT	1	93.799	93.799	119.5	significant
RT	2	16.076	8.038	10.2	significant
BT × *RT*	2	123.027	61.514	78.4	significant
VS	2	66.346	33.173	42.3	significant
DR	1	6.309	6.309	8.0	significant
Res	9	7.067	0.785		
Total	17	312.624			

Table 11.24 ANOVA summary for *TPM* (case-study 11.4)

Source	df	SS	MSS
BT	1	66.125	66.125
RT	2	107.771	53.886
BT × RT	2	159.396	79.698
VS	2	2.083	1.042
PC	2	2392.333	1196.167
[LP, DR]	2	88.563	44.282
SP	2	10.396	5.198
EP	2	121.188	60.594
Res	2	19.770	9.885
Total	17	2967.625	

that is, a factor which can be manipulated to bring the mean response on target, in this case, at 100 ohms per square inch.

11.3.6 Confounding technique

When one needs to study numerous factors and, due to a restrictive experimentation capability, none of the techniques covered so far can produce a satisfactory design enabling the independent assessment of all factor effects, then, as a last resort, the confounding method is followed. For example, there might be occasions when one needs to study the effects of numerous multilevel sources totalling, say, n degrees of freedom, but the only affordable designs are those which allow for m degrees of freedom, where $m < n$.

Prior experience and engineering judgment will then have to play a role in identifying those factors which are not expected to have a significant effect. The effects of these factors will then be allowed to be confounded (confused).

For example, 2 of these factors, say A and B, with two levels each, will be assigned to a single two-level column by forming the two-level factor AB with levels

$$AB(1) = A(1)B(1) \quad \text{and} \quad AB(2) = A(2)B(2)$$

If, during the analysis, the effect of AB is found to be insignificant, it can be assumed that neither A nor B is significant. However, if AB is found to have a significant effect, it is always possible that either A or B, or both A and B, could be significant, and an additional experiment might be necessary in order to separate their effects.

Nevertheless, in the presence of numerous factors, especially during initial screening, this method can be followed, even by combining more than 2 factors together. This can reduce a prohibitively large number of sources to a manageable set of effects which may (or may not) include some confounded effects. Once this reduction is achieved, subsequent experimentation may then be possible to enable more detailed study and proper assessment.

11.3.7 Compounding technique

There are many occasions when the responses of interest are numerous. It is possible to perform many types of study (as many as the number of responses) using the same design and performing only one experiment, by assigning many factors to the same column in the design. During the analysis of a particular response, only the appropriate sources related to this response are considered.

For example, suppose there are three responses of interest $R1$, $R2$ and $R3$ with which 9 two-level factors $A, B, ..., I$ are related in the manner shown in Table 11.25. The asterisk in the table signifies that the associated factor has, or may have, an influence on the corresponding response. Table 11.26 shows how 14 main effects and 3 interaction effects could be studied with the expense of only 8 experimental trials using the $OA_8(2^7)$ design. The number of replications per trial could differ depending on the response under consideration. Different ANOVA analyses would be performed, one for each response.

11.3.8 Choosing the factor levels

One of the most important steps that has to be taken before experimentation is the proper selection of factor levels. Appropriately chosen levels can greatly enhance the efficiency of an experimental study. Careful consideration of the experimental range for each factor, and of the interrelationships between

Table 11.25 Factors and related responses

	Factors								
	A	*B*	*C*	*D*	*E*	*F*	*G*	*H*	*I*
R1	*	*	*	*	*				
R2		*		*			*	*	
R3	*			*		*		*	*

Table 11.26 Assignment by compounding

	Column						
	1	2	3	4	5	6	7
R1	*A*	*B*	*C*	*D*	e	*B* × *D*	*E*
R2	*G* × *H*	*B*	e	*D*	*B* × *H*	*G*	*H*
R3	*A*	e	e	*D*	*F*	*I*	*H*

Trial									Data	
								R1	R2	R3
1	1	1	1	1	1	1	1	.	.	.
2	1	1	1	2	2	2	2	.	.	.
.	.	.	.	.	.	.	.	.	.	.
.	.	.	.	.	.	.	.	.	.	.
8	2	2	1	2	1	1	2	.	.	.

factors, can help towards a proper choice of levels. If from past experience it is known that a particular range is unusable or prohibitive in terms of cost, low yield etc., it should not be used for the experiment. This will eliminate the possibility of failed trials or useless information.

Careful consideration should also be given to whether or not the range of a particular factor differs according to the levels of another factor. If such interrelationships exist, the levels of one of the factors should be defined in a different way for every level of the other factors. For example, in chemical reaction experiments, it is common that the range of the reaction time (say, A) varies according to the levels of the temperature (say, B) used. One could then define the levels of the two-level factor A in the manner indicated by the following (hypothetical) example:

	$A(1)$	$A(2)$
$B(1) = 50\,^{\circ}C$	6 hours	8 hours
$B(2) = 60\,^{\circ}C$	5 hours	7 hours
$B(3) = 70\,^{\circ}C$	4 hours	6 hours

Data analysis is conducted in the usual manner.

Forming the levels of A as above, in addition to avoiding experiments in an unnecessary or unusable range, most importantly cancels the interaction between A and B for this particular experiment. Cancellation of interactions (in this way) can considerably enhance the precision of data analysis and facilitate the choice of an affordable experimental design.

Strictly speaking, it is never the case that there is no interaction between the factors under study. It is usually the case that the effect of every factor, say A, depends on other conditions B, C, ... Nevertheless, as long as the interrelationships between the factors under study are logically considered before experimentation, it is possible to contrive monotonicity in the factorial effects and additivity in the response model for this particular experiment.

In Taguchi's opinion, when monotonicity or additivity of factorial effects does not hold, it is because insufficient research has been carried out on the interrelationships between the factors. Taguchi actually believes that 'as long as it is not possible to minimize interactions between the controllable factors, it is impossible to render the experiment efficient'. He recommends that experiments are designed with emphasis on main effects. As far as possible, past engineering experience should play a role in the selection of characteristics with minimal interactions. He believes that interaction is not a matter of assignment, but should be dealt with 'by changing to characteristic values possessing additivity or monotonicity, and by consideration of interrelationships between the levels chosen for the different factors, prior to experimentation'.

The designs OA_{12}, OA_{18} and OA_{36} are among specially designed arrays in which interactions are distributed more or less uniformly among all columns; this enables the researcher to focus on main effects, and contributes towards greater efficiency and reproducibility of small scale experimentation.

11.3.9 Dealing with mixture experiments

When experiments involve the mixing of various substances, in percentages that have to sum up to 100, the factor levels can be formed by one of the two following methods.

Expanding–shrinking method

Assuming that the ranges of the various substances have been decided upon, and initial levels have been formed and assigned on the basis of a suitable experimental design, the initial levels are allowed to expand or shrink appropriately so that they can add up to 100 for each experimental design. For example, suppose that 4 three-level factors (substances) are assigned to the 4 columns of $OA_9(3^4)$ with the following initial levels (in percentages):

Factors	Levels		
	1	2	3
A	20	35	45
B	18	20	50
C	17	25	25
D	15	20	15

Since the first trial of $OA_9(3^4)$ – see Appendix C – constitutes an experiment in which all factors appear in their first level, the total of the initial levels for the first trial will amount to

$$20 + 18 + 17 + 15 = 70\%$$

and not 100%. To perform this experimental trial, we first expand its levels appropriately enough to add up to 100; to do this, we multiply each of the original values (for the levels) by 100/70. So, for the first trial of $OA_9(3^4)$, the following expanded levels will be used:

$A(1)'$	$B(1)'$	$C(1)'$	$D(1)'$
$20 \times \dfrac{100}{70} = 28.6\%$	$18 \times \dfrac{100}{70} = 25.7\%$	$17 \times \dfrac{100}{70} = 24.3\%$	$15 \times \dfrac{100}{70} = 21.4\%$

In general, before we perform a particular trial, every level is multiplied by

$$\frac{100}{k}$$

where k is the total sum of the initial levels associated with this trial. For example, for the first trial of the $OA_9(3^4)$ considered above, $k = 70$, and the multiplication by 100/70 causes the expansion of the initial levels for this trial. For the last trial of $OA_9(3^4)$ we initially have

$$A(3) + B(3) + C(2) + D(1) = 45 + 50 + 25 + 15 = 135$$

and the multiplication by 100/135 will have as an effect the shrinking of the initial values into

$$A(3)' = 45 \times (100/135) = 33.3\% \qquad B(3)' = 37\%$$
$$C(2)' = 18.5\% \qquad D(1)' = 11.1\%$$

so that they sum up to 100%.

Planning out method

One of the substances is chosen not to be considered as a factor, so that it can be used as a remainder to bring the sum total of the levels of the other factors up to 100%. For example, in the hypothetical case considered in the previous section, substance A can be used as a remainder entering the experimental trial with a proportion of 50% when B, C and D are all at level 1, or with a proportion of 35% when B, C and D are all at level 2 etc. To ensure that the level total of the other factors does not exceed 100%, the substance used as the remainder is usually the one with the greatest quantity. However, this should not be taken as a rule. For example, if a substance is to be studied in terms of quantity as well as in terms of type, or is considered in combination with another substance for the purpose of cancelling their interaction, then it should not be used as a remainder, despite being the substance with the greatest quantity.

■ 11.4 From Deming to Taguchi and vice versa

It has been said that if Deming's teachings inspired a revolution in the old management culture, Taguchi's approach is an inspired evolution; an evolution of valuable statistical techniques which have their origins in the practices of Roland Fisher at Rothamstead Agricultural Station in the 1920s. These are the very same techniques as those on which Deming's principles are based. Deming advocates the implementation of a statistical quality management approach. He considers it critical that top managers acquire knowledge, or at least a clear appreciation, of the usefulness of statistical tools for achieving enhanced quality and increased productivity.

Another obvious connection is the similarity in their basic objectives. Deming provides a road map which can lead to the satisfaction of the customer, the creation of a happy working environment for the employee (through cooperation, job satisfaction, breaking down of barriers, elimination of fear), the safeguarding of jobs, the creation of more jobs etc. In other words, 'serving society in the best possible way'. Taguchi's main objective lies in his definition of quality (or non-quality): 'Quality is the amount of damage incurred to society from the moment the product has left the factory.' By 'society' he means the customer as well as the employees of the company; because, if the customer suffers, the whole company will eventually suffer through rework, guarantee costs, loss of reputation, of market share, and eventually loss of jobs. So, serving society is also Taguchi's aim.

When it comes to Deming's fourteen points for management, some other truths underlying Taguchi's philosophy can easily be detected. Indeed, if we look at the fourteen points as examples of statistical thinking, every one of them demands a real understanding of variation and an adequate appreciation of the damage which variation causes. Utilization of Taguchi's loss function can satisfy both the above demands.

Deming strongly advocates constancy of purpose for continuous improvement of product and services. Statistically speaking, the problem of establishing constancy and maintaining consistency of purpose can be related to Taguchi's problem of achieving the mean (target) and minimizing dispersion (variability) around the mean. Indeed, simply establishing constancy of purpose is equivalent to setting a course towards the target and achieving it; it is a necessary condition for business success, but is not sufficient. Maintaining long-term consistency is equivalent to striving for a reduction of the spread around the course so that the target is consistently achieved. As with any problem about variability, the cause of non-quality is usually the more difficult to resolve. But one should always keep trying.

The main steps for action advocated by both men are almost identical. Recall Deming's essential ongoing activities (see Section 2.4.3) and the PDCA (plan–do–check–act) cycle – see Figure 11.6. Deming's plan stage matches the activities Taguchi recommends for the brainstorming stage, perhaps the most important stage of the whole Taguchi procedure. This is when clear statements of the problems are established, the objective, the output characteristics and methods of measurement are determined, the controllable and uncontrollable factors of interest are defined, and the appropriate experiments are designed.

The do stage in Taguchi terms is equivalent to performing the experiments, analysing the resulting data and interpreting the results. This is where

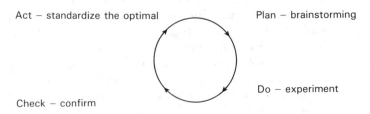

Figure 11.6 The Deming and Taguchi cycle

the variability control factors are determined and their optimal levels are selected so that the variability in the process/product performance is minimized. The target control factors are also determined and their settings are selected so that the mean response attains its desired value. A prediction of the process performance under the optimal settings will also take place at this stage.

Taguchi's equivalent action to the check stage is the running of a confirmatory experiment in order to verify predicted results. It is essential that it takes place, in order to confirm that the new parameter settings do indeed improve the performance. Confirmation will alleviate concerns about the possibility of a wrong choice of the factors to be studied or of experimental design, and about wrong assumptions in the underlying response model.

Corrective action can follow, based on the lessons learned so far (act). Changes should be adopted or abandoned in line with the results of the previous stage. A study of the current situation should take place, standardizing any improvements and properly documenting any good new processes and innovative ideas. Following a successful confirmation Taguchi experiment, this means that the optimal settings will, from there on, become the standard. They should be carefully documented and communicated, so that changes to the new settings become irreversible. This is the only way of holding the gains.

Deming does not consider it sufficient merely to solve problems, big or small. He is seeking a major transformation in the current practices of Western management. He suggests that a basis for this transformation is provided by his fourteen points, whose adoption and implementation would be a sign that 'the management intend to stay in business and aim to protect investors and jobs.' The common denominator between Deming's fourteen points and Taguchi's main principles is the importance of a never-ending effort towards variation reduction. Understanding that variation affects everything, not only in production but in all sectors of an organization, is one part of the profound knowledge that Deming tries to convey. Evaluating and predicting the damage that this variation causes, is the basis of Taguchi's efforts.

But, apart from the common elements inherent in Deming's and Taguchi's teachings, there are also many complementary ones. For example, if one of Deming's main achievements has been to convince companies to shift quality improvement backwards from inspection to statistical control of production processes, Taguchi's has been to make the further step back from production to design, in an attempt to make the design robust against variability downstream in both production and the user environment. This is in complete agreement with Deming's belief that reducing variation is the key to improving quality, to decreasing quality costs, and therefore for survival in this new economic age (created by Japan).

On the whole, Deming's and Taguchi's methods are complementary. Deming mainly provides a theory for management; Taguchi provides some important techniques that management can use to solve chronic problems. Theory and techniques are both necessary for management.

Without techniques for eliminating chronic waste, there is no hope for improvement, breakthrough and innovation, the necessities for survival in this new economic age. On the other hand, experience without theory teaches us nothing. Management attitudes need to change for any innovative technique to be established. It it hopeless to attempt to introduce Taguchi techniques, before the ground has been prepared by the senior management.

For example, without management's commitment, there is no hope that you will be allowed to perhaps stop the manufacturing process, if necessary, to perform the experiments that Taguchi demands. Deming can certainly help here: adaptation of his points by upper management will allow for innovation, for risk-taking, for experimental research, development and application of innovative techniques. He provides the theory for managing the business; the excuse that such a theory does not exist is no longer available. Deming's theory can lead to a total transformation of an outdated management culture into a total quality management (TQM) culture. It is actually evident that the Deming path to quality management is implicit in a TQM culture.

Deming provides a philosophy of management, a theory of management and specific powerful rules capable of transforming any company culture into a true TQM culture. On the other hand, the innovative techniques of SPC and those advocated by Taguchi provide the means for technically improving any process in a total sense, in its every stage from design to production and maintenance, and also for keeping the improved processes under control.

It is worthwhile finishing this section with a note of warning. The principles of Deming and Taguchi need to be clearly and properly understood before any attempt is made to implement them. Another common element in the philosophies of the two men is that certain points in both philosophies have been misinterpreted by people who have hurried the learning process. For example, one manager who completely misunderstood Deming's Point 3 (cease dependence on inspection) completely abolished inspection, with disastrous results. And (many) people still think that Taguchi does not believe in interactions and prefers to ignore them in his studies. This could not be further from the truth, something that becomes very clear from the following quotation: 'If one assumes a linear model thinking it correct, then one is a man removed from natural science or reality, and commits the mistake of standing just upon mathematics which is nothing but idealism.'

The management principles and process control methods associated with the work of W.E. Deming, together with Taguchi's methodology, which can certainly help towards a better understanding of the relationship between statistical and engineering science, are a long overdue revolution in quality improvement for products as well as for services. Whether these ideas can force changes in the direction of successful ways of working in Europe will be interesting and exciting to observe.

12 Taguchi's Recommended Analysis Techniques

The truth is rarely pure and never simple.
Oscar Wilde

In this chapter we outline some non-standard analysis techniques recommended by Taguchi for promoting the efficiency of an experimental study. The concept of *contribution ratios* is mentioned; this is a measure that can play an important role in *tolerance analysis* (see Chapter 14). A technique for predicting the future process performance under certain conditions is described, concentrating on the aspect of *discount (β) coefficients* which are used to improve estimation. For the analysis of categorical and ranked-type data Taguchi recommends *accumulating analysis*, which is also discussed.

■ 12.1 Net variation and contribution ratio

According to Taguchi, the use of the *F*-ratios in an ANOVA analysis is only helpful for the qualitative evaluation of whether factorial effects exist. What is needed is a quantitative evaluation, something that can be achieved through the use of contribution ratios. Generally speaking, the contribution ratio of a source (main factor effect, interaction etc.) is its contribution (in percentage terms) to the total variability of the experimental results. One of the main uses of the contribution ratio is in the field of tolerance design (to be explained in Chapter 14).

As explained in Chapter 7, the mean sum of squares for a particular effect (in an ANOVA table) is defined as the ratio of the sum of squares of the effect to its degrees of freedom. For example, for the (main or interaction) effect A we have

$$MSS_A = \frac{SS_A}{df_A}$$

and for the residual:

$$MSS_e = \frac{SS_e}{df_e}$$

with SS_e being the residual (error) sum of squares. MSS_e is otherwise known as the error variance.

In testing for significance of the effect of A, the following F-ratio is calculated:

$$F_A = \frac{MSS_A}{MSS_e} = \frac{SS_A}{df_A \times MSS_e}$$

If the effect of the source A were negligible, the value F_A should be about 1, that is, SS_A should be about $df_A \times MSS_e$. Therefore, the net effect of A could be estimated from

$$SS'_A = SS_A - df_A \times MSS_e$$

SS'_A is called the net variation (or pure variation) of the source A. The net variation for the error, SS_e, is obtained by subtracting the net variations of all the available sources from the total sum of squares SS_{tot}.

Having calculated the net variation of a particular source, we can now estimate the extent to which this source affects the experimental results, in other words, the portion of the whole experimental variation that the source is responsible for. This is achieved by dividing the source's net variation by SS_{tot}; the contribution ratio is thus obtained, which, in percentage terms, is given (for example, for source A) by the following:

$$Cr_A = \frac{SS'_A}{SS_{tot}} \times 100 = \frac{SS_A - df_A \times MSS_e}{SS_{tot}} \times 100$$

We similarly have

$$Cr_e = \frac{SS'_e}{SS_{tot}} \times 100$$

The above also covers the case of a pooled error variation component.

It is sufficient to calculate only the contribution ratios of the significant sources.

The ANOVA table for case-study 11.2 (optical fibres experiment, page 318) is reproduced in Table 12.1 with the contribution ratios of the most important sources also shown. For example, for the source PS (pulling speed) we have

$$SS'_{PS} = SS_{PS} - df_{PS} \times MSS_e = 0.32 - 1 \times 0.0069 = 0.3131$$

and

$$Cr_{PS} = \frac{SS'_{PS}}{SS_{tot}} \times 100 = \frac{0.3131}{0.4267} \times 100 = 73.4\%$$

Table 12.1 ANOVA for case-study 11.2

Source	df	SS	MSS	F-ratio	Cr
PS	1	0.32	0.32	46.4	73.4%
BW	1	0.061	0.061	8.84	12.7%
PG	1	0.005 p			
PT	1	0.0181	0.0181	2.62	2.6%
IT	1	0.0004 p			
AP	1	0.0169 p			
Res (p)	4	0.0276	0.0069		11.3%
Total	7	0.4267			100.0%

It is clear from the *Cr* column of Table 12.1 that the highest contributors to the variability of the experimental results are the burner width (*BW*) and the pulling speed (*PS*), with the pulling speed accounting for more than 73% of the total variation in the light loss of the optical fibre couplers used in the experiment.

Contribution ratios can be similarly calculated and interpreted for interaction effects (of any order).

■ 12.2 Estimation of process performance

When the analysis of some experimental results has indicated the optimal settings for the studied parameters, estimation of the process's future performance under optimal process conditions is usually required. A method of predicting long-run (average) process performance would be particularly useful in hypothetical situations when cost restrictions prohibit the setting of a particular factor at its optimal level, and a different (suboptimal) setting needs to be considered and its effect on long-run process performance evaluated.

Since every estimation procedure has to be based on experimental results, the estimated performance average can be considered valid only under the assumption that the experimental state continues. For example, fixed causes (of variation) at the time of the experiment will have to be assumed to remain fixed. However, changes in the state of experimentation cannot be helped; but it is still possible to assume that the differences between the optimal process performance (that estimated under optimal factor levels) and that estimated under other combinations of levels will remain approximately the same.

Taguchi suggests a simple estimation formula based on individual differences between the average of the chosen factor levels and the overall mean. For example, suppose we are interested in estimating the long-run (average) yield, μ, of a process, on the basis of the results of an experiment which indicated that factors A and B were significant with optimal levels $A(4)$ and $B(1)$. Suppose that $\bar{A}_4$ represents the average yield at level $A(4)$, easily calculated by averaging all the data values obtained when factor A was at its level 4. Suppose also that $\bar{B}_1$ is the average at level $B(1)$ and M represents the grand average of all experimental results. The long-run process average under the optimal levels $A(4)$ and $B(1)$ can be estimated by

$$\hat{\mu} = M + (\bar{A}_4 - M) + (\bar{B}_1 - M)$$

In other words,

long-term average yield = (mean of all the experimental values)
+ (increase in yield above M when $A(4)$ is selected)
+ (increase in yield above M when $B(1)$ is selected)

The above formula can incorporate not just main effects, but also interaction effects, assuming that such effects are significant and that averages for the selected interaction levels are available. In general,

$$\hat{\mu} = M + \Sigma \text{ (average of selected source level} - M) \tag{12.1}$$

Sources which are not important (statistically insignificant) can be disregarded since their inclusion in formula (12.1) will have only a minor effect on the estimate.

Clearly $\hat{\mu}$ is only an estimate of the real process average μ under the selected conditions (assuming that the state of experimentation continues). Confidence limits for μ can be constructed on the basis of the estimate and the error variance obtained through ANOVA. Indeed, $(100 - \alpha)\%$ confidence limits can be obtained using the formula

$$\hat{\mu} \pm \sqrt{F(1, df_e; \alpha) \times MSS_e \times (1/n_e)} \tag{12.2}$$

where MSS_e represents the mean sum of squares for the residual variance (error variance), df_e are the residual degrees of freedom, $F(1, df_e; \alpha)$ is the critical value from the F-tables depending on 1 and df_e degrees of freedom at level of significance α, and n_e represents the *effective number of replications*, to be described in Section 12.3.

■ 12.3 Effective number of replications

Taguchi's general formula for the effective number of replications is as follows:

$$n_e = \frac{N}{DC + \Sigma \ (ED)} \tag{12.3}$$

where N is the total number of data values (the size of the experiment), DC represents the effective number of degrees of freedom attributable to the correction factor (usually the value of 1 except in the case of accumulating analysis – see Section 12.5), and $\Sigma (ED)$ is the total effective number of degrees of freedom attributable to the sources that have not been disregarded in estimating the process average. The value of ED for each source depends on the experimental design used; some representative cases are as follows:

1. For the case of orthogonal designs, the effective number of degrees of freedom is simply the usual number of degrees of freedom. For example, if A is a k-level factor, then

    $$ED_A = k - 1$$

    or, if B is another factor with m levels, ED for the interaction effect $A \times B$ is

    $$ED_{A \times B} = (k - 1)(m - 1)$$

2. When a factor it assigned to a column using the dummy-level technique (see Section 11.3.2), its effective number of replications is given by

    $$ED = \frac{\text{number of column levels}}{\text{number of repetitions of dummy levels}} - 1$$

    For example, suppose we assigned to the four-level columns of $OA_{16}(4^5)$ a three-level factor A, a four-level factor B and 2 two-level factors C and D; using the dummy-level technique we repeat one of the levels of A twice, and one of the levels of C and D three times. Therefore,

    $$ED_A = \tfrac{4}{2} - 1, \qquad ED_C = ED_D = \tfrac{4}{3} - 1$$

    Assuming r replications per trial, and assuming that the effects of A, B, C are not disregarded, we have

    $$n_e = \frac{16r}{1 + (\tfrac{4}{2} - 1) + (\tfrac{4}{3} - 1) + (\tfrac{4}{3} - 1)} = \frac{16r}{4 + \tfrac{4}{3}}$$

3. When the assignment of factors takes place using relatively complicated techniques, such as the trans-factor technique (see Section 11.3.3) or the idle-column technique (Section 11.3.4), the calculation of the effective number of replications needed in formula (12.2) is rather complex. For these cases, instead of (12.2), Taguchi suggests the following simple approximate formula for confidence limits of $\hat{\mu}$:

    $$\hat{\mu} \pm 3\sqrt{MSS_e}$$

■ 12.4 Discount (β) coefficients

Taguchi suggests that significance testing should only be considered as a preparatory stage for performing a better estimation. In fact, he suggests that accepting significance for an effect with total confidence just because its F-ratio happens to be slightly greater than a critical value (from the F-tables), and completely disregarding an effect if its F-ratio happens to be slightly less than this critical value, is 'a total departure from common sense'. He also suggests that the usefulness of F-ratios lies only in their role as a substitute for the discount (or β) coefficients which can be used to improve formula (12.1), that is, improve estimation of the long-term average performance.

The discount coefficients arose out of Taguchi's belief that every estimate of a parameter is usually an overestimate of the true value of that parameter. There is, therefore, a need for some discounting. For example, if we are interested in the difference between two levels of factor A whose true mean values are respectively μ_1 and μ_2, then we can estimate this difference by $\bar{A}_1 - \bar{A}_2$, which is an overestimate of the true difference $\mu_1 - \mu_2$. To improve on the estimate, we need a discount coefficient β which, when applied to the initial estimate, would increase its precision. Such a coefficient would minimize the mean square of

$$D = \beta(\bar{A}_1 - \bar{A}_2) - (\mu_1 - \mu_2)$$

and could, therefore, be estimated using the method of least squares. Generally speaking, the method of least squares can be employed to estimate the discount coefficient $\beta(\hat{P})$ of a parameter $\hat{P}$, which, when multiplied by $\hat{P}$, produces a better estimate for the real P. $\hat{P}$ could be a linear combination either of data values (such as the grand average M) or of level averages (such as $A_1 - A_2$, $A_1 - M$ etc.).

It can be shown that, by minimizing the mean square of the error

$$D = \beta(\hat{P}) \times \hat{P} - P$$

we obtain

$$\beta(\hat{P}) = 1 - \frac{1}{F_P} \tag{12.4}$$

where F_P is the F-ratio of the parameter $\hat{P}$ (ratio of the variance of $\hat{P}$ to the error variance MSS_e). Since the variance of $\hat{P}$ will normally be a variation component associated with one degree of freedom, we have

$$F_P = \frac{SS_P}{MSS_e}$$

with SS_P representing the sum of squares for P. Note that, when the variance ratio F_P approaches infinity, the value of $\beta(\hat{P})$ approaches 1. On the other hand, when F_P approaches 1, $\beta(\hat{P})$ approaches zero. When F_P is less than 1, $\beta(\hat{P})$ is regarded as zero. In general,

$$\beta(\hat{P}) = \begin{cases} 1 - \dfrac{1}{F_P} & \text{when } F_P > 1 \\ 0 & \text{when } F_P \leqslant 1 \end{cases}$$

The above indicates Taguchi's wish not to disregard any effect unless its variance ratio is less than 1. However, he is also reluctant to accept any estimation at its full value (hence the discounting) even if there is a high degree of significance. For example, if the F-ratio is as high as 10, he advises taking 0.9 times the effect observed during experimentation, as a more reliable estimate of the real effect. This is because he believes it is very rare that an effect greater than that observed in the experiment will be experienced in reality; in most cases, less than the expected effect is observed, which justifies the discounting during estimation.

From the above it becomes clear that the aim of the β coefficients is the improvement of the reliability of the estimation formulae (12.1) and (12.3) (and therefore (12.2)), which now take the form

$$\mu_\beta = M \times \beta(M) + \Sigma \ \{(P) \times \beta(P)\} \tag{12.5}$$

and

$$n_{e,\beta} = \frac{N}{\beta(DC) + \Sigma \ \{(ED) \times \beta(P)\}} \tag{12.6}$$

where by P we now mean the relationship $P =$ (average of selected source level $- M$) and the sum Σ is over sources that have not been disregarded in estimating $\hat{\mu}$. Note that when $P = M$, then $\beta(M) = 1 - 1/F_M$, where $F_M = CF/MSS_e$.

■ 12.5 Accumulating analysis

For the analysis of ranked data, categorized into a certain number of classes according to their importance or their properties (for example into 'bad', 'fair', 'good' and 'excellent'), or for the analysis of characteristic values which, although fundamentally continuous, have been divided into a number of groups depending on their magnitude, Taguchi recommends the method of accumulating analysis. The technique can also be used to analyse data which are mixed categorical–continuous.

The procedure to follow for such an analysis will be described through a case study.

CASE STUDY 12.1

A mixture experiment took place in order to determine the appropriate formulation for a particular type of ink used in ink-jet printers, so that high adhesion and low drying time could be achieved. We will concentrate on the objective of high adhesion on metal and plastic substrates. The substrates used were mylar film (plastic) and plated steel (metal).

There were 6 substances (factors) of interest:

MeOH, resin, dye, PM, carbitol and water

The planning out method for a mixture experiment (see Section 11.3.9) was followed. MeOH was the largest ingredient and was therefore used as a remainder, entering every experimental trial in a proportion large enough to bring the sum total of the levels of the other factors up to 100%. The $OA_8(2^7)$ was used to study the effects of the other five substances and two interactions, between dye and carbitol and between dye and PM. The proportions for each substance, according to the experimental design used, are shown in Table 12.2.

The adhesive ability of the ink formulation for each experimental trial was tested after a code had been printed on the substrates using ten samples of ink; five samples were on plastic and five on metal substrate. We can thus view the substrate-type as a noise factor simulated at two levels (plastic and metal).

The printed samples were stored overnight for a fixed period of time under constant storage conditions. After the overnight ageing, the adhesion was evaluated by rubbing the print with a suitable abrasive material and by counting the number of rubs needed to render the code illegible. If more than 26 rubs were needed, the ink-sample was considered of high adhesive quality. The data are shown in Table 12.3; the datum value '>26' indicates that more than 26 rubs were needed.

Table 12.2 Design for ink-formulation experiment

| | | Column | | | | | |
Trial	Substance: (factor)	1 Dye (A)	2 Carbitol (B)	4 PM (C)	6 Resin (D)	7 Water (E)	MeOH (remainder)
1		1.0	1.5	6.5	8.0	10	73%
2		1.0	1.5	9.5	12.0	20	56%
3		1.0	2.5	6.5	12.0	20	58%
4		1.0	2.5	9.5	8.0	10	69%
5		3.0	1.5	6.5	8.0	20	61%
6		3.0	1.5	9.5	12.0	10	64%
7		3.0	2.5	6.5	12.0	10	66%
8		3.0	2.5	9.5	8.0	20	57%

Table 12.3 Data values for the ink-formulation experiment

Trial	Data (Number of rubs)									
1	2	9	5	25	2	19	15	17	26	13
2	>26	11	20	11	>26	18	11	10	16	6
3	1	2	2	5	>26	11	1	2	4	3
4	15	3	3	19	>26	19	14	3	18	14
5	19	5	2	1	2	2	6	3	>26	4
6	9	6	8	7	3	5	3	7	2	1
7	>26	20	>26	20	>26	>26	>26	>26	24	10
8	>26	>26	1	15	19	>26	>26	26	3	>26

Analysis

The data are first divided into the following four categories:

Categories	Range of values
I	[1–10]
II	[11–18]
III	[19–26]
IV	[>26]

Clearly, category IV is the most desirable.

The frequency distribution per trial with reference to the four categories is shown in Table 12.4, which also shows the cumulative frequencies for all trials with reference to cumulative categories. The cumulative categories are denoted in parentheses; for example (III) means sum of categories I, II and III.

Using the values of Table 12.4 and the design of Table 12.2, the frequencies and cumulative frequencies for all factor levels can now be calculated and these are shown in Table 12.5. For example, the cumulative frequency of the second level of factor A under category (III) is obtained by summing the cumulative frequencies under (III) from Table 12.4 for the last 4 trials. Note that the cumulative frequency in category (IV) for a particular level is the total number of tests performed for that level.

To estimate the variation effects for each source, we first calculate a weighted variation component $W(c)$ with reference to each cumulative category (c). Such calculation is not necessary for category (IV). The W's are defined as

$$W(c) = \frac{1}{P(c)(1 - P(c))}$$

where $P(c)$ is the proportion of data in cumulative category (c). For example, if $(c) = $ (I), from the sum totals of Table 12.5(b) we have

$$W(I) = \frac{1}{P(I)(1 - P(I))} = \frac{1}{\frac{38}{80}(1 - \frac{38}{80})} = \frac{80^2}{38(80-38)} = 4.01$$

Similarly,

$$W(II) = \frac{80^2}{52(80 - 52)} = 4.4$$

and

$$W(III) = \frac{80^2}{63(80 - 63)} = 5.98$$

Table 12.4 Categories for accumulating analysis

Trial	Frequencies				Cumulative frequencies			
	I	II	III	IV	(I)	(II)	(III)	(IV)
1	4	3	3	0	4	7	10	10
2	2	5	1	2	2	7	8	10
3	8	1	0	1	8	9	9	10
4	3	4	2	1	3	7	9	10
5	8	0	1	1	8	8	9	10
6	10	0	0	0	10	10	10	10
7	1	0	3	6	1	1	4	10
8	2	1	1	6	2	3	4	10

Table 12.5 Frequencies for factor levels in accumulating analysis

Levels	a: Frequencies				b: Cumulative frequencies			
	I	II	III	IV	(I)	(II)	(III)	(IV)
$A(1)$	17	13	6	4	17	30	36	40
$A(2)$	21	1	5	13	21	22	27	40
$B(1)$	24	8	5	3	24	32	37	40
$B(2)$	14	6	6	14	14	20	26	40
$C(1)$	21	4	7	8	21	25	32	40
$C(2)$	17	10	4	9	17	27	31	40
$D(1)$	17	8	7	8	17	25	32	40
$D(2)$	21	6	4	9	21	27	31	40
$E(1)$	18	7	8	7	18	25	33	40
$E(2)$	20	7	3	10	20	27	30	40
$A(1)B(1)$	6	8	4	2	6	14	18	20
$A(1)B(2)$	11	5	2	2	11	16	18	20
$A(2)B(1)$	18	0	1	1	18	18	19	20
$A(2)B(2)$	3	1	4	12	3	4	8	20
$A(1)C(1)$	12	4	3	1	12	16	19	20
$A(1)C(2)$	5	9	3	3	5	14	17	20
$A(2)C(1)$	9	0	4	7	9	9	13	20
$A(2)C(2)$	12	1	1	6	12	13	14	20
Sum totals	38	14	11	17	38	52	63	80

By using the weights $W(c)$, the analysis of variance proceeds as follows.

The correction factor $CF(c)$ for each cumulative category (c) is weighted by the corresponding weight $W(c)$ and an overall CF is calculated as

$$CF = CF(I) \times W(I) + CF(II) \times W(II) + CF(III) \times W(III)$$

$$= \frac{38^2}{80} \times 4.01 + \frac{52^2}{80} \times 4.4 + \frac{63^2}{80} \times 5.98 = 517.78 \qquad (df = 3)$$

The number of degrees of freedom corresponding to the overall CF is 3, the same as the number of cumulative categories being analysed.

On the same basis,

$$SS_{tot} = (SS_{tot(I)}) \times W(I) + (SS_{tot(II)}) \times W(II) + (SS_{tot(III)}) \times W(III)$$

Now,

$$SS_{tot(I)} = \Sigma\ y^2(I) - CF(I)$$

The data value 'y' is a binary data value; this is because y either has the value of 1 (belongs to category (I)) or 0 (does not belong to (I)). Therefore

$$\Sigma\ y^2 \text{ for (I)} = \Sigma\ 1^2 \text{ over (I)} = 38$$

So

$$SS_{\text{tot(I)}} = 38 - \frac{38^2}{80} = 38(1 - \tfrac{38}{80}) = \frac{80}{W(I)}$$

and so

$$SS_{\text{tot(I)}} \times W(I) = 80$$

The same relationship applies for categories (II) and (III). Therefore,

$$SS_{\text{tot}} = 80 + 80 + 80 = 240 \qquad (df = 3 \times 79)$$

For the sum of squares for the sources, similar principles apply. For example,

$$SS_A = SS_{A(I)} \times W(I) + SS_{A(II)} \times W(II) + SS_{A(III)} \times W(III) \qquad (df = 1 \times 3 = 3)$$

and using the results from Table 12.5(b),

$$SS_A = \left(\frac{17^2 + 21^2}{40} - \frac{38^2}{80}\right) \times 4.01 + \left(\frac{30^2 + 22^2}{40} - \frac{52^2}{80}\right) \times 4.4$$

$$+ \left(\frac{36^2 + 27^2}{40} - \frac{63^2}{80}\right) \times 5.98 = 10.377 \qquad (df = 3)$$

Similarly, we find

$$SS_B = 21.977, \qquad SS_C = 1.097, \qquad SS_D = 1.097, \qquad SS_E = 1.093$$

$$SS_{A \times B} = \frac{(6^2 + 11^2 + 18^2 + 3^2) \times W(I) + \cdots + (18^2 + 18^2 + 19^2 + 8^2) \times W(III)}{20}$$

$$- CF - SS_A - SS_B = 43.175 \qquad (df = 1 \times 3 = 3)$$

and

$$SS_{A \times C} = 7.665 \qquad (df = 3)$$

Finally, by subtraction,

$$SS_e = SS_{\text{tot}} - (SS_A + \cdots + SS_{A \times C}) = 153.519 \qquad (df = 3 \times 72 = 216)$$

The ANOVA summary is shown in Table 12.6. This indicates that substances A (dye) and B (carbitol) are significant in the ink formulation for high adhesive capability. Moreover, the dye used seems to interact significantly with carbitol as well as with PM, something that renders PM another significant factor.

Using the values for the factor levels shown in Table 12.5(a) (in particular for category IV), we can decide on a tentative ink formulation as

$$A(2)B(2)C(1)D(2)E(2)$$

which translates into percentages for the ingredients as

dye (3%), carbitol (2.5%), PM (6.5%), resin (12%), water (20%)

and for the remainder

MeOH (56%)

Table 12.6 ANOVA summary for accumulating analysis

Source	df	SS	MSS	F-ratio	
(*A*) Dye	3	10.377	3.46	4.9	Significant
(*B*) Carbitol	3	21.977	7.33	10.3	Significant
A × *B*	3	43.175	14.39	20.2	Significant
(*C*) PM	3	1.097	0.37	0.5	
A × *C*	3	7.665	2.56	3.6	Significant
(*D*) Resin	3	1.097	0.37	0.5	
(*E*) Water	3	1.093	0.36	0.5	
Residual	216	153.519	0.711		
Total	237	240			

There have been many objections to the method of accumulating analysis from many notable statisticians: see Box and Jones (1986) and Hamada and Wu (1986). An obvious disadvantage of the method is the fact that the frequencies of the cumulative categories are not independent. As a result, spurious effects might be detected and small real effects can be detected for the wrong reason. Indeed, during the analysis it was shown that SS_{tot} = (number of categories being analysed) × (total number of measured values). Therefore, SS_{tot} = constant invariably. Then, for example in a two-factor experiment, SS_e = constant − SS_A − SS_B, and, consequently, testing for the significance of A, the distribution of the F_A-ratio statistic depends on factor B. In fact, as Hamada and Wu (1986) have shown, when fractional designs are utilized, the statistic used in testing for significance of a particular factor depends on all the other factors being studied.

Another disadvantage of the technique becomes apparent when it is used in continuous type data: by grouping such data, valuable information is being lost. It is therefore recommended that, when accumulating analysis is to be used, the ordered categories should be refined as far as possible, a balanced design should be used for the experiment and the technique should be avoided when only continuous data are available.

13 Performance Measures

However certain our expectations, the moment foreseen may be unexpected when it arrives.

T.S. Eliot

In this chapter we suggest a simple method for determining a statistical measure which will reflect the variability in the response of interest. The analysis of such a measure can lead to the clearer identification of those controllable factors and their optimal setting, which can minimize the undesired effects of the factors which are uncontrollable.

■ 13.1 Introduction

As was explained in Section 11.2, Taguchi concentrates his efforts on the minimization of the variability caused by the effect of uncontrollable (noise) factors on the response. During experimentation, before or independently of production (off line), the effects of noise factors are simulated and an optimum combination of easy to control factors is determined so that robustness (insensitivity to the effects of noise) is achieved.

The results of the (statistically designed) experimental trials are used to compute certain performance measures which quantify quality. An analysis of the noise performance measure (*NPM*), which is a measure of the process variability, will identify the variability control factors and also the optimal combined setting which will minimize variability. An analysis of the target performance measure (*TPM*), which is a measure of the process mean, will reveal which of the controllable factors, which are not variability control factors, have a large effect on the mean response – the target control factors; these can subsequently be manipulated to bring the mean response to the target value. One such factor (ideally with a linear effect) will be sufficient to achieve the process target and subsequently control the process on target. The important thing is that this factor affects only the mean response and not the variability. It is clear, therefore, that the performance measures should be chosen so that there is as little overlap as possible between the group of variability control factors and the target control factors.

It is generally accepted that the sample mean of the observations in each experimental trial is a sufficient measure for reflecting the average response, and can thus be used for the identification of those factors that affect the mean. It is, therefore, evident that a proper choice of *NPM*, that is, of a measure reflecting only the variability in the response, is crucial, if one seeks for clear-cut results from a Taguchi-type analysis.

The task of eliminating 'cross-talk' between variability control and target control factors becomes easier if the analysis of the results takes place on a scale (data-transformed setting) that the performance model (functional relationship relating the chosen *TPM* or *NPM* with the controllable factors) is as simple as possible. The degree of interdependence between model simplicity and appropriate choice of performance measures will become evident later in this chapter.

■ 13.2 Ensuring simplicity of the model structure

Studies of non-linear effects have frequently been neglected in many industrial experiments, mainly because of restricted capability to carry out an adequate number of experimental trials. Another reason could be the inability sometimes to explain, say, a high-order interaction, if such an effect were found to be statistically significant; and, of course, it would be much easier and more convenient to have to deal with only a linear (main-effects) response model, especially if such a model were to be used for forecasting purposes. Two approaches dealing with non-linear effects have been recommended in the past. One concerns the pre-experimental stage (the Taguchi approach) and the other the post-experimental analysis stage (the data-transformation approach).

13.2.1 The Taguchi approach

Taguchi strongly believes that a careful consideration of the experimental range for each factor and of the interrelationships between factors, before experimentation (at the brainstorming stage), can help towards an appropriate choice of factor levels, which can greatly enhance the efficiency of an experimental study. On the basis of past experience, one should always consider whether or not the range of a particular factor depends on the levels of another factor. If such a relationship is suspected to exist, the levels of one of the factors should be defined in a different way for every level of the other related factors. This has the advantage of cancelling the interaction effects between the interrelated factors for that particular experiment, as well as avoiding experiment in an unnecessary or unusable range.

It is, of course, naive to expect that non-linear (interaction, quadratic etc.) effects (if any) will disappear in real terms. But as long as the possible interrelationships between the factors are considered logically, prior to experimentation, it is always feasible to contrive that there will be monotonicity to the factorial effects and additivity in the response model for the proposed experiment.

13.2.2 The data-transformation approach

A technique which could help in the choice of a data transformation likely to satisfy certain statistical assumptions (normality, constancy of error variance), as well as simplicity of response model, is that described in an important paper by Box and Cox (1964). It can be summarized as follows.

For any real λ (usually between -2 and $+2$), transform the original data into

$$
y^\lambda = \begin{cases} \dfrac{y^\lambda}{\lambda \dot{y}^{(\lambda-1)}} & \text{if } \lambda \neq 0 \\[2ex] \dot{y} \log(y) & \text{if } \lambda = 0 \end{cases} \tag{13.1}
$$

where $\dot{y}$ is the geometric mean (the nth root of the product of the n observations) of all the observations.

Then tabulate against every λ the residual (error) sum of squares (SS_e) from the ANOVA of the corresponding transformed data, assuming the simplest model possible, for example, a linear model for quantitative factors or an additive (main-effects) model for qualitative factors.

The value of λ, say λ_{BC}, corresponding to the minimum of SS_e will direct us as to what transformation is needed. For example, if $\lambda_{BC} = 1$ then no transformation is needed; if $\lambda_{BC} = 1/2$ then a square root transformation is needed; if $\lambda_{BC} = 0$ then a log-transformation is needed etc.

The main problem with the Box–Cox transformation is that it could be heavily biased by the requirement for simplicity (linearity) in the model structure, and in such a case, it could actually induce in the λ_{BC}-transformed scale a functional dependence between the sample variance and the sample mean of each experimental trial; in other words, it could induce a mean bias in the *NPM*, something that one should try to avoid if a clear-cut Taguchi analysis is aimed for. Such an eventuality with the Box–Cox type of transformations was demonstrated in Logothetis (1990).

■ 13.3 Avoiding a mean-variance dependence

A functional dependence between the trial mean and trial variance of the experimental results, apart from violating the statistical assumption of constancy of the error variance, inhibits the clear-cut classification of which factors affect the mean response and which affect the variability in the response, the basis of Taguchi's technique. An appropriate data-transformation would alleviate the above problems, provided that such a transformation is mainly oriented towards achievement of a mean-variance independence.

If the functional relationship between trial mean μ and trial variance σ^2 in the original scale is known to be, say

$$\sigma = f(\mu) \tag{13.2}$$

it can then be shown that the transformation T, which is supposed to make the trial variance in the transformed scale constant, c^2 say, approximately satisfies (see also Logothetis, 1988)

$$T(\mu) \simeq \int \frac{c}{f(\mu)} \, d\mu \tag{13.3}$$

The above is a rough approximation but it can nevertheless direct us to what T should be in special cases. For example, if

$$f(\mu) = k\mu^\beta \tag{13.4}$$

then from (13.3)

$$T(\mu) \simeq \begin{cases} C_1\mu^{1-\beta} & \text{if } \beta \neq 1 \\ C_1 \log(\mu) & \text{if } \beta = 1 \end{cases} \quad (k, C_1 = \text{constants})$$

that is, we need a transformation to the power of $(1 - \beta)$ if $\beta \neq 1$, and the log-transformation if $\beta = 1$. In other words, if $\lambda = 1 - \beta$ we need a transformation to the power of λ if $\lambda \neq 0$, and the log-transformation if $\lambda = 0$. This can be shown to be equivalent to the Box–Cox family of transformations (13.1) with $\lambda = 1 - \beta$.

One way to establish whether (13.4) is a reasonable approximation, is to estimate β through the least-squares estimator b in the relationship between the sample mean $\bar{y}_i$ and sample standard deviation s_i:

$$\log(s_i) = \log(a) + b \log(\bar{y}_i) + e_i, \quad i = 1, ..., n \tag{13.5}$$

(n is the number of experimental trials) with its significance indicated through the t-ratio for b (see Section 6.7.2).

■ 13.4 Choosing the noise performance measure

A data-transformation chosen appropriately enough to alleviate the mean-variance dependence problem can simultaneously help in answering the question as to which noise performance measure (*NPM*) to analyse. Indeed, since there will be no question of any functional dependence between the trial variance σ_T^2 and the trial mean μ_T in the transformed scale, we only need to analyse

$$\log_{10}(\sigma_T)^2$$

for the determination of the variability control factors, and μ_T for the determination of the target control factors. In practice we use

$$NPM = -10\ \log_{10}(s_T)^2$$

and

$$TPM = \bar{y}_T$$

where $(s_T)^2$ and $\bar{y}_T$ are respectively the sample trial variance and sample trial mean in the transformed scale.

If a transformation is difficult to determine and applied to the original scale (such as when (13.3) is difficult to solve), but the functional relationship (13.2) is nevertheless known, then the appropriate *NPM* to use in the original scale should be a function of $\sigma/f(\mu)$, because only then can the measure reflecting variability be unbiased by the mean μ. In practice we use (in the original scale)

$$NPM = 10\ \log_{10}\left(\frac{f(\bar{y})}{s}\right)^2$$

and

$$TPM = \bar{y}$$

For example, if (13.4) holds, that is if

$$f(\mu) = k\mu^\beta$$

with β estimated by b through (13.5), that is, through

$$\log(s_i) = \log(a) + b\ \log(\bar{y}_i) + e_i \qquad i = 1, \ldots, n$$

then

$$NPM = 10\ \log_{10}\left(\frac{\bar{y}^b}{s}\right)^2 \tag{13.6}$$

Note that when $b = 1$, the measure (13.6) is equivalent to Taguchi's signal to noise ratio (*SNR*), whose use is recommended for 'nominal is best' (there is a target value to be achieved in the response) situations.

Formula (13.6), estimated through (13.5), provides a convenient way of determining the appropriate noise performance measure, thus avoiding not only the need for data-transformation but also, more importantly, the 'cross-talk' between the variability control and target control factors.

We can use the data of case-study 11.4 (Section 11.3.5, Table 11.21), reproduced in Table 13.1, to demonstrate the above technique.

Table 13.1 Sample means and standard deviations for case-study 11.4

Trial	Sample mean $\bar{y}$	Sample standard deviation s
1	69.25	4.03
2	87.00	3.92
3	101.50	9.30
4	75.50	5.80
5	90.75	5.74
6	106.75	11.64
7	98.00	2.94
8	115.25	2.50
9	84.00	3.74
10	110.00	3.65
11	71.25	1.71
12	84.75	2.50
13	90.00	2.58
14	94.75	1.70
15	80.50	3.00
16	100.25	4.03
17	79.00	2.83
18	83.00	4.16

Table 13.1 shows the sample mean and standard deviations for each of the 18 trials of the experiment. Using the technique of linear regression analysis (see Section 6.7.2) we can determine the regression model between $\log(s)$ and $\log(\bar{y})$ as follows:

$$\log(\bar{s}) = -2.49 + 0.844 \log(\bar{y}) \qquad (df = 16)$$

that is, $b = 0.844$. We can also estimate the standard error of b as $SE(b) = 0.842$, and so the t-ratio of b is

$$t(b) = \frac{b}{SE(b)} = 1.002$$

which shows the non-significance of b. This means that we can accept that for the real β (which is estimated by b) $\beta \simeq 0$. Consequently, from (13.6), we can accept the use of

$$NPM = -10 \log_{10}(s^2)$$

in the original scale. However, apart from the value of 0 for β, we can also accept any other value of β in the 95% confidence interval for β given by

$$b \pm t(df; 5\%)SE(b)$$

where, from the t-tables

$$t(df; 5\%) = t(16; 5\%) = 2.12$$

Therefore, we can accept any value for b in the interval $\{-0.94, 2.26\}$.

This means that we can accept either

$$NPM = -10 \log_{10}(s^2) \qquad (b = 0)$$

or

$$NPM = 10 \log_{10}\left(\frac{\bar{y}}{s}\right)^2 = SNR \qquad (b = 1)$$

or even

$$NPM = 10 \log_{10}\left(\frac{\bar{y}^2}{s}\right)^2 \qquad (b = 2)$$

and the conclusions from the ANOVA analysis of the *NPM* will be the same. Recall that in case-study 11.4 we used the *SNR* as recommended by Taguchi but, in fact, we could have used any of the above three *NPM* measures, obtaining similar conclusions.

■ 13.5 On Taguchi's recommended measures

In Section 11.2, three noise performance measures were mentioned, as recommended by Taguchi. When a specific target for the response was to be met (nominal is best), the signal to noise ratio was suggested, expressed in practice by

$$SNR = 10 \log_{10}(\bar{y}^2/s^2)$$

where $\bar{y}$ and s are respectively the sample mean and sample standard deviation of the (n) observations in each trial.

It has already been observed that the *SNR* is a special case of formula (13.6) when $b = 1$. It is therefore evident that the use of *SNR* is appropriate only when there is a functional relationship between the sample trial variance and mean of the form

$$s \simeq k\bar{y}$$

that is, when s is directly proportional to $\bar{y}$ in the original scale. In any other case for nominal is best situations, the use of *SNR* will induce a mean bias in the analysis for the determination of the variability control factors.

The possibility of the existence of a mean bias in the noise performance measure becomes even more apparent when we consider Taguchi's recommended measure for 'lower is best' situations:

$$\eta = -10 \log_{10}\left\{\frac{1}{n} \sum y^2\right\}$$

Note that

$$\frac{1}{n} \sum y^2 = (\bar{y})^2 + \frac{n-1}{n} s^2 \tag{13.7}$$

The above relationship shows how the measure η confounds location effects arising from changes in the trial mean $\bar{y}$ with dispersion effects arising from changes in the trial variance s^2. Particularly in the cases when $\bar{y}$ is large in comparison to s, analysing η is the same as reanalysing $\bar{y}$, and is therefore unnecessary. So the use of η by a non-statistician is at best a duplication of effort and at worst the cause of confusion since it confounds dispersion with location effects, which could result in an ambiguity in classification between variability control and target control factors.

The same argument applies to the use of the measure ϑ that Taguchi recommends when the response is 'the larger the better':

$$\vartheta = -10 \log_{10} \left\{ \frac{1}{n} \sum y^{-2} \right\}$$

Indeed, note that

$$\frac{1}{n} \sum y^{-2} \approx 3 \frac{s^2}{\bar{y}^4} + \frac{1}{\bar{y}^2}$$

and it is obvious how much $\bar{y}$ can affect ϑ.

An example of the confusion caused by the indiscriminate use of Taguchi's performance measures can be found in the study described by Bandurek *et al.* (1988), concerning a Taguchi experiment which attempted to optimize the process of the placement of surface mount components on circuit boards.

The initial analysis had the objective of determining which of the controllable factors could affect (minimize) the variability caused by the effects of the noise factors, but a lack of significance was noted for all the controllable factors under investigation. Among other reasons, this could be either due to an inadequate brainstorming stage (that is, to a decision to investigate an insufficient or irrelevant number of controllable factors), or due to a strong day effect (block-factor effect) which was noted but never accounted for in the analysis, or due to strong systematic effects from noise factors. It was decided to investigate the latter further, and an analysis of noise factors was performed by treating the controllable-factor combinations as replications of each noise-factor combination. Taguchi's recommended measure η was used and renamed, perhaps justifiably, by the authors, noise to signal ratio, as it was summed over the columns of the complete parameter design rather than the rows.

Figure 13.1 (taken from Figure 7 of Bandurek *et al.*, 1988) shows graphically the effects of 5 noise factors on η and on the mean response $\bar{y}$. It is immediately obvious that the graphs for η are almost complete mirror images of those for $\bar{y}$. In fact, had the authors analysed $-\bar{y}$, the graphs would have

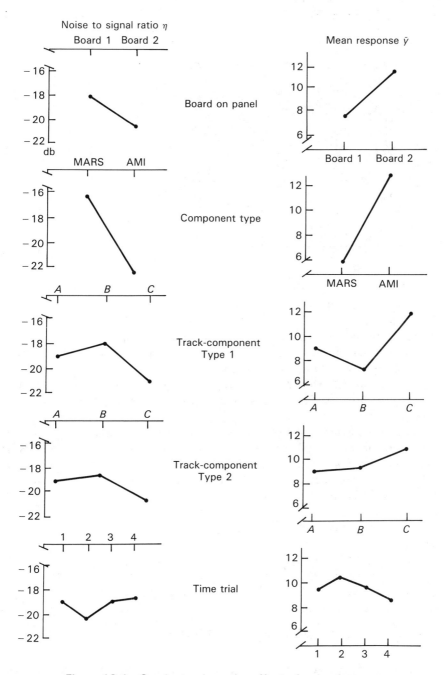

Figure 13.1 Graphs to show the effect of noise factors

Table 13.2 S/N ratio decomposition

η	$\bar{y}$	$\bar{y}^2$	$[(n-1)/n]\,s^2$	$(\bar{y}^2)/\{[(n-1)/n]\,s^2\}$
−21.60	11.06	122.32	22.22	5.5
−20.18	8.75	76.56	27.67	2.8
−20.21	9.31	86.68	18.28	4.7
−20.19	9.19	84.46	20.02	4.2
−20.68	9.00	81.00	35.95	2.3
−20.76	9.34	87.23	31.89	2.7
−19.17	8.34	69.56	13.05	5.3
−21.07	9.63	92.74	35.20	2.6
−22.23	11.50	132.25	34.86	3.8
−20.57	9.44	89.11	24.91	3.6
−21.35	10.25	105.06	31.40	3.4
−22.09	11.50	132.25	29.56	4.5
−20.75	8.75	76.56	42.29	1.8
−20.79	8.88	78.85	41.10	1.9
−20.28	8.81	77.60	29.04	2.7
−19.79	8.44	71.23	24.05	3.0

been almost identical to those of η. This demonstrates clearly how a relatively large value of $\bar{y}$ can bias the analysis of η because of the relationship (13.7). This makes it impossible to distinguish between what affects the variability in the performance and what affects its average performance.

Looking at Figure 13.1, we note that the first 3 noise factors strongly affect both the variability in the response as well as the mean response. This could be completely wrong since a proper measure reflecting purely the variability, not biased by the mean (such as an *NPM* determined by (13.6)), was never analysed.

A numerical demonstration of how much $\bar{y}$ can bias η, can be seen in the data used for the analysis of the controllable factors in the same case-study (see Bandurek *et al.* (1988), Table IV). If we 'dissolve' the S/N ratio η using (13.7), we can find (see Table 13.2) that the part $(\bar{y})^2$ is more than two and a half times larger than the part

$$\frac{n-1}{n}\,s^2$$

in 13 out of 16 experimental trials!

■ 13.6 An illustration of Taguchi's techniques

The rest of this chapter will consist of a case study reporting one of the first applications of the Taguchi technique to a real-life chemical engineering situation.

CASE STUDY 13.1

Plasma-deposited silicon is often used as a protective mask for micromechanical structures etched in silicon using aqueous alkali solutions; it is not a stoichiometric chemical compound but has a range of compositions, depending on the deposition variables. The resistance of the silicon nitride to hot aqueous alkali is largely controlled by the chemical composition and porosity of the film. Plasma-deposited films usually contain large amounts of hydrogen, which may be bonded to the silicon or the nitrogen atoms. The concentration of hydrogen and the ratio of silicon to nitrogen may determine the resistance to aqueous alkali. The composition, deposition rate and physical properties of plasma-deposited silicon nitride are controlled by a number of variables, including the plasma excitation frequency, the electrode spacing, the power density, the total pressure, the gas composition, the temperature and the pumping speed.

For complicated cases of multivariate multiresponse processes such as this, a systematic experimental procedure should be adopted followed by statistical analysis of measures clearly reflecting the variability in each response. For the same experiment, a different *NPM* might be required for each response of interest. It is therefore important to be able to choose the proper noise performance measure, and this should be determined by the data themselves, perhaps using the technique described in this chapter.

We report on one of the first applications of the Taguchi technique in GEC's Hirst Research Centre. We will concentrate on the cost-effectiveness of the technique in the characterization and optimization of a newly installed plasma deposition process, which is described next.

The process

Plasma-deposited silicon nitride is used to protect the support rims of microwave power-sensor devices from an electrochemical etch-stop process used to form the active silicon webs (see Figure 13.2). After front-face processing of these devices has been completed, the three-inch wafers are lapped and polished to a thickness of 100 μm. After cleaning, silicon nitride is deposited on the backs of the wafers and defined using conventional photolithography and plasma-etch techniques. The wafers are then etched in 5 M potassium hydroxide solution at 70 $^{\circ}$C with a 2 V bias applied to the front face of the wafers. The etch proceeds until a 5 μm silicon web is formed, strengthened by a 100 μm thick support rim, as shown in Figure 13.2. Until now it has not been possible to optimize the silicon nitride deposition part of this process, and the yields of devices from the electrochemical etch process have been anything between 0 and 95%.

All the failures at this stage have been due to the alkali solution attacking the silicon nitride rims. As this was clearly unacceptable, a dedicated plasma deposition kit was purchased so that the process could be developed. It is not practicable to obtain an accurate and quantitative measure of the etch-resistance of silicon nitride layers to hot potassium hydroxide solution and it is therefore necessary to use indirect methods. Thickness, refractive index, Fourier transform infrared measurements and etch characteristics give information about chemical stability, uniformity and control of the process. Although it is necessary to use wafers which have been thinned to 100 μm for the microwave power-sensor

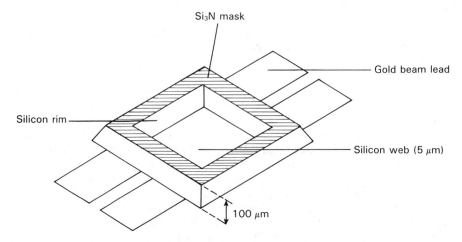

Figure 13.2 Schematic diagram of device

application, standard thickness wafers have been included in the study since this technique could be useful in other applications, for example pressure sensors, accelerometers, micron valves etc.

Controllable variables

Seven controllable variables were identified as being important for study, of which 5 were quantitative and studied at three levels, whereas 2 were qualitative and studied at two levels. These are shown in Table 13.3.

Response variables

Five responses were of interest, as follows (in order of importance):

R1: resistance to etching in aqueous alkali (KOH-etch resistance). This is measured using optical microscopy and given as the percentage of the silicon nitride rim remaining intact after etching. This needs to be optimized to as high a value as possible.

R2: thickness. The film thickness (in Ångstroms) was measured at 5 points on each wafer using interferometry. The target value could not be specified prior to experiment, but variation across the wafer needs to be minimized.

R3: refractive index. The refractive index of the films was measured at 5 points on each wafer using ellipsometry. As with thickness, the target value could not be specified prior to experiment, but variation across the wafer needs to be minimized.

R4: plasma-etch performance. In order to define the protective back mask, the photolithed silicon nitride is etched in a CF_4 plus O_2 plasma. The film must etch, and undercut must be minimized. The performance has been recorded as a binary response, with 1 representing a successful etching and 0 a failure to etch.

Table 13.3 Controllable variables and levels for case-study 13.1

ST Substrate thickness (standard thickness wafers as well as wafers thinned to 100 μm were included in the study): two levels, standard, thin

PR Pressure of the reaction chamber (mTorr): three levels, 320, 350, 380

PO The RF power supplied to the chamber (W): three levels, 20, 50, 80

CO The silane flow-rate which largely controls the gas composition (sccm): three levels, 5, 10, 15

PC Plasma conditioning of the chamber (the use or not of N_2 plasma prior to deposition): two levels, with N_2 plasma, without

TE The temperature of the lower electrode on which the substrate is supported ($^\circ$C): three levels, 100, 200, 300

GT The growth time of the silicon nitride layer (min): three levels, 30, 60, 90

R5: D-bow. This is the change in bow which is given from north to south and from west to east across the wafer. Measurements are carried out before and after deposition of silicon nitride.

Experimental design

The 7 variables were assigned to the $OA_{18}(2 \times 3^7)$ orthogonal design, as shown in Table 13.4. This is a highly fractional but efficient design for dealing with 7 three-level factors and 1 two-level factor using only 18 experimental trials. Column 3 was left unassigned. Note that, although factor *PC* is a two-level factor, it was assigned to column 6 using the dummy-level technique (see Section 11.3.2).

Table 13.4 Experimental design for case-study 13.1

Trial	Column							
	1	2	3	4	5	6	7	8
	ST	PR		PO	CO	PC	TE	GT
1	1	1	1	1	1	1	1	1
2	1	1	2	2	2	2	2	2
3	1	1	3	3	3	3 (= 2)	3	3
4	1	2	1	1	2	2	3	3
5	1	2	2	2	3	3 (= 2)	1	1
6	1	2	3	3	1	1	2	2
7	1	3	1	2	1	3 (= 2)	2	3
8	1	3	2	3	2	1	3	1
9	1	3	3	1	3	2	1	2
10	2	1	1	3	3	2	2	1
11	2	1	2	1	1	3 (= 2)	3	2
12	2	1	3	2	2	1	1	3
13	2	2	1	2	3	1	3	2
14	2	2	2	3	1	2	1	3
15	2	2	3	1	2	3 (= 2)	2	1
16	2	3	1	3	2	3 (= 2)	1	2
17	2	3	2	1	3	1	2	3
18	2	3	3	2	1	2	3	1

One wafer was used for each trial. For the responses of thickness and refractive index, 5 measurements were taken at 5 wafer sites. One observation per trial was available for the resistance and etch-performance responses. The experimental data are shown in Table 13.5.

Analysis of results

The conclusions of the experiment were based on the results of the analyses for responses $R1$, $R2$ and $R3$ only.

Analysis of R1

The KOH-etch resistance response was the first to be analysed, being the most important. As only one data value per trial was available, it was not possible to obtain an *NPM* value for analysis. We view the single trial value as the value of the *TPM* measure for that trial.

A simple way of analysing the response data is to calculate the average response for each factor level and plot the results. For example, in order to find the average resistance value corresponding to level 1 of *ST* (substrate thickness), we calculate the average of all data values for those experimental trials corresponding to code 1 in the first column of the array of Table 13.4, that is, the first 9 trials. So the average resistance at level $ST(1)$ is

$$(50 + 99 + \cdots + 90)/9 = 71.4$$

and for $ST(2)$

$$(80 + 80 + \cdots + 80)/9 = 61.1$$

A large difference between these values will be indicative of a significant effect due to factor *ST*. How large is 'large' is a matter of statistical practice, but a relative comparison of all the factor-effects can be carried out by plotting the averages of all factor levels on the same chart. For the KOH-resistance this is shown in

Table 13.5 Summary of measurement data for case-study 13.1

Trial	Thickness (Å)					Refractive index					KOH-etch Resistance (%)
	Top	Centre	Flat	Right	Left	Top	Centre	Flat	Right	Left	
1	3028	2641	2936	2968	2961	1.739	1.726	1.732	1.741	1.742	50
2	8666	8221	8479	8503	8350	1.694	1.70	1.700	1.724	1.744	99
3	15327	15804	13539	12084	14814	1.870	1.770	2.125	2.379	1.983	99
4	5006	4989	4060	4211	4279	1.997	1.933	2.484	2.398	2.368	90
5	4970	4926	4989	4990	5193	1.787	1.762	1.769	1.797	1.695	95
6	13318	12065	14363	13701	13299	1.875	1.8	1.671	1.802	1.839	0
7	15766	—	15470	16094	15641	1.814	—	1.782	1.785	1.783	90
8	5016	5299	4548	6240	4790	2.037	1.862	2.235	1.639	2.110	30
9	7054	6697	7060	7106	6967	1.789	1.801	1.792	1.777	1.786	90
10	5260	5331	5181	5172	5174	1.848	1.841	1.872	1.843	1.855	80
11	4658	4725	5051	4120	4357	1.780	1.812	1.748	1.802	1.798	80
12	13357	13181	12972	13671	13602	1.996	1.727	2.169	1.224	1.135	0
13	6221	6202	6189	6225	6201	2.538	1.909	1.907	1.903	1.912	80
14	18978	17977	16357	18372	—	1.775	1.773	1.792	1.758	—	5
15	2468	2510	2418	2515	2423	1.894	1.843	1.826	1.814	1.780	90
16	11486	11906	12017	12079	12099	1.756	1.764	1.726	1.734	1.731	50
17	9590	13137	10034	8120	8330	1.818	1.827	1.832	1.545	1.864	85
18	4545	4204	4239	4605	4596	1.845	1.868	1.847	1.711	1.664	80

Figure 13.3. The values for the level averages are taken from Table 13.6. It can be seen from Figure 13.3 that, in relation to the rest of the factors, *PO*, *CO*, *PC* and *TE* significantly affect the KOH-resistance. This can be confirmed by the statistical analysis of variance (ANOVA) for this response, shown in Table 13.7. Since the ideal value for the KOH-resistance is 'as high as possible' (100%), it can be seen from Figure 13.3 that the optimal levels for the significant factors are as shown in Table 13.8.

Analysis of R2

The 5 measurements taken on each trial were used to calculate the sample mean $\bar{y}$ and the sample standard deviation s per trial, which are shown in Table 13.9. Following the technique suggested in Section 13.4, we perform a

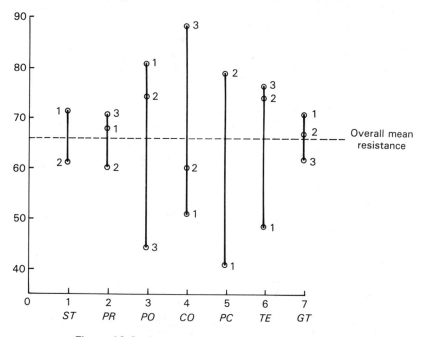

Figure 13.3   Level averages for resistance (*TPM*)

Table 13.6   Level averages for the KOH-etch response

Factor	Level averages (for *TPM*)		
	1	2	3
ST	71.4	61.1	
PR	68.0	60.0	70.8
PO	80.8	74.0	44.0
CO	50.8	59.8	88.2
PC	40.8	79.0	
TE	48.3	74.0	76.5
GT	70.8	66.5	61.5

C

Table 13.7 ANOVA summary for the KOH-resistance response

Source	df	SS	MSS	F-ratio	Cr
ST	1	480.5	480.5	1.43	0.7%
PR	2	378.8	189.4	0.56	
PO	2	4606.8	2303.4	6.85	**19.0%
CO	2	4555.1	2277.6	6.77	**18.8%
PC	1	5826.8	5826.8	17.33	**24.9%
TE	2	2916.8	1458.4	4.34	**10.8%
GT	2	261.8	130.9	0.39	
Residual	5	1681.0			25.8%
Total	17	20707.6			100.0%

Table 13.8 Optimal factor levels for resistance to KOH-etch

Factor	Optimal level
PO	1 (20 W) or 2 (50 W)
CO	3 (15 sccm)
PC	2 (no N_2 plasma)
TE	3 (300 $^\circ$C) or 2 (200 $^\circ$C)

Table 13.9 Trial means and standard deviations for thickness

Trial	Sample mean ($\bar{y}$)	Sample standard deviation (s)	NPM
1	2906.8	152.38	25.61
2	8443.8	167.75	34.04
3	14313.6	1515.80	19.56
4	4509.0	452.97	19.96
5	5013.6	103.59	33.70
6	13349.2	837.29	24.05
7	15742.8	263.73	35.52
8	5178.6	655.01	17.96
9	6976.8	164.29	32.56
10	5223.6	70.35	37.41
11	4582.4	357.26	22.16
12	13356.6	290.61	33.25
13	6207.6	15.03	52.32
14	17921.0	1120.99	24.08
15	2466.8	46.07	34.57
16	11917.4	252.61	33.48
17	9842.2	2013.01	13.79
18	4437.8	199.16	26.96

regression analysis between $\log(s)$ as the dependent variable and $\log(\bar{y})$ as the independent variable (see Section 6.7.2) in order to estimate the model

$$\log(s) = a + b \log(\bar{y}) \qquad (df = 16)$$

We find

$$a = -4.503 \quad \text{and} \quad b = 1.132 \quad \text{with} \quad SE(b) = 0.44$$

and so for the t-ratio of b

$$t(b) = 2.6$$

This indicates a significant value of $\beta \approx 1$, which in turn indicates (see Section 13.4) either the need of a log-transformation of the data ($\lambda = 1 - \beta = 1 - 1 = 0$) or the use in the original scale of

$$NPM = 10 \, \log_{10}\left(\frac{\bar{y}^b}{s}\right)^2 = 10 \, \log_{10}\left(\frac{\bar{y}}{s}\right)^2 = SNR$$

The values of the *NPM* are also shown in Table 13.9.

An analysis of the *NPM* can determine the variability control factors, that is, those controllable factors that have a large effect on the within wafer variability as far as thickness is concerned. The optimal levels of these factors are the levels with the maximum *NPM* (on average), that is, with the minimum variability.

The level averages (for *NPM*) are shown in Table 13.10. On the basis of these, Figure 13.4 can be constructed.

Table 13.10 *NPM* level averages for the thickness response

Factor	Level averages (for *NPM*)		
	1	2	3
ST	27.0	30.9	
PR	28.7	31.4	26.7
PO	24.8	36.0	26.1
CO	26.4	28.9	31.6
PC	27.8	29.5	
TE	30.4	29.9	26.5
GT	29.4	33.1	24.2

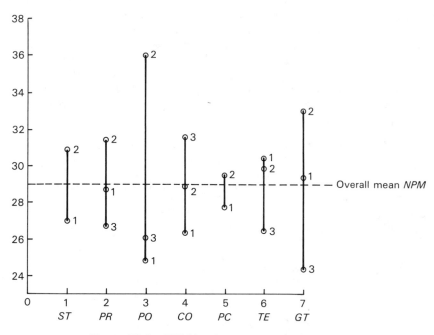

Figure 13.4 *NPM* level averages for thickness

There is evidence from Figure 13.4 that there is a significant effect on the thickness variability from factors PO and GT and, to a lesser degree, from PR and CO. It is clear from Table 13.10 that the optimal levels for these factors are

$$PR(2) \quad PO(2) \quad CO(3) \quad GT(2)$$

As a target performance measure we can use $TPM = \bar{y}$, whose analysis has shown that the only factor which significantly affects the TPM (and not the NPM) is factor TE. Therefore, TE can be viewed as a target control factor, whereas PR, PO, CO and GT are variability control factors.

Analysis of R3

A procedure similar to that for the thickness response was followed in order to analyse the 5 refractive index measurements on each of the 18 wafers. The analysis identified factor PC as a variability control factor, with optimal level for minimum variability at the second level, and TE as the only target control factor.

Estimation

On the basis of the results of the above analyses, a decision was taken to set the factors at the following combination: ST at level 1 (the effect of this factor is insignificant); PR at level 2; PO at level 2; CO at level 3; PC at level 2; TE at level 3; and GT at level 2. Note that this combination of factor levels (1, 2, 2, 3, 2, 3, 2) was not one of the 18 combinations tried in the experiment. This was to be expected because of the high fractionality of the experimental design used (18 out of $2^2 \times 3^5 = 972$ possible combinations). The target value for the most important response – resistance to KOH-etching – is obviously 100%. It would be interesting to have an estimate of the long-term average value of this response under the optimal conditions.

Using Taguchi's estimation formula (see Chapter 12) based on the level averages and the associated 'β coefficients' (using Tables 13.6 and 13.7), an estimate of the long-term performance for $R1$ under the optimal conditions is given by formula (12.5), which yields

$$R1 = M \times \beta(M) + (ST_1 - M) \times \beta(ST) + (PO_2 - M) \times \beta(PO) + (CO_3 - M) \times \beta(CO)$$
$$+ (PC_2 - M) \times \beta(PC) + (TE_3 - M) \times \beta(TE)$$

where M is the grand average, and $\beta(P)$ is the β coefficient (see Section 12.4) of factor P defined by

$$\beta(P) \begin{cases} 1 - 1/F_P & \text{when the } F\text{-ratio for } P \text{ is positive} \\ 0 & \text{otherwise} \end{cases}$$

We can find $M = 66.27$ with $\beta(M) = 1 - 1/F_M$ where $F_M = C_F/MSS_e = 79069.39/336.2 = 235.19$ and so $\beta(M) = 1 - 1/235.19 = 0.996$.
Also from Table 13.7,

$$\beta(ST) = 1 - 1/1.43 = 0.3, \qquad \beta(PO) = 1 - 1/6.85 = 0.854,$$
$$\beta(CO) = 0.852, \qquad \beta(PC) = 0.942 \quad \text{and} \quad \beta(TE) = 0.77.$$

Therefore

$$R1 = 66.27 \times 0.996 + (71.4 - 66.27) \times 0.3 + (74 - 66.27) \times 0.854$$
$$+ (88.2 - 66.27) \times 0.852 + (79 - 66.27) \times 0.942$$
$$+ (76.5 - 66.27) \times 0.77$$
$$= 112.7$$

Confidence limits on the above estimate can be calculated using formulae (12.2) and (12.6) as

$$R1 \pm \sqrt{F(1, df_e; \alpha) \times MSS_e \times (1/n_e)}$$

where

$$F(1, df_e; \alpha) = F(1, 5; 5\%) = 6.61 \qquad MSS_e = 336.2$$

and (because of (12.6))

$$n_e = \frac{18}{1 + 1 + 2 + 2 + 0.5 + 2} = 2.118$$

Therefore a 95% confidence interval for the KOH-etch resistance is given by 112.7 ± 32.4, that is anything from 80.3% to 100%. Estimates for the other two responses (thickness and refractive index), for which no targets had been specified, can similarly be obtained.

Conclusions

Confirmation trials took place at the recommended setting which was confirmed as the optimal. Subsequent monitoring under the optimal conditions has shown the following:

1. Resistance to KOH-etching: 97% ± 1%. In comparison with results prior to the experiment (66% ± 35%), this represents a 50% improvement in the average yield of the devices, with a 35-fold reduction in yield variability.
2. An average thickness of 4220 Å and a standard deviation of 79.2 Å were experienced. This average compared well with the predicted estimate and the standard deviation indicates a 7-fold reduction in thickness variability on previous results.
3. An average refractive index of 1.887 and a standard deviation of 0.0059 were recorded. This average compared well with the predicted estimate and the standard deviation indicates an 8-fold reduction in thickness variability on previous results.
4. Plasma-etch performance: 100% success in etching has been noticed, whereas up to 15% failures in etching were experienced before the experiments.
5. D-bow changes from $-0.6 \, \mu m$ to $-4.4 \, \mu m$ were experienced. This represents a 9-fold improvement in the range of the previous bow-changes (from $-20 \, \mu m$ to $+15 \, \mu m$).

14 Taguchi's Non-Standard Techniques

There were things which he stretched, but mainly he told the truth.

Mark Twain

■ 14.1 Introduction

In performing life tests, the experimenter is interested in estimating the survival period of a particular product unit under certain conditions which are simulated in an experimental environment. Life tests are not necessarily destruction tests; if the duration of the testing period is predetermined, some of the test units could survive the duration of the experiment. When the resulting data are expressed in the continuous mode of the length of life for each unit, with the additional specification on whether the unit failed or survived for the whole of the testing period, Weibull analysis (see section 8.19) is usually performed to assess the reliability of the product unit. However, such an analysis requires the satisfaction of the assumption that the failure distribution of the unit follows a Weibull-type probability distribution.

A technique for life-test analysis which does not require such an assumption, is the method of *minute analysis* (or minimum-unit analysis or minute-accumulating analysis) recommended by Taguchi, whereby not only the effects of the factors affecting the unit's survival can be assessed, but the survival distribution function can also be estimated. Considering the characteristic value as an estimate of a point in the life-distribution function, the method allows the expression of any value, even of a continuous nature, by two classes of categorization, 'exists' and 'does not exist', at each point of the coordinate. Thus a unified analysis method is suggested, as claimed by Taguchi, to simultaneously be able to:

1. Deal with any type of characteristic value (continuous, discrete or categorized).

2. Estimate the distribution function.

3. Test not only differences of mean values but also differences of distribution due to dispersion.

4. Perform significance testing on factors that might be involved in the life-test experiment.

Although the method can certainly deal with any type of characteristic value, (1), and can go some way towards achieving an estimate of the survival rate curve at each minimum unit, (2), to this author the ability of the method to identify dispersion effects, (3), is rather doubtful. This is simply because the analysis method followed is almost identical to the conventional method of analysis for a mean response (see Section 14.2.1); at the stage where it differs, it makes use of pseudo-data which are not statistically independent, something which invalidates the statistical analysis involved at this stage.

These points raise the question of whether, for purposes of significance testing of factors involved, (4), the relatively more complicated method of minute analysis is really necessary, when perhaps the simpler two-stage analysis approach (separate lifetime analysis of a mean measure and a variability measure), originated by Taguchi himself, might be more appropriate and more informative. Experimentally involving factors that could affect survival is of paramount importance, because it utilizes the idea that the engineer can experimentally improve product reliability instead of just passively describing the probability of failure over time. It is equally important, therefore, that the life-data analysis involved should be statistically valid and as simple and informative as possible.

Using an actual case-study we will fully describe the method of minute analysis (Section 14.2) and propose a simpler alternative (Section 14.3) which, although it fully adheres to innovative Taguchi principles, avoids (in the case of survival testing) the statistical drawbacks of minute analysis; these drawbacks will be outlined in Section 14.4.

In this chapter, we will also follow Taguchi's recommendations for managing the component tolerances (Section 14.5). Within a product, every component is subject to tolerances which can be the source of unacceptable variation in the product's functional performance, and hence the cause of low quality. The usual approach to dealing with this problem has been the arbitrary tightening of component tolerances through appropriate arrangements with the component suppliers, resulting in increased production costs and inevitably higher sale prices for the product. However, high quality need not necessarily mean higher prices, provided that a rational (re-)design, after statistical analysis, of component tolerances takes place, balancing the cost of tightening crucial tolerances with the savings from relaxing non-crucial ones.

In the rest of this chapter, Taguchi's approach, based on the above principle, will be demonstrated with an actual case-study which had as its objective the optimization of a filter circuit used in television transmitters. A general methodology which is potentially applicable to any kind of product unit which is subject to the undesired effects of component tolerances will thus be proposed.

■ 14.2 Minute analysis and life testing

The method is based on the breakdown of the testing period into regular intervals of a specific duration called minimum units (minutes) or cycles. The duration of a minimum unit depends on the problem under investigation. For example, in discussing the life of small light bulbs, one or two hours will probably be used as the minimum unit. In other cases, the minimum unit could be anything from a second, one day etc. to a year or more. In cases of accelerated ageing, a minimum unit of one hour could represent the length of a year etc. Essentially, the method constitutes an investigation of at which minimum unit the end of life occurred with regard to the test-piece used in the experiment. The data are expressed in binary form with 1 (0) signifying that the test unit will still adequately function (not function) at the end of a particular cycle.

The division of the test period into minimum units, $\omega(1), ..., \omega(n)$ say, introduces an additional factor, the minimum-unit factor, or cycle factor or ω-factor, with n levels. It also introduces an additional error component, the between-minutes error or ω-order error. These will have to be considered during analysis.

The ANOVA is performed in the usual way but bearing in mind that:

1. There are now three components of error variance to be considered:
   (a) the interexperiment error (first-order or between-experiments error);
   (b) the replication error (second-order or within-experiment or between-replications error) in cases where trials are replicated; and
   (c) the ω-order (between minimum units) error.
2. The replication error (if it exists), the ω-factor and any ω-related effects (such as interactions between the ω-factor and the other factors) are tested for significance against the ω-order error.

If we start with, say, N data values y_i, representing lifetimes, by introducing the n-level minute factor, we replace the N lifetime values y_i with $N \times n$ data values m_{ij}, $i = 1, ..., N$; $j = 1, ..., n$, in binary form 1 or 0, so that for each $i = 1, ..., N$

$$y_i = m_{i1} + m_{i2} + \cdots + m_{in} \tag{14.1}$$

The problem, of course, arises that these binary data values are not independent; they are simply a subdivision of the original lifetime values into values satisfying (14.1); up to one point they are all 1 and beyond this point they are all 0. In other words, we introduce a pseudo-random repetition of values correlated with each other and not even normally distributed. These statistical irregularities do not affect the analysis and significance testing of the *non ω-related* effects. Indeed, the conclusions drawn from a conventional statistical analysis of the lifetime data values y_i, as far as the significance (of main effects and interactions) of the factors involved in the experiment is concerned, are identical to the conclusions drawn by analysing the binary data values m_{ij}. For example, it can be easily shown that because of (14.1) the sums of squares of a factor effect using the y_i's ($i = 1, ..., N$) is n times the sum of squares of the same factor effect using the m_{ij}'s ($i = 1, ..., N; j = 1, ..., n$).

However, because of the correlation and non-normality of the m_{ij}'s (within each y_i), any statistical analysis of the ω-related effects (such as the ω-factor effect and the interactions between the ω-factor and the other factors) is seriously invalidated. Apart from that, the question arises of whether significance testing of the ω-related effects is really necessary. Taguchi himself says that:

> In terms of testing, the main effect of the ω-factor can always be regarded as significant, and it is unnecessary to test each time.... Also when the main effect of a factor A is not significant, it means that (the interaction) $A \times \omega$ is testing whether or not the shape of the distribution differs between the levels of A, and in this case, it means it is not significant.

Conversely, when A is significant, there is a large difference (in the response) between the levels of A, and the same should be expected for the shape of the distribution. Therefore, in a minute analysis, the only ω-related sources expected to have a significant effect are those of the ω-factor, and of the interactions between the ω-factor and the *other significant* factors; and this always turns out to be true!

This author believes that a simpler, more statistically valid and more informative approach to life-testing analysis is the two-stage approach recommended originally by Taguchi himself, whereby two separate analyses, one for the mean response and one for the variability in the response, are carried out (see Section 14.3), with the characteristic under analysis being the lifetime values and not the binary minutes. The statistical drawbacks of minute analysis can thus be avoided, and more information gained not only on what affects the mean lifetime but also on what affects dispersion in the lifetimes.

CASE STUDY 14.1

A study on semiconductor component susceptibility took place utilizing Taguchi's principles. The response of interest was the minimum RF power (in dB's with respect to a mW, dBm) required to cause disruption in the semiconductor circuit under test. Four parameters (factors) have been studied, 3 at five levels and 1 at two levels:

Factor	Description	Level				
		(1)	(2)	(3)	(4)	(5)
$F1$	Frequency (GHz)	8	10	12	14	16
$F2$	Pulse width (ns)	10^2	10^3	10^4	10^5	10^6
$F3$	Duty cycle (%)	1	10	20	50	90
$F4$	Orientation	Vertical	Vertical	Vertical	Horizontal	Horizontal

C

Table 14.1 Experimental design used

Trial	F1	F2	F3	F4		Data		Total
1	1	1	1	1(1)	36	33	31	100
2	1	2	2	2(1)	23	23	22	68
3	1	3	3	3(1)	27	23	23	73
4	1	4	4	4(2)	23	21	22	66
5	1	5	5	5(2)	22	18	20	60
6	2	1	2	3(1)	25	24	25	74
7	2	2	3	4(2)	23	22	22	67
8	2	3	4	5(2)	23	22	22	67
9	2	4	5	1(1)	22	19	20	61
10	2	5	1	2(1)	26	24	26	76
11	3	1	3	5(2)	27	25	25	77
12	3	2	4	1(1)	27	26	27	80
13	3	3	5	2(1)	26	24	25	75
14	3	4	1	3(1)	36	34	36	106
15	3	5	2	4(2)	27	26	26	79
16	4	1	4	2(1)	28	27	33	88
17	4	2	5	3(1)	27	25	31	83
18	4	3	1	4(2)	35	35	34	104
19	4	4	2	5(2)	33	31	32	96
20	4	5	3	1(1)	30	27	35	92
21	5	1	5	4(2)	36	37	37	110
22	5	2	1	5(2)	37	40	36	113
23	5	3	2	1(1)	39	37	37	113
24	5	4	3	2(1)	37	33	36	106
25	5	5	4	3(1)	33	31	33	97
								2131

The experimental design used is shown in Table 14.1. Note that Taguchi's dummy-level technique (see Chapter 11) was utilized in order to assign the two-level factor $F4$ to a five-level column. Table 14.1 allows the study of 3 five-level factors $(F1, F2, F3)$ and 1 two-level factor $(F4)$ with the expense of only 25 experimental trials instead of the 250 $(= 5 \times 5 \times 5 \times 2)$ that would otherwise be needed.

Three transistors were used for each trial. Table 14.1 shows the resulting data. Each data value (minimum power required to cause disruption) can be considered as a lifetime value; for calculation purposes it can be assumed that the values can range from 0 to 52 dBm. As the power level is increased from 0 no undesired effect is observed until the level reaches that shown in the data columns of Table 14.1. The no-effect condition can be taken to be a '1' state. At the level shown in the table a disruptive effect is observed and this can be taken to be a '0' state. The 0 state is then held as the level is increased to the maximum level of 52. For example, for an effect occurring at 36 dBm

Power level	0	1	2	...	34	35	36	37	38	...	52
State	1	1	1	...	1	1	0	0	0	...	0

A breakdown of the lifetime value in values of binary form as above, allows the application of Taguchi's minute analysis (Section 14.2.1). Here the minutes (minimum units) are the 53 power levels (in dBm). Using a more conventional

Taguchi approach, the actual lifetime data values of Table 14.1 will be reanalysed in Section 14.3. Section 14.4 includes the basic conclusions and recommendations.

14.2.1 Minute analysis of the survival data

This method is based on the breakdown of the testing period into regular intervals of a specific duration called minimum units (minutes) or cycles. The duration of a minimum unit depends on the problem under investigation. In case-study 14.1 the 53 steps (from 0 to 52 dBm) of the RF power are considered as minutes of 1 dBm each. The method constitutes an investigation into at *which* minimum unit a disruption took place in the semiconductor circuit under test. The data are expressed in binary form (1 or 0) with 1 signifying that the transistor was functioning without disruptions, and a 0 indicating a disruption.

The maximum cycle with a data value of 1 can only be 40 (see Table 14.1). For practical reasons we will be dealing with 40 minutes; in other words, we only consider the cycles for which at least one experimental test-piece was functioning without disruption (the conclusions would be exactly the same as if we considered all 53 minutes). The division of the testing period into minutes $\omega(1), ..., \omega(40)$, introduces an additional factor, the ω-factor with 40 levels. This will have to be taken into consideration as shown below. The total number of observations N is considered to be equal to the total number of binary data values, that is,

$$N = \text{(minutes or trials)} \times \text{(number of replications)} \times \text{(number of minutes)}$$
$$= 25 \times 3 \times 40 = 3000$$

So the total number of degrees of freedom is

$$df_{tot} = N - 1 = 2999$$

First calculate the correction factor CF:

$$CF = \frac{\text{(total sum of values)}^2}{N} = \frac{(2131)^2}{3000} = 1513.72$$

Then the total sum of squares

$$SS_{tot} = \text{(total sum of squared values)} - CF = (1^2 + \cdots + 1^2) - CF$$
$$= 2131 - 1513.72 = 617.28$$

The sum of squares due to $F1$ can be found as

$$SS(F1) = \frac{\text{(sum in level 1 of } F1)^2}{\text{number of values in level 1}} + \cdots + \frac{\text{(sum in level 5 of } F1)^2}{\text{number of values in level 5}}$$
$$- CF$$
$$= \frac{(367)^2 + (345)^2 + (417)^2 + (453)^2 + (539)^2}{600} - 1513.72 = 40.435$$

(Note that $367 = 100 + 68 + 73 + 66 + 60$: see Table 14.1.)

Similarly,

$$SS(F2) = \frac{(449)^2 + (411)^2 + (432)^2 + (435)^2 + (404)^2}{600} - 1513.72 = 2.258$$

$$SS(F3) = \frac{(499)^2 + (430)^2 + (415)^2 + (398)^2 + (389)^2}{600} - 1513.72 = 12.698$$

Also

$$SS(F4) = \frac{(\text{sum in level 1})^2}{\text{number of values in level 1}} + \frac{(\text{sum in level 2})^2}{\text{number of values in level 2}}$$

$$- CF$$

$$= \frac{(1292)^2}{1800} + \frac{(839)^2}{1200} - 1513.72 = 0.2497$$

The degrees of freedom for the factors are one less than the number of levels. So

$$df(F1) = 5 - 1 = 4 = df(F2) = df(F3)$$

and

$$df(F4) = 2 - 1 = 1$$

The sum of squares for the interexperimental error e_1 is found as (see Table 14.1):

$$SS(e_1) = \frac{(100)^2 + (68)^2 + \cdots + (97)^2}{120} - CF - SS(F1) - SS(F2)$$

$$- SS(F3) - SS(F4)$$

$$= 3.164$$

Also (see Table 14.1):

$$SS(e_2) = \left\{ \frac{36^2 + 33^2 + 31^2}{40} - \frac{100^2}{120} \right\} + \cdots + \left\{ \frac{33^2 + 31^2 + 33^2}{40} - \frac{97^2}{120} \right\}$$

$$= 3.6997 \qquad (df(e_2) = 25 \times 39 = 975)$$

To calculate the ω-related sum of squares we need to express the data in the form depicted in Table 14.2. The rows correspond to the 25 experimental trials and the columns correspond to the 40 levels of the ω-factor. In the first row (trial 1) we see that three transistors were functioning without disruption up to the 31st cycle, two up to the 33rd cycle and one up to the 36th cycle: similarly for the other trials. In this way we can now calculate the sum of squares for the ω-related effects.

Table 14.2 Data needed to calculate the ω-related sum of squares

Trial	1	2	...	17	18	19	20	21	22	23	24	25	26	27	28	29	30	31	32	33	34	35	36	37	38	39	40
1	3	3	...	3	3	3	3	3	3	3	3	3	3	3	3	3	3	3	2	2	1	1	1	0	0	0	0
2	3	3	...	3	3	3	3	3	3	2	0	0	0	0	0	0	0	0	0	0	0	0	0	0	0	0	0
.	.	.	...	.	.																						.
.	.	.	...	.	.																						.
5	3	3	...	3	3	2	2	1	1	0	0	0	0	0	0	0	0	0	0	0	0	0	0	0	0	0	0
6	3	3	...	3	3	3	3	3	3	3	3	2	0	0	0	0	0	0	0	0	0	0	0	0	0	0	0
.	.	.																									.
.	.	.																									.
15	3	3		3	3	3	3	3	3	3	3	3	3	1	0	0	0	0	0	0	0	0	0	0	0	0	0
16	3	3		3	3	3	3	3	3	3	3	3	3	2	1	1	1	1	1	1	0	0	0	0	0	0	0
.	.	.		.																							.
.	.	.		.																							.
22	3	3		3	3	3	3	3	3	3	3	3	3	3	3	3	3	3	3	3	3	3	2	1	1	1	
.	.			.																							.
.	.			.																							.
25	3	3		3	3	3	3	3	3	3	3	3	3	3	3	3	3	2	2	0	0	0	0	0	0	0	0
Total	75	75	...	75	75	74	73	71	70	62	55	53	45	40	32	31	31	30	26	25	19	17	14	8	2	2	1

$$SS(\omega) = \frac{75^2 + 75^2 + \cdots + 75^2 + 74^2 + 73^2 + 71^2 + \cdots + 2^2 + 1^2}{75} - CF$$

$$= 369.725 \qquad (df = 40 - 1 = 39)$$

$$SS(F1 \times \omega) = \frac{(F1(1) \times W(1))^2 + \cdots + (F1(5) \times W(1))^2}{15}$$
$$\frac{+ \cdots + (F1(1) \times W(40))^2 + \cdots + (F1(5) \times W(40))^2}{15}$$
$$- CF - SS(F1) - SS(W)$$

$$= \frac{(15)^2 + \cdots + (15)^2 + \cdots + 0^2 + 1^2}{15} - 1513.72 - 40.435$$

$$- 369.725$$

$$= 79.52 \qquad (df = df(F1) \times df(\omega) = 4 \times 39 = 156)$$

Similarly

$$SS(F2 \times \omega) = 14.097 \qquad df = 156$$

$$SS(F3 \times \omega) = 24.99 \qquad df = 156$$

and

$$SS(F4 \times \omega) = 3.767 \qquad df = 1 \times 39 = 39$$

Table 14.3 ANOVA for minute analysis

Source	df	SS	$MSS = SS/df$	F-ratio	
$F1$	4	40.435	10.11	$10.11/0.29$	$= 35^*$
$F2$	4	2.258	0.56		1.9
$F3$	4	12.698	3.17		11^*
$F4$	1	0.2497	0.25		0.8
e_1	11	3.164	0.29	$0.29/0.0038$	$= 76.3^*$
e_2	975	3.6997	0.0038	$0.0038/0.043 =$	0.09
ω	39	369.725	9.48	$9.48/0.043$	$= 220.5^*$
$F1 \times \omega$	156	79.52	0.51		11.9^*
$F2 \times \omega$	156	14.097	0.09		2.1
$F3 \times \omega$	156	24.99	0.16		3.7^*
$F4 \times \omega$	39	3.767	0.1		2.3
e_3	1454	62.677	0.043		
Total	2999	617.28			

Table 14.4 ANOVA for the lifetime values

Source	df	SS	F-ratio
$F1$	4	1617.4	35^*
$F2$	4	90.3	1.9
$F3$	4	507.9	11^*
$F4$	1	9.98	0.8
e_1	11	126.6	3.9^*
e_2	50	148.0	

Finally, the sum of squares for e_3 can be found by subtraction from the total sum of squares of all calculated so far. The ANOVA table is given in Table 14.3.

From this we can see that factors $F1$ and $F3$ are significant. The ω-factor and its interactions with $F1$ and $F3$ are also significant, which was to be expected. The optimal settings for $F1$ and $F3$ can easily be found to be level 5 for $F1$ and level 1 for $F3$. These are the levels which on average produced the highest cycle value.

If we analyse the lifetime values of Table 14.1 in the conventional way, we will obtain the results given in Table 14.4. Note that the conclusions of Table 14.4 are identical to those depicted in Table 14.3 (above the dotted line). This is simply because the sums of squares appearing in Table 14.4 are all 40 times the corresponding sum of squares of Table 14.3 (40 is the number of levels of the minute ω-factor). Note that in both tables all factor effects are tested against the interexperimental error e_1 because e_1 is significant when tested against the replication error e_2.

■ 14.3 A conventional Taguchi analysis

A measure reflecting the mean response (target performance measure – *TPM*) and a measure reflecting the variability (noise performance measure – *NPM*) in the response are analysed. The response is the minimum RF power level required to cause disruption to the transistors and so the data to be analysed are the lifetime values of Table 14.1. We first calculate the arithmetic mean $\bar{x}$ and standard deviation S of the three lifetime data values in each trial.

Following the approach described in Chapter 13, the performance measures are determined to be: $TPM = \bar{x}$; $NPM = -20 \log_{10}(S)$. An analysis of the *TPM* produces the ANOVA table given in Table 14.5. An analysis of the *NPM* yields Table 14.6.

Tables 14.5 and 14.6 show that factors *F*1 and *F*3 have a significant effect on the mean response, whereas *F*4 has an effect on the variability in the response. It can easily be shown that the optimal levels for *F*1 and *F*3 for achieving the best response (highest survival) are level 5 for *F*1 and level 1 for *F*3. The best level for *F*4 for minimum variability is level 2. Factor *F*2 has no effect and can be set at its most economical level.

Note that the effect of *F*4 on dispersion was not apparent in the minute analysis of Section 14.2. Following the conventional estimation procedure recommended by Taguchi, a 95% confidence interval for the long-term (average) survival time at the optimal settings can be found to be given by 40.8 ± 2.6, that is from 38.2 dBm to 43.4 dBm. So under the best conditions, 95% of the transistors are expected to function without disruption up to an RF power level of at least 38.2 dBm with a maximum of 43.4 dBm.

Table 14.5 ANOVA for *TPM*

Source	df	SS	MSS	F-ratio
*F*1	4	539.13	134.78	35.2[*]
*F*2	4	30.11	7.53	2.0
*F*3	4	169.31	42.33	11.1[*]
*F*4	1	3.33	3.33	0.9
Res	11	42.18	3.83	
Total	24	784.06		

Table 14.6 ANOVA for *NPM*

Source	df	SS	MSS	F-ratio
*F*1	4	241.63	60.41	2.5
*F*2	4	24.92	6.23	0.3
*F*3	4	143.7	35.93	1.5
*F*4	1	87.55	87.55	3.6 (significant at 10% level)
Res	11	265.12	24.1	
Total	24	762.92		

■ 14.4 A perspective

In comparison with the minute analysis of Section 14.2 the two-stage analysis of Section 14.3 has certain advantages which cannot be overlooked:

1. Simplicity: it does not require the breakdown into minimum units (Table 14.2) needing a separate analysis (the part of Table 14.3 below the dotted line) whose conclusions are expected in advance.
2. It is more informative: it provides additional information about factors affecting dispersion (such as $F4$), something which is not apparent in the minute analysis of Table 14.3.
3. Statistical validity: it avoids the statistical drawbacks of dependence and non-normality inherent in the minimum units.

The most obvious of these drawbacks is the arbitrary introduction of the extra degrees of freedom which heavily depend upon the adopted decision on the size of the minimum units. For example, in the case-study considered, if the minute was defined to be a power of 5 dBm, instead of 1 dBm, one would only have to deal with 600 degrees of freedom instead of 3000. On the other hand, if a measurement scale of 0.1 dBm was used, one would be overwhelmed with 30,000 degrees of freedom! In any case, these are not degrees of freedom in the statistical sense of independent values, which makes the testing and validity of the ω-related effects rather dubious.

Moreover, for estimating the future average performance, the method which followed the analysis of Section 14.3 simply utilized the average responses corresponding to the optimal levels of the significant factors and the error variance of Table 14.5. However, an estimation following the minute analysis (of Section 14.2) would have additionally involved:

1. The optimal cycle, that is, the best level of the ω-factor.
2. The optimal interaction levels between the ω-factor and the significant factors $F1$ and $F3$.
3. The ω-order error variance, that is, the error variance associated with the pseudo-repetitions of the minimum units.
4. The logit-transformation, a transformation of proportions into decibels (and vice versa), which Taguchi recommends when one is dealing with proportions (as in the case of the minute analysis) in order to avoid unrealistic estimation results (such as negative probabilities).

The additional complication involved in the minute-analysis method, coupled with the statistical inflexibility of the pseudo-binary data values (the minimum units) which are forcibly introduced, makes the advantages of the simpler two-stage approach of Section 14.3 even more apparent. This approach is the type of analysis originated by Taguchi himself, and is strongly recommended as the best alternative to minute analysis.

■ 14.5 Taguchi's tolerance design

When designing electronic circuits, in order to achieve the aim of understanding how the variability in input affects variability in the output, certain simulation techniques have been developed. Assuming the existence of a reliable functional relationship between the input variables and the output response, the usual simulation procedure makes use of Monte Carlo methods, which may require a relatively large computer capability and availability. Whether a functional model is available or not, Taguchi recommends the use of experimental design as the most important tool in the following two-stage procedure.

> *Stage 1*: Parameter design through tolerance analysis is the most important phase of circuit design work and has the objective of selecting optimum nominal settings of the circuit's components, so that the response of interest is stable (of low variability) despite the use of highly variable, inexpensive components, and even if the system and environmental parameters change. At this stage, the tolerance specifications of the system components remain unchanged but are analysed in order to determine ways to make the circuit insensitive to their effects.

> *Stage 2*: Tolerance (re-)design: This is the stage when decisions are made as to how much variability to allow in component parts. A rational tightening of tolerance specifications of most crucial components takes place, so that further robustness and stability is achieved in the response of interest. Of course, setting tight tolerances might inevitably lead to additional costs, so this should take place only after stage (1), if necessary, that is, only if the required robustness has not been achieved using existing tolerance levels during the parameter-design stage. Nevertheless, additional cost at this stage might be avoided by relaxing the tolerance specifications of the least crucial components.

For such cost-effective respecification of tolerances, Taguchi recommends the use of the contribution ratios (Section 12.1) to be explained below.

We will apply the above two-stage procedure to the optimization of a low pass active filter for which a reliable functional model (relating the input parameters with the output response) was available; this meant that simulated computer experimentation was possible. A general methodology will thus become apparent, applicable to non-simulated situations as well as to areas other than circuit design.

■ CASE STUDY 14.2

A RC630 low pass active filter, part of the television transmit circuit (see Figure 14.1), was to be studied. The response of interest is the *gain*, which at a

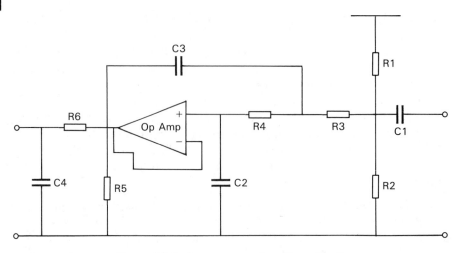

Figure 14.1 Low pass active filter circuit

certain frequency f is defined in decibels (dB) as

$$G(f) = 10 \log_{10}\{V(f)\}^2$$

where $V(f)$ can be calculated on the basis of the resistance of 6 resistors R1–R6 and the capacitance of 4 capacitors C1–C4 which comprise the circuit. For a proper performance of the circuit, it is required that the gains at frequencies 2.55 KHz and 1 KHz should consistently satisfy

$$-2 \text{ dB} \leqslant G(2.55 \text{ KHz}) - G(1 \text{ KHz}) \leqslant 1 \text{ dB}$$

or equivalently

$$0.7943 \leqslant Y = \frac{V(2.55 \text{ KHz})}{V(1 \text{ KHz})} \leqslant 1.122$$

Since a functional model relating input (resistance and capacitance) to output (Y) was available, it was possible to perform computer simulation experiments using experimental design techniques. Taguchi's two-stage approach was followed with the objective of determining the optimal nominal levels of the resistors and capacitors, and if necessary their optimal tolerance specifications, so that Y achieved the target response with minimum variability.

Parameter design through tolerance analysis

Three important components were studied at this stage, the resistor R6 and the capacitors C2 and C3, which were allowed to vary at three nominal levels each. Past information was available indicating that:

1. These three components were not interacting with each other.
2. The other components had to be set at fixed nominal levels predetermined as optimal.

Low-cost tolerances were used at these stages. The nominal and tolerance levels studied are shown in Table 14.7. The resistance values are given in KΩ and the capacitance values in nF $(= 10^{-9}$ F).

Experimental design

The general experimental set up is the same as that shown in Figure 11.4 (page 302). It consists of an inner array and an outer array. The parameters, when viewed as controllable factors, are assigned (with their nominal levels) to the columns of the inner array. For each trial run (nominal-level combination) of the inner array, a number of response values Y will be calculated (using the functional model) by systematically varying all the parameters within their tolerance specification. This systematic change of all the parameters around their nominal values will be directed by the outer array to which the parameters, when viewed as noise factors, will be assigned.

Taguchi recommends orthogonal arrays (OA); such arrays allow the factors to have different numbers of test settings (level) and also have a pairwise balancing property: every level of a factor occurs with every level of all other factors the same number of times. Fractional orthogonal arrays minimize the number of trial runs while keeping the pairwise balancing property. The $OA_9(3^4)$ was chosen as the inner array; the controllable factors R6, C2 and C3 were assigned in their nominal levels as shown, in Table 14.8. The full outline of the inner array using

Table 14.7 Nominal and tolerance levels

Circuit parameters as controllable factors	Nominal levels			Circuit parameters as noise factors	Tolerance levels (% from nominal)	
	1	2	3		1	2
R1		27	(fixed)	R1′	− 2	+ 2
R2		27	(fixed)	R2′	− 2	+ 2
R3		22	(fixed)	R3′	− 2	+ 2
R4		22	(fixed)	R4′	− 2	+ 2
R5		56	(fixed)	R5′	− 2	+ 2
R6	20	22	24	R6′	− 2	+ 2
C1		100	(fixed)	C1′	− 10	+ 10
C2	0.82	1	1.2	C2′	− 5	+ 5
C3	6.8	8.2	10	C3′	− 5	+ 5
C4		4.7	(fixed)	C4′	− 5	+ 5

Table 14.8 $OA_9(3^4)$ for inner array

Trial run	Controllable factors			
	C3	R6	C2	
1	1	1	1	1
2	1	2	2	2
3	1	3	3	3
4	2	1	2	3
5	2	2	3	1
6	2	3	1	2
7	3	1	3	2
8	3	2	1	3
9	3	3	2	1

the three nominal values due to be studied for R6, C2 and C3, is shown in Table 14.9. All the other parameters (R1–R5, C1, C4) are fixed at the pre-determined values (see Table 14.7). Note that there are only 9 nominal-level combinations (trial runs) out of 27 possible combinations.

The 10 circuit components were viewed both as controllable and as noise factors: controllable because the experimenter was free to choose among certain nominal values, and noise because of the effect of their tolerances (the deviations from the nominal), which was the cause of variability in the circuit's performance. Note that the tolerances were $\pm 2\%$ from the nominal level for the resistors, and $\pm 5\%$ for the capacitors except in the case of the capacitor C1 with $\pm 10\%$ from nominal.

As outer array, the $OA_{12}(12^{11})$ was used, on which all 10 parameters, viewed as noise factors, were assigned in their tolerance levels as shown in Table 14.10. For example, since R1 is fixed at the nominal value of 27 KΩ, then

Level 1 of R1' in outer array is 26.46 (nominal -2%)
Level 2 of R1' in outer array is 27.54 (nominal $+2\%$)

If C3 in the inner array is at nominal level 1 (6.8 nF) then

Level 1 of C3' in outer array is 6.46 (nominal -5%)
Level 2 of C3' in outer array is 7.14 (nominal $+5\%$)

Table 14.9 Inner array using nominal values

Trial run	Controllable factors		
	C3	R6	C2
1	6.8	20	0.82
2	6.8	22	1.00
3	6.8	24	1.20
4	8.2	20	1.00
5	8.2	22	1.20
6	8.2	24	0.82
7	10.0	20	1.20
8	10.0	22	0.82
9	10.0	24	1.00

Table 14.10 $OA_{12}(3^{11})$ for outer array

Replication run	Noise factors									
	R1'	R2'	R3'	R4'	R5'	R6'	C1'	C2'	C3'	C4'
1	1	1	1	1	1	1	1	1	1	1 1
2	1	1	1	1	1	2	2	2	2	2 2
3	1	1	2	2	2	1	1	1	2	2 2
4	1	2	1	2	2	1	2	2	1	1 2
5	1	2	2	1	2	2	1	2	1	2 1
6	1	2	2	2	1	2	2	1	2	1 1
7	2	1	2	2	1	1	2	2	1	2 1
8	2	1	2	1	2	2	2	1	1	1 2
9	2	1	1	2	2	2	1	2	2	1 1
10	2	2	2	1	1	1	1	2	2	1 2
11	2	2	1	2	1	2	1	1	1	2 2
12	2	2	1	1	2	1	2	1	2	2 1

Similarly for the other inner array levels of C3 and for the levels of the other circuit parameters. Tables 14.11 and 14.12 show the outer array for the 1st and 9th trial run of the inner array respectively, using the actual tolerance levels. Note that there are only 12 tolerance level combinations (replication runs) out of $2^{10} = 1024$ possible.

Results

The 12 replication runs (from the outer array) at each of the 9 trial runs (of the inner array) provided the data values of Y, for the calculation of a measure reflecting the mean response (target performance measure – *TPM*) and a measure reflecting the variability in the response (noise performance measure – *NPM*) at each trial run. For the 1st and 9th trial run, the Y data are shown in Tables 14.11 and 14.12 respectively. First, the sample mean $\bar{Y}$ and sample standard deviation S for each of the 9 trial runs have been calculated, and these are shown in Table 14.13.

Table 14.11 Outer array for trial 1 of inner array

Replication	Noise factor										
	R1′	R2′	R3′	R4′	R5′	R6′	C1′	C2′	C3′	C4′	Y data
1	26.46	26.46	21.56	21.56	54.88	19.6	90	0.78	6.46	4.46	0.9174
2	26.46	26.46	21.56	21.56	54.88	20.4	110	0.86	7.14	4.94	0.8706
3	26.46	26.46	22.44	22.44	57.12	19.6	90	0.78	7.14	4.94	0.9177
4	26.46	27.54	21.56	22.44	57.12	19.6	110	0.86	6.46	4.46	0.8945
5	26.46	27.54	22.44	21.56	57.12	20.4	90	0.86	6.46	4.94	0.8413
6	26.46	27.54	22.44	22.44	54.88	20.4	110	0.78	7.14	4.46	0.9444
7	27.54	26.46	22.44	22.44	54.88	19.6	110	0.86	6.46	4.94	0.8554
8	27.54	26.46	22.44	21.56	57.12	20.4	110	0.78	6.46	4.46	0.9071
9	27.54	26.46	21.56	22.44	57.12	20.4	90	0.86	7.14	4.46	0.9030
10	27.54	27.54	22.44	21.56	54.88	19.6	90	0.86	7.14	4.46	0.9193
11	27.54	27.54	21.56	22.44	54.88	20.4	90	0.78	6.46	4.94	0.8663
12	27.54	27.54	21.56	21.56	57.12	19.6	110	0.78	7.14	4.94	0.9157

Table 14.12 Outer array for trial 9 of inner array

Replication	Noise factor										
	R1′	R2′	R3′	R4′	R5′	R6′	C1′	C2′	C3′	C4′	Y data
1	26.46	26.46	21.56	21.56	54.88	23.52	90	0.95	9.5	4.46	0.7943
2	26.46	26.46	21.56	21.56	54.88	24.48	110	1.05	10.5	4.94	0.6130
3	26.46	26.46	22.44	22.44	57.12	23.52	90	0.95	10.5	4.94	0.6599
4	26.46	27.54	21.56	22.44	57.12	23.52	110	1.05	9.5	4.46	0.6717
5	26.46	27.54	22.44	21.56	57.12	24.48	90	1.05	9.5	4.94	0.6315
6	26.46	27.54	22.44	22.44	54.88	24.48	110	0.95	10.5	4.46	0.6798
7	27.54	26.46	22.44	22.44	54.88	23.52	110	1.05	9.5	4.94	0.6165
8	27.54	26.46	22.44	21.56	57.12	24.48	110	0.95	9.5	4.46	0.7588
9	27.54	26.46	21.56	22.44	57.12	24.48	90	1.05	10.5	4.46	0.6073
10	27.54	27.54	22.44	21.56	54.88	23.52	90	1.05	10.5	4.46	0.6186
11	27.54	27.54	21.56	22.44	54.88	24.48	90	0.95	9.5	4.94	0.7224
12	27.54	27.54	21.56	21.56	57.12	23.52	110	0.95	10.5	4.94	0.7248

Table 14.13   Trial means, standard deviations and NPM values for Y

Trial run	Sample mean $\bar{y}$	Sample standard deviation S	$NPM = -10 \log_{10}(S^2)$
1	0.8960	0.03097	30.18
2	0.7725	0.03445	29.26
3	0.6348	0.03774	28.46
4	0.7970	0.04935	26.13
5	0.6172	0.04945	26.12
6	0.8731	0.03502	29.11
7	0.5549	0.05862	24.64
8	0.9059	0.05754	24.80
9	0.6749	0.06264	24.06

Analysis

Following the techniques described in Chapter 13 the appropriate *TPM* and *NPM* were determined to be

$$TPM = \bar{Y}$$
$$NPM = 10 \log_{10}(S^2)$$

The values of *NPM* for the 9 trial runs are also shown in Table 14.13.

An ANOVA for the above *NPM* has shown that C3 significantly affects the *NPM* and therefore the variability in the response *Y*. So C3 can be considered as a variability control factor with optimal level 1; this is the level with maximum *NPM*, that is, minimum value of *S*. An ANOVA for the *TPM* has shown C2 to be highly significant. Since C2 does not affect the variability, it can be considered as a target control factor and can be manipulated to bring the mean response of *Y* towards its target. Level 1 has been shown to be the optimal for this purpose. The factor R6 did not seem to affect either the *TPM* or the *NPM*.

Confirmation

The analysis of the results has shown level 1 to be the optimum for both C2 and C3. For R6, level 1 was also chosen. Keeping all the other parameters at the predetermined fixed settings, and keeping R6, C2 and C3 at their level 1, some confirmation trials have shown that *Y* indeed achieved its target with minimum variability. In fact, in comparison to results before the parameter-design stage a 30% reduction in variability has been achieved, which has ensured consistency of the *Y* response within the required range.

■ 14.6 Tolerance (re-)design

If the variability in the response at an optimal setting determined during the parameter-design stage is still unacceptable, a further improvement can be achieved through a rational reduction of certain tolerances. The additional costs incurred may be offset by simultaneously relaxing the tolerances of non-crucial components. Such a cost-effective respecification of tolerances can be achieved through the utilization of Taguchi's contribution ratios.

Suppose it is required to reduce the variance of Y to 50% of what it was at the optimal component setting determined in the parameter-design stage. To achieve this we first need to determine which of the circuit's components are the most crucial in affecting a change in variability levels. For this, we need to study the effect of the *existing* tolerance levels and determine how much each component contributes to the total variability at the optimal setting. So, we will view all the components as noise factors and consider an outer array corresponding to the current optimal setting. Additional noise factors not included previously might be included for study at this stage; for our case we considered only the previously studied noise factors $R1'-R6'$, $C1'-C4'$ and assigned them on the $OA_{12}(2^{11})$ as before, using the existing tolerance levels. This coincided with the outer array of Table 14.11; this was because the optimal setting of the controllable factors coincided with trial 1 of the inner array.

The resulting 12 data values (see Table 14.11) were analysed and the ANOVA results are shown in Table 14.14.

Note that the contribution ratio P_F for each factor is also given in Table 14.14; this is defined by

$$P_F = \frac{SS_F - df_F \times MSS_{res}}{SS_{tot}} \times 100$$

where $MSS_{res} = SS_{res}/df_{res}$, with SS_F representing the sum of squares for F corresponding to df_F degrees of freedom.

Since it is required to reduce the existing variability by 50%, the reassignment of the tolerances can be decided upon using the following tolerance equation:

$$50 = [1/A(R1)]^2 P_{R1} + \cdots + [1/A(C4)]^2 P_{C4} + P_{res} \qquad (14.2)$$

where '$1/A(F)$' represents a reduction to $1/A(F)$ of the existing tolerance specification of factor F. For example, by $A(F) = 1$ we mean that the tolerance of F will remain the same, where $A(F) = 2$ we mean a reduction to $1/2$ of the existing F-tolerance, that is $\pm 10\%$ reduced to $\pm 5\%$.

Of course there are many combinations of $A(R1), ..., A(R6)$, $A(C1), ..., A(C4)$ which would satisfy formula (14.2). This is a flexibility which should be welcomed, since cost considerations can be more easily taken into account when deciding on the final choice. In our case, we clearly see that tightening of the tolerances for C2, C3 and C4 will have the greatest effect on the Y variability because these parameters contribute the most in the ANOVA of Table 14.14.

For example, if we reduce the tolerances of C2, C3, C4 to $2/3$ of the existing specification, from $\pm 5\%$ to $\pm 3.33\%$ $(A(C2) = A(C3) = A(C4) = 3/2)$, and in order to avoid any additional cost, we relax the tolerance of all the

Table 14.14 ANOVA for Y at optimal setting

Component	df	SS	Contribution ratio (%)
R1	1	0.0000304	0.286
R2	1	0.00000884	0.08
R3	1	0.00002611	0.245
R4	1	0.00000817	0.075
R5	1	0.0000029	0.025
R6	1	0.0006351	0.060
C1	1	0.0000429	0.405
C2	1	0.0028367	26.9
C3	1	0.0029673	28.14
C4	1	0.0039858	37.8
Res	1	0.00000023	5.98
Total	11	0.0105445	100.00

resistors by a factor of 2 $(A(R1) = \cdots = A(R6) = 1/2)$, the new variability target will be achieved; indeed, by allowing

$$A(R1) = \cdots = A(R6) = 1/2, \quad A(C1) = 1, \quad A(C2) = A(C3) = A(C4) = 3/2$$

the right-hand side of formula (14.2), using the contribution ratios of Table 14.14, yields a value of 50.7 as required. A model trial run of the optional setting with the tolerances respecified as above, confirmed the tolerance-equation prediction.

■ 14.7 Conclusion

It is evident that the area of circuit design can greatly benefit from the application of Taguchi's parameter design and tolerance redesign. Improvement and robustness in design can be efficiently obtained using only low-cost components with wide tolerances. Further robustness can be achieved by a rational reduction of crucial tolerances with the minimum additional cost. Whether a reliable response model is available or not, the use of well-designed experiments is strongly recommended in order to improve design robustness against the effects of components' tolerances, followed by the use of tolerance equations, which can help in the cost-effective respecification of tolerances. Managing the subject of tolerances in this way, has already been proved extremely effective in avoiding arbitrary and panic actions, as well as a great deal of additional expense.

If one assumes a linear model (i.e. no interactions), thinking it correct, then one is a man removed from natural science or reality, and commits the mistake of standing just upon mathematics which is nothing but idealism.

G. Taguchi

In this chapter we evaluate alternative techniques to fractional experimentation and analysis, in particular those recommended by Dorian Shainin. His methods for variable identification and variation reduction at the on-line and off-line stage of a production process are described and assessed in relation to other methods for off-line quality control and on-line improvement.

Dorian Shainin, an American quality consultant, strongly objects to the use of fractional factorials for experimentation (see Shainin and Shainin, 1988). Instead, he proposes a set of procedures which have as an objective the identification and removal of the majority of the sources of variation down to a manageable number (4 or 5), at which time he allows the use of full factorials. In this chater, we provide a perspective on those particular procedures which are relevant to special forms of experimentation. His approach will be viewed in relation to other quality improvement techniques, in particular those recommended by Genichi Taguchi (see Chapter 11).

■ 15.1 Shainin's approach to experimentation

The colourful world of D. Shainin is adequately revealed in K.R. Bhote's book on *World Class Quality* (see Bhote, 1988). Shainin rates the sources of variation in order of importance into the Red X, the Pink X and the Pale Pink X types of variables, which he attempts to identify and remove through a series of techniques, largely invented by him. Some of these techniques are related to specific forms of experimentation and are briefly described below (see also Bhote, 1988); following each description, an assessment and critique will be given.

15.1.1 Component search

This technique is applicable in assembly operations, where measurable good and bad units are found, capable of easy disassembly and reassembly.

Stage 1

1. A good and a bad unit are selected at random (from a sufficient number of good and bad units), and a parameter representing their performance is measured. Denote these measurements by $G1$ (for the good unit) and $B1$ (for the bad unit).
2. Disassemble and reassemble both units and remeasure them. Denote the results as $G2$ and $B2$ respectively.
3. Calculate the following:

$$D = \frac{G1 + G2}{2} - \frac{B1 + B2}{2}$$

and

$$d = \frac{G1 - G2}{2} + \frac{B1 - B2}{2}$$

If the ratio D/d is larger than five, then 'a significant and repeatable difference between the good and bad units is established'.
4. Based upon engineering judgment, rank the likely component problems in descending order of importance.

Stage 2

1. Switch the top-ranked component from the good unit with the corresponding component in the bad unit. Measure the two assemblies. If there is a complete reversal in the outputs, this component could be in the Red X family and the search can stop; if there is a partial reversal, the component could be in the Pink X or Pale Pink X family; otherwise the component is unimportant.
2. Restoring the component to its original position, the switching and measurement process is repeated with the remaining (lower-ranked) components, until a complete reversal of the results takes place.
3. Assuming that some important variables (components) have been identified, then: capping runs are conducted, with these variables banded together in the good and bad assemblies, to verify their importance; using all the data gathered, a factorial analysis takes place of the most important variables, for a quantitative determination of main and interaction effects; to avoid the occurrence of bad units in the future, agreements with the components' suppliers take place so that the tolerances of the important components are redesigned and tightened.

Assessment

The deviation of the component's value away from its nominal (component tolerance) can cause a unit to fail. The component search technique attempts to identify the components whose allowed tolerance was too wide for that particular (bad) unit; when the identification is achieved, the suppliers are asked to tighten up those tolerances. However, the random choice of a single bad unit does not guarantee that all important tolerances (Red X) will reveal themselves. For example, let us assume that both the allowed tolerances of two components, A and B, was too wide. A particular unit can be bad because:

1. Either, A's value happens to be at the extreme of its tolerance and B's value at its nominal.
2. Or, B's value is at the extreme of its tolerance and A's value at its nominal.
3. Or, A and B are both reasonably close to their nominals but the interaction of these (small) deviations causes the unit to fail.
4. Or, both A and B happen to be at the extremes of their allowed tolerance.

In three out of the above four cases (1–3), the technique would not reveal that both A and B are important. In particular in (3), it would wrongly indicate another component as being in the Red X. This heavy reliance on (randomly) selecting a proper and fully informative bad unit, is one of the weakest points of this particular technique.

The technique falls short of providing any statistical justification for the $5:1$ rule, that is, of explaining why the ratio D/d being larger than five denotes a significant and repeatable difference between (presumably all) good and bad units. What happens when D/d is less than five? Does one then continue testing every bad unit? What does one do if no bad unit satisfies the $5:1$ rule? What if $D/d = 4.99$?

The technique very much resembles the 'change one factor at a time' method of experimentation. Indeed, if we call the process of disassembly/reassembly/measurement an experimental trial, a separate trial is involved with each switching of a single component from the bad to the good unit (and vice versa), with the rest of the components remaining fixed at their original position. For example, assuming that all possible problematic components will reveal themselves in the chosen bad unit (something needing a lot of luck), let us suppose that seven components, $A, B, ..., G$, have been ranked, in order of perceived importance, as the likely problematic ones. Define that each component is in condition 1 if it originates from the good unit, and in condition 2 if it originates from the bad unit. The trials involved are then as shown in Table 15.1.

Apart from the capping runs, the trials of Table 15.1 represent versions of the one factor at a time method (performed twice). The unreliability of this method is well known, as it relies heavily on information obtained when every variable, except one, is fixed – something that does not guarantee the

Table 15.1 Shainin's experimental set up

Trial	A	B	C	D	E	F	G	Comments
1	1	1	1	1	1	1	1	Initial measurement of good unit
2	2	2	2	2	2	2	2	Initial measurement of bad unit
3	1	1	1	1	1	1	1	Measurement after dis/reassembly
4	2	2	2	2	2	2	2	Measurement after dis/reassembly
5	2	1	1	1	1	1	1	Switch A from bad to good
6	1	2	1	1	1	1	1	Restore A, switch B etc.
7	1	1	2	1	1	1	1	
8	1	1	1	2	1	1	1	
9	1	1	1	1	2	1	1	
10	1	1	1	1	1	2	1	
11	1	1	1	1	1	1	2	
12	1	2	2	2	2	2	2	Switch A from good to bad
13	2	1	2	2	2	2	2	Restore A, switch B etc.
14	2	2	1	2	2	2	2	
14	2	2	2	1	2	2	2	
15	2	2	2	2	1	2	2	
16	2	2	2	2	2	1	2	
17	2	2	2	2	2	2	1	
18	Capping run of important components banded in good unit							
19	Capping run of important components banded in bad unit							

reproducibility of the measured effects at settings different from the fixed ones examined.

A much better alternative would be to follow the trials suggested by the fractional orthogonal design of Table 15.2. In such a design, every level of a factor occurs with every level of all other factors the same number of times (see also Appendices B and C).

The experimental design of Table 15.2 (strongly recommended by Taguchi) would be more reliable, statistically valid and would require less than

Table 15.2 Orthogonal array $OA_8(2^7)$

Trial	A	B	C	D	E	F	G
1	1	1	1	1	1	1	1
2	1	1	1	2	2	2	2
3	1	2	2	1	1	2	2
4	1	2	2	2	2	1	1
5	2	1	2	1	2	1	2
6	2	1	2	2	1	2	1
7	2	2	1	1	2	2	1
8	2	2	1	2	1	1	2

half the experimental effort. Moreover, in order to avoid the pitfalls expressed in the assessments above, the conditions 1 and 2 in the design should deliberately represent component values at nominal (level 1) and at the extreme of the allowed tolerance (level 2) for each component (deliberate simulation of worst cases – the Taguchi approach), and a proper statistical analysis of the results should follow. Of course, the array of Table 15.2 does not allow the study of any interaction effects among $A, ..., G$, but nor does the set up of Table 15.1.

It might be argued that the advantage of the set up of Table 15.1 over that of Table 15.2 is that it does not require any off-line (pre-production) experimentation; the experimental units are being picked up from the ongoing production line. However, even assuming that the good and bad units are properly chosen, the effort and time involved in the whole procedure is far greater than the effort needed in deliberately producing 8 units simulating the set up of Table 15.2 and then analysing the performance data.

The technique does not offer any suggestions on what one can do to remove the undesired effects of the component tolerances instead of demanding their tightening from the suppliers – usually a very costly approach; nor does it specify how much tightening of the important tolerances is required. Taguchi's cost-effective tolerance analysis and redesign approach can certainly offer the needed answers. Such an approach would not even require any further experimentation; it would simply utilize the data corresponding to Table 15.2 (see Section 14.6).

15.1.2 Variables search

The technique is very similar to the component search technique. The subject of investigation here is process variables/factors (instead of unit components) for which the best and worst levels are expected to be known. The process output response is assumed to be measurable.

Stage 1

1. Based on engineering judgment select and list the most important factors in descending order of perceived importance, and assign to them a best and a worst level.
2. Run two experiments with all the factors at their best level, resulting in the good response outputs $G1$ and $G2$, and two more experiments with all the factors at their worst level, resulting in the bad outputs $B1$ and $B2$.
3. The $5:1$ rule is applied with D and d defined exactly as in Section 15.1.1 (note the similarity with stage (1) of component search). If the ratio D/d is larger than 5, 'the "Red X" is captured as being one or more of the factors considered in the first step'. If the ratio D/d is less than 5, either go back to the beginning and select other factors or levels, or run full factorial experiments in groups of four factors at a time.

Stage 2

1.   Using the important factors determined in stage (1), an experiment is run with the top-ranked factor, say A, at its worst level and all the other factors at their best level. If there is a complete reversal in the output in comparison to the best results of stage (1), then A is in the Red X; otherwise, A is in the Pink X (partial reversal) or unimportant. The result should be confirmed by running another experiment with A at its best level and the other factors at their worst level, and comparing with the worst results of stage (1).
2.   The experimentation continues in the same way for the rest of the factors. Finally, capping runs are conducted for confirmation purposes with the significant factors at their best level and the insignificant ones at their worst level (and vice versa). Using the data collected, a factorial analysis is performed on the Red X factors to quantify main and interaction effects.
3.   The tolerances of the unimportant components are relaxed in the expense of the redesign or tighter control of the important components (associated with the significant factors) after supplier agreement.

Assessment

Recall that in the component search technique, there was a heavy reliance on the lucky choice of a proper bad unit which would reveal all the information needed. Similarly, in the variables search, there is a heavy reliance on the ability to know the most important factors in advance, in order of importance, as well as their best and worst levels. But, if the engineers knew all these in advance, there would be no quality problem in the first place, nor any need for experimentation!

It is ironic, however, that Shainin seems to continuously rely on engineering judgment and experience when, at the same time, he always suggests that the engineer's opinion is often wrong. To quote him, 'Don't let the engineers do the guessing; let the parts do the talking' (Bhote (1988), p. 74), or, 'talk to the parts, they are smarter than the engineers!' (Bhote (1988), p. 23). And yet, in the variable search technique, the so-called 'Rolls Royce of variation reduction' (Bhote (1988), Chapter 9), the second stage can never be reached unless the engineers are smart enough! Otherwise, numerous brainstormings, followed by initial runs at the best and worst levels, followed by endless full factorial experiments, have to take place before Stage 2 is allowed to start.

And even when Stage 2 starts, the similarity with the costly and unreliable one factor at a time method is obvious, exactly as in Section 15.1.1. In fact, all the arguments brought against the component search technique can also be brought against the variables search technique and do not need repeating.

15.1.3 Full factorials

The idea of full factorial experiments is, of course, not Shainin's. The objective is to concentrate on the most important variables, up to a maximum of four, from the Red X or Pink X family, and quantify every main effect and interaction (of any order) between them.

Description

1. Select the 4 factors to be investigated, based on previous homing-in experiments and/or engineering judgment. Select two levels for each factor.
2. Run a full factorial experiment (every possible combination of the levels of the 4 factors – 16 trials – tested in a random order). Repeat the whole experiment for a second time, so that there are two replications per trial (32 trials altogether).
3. Perform a statistical analysis on the data, thus quantifying the significance (or non-importance) of every main effect and interaction, and determining the optimal settings (from those considered) of the 4 factors.

Assessment

There is nothing wrong with the idea of performing full factorial experiments, assuming a limitless experimental capability or a very small number of two-level factors under study. Shainin relies on the latter, believing that his variable reduction techniques will achieve the homing-in to only 4 important factors. If that fails, he relies (yet again) on engineering judgment. Nevertheless, assuming the existence of only four important variables, a fourth-order interaction is not only extremely difficult to explain, it is, in the overwhelming majority of the cases, insignificant. The same argument applies even to third-order interactions, apart from cases of mixture experiments in the chemical industry. There is not much justification for using full factorials just on the remote possibility that some high-order interactions may be significant. This can be proved to be a highly expensive exercise, especially if more than two levels need to be studied. For example, 4 factors at three levels each in a replicated full factorial would require 162 experimental trials.

Returning to the two-level case, instead of the 32 trials required by a 4-factor full factorial experiment with a repetition, one could utilize the design of Table 15.2 (twice), which would allow the independent study of all 4 main effects and up to 3 two-way interactions, at the expense of only 16 trials (half the effort). Even if there were an experimental capability of 32 trials, it would still be better to repeat the set up of Table 15.2 4 times, rather than repeat the full factorial once. Then, the 4 replications in each of the 8 trials of Table 15.2 could be adequate for a Taguchi-type analysis; this would allow the additional study and determination of what can control and minimize variability (the effect of the noise factors) at each trial, not only what controls the mean response at each trial, as in Shainin's full factorial practices.

On the important subject of interactions, depending on the number of factors, fractional orthogonal arrays exist which can also study a certain number of interactions, without having to resort to a full factorial: see, for example, Appendix C.

15.1.4 Conclusion

The strength of Shainin's techniques for variation reduction through experimentation lies in the fact that they are very easy to learn and can be applied in ongoing processes, even during full production (on line). Nevertheless, the time, effort and experimental capability required could still be utilized more constructively by following an off-line (not necessarily meaning preproduction) approach. Moreover, despite their apparent simplicity (which stems from the fact that they are, most of the time, simple versions of the one factor at a time method), Shainin's techniques do not seem to offer a serious alternative to other well-established (and simple enough) experimental design and statistical analysis techniques. In fact, they could be more costly, time consuming and unreliable than, say, Taguchi's recommended techniques, or those under the banner of evolutionary operation (see Section 15.2), an excellent procedure for continuous on-line process improvement.

Shainin's recommended procedures for experimentation and analysis suffer from the same problems associated with the ineffective one factor at a time method and/or with those techniques which concentrate only on the mean response (rather than on the mean as well as on the variability in the response) and heavily rely on costly agreements with the suppliers for tightening up tolerances as the only way of improving quality. On the other hand, Taguchi's approach deals with all the above problems in a cost-effective way which, although by no means perfect (see Box *et al.*, 1988), is still more powerful, more statistically valid and more robust.

Nevertheless, Shainin is to be commended for stressing the importance of statistically designed experiments for improving processes. But before embarking on a blind application of his techniques, one should first objectively compare them with other more established and statistically valid methods. Allowing for some optimism, Shainin's methods could perhaps have some applicability in processes for which a high level of quality has already been achieved. This is when one could reasonably hope to be able, for example, to pick up a proper bad unit revealing all the information needed in the component search technique, or, in the variables search, one could then expect the engineers to be able to identify the few crucial factors with their best/worst levels. Since in a quality process only a few bad units are produced, and most of the process parameters are already at an optimum and robust setting, it would indeed be relatively easy to pinpoint the causes of trouble and even full factorial experimentation is possible. But, unfortunately, as almost all newly commissioned processes and most of the existing ones are usually still in the Dark Ages of quality (at least in the West), we cannot afford to be overoptimistic.

■ 15.2 Evolutionary operation

A method developed in the late 1950s by Professor G.E.P. Box and his co-workers, goes under the broad heading of evolutionary operation (EVOP): see Box (1957). The technique can be seen as a step-by-step search for an optimum set of operating conditions within the range of operability of a process *while it is currently running*. EVOP arose out of the need to study the behaviour of a production process with the minimum possible disturbance to it.

The procedure consists of running a simple experiment, with the process variables being controlled within a short distance of their current settings, without disturbing the process operation. The principles of experimental design are applied, with response data being gathered at the various design points (what we used to call trials before) of an array (usually a two-level full factorial) including a centre point. By taking a point at the centre of, say, a 2^2 factorial, we can check on a change in the mean response by comparing the result at this point with the results at the four points around the vertices of the square: see Figure 15.1.

When the data at all design points have been gathered, one cycle is said to have been completed. Subsequent cycles are completed until a significant change (shift, improvement, increase in yield or a variable effect shown as significant) in the process is detected. At this point one phase is said to have been completed. The decision is then taken to change the current operating conditions in a direction that should improve the yield. The new optimum conditions become the new centre design point and a new phase is begun. This procedure can go on continually during production, the objective being to always move in the direction of an optimum response.

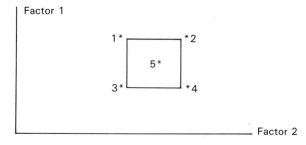

Figure 15.1 2^2 factorial with a centre point

EVOP's greatest advantage is that the engineer only needs to learn the basic fundamentals of the method and can then apply it almost at once. It contains all the elements for success which statistical experimental design and analysis can devise; it is cost-effective and also adheres to the extremely important principle of never-ending effort for improvement. EVOP's basic ideas can motivate engineers and managers to introduce in their manufacturing processes more advanced statistical procedures, such as the use of multi-factorial fractional designs, time-series analysis, SPC, forecasting models and even Taguchi's non-standard (off-line) techniques (exploration of noise space, analysis of noise performance measures etc.), all during production (on line) with the minimum of disturbance in the process.

An ideal matrimony, therefore, exists between on-line and off-line principles for quality control and continuous improvement, offering a perfect integration of the most important ideas contained in this book.

Sources of Further
Information (Part IV)

Bandurek, G., Disney, J. and Bendell, A. (1988), 'Application of Taguchi methods to surface mount process', *Quality and Reliability Engineering International*, **4**, pp. 171–81.

Barker, T.B. (1986), 'Quality engineering by design: Taguchi's philosophy', *Quality Progress*, December, pp. 32–42.

Bendell, A. (1989) (ed.), *Taguchi Methods: Proceedings of the 1988 European Conference*, Elsevier Applied Science Publications: London and New York.

Bendell, A., Disney, J. and Pridmore, W.A. (1989) (eds.), *Taguchi-methods: Applications in world industry*, IFS Publications/Springer-Verlag: Kempston.

Bhote, K.R. (1988), *World Class Quality*, AMA Management Briefing, AMA Membership Publications Division: New York.

Box, G.E.P. (1957), 'Evolutionary operation: a method for increasing industrial productivity', *Applied Statistics*, VI.

Box, G.E.P. (1966), 'A simple system of evolutionary operations subject to empirical feedback', *Technometrics*, **9**, pp. 10–26.

Box, G.E.P. (1988), 'Signal-to-noise ratios, performance criteria and transformations' (with discussion), *Technometrics*, **30**, pp. 1–40.

Box, G.E.P. and Cox, D.R. (1964), 'An analysis of transformations' (with discussion), *Journal of the Royal Statistical Society*, B, **26**, pp. 211–46.

Box, G.E.P. and Draper, N.R. (1969), *Evolutionary Operation: A statistical method for process improvement*, Wiley: New York.

Box, G.E.P. and Fung, C.A. (1986), 'Minimising transmitted variation by parameter design', *Studies in Quality Improvement, Report No. 8*, University of Wisconsin: Madison, WI.

Box, G.E.P. and Jones, S. (1986), 'An investigation of the method of accumulation analysis', Report no. 19, Center for Quality and Productivity Improvement, University of Wisconsin: Madison, WI.

Box, G.E.P. and Meyer, R.D. (1986), 'An analysis of unreplicated fractional factorials', *Technometrics*, **28**, pp. 11–18.

Box, G.E.P., Bisgaard, S. and Fung, C. (1988), 'An explanation and critique of Taguchi's contributions to quality engineering', *Quality and Reliability Engineering International*, **4**, pp. 123–31.

Deming, W.E. (1986), *Out of the Crisis*, MIT Center of Advanced Engineering Study: Cambridge, MA.

Dey, A. (1985), *Orthogonal Fractional Factorial Designs*, Wiley Eastern: New Delhi.

Dey, A. (1986), *Theory of Block Designs*, Wiley Eastern: New Delhi.

Earley, L.A. (1988), *Quality by Design: Taguchi methods in US industry*, ASI Press: Dearborn, MI.

Hamada, M. and Wu, C.F.J. (1986), 'A critical look at accumulation analysis and related methods', *Report no. 20*, Center for Quality and Productivity Improvement, University of Wisconsin: Madison, WI.

Jebb, A. and Wynn, H.P. (1989), 'Robust engineering design, post-Taguchi', *Philosophical Transactions of the Royal Society*, **327**, pp. 605–16.

Kackar, R.N. (1985), 'Off-line quality control, parameter design and the Taguchi method', *Journal of Quality Technology*, **17**, pp. 176–88, discussion, pp. 189–209.

Leon, R.V., Shoemaker, A.C. and Kackar, R.N. (1987), 'Performance measures independent of adjustment', *Technometrics*, **29**, pp. 253–85.

Logothetis, N. (1987), 'Off-line quality control and ill-designed data', *Quality and Reliability Engineering International*, **3**, pp. 227–38.

Logothetis, N. (1988), 'The role of data-transformation in the Taguchi analysis, *Quality and Reliability Engineering International*, **4**, pp. 49–61.

Logothetis, N. (1990), 'The Box–Cox transformations and the Taguchi method', *Applied Statistics, J.R.S.S (C)*, **39**, pp. 31–48.

Logothetis, N. and Wynn, H.P. (1989), *Quality through Design: Experimental design, off-line quality control and Taguchi's contributions*, Clarendon Press: Oxford.

Nair, V.N. and Pregibon, D. (1986), 'A data-analysis strategy for quality engineering experiments' *AT & T Technical Journal*, **65**, pp. 73–84.

Phadke, M.S. (1986), 'Design optimisation case studies', *AT & T Technical Journal*, **65**, pp. 51–68.

Phadke, M.S. (1989), *Quality Engineering using Robust Design*, Prentice Hall: Englewood Cliffs, NJ.

Phadke, M.S., Kackar, R.N., Speeney, D.V. and Grieco, M.I. (1983), 'Off-line quality control in integrated circuit fabrication using experimental design', *Bell System Technical Journal*, **62**, pp. 1273–1309.

Plackett, R.L. and Burman, J.P. (1946), 'The design of optimum multifactorial experiments', *Biometrica*, **33**, pp. 305–25.

Ross, P.J. (1988), *Taguchi Techniques for Quality Engineering*, McGraw-Hill: New York.

Shainin, D. and Shainin, P. (1988), 'Better than Taguchi orthogonal tables', *Quality and Reliability Engineering International*, **4**, pp. 143–9.

Taguchi, G. (1986), *Introduction to Quality Engineering*, Asian Productivity Organization: Tokyo.

Taguchi, G. (1987), *Systems of Experimental Design: (Vols 1 and 2)*, Unipub/Kraus International Publications: New York.

Taguchi, G. and Konishi, S. (1987), *Taguchi Methods: Orthogonal arrays and linear graphs; tools for quality engineering*, ASI: Dearborn, MI.

Taguchi, G. and Wu, Y.-I. (1985), *Introduction to Off-Line Quality Control*, Central Japan Quality Control Association: Tokyo; also available from ASI: Dearborn, MI.

Appendix A
Statistical Tables

What is all knowledge too but recorded experience and a product of history?

Thomas Carlyle

Table A1 Critical values for the t-test

| | Significance level | | | | | |
| | Two-sided | | | One-sided | | |
Degrees of freedom	10% (0.10)	5% (0.05)	1% (0.01)	10% (0.10)	5% (0.05)	1% (0.01)
1	6.31	12.71	63.66	3.08	6.31	31.82
2	2.92	4.30	9.92	1.89	2.92	6.97
3	2.35	3.18	5.84	1.64	2.35	4.54
4	2.13	2.78	4.60	1.53	2.13	3.75
5	2.02	2.57	4.03	1.48	2.02	3.36
6	1.94	2.45	3.71	1.44	1.94	3.14
7	1.89	2.36	3.50	1.42	1.89	3.00
8	1.86	2.31	3.36	1.40	1.86	2.90
9	1.83	2.26	3.25	1.38	1.83	2.82
10	1.81	2.23	3.17	1.37	1.81	2.76
11	1.80	2.20	3.11	1.36	1.80	2.72
12	1.78	2.18	3.06	1.36	1.78	2.68
13	1.77	2.16	3.01	1.35	1.77	2.65
14	1.76	2.15	2.98	1.35	1.76	2.62
15	1.75	2.13	2.95	1.34	1.75	2.60
16	1.75	2.12	2.92	1.34	1.75	2.58
17	1.74	2.11	2.90	1.33	1.74	2.57
18	1.73	2.10	2.88	1.33	1.73	2.55
19	1.73	2.09	2.86	1.33	1.73	2.54
20	1.72	2.08	2.85	1.32	1.72	2.53
25	1.71	2.06	2.78	1.32	1.71	2.49
30	1.70	2.04	2.75	1.31	1.70	2.46
40	1.68	2.02	2.70	1.30	1.68	2.42
60	1.67	2.00	2.66	1.30	1.67	2.39
120	1.66	1.98	2.62	1.29	1.66	2.36
Infinite	1.64	1.96	2.58	1.28	1.64	2.33

Table A2.1 Critical values for the *F*-test (two-sided) at 5% significance level and 1% significance level

Degrees of freedom for denominator	Degrees of freedom for numerator														
	1	2	3	4	5	6	7	8	9	10	12	15	20	60	Infinity
5% significance level															
1	647.80	799.50	864.20	899.60	921.80	937.10	948.20	956.70	963.30	968.60	976.70	984.90	993.10	1010.00	1018.00
2	38.51	39.00	39.17	39.25	39.30	39.33	39.36	39.37	39.39	39.40	39.41	39.43	39.45	39.48	39.50
3	17.44	16.04	15.44	15.10	14.88	14.73	14.62	14.54	14.47	14.42	14.34	14.25	14.17	13.99	13.90
4	12.22	10.65	9.98	9.60	9.36	9.20	9.07	8.98	8.90	8.84	8.75	8.66	8.56	8.36	8.26
5	10.01	8.43	7.76	7.39	7.15	6.98	6.85	6.76	6.68	6.62	6.52	6.43	6.33	6.12	6.02
6	8.81	7.26	6.60	6.23	5.99	5.82	5.70	5.60	5.52	5.46	5.37	5.27	5.17	4.96	4.85
7	8.07	6.54	5.89	5.52	5.29	5.12	4.99	4.90	4.82	4.76	4.67	4.57	4.47	4.25	4.14
8	7.57	6.06	5.42	5.05	4.82	4.65	4.53	4.43	4.36	4.30	4.20	4.10	4.00	3.78	3.67
9	7.21	5.71	5.08	4.72	4.48	4.32	4.20	4.10	4.03	3.96	3.87	3.77	3.67	3.45	3.33
10	6.94	5.46	4.83	4.47	4.24	4.07	3.95	3.85	3.78	3.72	3.62	3.52	3.42	3.20	3.08
12	6.55	5.10	4.47	4.12	3.89	3.73	3.61	3.51	3.44	3.37	3.28	3.18	3.07	2.85	2.72
15	6.20	4.77	4.15	3.80	3.58	3.41	3.29	3.20	3.12	3.06	2.96	2.86	2.76	2.52	2.40
20	5.87	4.46	3.86	3.51	3.29	3.13	3.01	2.91	2.84	2.77	2.68	2.57	2.46	2.22	2.09
60	5.29	3.93	3.34	3.01	2.79	2.63	2.51	2.41	2.33	2.27	2.17	2.06	1.94	1.67	1.48
Infinity	5.02	3.69	3.12	2.79	2.57	2.41	2.29	2.19	2.11	2.05	1.94	1.83	1.71	1.39	1.00

Table A2.1 (Continued)

Degrees of freedom for denominator	Degrees of freedom for numerator														
	1	2	3	4	5	6	7	8	9	10	12	15	20	60	Infinity
1% significance level															
1	16211	20000	21615	22500	23056	23437	23715	23925	24091	24224	24426	24630	24836	25253	25465
2	198.50	199.00	199.20	199.20	199.30	199.30	199.40	199.40	199.40	199.40	199.40	199.40	199.40	199.50	199.50
3	55.55	49.80	47.47	46.19	45.39	44.84	44.43	44.13	43.88	43.69	43.29	43.08	42.78	42.15	41.83
4	31.33	26.28	24.26	23.15	22.46	21.97	21.62	21.35	21.14	20.97	20.70	20.04	20.17	19.61	19.32
5	22.78	18.31	16.53	15.56	14.94	14.51	14.20	13.96	13.77	13.62	13.38	13.15	12.90	12.40	12.14
6	18.63	14.54	12.92	12.03	11.46	11.07	10.79	10.57	10.39	10.25	10.03	9.81	9.59	9.12	8.88
7	16.24	12.40	10.88	10.05	9.52	9.16	8.89	8.68	8.51	8.38	8.18	7.97	7.75	7.31	7.08
8	14.69	11.04	9.60	8.81	8.30	7.95	7.69	7.50	7.34	7.21	7.01	6.81	6.61	6.18	5.95
9	13.61	10.11	8.72	7.96	7.47	7.13	6.88	6.69	6.54	6.42	6.23	6.03	5.83	5.41	5.19
10	12.83	9.43	8.08	7.34	6.87	6.54	6.30	6.12	5.97	5.85	5.66	5.47	5.27	4.86	4.64
12	11.75	8.51	7.23	6.52	6.07	5.76	5.52	5.35	5.20	5.09	4.91	4.72	4.53	4.12	3.90
15	10.80	7.70	6.48	5.80	5.37	5.07	4.85	4.67	4.54	4.42	4.25	4.07	3.88	3.48	3.26
20	9.94	6.99	5.82	5.17	4.76	4.47	4.26	4.09	3.96	3.85	3.68	3.50	3.32	2.92	2.69
60	8.49	5.79	4.73	4.14	3.76	3.49	3.29	3.13	3.01	2.90	2.74	2.57	2.39	1.96	1.69
Infinity	7.88	5.30	4.28	3.72	3.35	3.09	2.90	2.74	2.62	2.52	2.36	2.19	2.00	1.53	1.00

Table A2.2 Critical values for the *F*-test (one-sided)

Degrees of freedom for denominator	α	Degrees of freedom for numerator											
		1	2	3	4	5	6	7	8	9	10	11	12
1	0.10	39.9	49.5	53.6	55.8	57.2	58.2	58.9	59.4	59.9	60.2	60.5	60.7
	0.05	161	200	216	225	230	234	237	239	241	242	243	244
2	0.10	8.53	9.00	9.16	9.24	9.29	9.33	9.35	9.37	9.38	9.39	9.40	9.41
	0.05	18.5	19.0	19.2	19.2	19.3	19.3	19.4	19.4	19.4	19.4	19.4	19.4
	0.01	98.5	99.0	99.2	99.2	99.3	99.3	99.4	99.4	99.4	99.4	99.4	99.4
3	0.10	5.54	5.46	5.39	5.34	5.31	5.28	5.27	5.25	5.24	5.23	5.22	5.22
	0.05	10.1	9.55	9.28	9.12	9.10	8.94	8.89	8.85	8.81	8.79	8.76	8.74
	0.01	34.1	30.8	29.5	28.7	28.2	27.9	27.7	27.5	27.3	27.2	27.1	27.1
4	0.10	4.54	4.32	4.19	4.11	4.05	4.01	3.98	3.95	3.94	3.92	3.91	3.90
	0.05	7.71	6.94	6.59	6.39	6.26	6.16	6.09	6.04	6.00	5.96	5.94	5.91
	0.01	21.2	18.0	16.7	16.0	15.5	15.2	15.0	14.8	14.7	14.5	14.4	14.4
5	0.10	4.06	3.78	3.62	3.52	3.45	3.40	3.37	3.34	3.32	3.30	3.28	3.27
	0.05	6.61	5.79	5.41	5.19	5.05	4.95	4.88	4.82	4.77	4.74	4.71	4.68
	0.01	16.3	13.3	12.1	11.4	11.0	10.7	10.5	10.3	10.2	10.1	9.96	9.89
6	0.10	3.78	3.46	3.29	3.18	3.11	3.05	3.01	2.98	2.96	2.94	2.92	2.90
	0.05	5.99	5.14	4.76	4.53	4.39	4.28	4.21	4.15	4.10	4.06	4.03	4.00
	0.01	13.7	10.9	9.78	9.15	8.75	8.47	8.26	8.10	7.98	7.87	7.79	7.72
7	0.10	3.59	3.26	3.07	2.96	2.88	2.83	2.78	2.75	2.72	2.70	2.68	2.67
	0.05	5.59	4.74	4.35	4.12	3.97	3.87	3.79	3.73	3.68	3.64	3.60	3.57
	0.01	12.2	9.55	8.45	7.85	7.46	7.19	6.99	6.84	6.72	6.62	6.54	6.47
8	0.10	3.46	3.11	2.92	2.81	2.73	2.67	2.62	2.59	2.56	2.54	2.52	2.50
	0.05	5.32	4.46	4.07	3.84	3.69	3.58	3.50	3.44	3.39	3.35	3.31	3.28
	0.01	11.3	8.65	7.59	7.01	6.63	6.37	6.18	6.03	5.91	5.81	5.73	5.67
9	0.10	3.36	3.01	2.81	2.69	2.61	2.55	2.51	2.47	2.44	2.42	2.40	2.38
	0.05	5.12	4.26	3.86	3.63	3.48	3.37	3.29	3.23	3.18	3.14	3.10	3.07
	0.01	10.6	8.02	6.99	6.42	6.06	5.80	5.61	5.47	5.35	5.26	5.18	5.11
10	0.10	3.28	2.92	2.73	2.61	2.52	2.46	2.41	2.38	2.35	2.32	2.30	2.28
	0.05	4.96	4.10	3.71	3.48	3.33	3.22	3.14	3.07	3.02	2.98	2.94	2.91
	0.01	10.0	7.56	6.55	5.99	5.64	5.39	5.20	5.06	4.94	4.85	4.77	4.71
11	0.10	3.23	2.86	2.66	2.54	2.45	2.39	2.34	2.30	2.27	2.25	2.23	2.21
	0.05	4.84	3.98	3.59	3.36	3.20	3.09	3.01	2.95	2.90	2.85	2.82	2.79
	0.01	9.65	7.21	6.22	5.67	5.32	5.07	4.89	4.74	4.63	4.54	4.46	4.40
12	0.10	3.18	2.81	2.61	2.48	2.39	2.33	2.28	2.24	2.21	2.19	2.17	2.15
	0.05	4.75	3.89	3.49	3.26	3.11	3.00	2.91	2.85	2.80	2.75	2.72	2.69
	0.01	9.33	6.93	5.95	5.41	5.06	4.82	4.64	4.50	4.39	4.30	4.22	4.16

Degrees of freedom for numerator											
15	20	24	30	40	50	60	100	120	200	500	∞
61.2	61.7	62.0	62.3	62.5	62.7	62.8	63.0	63.1	63.2	63.3	63.3
246	248	249	250	251	252	252	253	253	254	254	254
9.42	9.44	9.45	9.46	9.47	9.47	9.47	9.48	9.48	9.49	9.49	9.49
19.4	19.4	19.5	19.5	19.5	19.5	19.5	19.5	19.5	19.5	19.5	19.5
99.4	99.4	99.5	99.5	99.5	99.5	99.5	99.5	99.5	99.5	99.5	99.5
5.20	5.18	5.18	5.17	5.16	5.15	5.15	5.14	5.14	5.14	5.14	5.13
8.70	8.66	8.64	8.62	8.59	8.58	8.57	8.55	8.55	8.54	8.53	8.53
26.9	26.7	26.6	26.5	26.4	26.4	26.3	26.2	26.2	26.2	26.1	26.1
3.87	3.84	3.83	3.82	3.80	3.80	3.79	3.78	3.78	3.77	3.76	3.76
5.86	5.80	5.77	5.75	5.72	5.70	5.69	5.66	5.66	5.65	5.64	5.63
14.2	14.0	13.9	13.8	13.7	13.7	13.7	13.6	13.6	13.5	13.5	13.5
3.24	3.21	3.19	3.17	3.16	3.15	3.14	3.13	3.12	3.12	3.11	3.10
4.62	4.56	4.53	4.50	4.46	4.44	4.43	4.41	4.40	4.39	4.37	4.36
9.72	9.55	9.47	9.38	9.29	9.24	9.20	9.13	9.11	9.08	9.04	9.02
2.87	2.84	2.82	2.80	2.78	2.77	2.76	2.75	2.74	2.73	2.73	2.72
3.94	3.87	3.84	3.81	3.77	3.75	3.74	3.71	3.70	3.69	3.68	3.67
7.56	7.40	7.31	7.23	7.14	7.09	7.06	6.99	6.97	6.93	6.90	6.88
2.63	2.59	2.58	2.56	2.54	2.52	2.51	2.50	2.49	2.48	2.48	2.47
3.51	3.44	3.41	3.38	3.34	3.32	3.30	3.27	3.27	3.25	3.24	3.23
6.31	6.16	6.07	5.99	5.91	5.86	5.82	5.75	5.74	5.70	5.67	5.65
2.46	2.42	2.40	2.38	2.36	2.35	2.34	2.32	2.32	2.31	2.30	2.29
3.22	3.15	3.12	3.08	3.04	3.02	3.01	2.97	2.97	2.95	2.94	2.93
5.52	5.36	5.28	5.20	5.12	5.07	5.03	4.96	4.95	4.91	4.88	4.86
2.34	2.30	2.28	2.25	2.23	2.22	2.21	2.19	2.18	2.17	2.17	2.16
3.01	2.94	2.90	2.86	2.83	2.80	2.79	2.76	2.75	2.73	2.72	2.71
4.96	4.81	4.73	4.65	4.57	4.52	4.48	4.42	4.40	4.36	4.33	4.31
2.24	2.20	2.18	2.16	2.13	2.12	2.11	2.09	2.08	2.07	2.06	2.06
2.85	2.77	2.74	2.70	2.66	2.64	2.62	2.59	2.58	2.56	2.55	2.54
4.56	4.41	4.33	4.25	4.17	4.12	4.08	4.01	4.00	3.96	3.93	3.91
2.17	2.12	2.10	2.08	2.05	2.04	2.03	2.00	2.00	1.99	1.98	1.97
2.72	2.65	2.61	2.57	2.53	2.51	2.49	2.46	2.45	2.43	2.42	2.40
4.25	4.10	4.02	3.94	3.86	3.81	3.78	3.71	3.69	3.66	3.62	3.60
2.10	2.06	2.04	2.01	1.99	1.97	1.96	1.94	1.93	1.92	1.91	1.90
2.62	2.54	2.51	2.47	2.43	2.40	2.38	2.35	2.34	2.32	2.31	2.30
4.01	3.86	3.78	3.70	3.62	3.57	3.54	3.47	3.45	3.41	3.38	3.36

(continued)

Table A2.2 (*Continued*)

Degrees of freedom for denominator	α	1	2	3	4	5	6	7	8	9	10	11	12
						Degrees of freedom for numerator							
13	0.10	3.14	2.76	2.56	2.43	2.35	2.28	2.23	2.20	2.16	2.14	2.12	2.10
	0.05	4.67	3.81	3.41	3.18	3.03	2.92	2.83	2.77	2.71	2.67	2.63	2.60
	0.01	9.07	6.70	5.74	5.21	4.86	4.62	4.44	4.30	4.19	4.10	4.02	3.96
14	0.10	3.10	2.73	2.52	2.39	2.31	2.24	2.19	2.15	2.12	2.10	2.08	2.05
	0.05	4.60	3.74	3.34	3.11	2.96	2.85	2.76	2.70	2.65	2.60	2.57	2.53
	0.01	8.86	6.51	5.56	5.04	4.69	4.46	4.28	4.14	4.03	3.94	3.86	3.80
15	0.10	3.07	2.70	2.49	2.36	2.27	2.21	2.16	2.12	2.09	2.06	2.04	2.02
	0.05	4.54	3.68	3.29	3.06	2.90	2.79	2.71	2.64	2.59	2.54	2.51	2.48
	0.01	8.68	6.36	5.42	4.89	4.56	4.32	4.14	4.00	3.89	3.80	3.73	3.67
16	0.10	3.05	2.67	2.46	2.33	2.24	2.18	2.13	2.09	2.06	2.03	2.01	1.99
	0.05	4.49	3.63	3.24	3.01	2.85	2.74	2.66	2.59	2.54	2.49	2.46	2.42
	0.01	8.53	6.23	5.29	4.77	4.44	4.20	4.03	3.89	3.78	3.69	3.62	3.55
18	0.10	3.01	2.62	2.42	2.29	2.20	2.13	2.08	2.04	2.00	1.98	1.96	1.93
	0.05	4.41	3.55	3.16	2.93	2.77	2.66	2.58	2.51	2.46	2.41	2.37	2.34
	0.01	8.29	6.01	5.09	4.58	4.25	4.01	3.84	3.71	3.60	3.51	3.43	3.37
20	0.10	2.97	2.59	2.38	2.25	2.16	2.09	2.04	2.00	1.96	1.94	1.92	1.89
	0.05	4.35	3.49	3.10	2.87	2.71	2.60	2.51	2.45	2.39	2.35	2.31	2.28
	0.01	8.10	5.85	4.94	4.43	4.10	3.87	3.70	3.56	3.46	3.37	3.29	3.23
30	0.10	2.88	2.49	2.28	2.14	2.05	1.98	1.93	1.88	1.85	1.82	1.79	1.77
	0.05	4.17	3.32	2.92	2.69	2.53	2.42	2.33	2.27	2.21	2.16	2.13	2.09
	0.01	7.56	5.39	4.51	4.02	3.70	3.47	3.30	3.17	3.07	2.98	2.91	2.84
40	0.10	2.84	2.44	2.23	2.09	2.00	1.93	1.87	1.83	1.79	1.76	1.73	1.71
	0.05	4.08	3.23	2.84	2.61	2.45	2.34	2.25	2.18	2.12	2.08	2.04	2.00
	0.01	7.31	5.18	4.31	3.83	3.51	3.29	3.12	2.99	2.89	2.80	2.73	2.66
60	0.10	2.79	2.39	2.18	2.04	1.95	1.87	1.82	1.77	1.74	1.71	1.68	1.66
	0.05	4.00	3.15	2.76	2.53	2.37	2.25	2.17	2.10	2.04	1.99	1.95	1.92
	0.01	7.08	4.98	4.13	3.65	3.34	3.12	2.95	2.82	2.72	2.63	2.56	2.50
120	0.10	2.75	2.35	2.13	1.99	1.90	1.82	1.77	1.72	1.68	1.65	1.62	1.60
	0.05	3.92	3.07	2.68	2.45	2.29	2.17	2.09	2.02	1.96	1.91	1.87	1.83
	0.01	6.85	4.79	3.95	3.48	3.17	2.96	2.79	2.66	2.56	2.47	2.40	2.34
200	0.10	2.73	2.33	2.11	1.97	1.88	1.80	1.75	1.70	1.66	1.63	1.60	1.57
	0.05	3.89	3.04	2.65	2.42	2.26	2.14	2.06	1.98	1.93	1.88	1.84	1.80
	0.01	6.76	4.71	3.88	3.41	3.11	2.89	2.73	2.60	2.50	2.41	2.34	2.27
∞	0.10	2.71	2.30	2.08	1.94	1.85	1.77	1.72	1.67	1.63	1.60	1.57	1.55
	0.05	3.84	3.00	2.60	2.37	2.21	2.10	2.01	1.94	1.88	1.83	1.79	1.75
	0.01	6.63	4.61	3.78	3.32	3.02	2.80	2.64	2.51	2.41	2.32	2.25	2.18

				Degrees of freedom for numerator							
15	20	24	30	40	50	60	100	120	200	500	∞
2.05	2.01	1.98	1.96	1.93	1.92	1.90	1.88	1.88	1.86	1.85	1.85
2.53	2.46	2.42	2.38	2.34	2.31	2.30	2.26	2.25	2.23	2.22	2.21
3.82	3.66	3.59	3.51	3.43	3.38	3.34	3.27	3.25	3.22	3.19	3.17
2.01	1.96	1.94	1.91	1.89	1.87	1.86	1.83	1.83	1.82	1.80	1.80
2.46	2.39	2.35	2.31	2.27	2.24	2.22	2.19	2.18	2.16	2.14	2.13
3.66	3.51	3.43	3.35	3.27	3.22	3.18	3.11	3.09	3.06	3.03	3.00
1.97	1.92	1.90	1.87	1.85	1.83	1.82	1.79	1.79	1.77	1.76	1.76
2.40	2.33	2.29	2.25	2.20	2.18	2.16	2.12	2.11	2.10	2.08	2.07
3.52	3.37	3.29	3.21	3.13	3.08	3.05	2.98	2.96	2.92	2.89	2.87
1.94	1.89	1.87	1.84	1.81	1.79	1.78	1.76	1.75	1.74	1.73	1.72
2.35	2.28	2.24	2.19	2.15	2.12	2.11	2.07	2.06	2.04	2.02	2.01
3.41	3.26	3.18	3.10	3.02	2.97	2.93	2.86	2.84	2.81	2.78	2.75
1.89	1.84	1.81	1.78	1.75	1.74	1.72	1.70	1.69	1.68	1.67	1.66
2.27	2.19	2.15	2.11	2.06	2.04	2.02	1.98	1.97	1.95	1.93	1.92
3.23	3.08	3.00	2.92	2.84	2.78	2.75	2.68	2.66	2.62	2.59	2.57
1.84	1.79	1.77	1.74	1.71	1.69	1.68	1.65	1.64	1.63	1.62	1.61
2.20	2.12	2.08	2.04	1.99	1.97	1.95	1.91	1.90	1.88	1.86	1.84
3.09	2.94	2.86	2.78	2.69	2.64	2.61	2.54	2.52	2.48	2.44	2.42
1.72	1.67	1.64	1.61	1.57	1.55	1.54	1.51	1.50	1.48	1.47	1.46
2.01	1.93	1.89	1.84	1.79	1.76	1.74	1.70	1.68	1.66	1.64	1.62
2.70	2.55	2.47	2.39	2.30	2.25	2.21	2.13	2.11	2.07	2.03	2.01
1.66	1.61	1.57	1.54	1.51	1.48	1.47	1.43	1.42	1.41	1.39	1.38
1.92	1.84	1.79	1.74	1.69	1.66	1.64	1.59	1.58	1.55	1.53	1.51
2.52	2.37	2.29	2.20	2.11	2.06	2.02	1.94	1.92	1.87	1.83	1.80
1.60	1.54	1.51	1.48	1.44	1.41	1.40	1.36	1.35	1.33	1.31	1.29
1.84	1.75	1.70	1.65	1.59	1.56	1.53	1.48	1.47	1.44	1.41	1.39
2.35	2.20	2.12	2.03	1.94	1.88	1.84	1.75	1.73	1.68	1.63	1.60
1.55	1.48	1.45	1.41	1.37	1.34	1.32	1.27	1.26	1.24	1.21	1.19
1.75	1.66	1.61	1.55	1.50	1.46	1.43	1.37	1.35	1.32	1.28	1.25
2.19	2.03	1.95	1.86	1.76	1.70	1.66	1.56	1.53	1.48	1.42	1.38
1.52	1.46	1.42	1.38	1.34	1.31	1.28	1.24	1.22	1.20	1.17	1.14
1.72	1.62	1.57	1.52	1.46	1.41	1.39	1.32	1.29	1.26	1.22	1.19
2.13	1.97	1.89	1.79	1.69	1.63	1.58	1.48	1.44	1.39	1.33	1.28
1.49	1.42	1.38	1.34	1.30	1.26	1.24	1.18	1.17	1.13	1.08	1.00
1.67	1.57	1.52	1.46	1.39	1.35	1.32	1.24	1.22	1.17	1.11	1.00
2.04	1.88	1.79	1.70	1.59	1.52	1.47	1.36	1.32	1.25	1.15	1.00

Table A3   (a) Area within the normal curve represented by the probabilities tolerated (b) Normal distribution probabilities (c) Special cases from the main table

Z	Probability	Z	Probability	Z	Probability	Z	Probability	Z	Probability	Z	Probability	Z	Probability	Z	Probability
0.00	0.5000	0.31	0.3783	0.62	0.2676	0.93	0.1762	1.24	0.1075	1.55	0.0606	1.86	0.0314	2.85	0.00219
0.01	0.4960	0.32	0.3745	0.63	0.2643	0.94	0.1736	1.25	0.1056	1.56	0.0594	1.87	0.0307	2.90	0.00187
0.02	0.4920	0.33	0.3707	0.64	0.2611	0.95	0.1711	1.26	0.1038	1.57	0.0582	1.88	0.0301	2.95	0.00159
0.03	0.4880	0.34	0.3669	0.65	0.2578	0.96	0.1685	1.27	0.1020	1.58	0.0571	1.89	0.0294	3.00	0.00135
0.04	0.4840	0.35	0.3632	0.66	0.2546	0.97	0.1660	1.28	0.1003	1.59	0.0559	1.90	0.0287	3.05	0.00114
0.05	0.4801	0.36	0.3594	0.67	0.2515	0.98	0.1635	1.29	0.0985	1.60	0.0548	1.91	0.0281	3.10	0.00097
0.06	0.4761	0.37	0.3557	0.68	0.2483	0.99	0.1611	1.30	0.0968	1.61	0.0537	1.92	0.0274	3.15	0.00082
0.07	0.4721	0.38	0.3520	0.69	0.2451	1.00	0.1587	1.31	0.0951	1.62	0.0526	1.93	0.0268	3.20	0.00069
0.08	0.4681	0.39	0.3483	0.70	0.2420	1.01	0.1562	1.32	0.0934	1.63	0.0516	1.94	0.0262	3.25	0.00058
0.09	0.4641	0.40	0.3446	0.71	0.2389	1.02	0.1539	1.33	0.0918	1.64	0.0505	1.95	0.0256	3.30	0.00048
0.10	0.4602	0.41	0.3409	0.72	0.2358	1.03	0.1515	1.34	0.0901	1.65	0.0495	1.96	0.0250	3.35	0.00040
0.11	0.4562	0.42	0.3372	0.73	0.2327	1.04	0.1492	1.35	0.0885	1.66	0.0485	1.97	0.0244	3.40	0.00034
0.12	0.4522	0.43	0.3336	0.74	0.2296	1.05	0.1469	1.36	0.0869	1.67	0.0475	1.98	0.0239	3.45	0.00028
0.13	0.4483	0.44	0.3300	0.75	0.2266	1.06	0.1446	1.37	0.0853	1.68	0.0465	1.99	0.0233	3.50	0.00023
0.14	0.4443	0.45	0.3264	0.76	0.2236	1.07	0.1423	1.38	0.0838	1.69	0.0455	2.00	0.0228	3.55	0.00019
0.15	0.4404	0.46	0.3228	0.77	0.2206	1.08	0.1401	1.39	0.0823	1.70	0.0446	2.05	0.0202	3.60	0.00016
0.16	0.4364	0.47	0.3192	0.78	0.2177	1.09	0.1379	1.40	0.0808	1.71	0.0436	2.10	0.0179	3.65	0.00013
0.17	0.4325	0.48	0.3156	0.79	0.2148	1.10	0.1357	1.41	0.0793	1.72	0.0427	2.15	0.0158	3.70	0.00011
0.18	0.4286	0.49	0.3121	0.80	0.2119	1.11	0.1335	1.42	0.0778	1.73	0.0418	2.20	0.0139	3.75	0.00009
0.19	0.4247	0.50	0.3085	0.81	0.2090	1.12	0.1314	1.43	0.0764	1.74	0.0409	2.25	0.0122	3.80	0.00007
0.20	0.4207	0.51	0.3050	0.82	0.2061	1.13	0.1292	1.44	0.0749	1.75	0.0401	2.30	0.0107	3.85	0.00006
0.21	0.4168	0.52	0.3015	0.83	0.2033	1.14	0.1271	1.45	0.0735	1.76	0.0392	2.35	0.0094	3.90	0.00005
0.22	0.4129	0.53	0.2981	0.84	0.2005	1.15	0.1251	1.46	0.0721	1.77	0.0384	2.40	0.0082	3.95	0.00004
0.23	0.4090	0.54	0.2946	0.85	0.1977	1.16	0.1230	1.47	0.0708	1.78	0.0375	2.45	0.0071	4.00	0.00003
0.24	0.4052	0.55	0.2912	0.86	0.1949	1.17	0.1210	1.48	0.0694	1.79	0.0367	2.50	0.0062		
0.25	0.4013	0.56	0.2877	0.87	0.1922	1.18	0.1190	1.49	0.0680	1.80	0.0359	2.55	0.0054		
0.26	0.3974	0.57	0.2843	0.88	0.1894	1.19	0.1170	1.50	0.0668	1.81	0.0351	2.60	0.0047		
0.27	0.3936	0.58	0.2810	0.89	0.1867	1.20	0.1151	1.51	0.0655	1.82	0.0344	2.65	0.0040		
0.28	0.3897	0.59	0.2776	0.90	0.1841	1.21	0.1131	1.52	0.0643	1.83	0.0336	2.70	0.0035		
0.29	0.3859	0.60	0.2743	0.91	0.1814	1.22	0.1112	1.53	0.0630	1.84	0.0329	2.75	0.0030		
0.30	0.3821	0.61	0.2709	0.92	0.1788	1.23	0.1093	1.54	0.0618	1.85	0.0322	2.80	0.0026		

Percentage points

	Two-sided			One-sided		
Significance level	10% (0.10)	5% (0.05)	1% (0.01)	10% (0.10)	5% (0.05)	1% (0.01)
	1.64	1.96	2.58	1.28	1.64	2.33

Table A4 Critical values of the product–moment correlation coefficient

Degrees of freedom	Two-sided test		One-sided test Significance level	
	5% (0.05)	1% (0.01)	5% (0.05)	1% (0.01)
2	0.950	0.990	0.900	0.980
3	0.878	0.959	0.805	0.934
4	0.811	0.917	0.729	0.882
5	0.754	0.875	0.669	0.833
6	0.707	0.834	0.621	0.789
7	0.666	0.798	0.582	0.750
8	0.632	0.765	0.549	0.715
9	0.602	0.735	0.521	0.685
10	0.576	0.708	0.497	0.658
11	0.553	0.684	0.476	0.634
12	0.532	0.661	0.457	0.612
13	0.514	0.641	0.441	0.592
14	0.497	0.623	0.426	0.574
15	0.482	0.606	0.412	0.558
20	0.423	0.537	0.360	0.492
30	0.349	0.449	0.296	0.409
40	0.304	0.393	0.257	0.358
60	0.250	0.325	0.211	0.295

Table A5 Coefficients of orthogonal polynomials

Number of levels K	Coefficients	W_1	W_2	W_3	W_4	W_5	W_6	W_7	W_8	W_9	W_{10}	$\Sigma_i W_i^2 = S$
2	Linear	-1	1									2
3	Linear	-1	0	1								2
	Quadratic	1	-2	1								6
4	Linear	-3	-1	1	3							20
	Quadratic	1	-1	-1	1							4
	Cubic	-1	3	-3	1							20
5	Linear	-2	-1	0	1	2						10
	Quadratic	2	-1	-2	-1	2						14
	Cubic	-1	2	0	-2	1						10
	Quartic	1	-4	6	-4	1						70
6	Linear	-5	-3	-1	1	3	5					70
	Quadratic	5	-1	-4	-4	-1	5					84
	Cubic	-5	7	4	-4	-7	5					180
	Quartic	1	-3	2	2	-3	1					28
7	Linear	-3	-2	-1	0	1	2	3				28
	Quadratic	5	0	-3	-4	-3	0	5				84
	Cubic	-1	1	1	0	-1	-1	1				6
	Quartic	3	-7	1	6	1	-7	3				154
8	Linear	-7	-5	-3	-1	1	3	5	7			168
	Quadratic	7	1	-3	-5	-5	-3	1	7			168
	Cubic	-7	5	7	3	-3	-7	-5	7			264
	Quartic	7	-13	-3	9	9	-3	-13	7			616
	Quintic	-7	23	-17	-15	15	17	-23	7			2184
9	Linear	-4	-3	-2	-1	0	1	2	3	4		60
	Quadratic	28	7	-8	-17	-20	-17	-8	7	28		2772
	Cubic	-14	7	13	9	0	-9	-13	-7	14		990
	Quartic	14	-21	-11	9	18	9	-11	-21	14		2002
	Quintic	-4	11	-4	-9	0	9	4	-11	4		468
10	Linear	-9	-7	-5	-3	-1	1	3	5	7	9	330
	Quadratic	6	2	-1	-3	-4	-4	-3	-1	2	6	132
	Cubic	-42	14	35	31	12	-12	-31	-35	-14	42	8580
	Quartic	18	-22	-17	3	18	18	3	-17	-22	18	2860
	Quintic	-6	14	-1	-11	-6	6	11	1	-14	6	780

Appendix B
Generating Vectors and
Blocks for Plackett
and Burman Designs

I recommend you to take care of the minutes; for hours will take care of themselves.

Earl of Chesterfield

Table B1 Table of generating vectors and blocks

(i) $(L = 2)$
   $N = 4$ (122)
   $N = 8$ (2221211)
   $N = 12$ (22122211121)
   $N = 16$ (222212122112111)
   $N = 20$ (2211222212121111221)
   $N = 24$ (22222121221122112121111)
   $N = 28$

212222111	121112112	221212212
221222111	112211211	122221221
122222111	211121121	212122122
111212222	112121112	212221212
111221222	211112211	221122221
111122222	121211121	122212122
222111212	112112121	212212221
222111221	211211112	221221122
222111122	121121211	122122211

   $N = 32$ (1111212122212211122222112212112)
   $N = 36$ (121222111222221222112111121121221121)
   $N = 40$ Double the design for $N = 20$
   $N = 44$ (2211212112221222221112122211111211122121221)
   $N = 48$ (222221222112121222112112212212211121212122111121111)
   $N = 52$

2	2121212121	2121212121	2121212121	2121212121	2121212121
2	1211111111	2211112222	2222112211	2211221122	2222221111
1	2212121212	2112122121	2121122112	2112211221	2121211212
2	1112111111	2222111122	1122221122	2222112211	1122222211
1	1222121212	2121121221	1221211221	2121122112	1221212112
2	1111121111	2222221111	2211221122	1122221122	1111222222
1	1212221212	2121211212	2112212112	1221211221	1212212121
2	1111111211	1122222211	1122112222	2211222211	2211112222
1	1212122212	1221212112	1221122121	2112212112	2112122121
2	1111111112	1111222222	2211221122	1122112222	2222111122
1	1212121222	1212212121	2112211221	1221122121	2121121221

(continued)

413

Table B1   (*Continued*)

$N = 56$ Double the design for $N = 28$

$N = 60$ (221222121211211222122221122222111112211112111221222121211121)

$N = 64$ Double the design for $N = 33$

$N = 68$ (2211212112211122221212222221121111212122212211111121211111222112212221)

$N = 72$ (2222222122212112212221112212122121112221211212112221112112221211112111111)

$N = 76$

2	21	21	21	21	21	21	21	21	21	21	21	21	21	21	21	21	21	21	21
2	12	11	22	11	11	22	22	11	22	11	11	11	11	22	22	22	11	22	22	22
1	22	12	21	12	22	21	21	12	21	12	12	12	12	21	21	21	12	21	21	21

21	21	21	21	21	21	21	21	21	21	21	21	21	21	21	21
22	11	22	22	22	11	11	11	11	22	11	22	22	11	11	22	11
21	12	21	21	21	12	12	12	12	21	12	21	21	12	12	21	12

$N = 80$

(222122112222121121122222212211112211121212121222112222112111111121221211112211211)

$N = 84$

(221221121222211122111212122222222121122212211211122212111111112121222112221111121221121)

$N = 88$ Double the design for $N = 44$

$N = 92$ See note at the end of this section

$N = 96$ Double the design for $N = 48$

$N = 100$

2	21212121212121	21212121212121	21212121212121
2	12111111111111	22112222112211	22111122221122
1	22121212121212	21122121122112	21121221211221
2	11121111111111	11221122221122	22221111222211
1	12221212121212	12211221211221	21211212212112
2	11111211111111	22112211222211	11222211112222
1	12122212121212	21122112212112	12212112122121
2	11111112111111	11221122112222	22112222111122
1	12121222121212	12211221122121	21122121121221
2	11111111121111	22112211221122	22221122221111
1	12121212221212	21122112211221	21211221211212
2	11111111111211	22222122112211	11222211222211
1	12121212122212	21211221122112	12212112212112
2	11111111111112	11222211221122	11112222112222
1	12121212121222	12212112211221	12122121122121

Table B1 *(Continued)*

21212121212121	21212121212121	21212121212121
22222211111122	22221111112222	22221122221111
21212112121221	21211212122121	21211221211212
22222222111111	22222211111122	11222221222211
21212121121212	21212112121221	12212112212112
11222222221111	22222222111111	11112222112222
12212121211212	21212121121212	12122121122121
11112222222211	11222222221111	22111122221122
12122121212112	12212121211212	21121221211221
11111122222222	11112222222211	22221111222211
12121221212121	12122121212112	21211212212112
22111111222222	11111122222222	11222211112222
21121212212121	12121221212121	12212112122121
22221111112222	22111111222222	22112222111122
21211212122121	21121212212121	21122121121221

21212121212121
22112211222211
21122112212112
11221122112222
12211221122121
22112211221122
21122112211221
22221122112211
21211221122112
11222211221122
12212112211221
22112222112211
21122121122112
11221122221122
12211221211221

(ii) $L = 3$

$N = 9$ (12331322)

$N = 27$ (112123223122211131323321333)

$N = 81$ (12222 31232 23231 31332 21312 21123 33132
11311 13333 21323 32321 21223 31213 31132 22123 11211)

(iii) $L = 5$

$N = 25$ (15223 21433 53125 54513 4424)

$N = 125$ (13332 15225 24245 23132 21355 42513 11555 31433
43232 43515 33154 42341 51144 45125 52535 32541 45514
22352 14112 22413 44345 45342 12441 23354 3121)

(iv) $L = 7$

$N = 49$ (12373 32716 43446 31524 22541 76266 72135 65536 14757 745)

Note: For the special case $L = 2$, $N = 92$, see Baumert, Golumb and Hall (1962). 'Discovery of a Hadamard matrix of order 92', *Bulletin of the American Mathematical Society*, **68**, 237–8.

Appendix C
Taguchi's Recommended
Designs and Interaction
Matrices

A state without the means of some change is without the means of its conservation.

Edmund Burke

This appendix contains the most commonly used orthogonal arrays and their associated triangular interaction tables; these arrays are strongly recommended by Taguchi (see also Taguchi and Konishi, 1987). Note that in some cases such as for $OA_4(2^3)$, $OA_9(3^4)$, $OA_{16}(4^5)$ and $OA_{25}(5^6)$, the interaction columns between any two columns are simply the other remaining columns in the array.

Although the interaction matrices provide only the columns for two-way interactions (see Section 7.4.4), indications on how to study other types of interactions are provided at the bottom of the arrays where lower case letters are used. For example, in a two-level array,

$$\begin{pmatrix} a \\ b \\ c \end{pmatrix}$$

at the bottom of a column means that the interaction $a \times b \times c$ can be assigned to this column. However if a, b, c are factors with more than two levels, three levels say,

$$\begin{pmatrix} a \\ b \\ c \end{pmatrix}$$

means the interaction of factor a with the *linear* components of b and c, that is, $a \times b_L \times c_L$, assuming b and c are quantitative factors. The quadratic components are indicated with a square, the cubic components with a power of 3 etc.

For example,

$$\begin{pmatrix} b \\ c^2 \\ d \end{pmatrix}$$

416

indicates the interaction of b with the *quadratic* component of c and the *linear* component of d. Also,

$$\binom{a}{b^3}$$

corresponds to the interaction of a with the cubic component of b (as in $OA_{25}(5^6)$), and so on.

Table C1 $OA_4(2^3)$

		Column	
Trial	1	2	3
1	1	1	1
2	1	2	2
3	2	1	2
4	2	2	1
	a	b	a
			b

Table C2 Interactions between columns for Table C1

		Column	
(Column)	1	2	3
	(1)	3	2
		(2)	1

Table C3 $OA_8(2^7)$

				Column			
Trial	1	2	3	4	5	6	7
1	1	1	1	1	1	1	1
2	1	1	1	2	2	2	2
3	1	2	2	1	1	2	2
4	1	2	2	2	2	1	1
5	2	1	2	1	2	1	2
6	2	1	2	2	1	2	1
7	2	2	1	1	2	2	1
8	2	2	1	2	1	1	2
	a	b	a	c	a	b	a
			b		c	c	b
							c

Table C4 Interactions between columns for Table C3

(Column)	Column						
	1	2	3	4	5	6	7
	(1)	3	2	5	4	7	6
		(2)	1	6	7	4	5
			(3)	7	6	5	4
				(4)	1	2	3
					(5)	3	2
						(6)	1

Table C5 $OA_{12}(2^{11})$

Trial	Column										
	1	2	3	4	5	6	7	8	9	10	11
1	1	1	1	1	1	1	1	1	1	1	1
2	1	1	1	1	1	2	2	2	2	2	2
3	1	1	2	2	2	1	1	1	2	2	2
4	1	2	1	2	2	1	2	2	1	1	2
5	1	2	2	1	2	2	1	2	1	2	1
6	1	2	2	2	1	2	2	1	2	1	1
7	2	1	2	2	1	1	2	2	1	2	1
8	2	1	2	1	2	2	2	1	1	1	2
9	2	1	1	2	2	2	1	2	2	1	1
10	2	2	2	1	1	1	1	2	2	1	2
11	2	2	1	2	1	2	1	1	1	2	2
12	2	2	1	1	2	1	2	1	2	2	1

Note: $OA_{12}(2^{11})$ is a specially designed array, in that interactions are distributed more or less uniformly to all columns. It should not be used to analyse interactions.

Table C6 $OA_{16}(2^{15})$

Trial	Column														
	1	2	3	4	5	6	7	8	9	10	11	12	13	14	15
1	1	1	1	1	1	1	1	1	1	1	1	1	1	1	1
2	1	1	1	1	1	1	1	2	2	2	2	2	2	2	2
3	1	1	1	2	2	2	2	1	1	1	1	2	2	2	2
4	1	1	1	2	2	2	2	2	2	2	2	1	1	1	1
5	1	2	2	1	1	2	2	1	1	2	2	1	1	2	2
6	1	2	2	1	1	2	2	2	2	1	1	2	2	1	1
7	1	2	2	2	2	1	1	1	1	2	2	2	2	1	1
8	1	2	2	2	2	1	1	2	2	1	1	1	1	2	2
9	2	1	2	1	2	1	2	1	2	1	2	1	2	1	2
10	2	1	2	1	2	1	2	2	1	2	1	2	1	2	1
11	2	1	2	2	1	2	1	1	2	1	2	2	1	2	1
12	2	1	2	2	1	2	1	2	1	2	1	1	2	1	2
13	2	2	1	1	2	2	1	1	2	2	1	1	2	2	1
14	2	2	1	1	2	2	1	2	1	1	2	2	1	1	2
15	2	2	1	2	1	1	2	1	2	2	1	2	1	1	2
16	2	2	1	2	1	1	2	2	1	1	2	1	2	2	1
	a	b	a	c	a	b	a	d	a	b	a	c	a	b	a
			b		c	c	b		d	d	b	d	c	c	b
							c				d		d	d	c
															d

Table C7 Interactions between two columns for Table C6

(Column)	Column														
	1	2	3	4	5	6	7	8	9	10	11	12	13	14	15
	(1)	3	2	5	4	7	6	9	8	11	10	13	12	15	14
		(2)	1	6	7	4	5	10	11	8	9	14	15	12	13
			(3)	7	6	5	4	11	10	9	8	15	14	13	12
				(4)	1	2	3	12	13	14	15	8	9	10	11
					(5)	3	2	13	12	15	14	9	8	11	10
						(6)	1	14	15	12	13	10	11	8	9
							(7)	15	14	13	12	11	10	9	8
								(8)	1	2	3	4	5	6	7
									(9)	3	2	5	4	7	6
										(10)	1	6	7	4	5
											(11)	7	6	5	4
												(12)	1	2	3
													(13)	3	2
														(14)	1

Table C8 $OA_{32}(2^{31})$

Trial	1	2	3	4	5	6	7	8	9	10	11	12	13	14	15	16	17	18	19	20	21	22	23	24	25	26	27	28	29	30	31
1	1	1	1	1	1	1	1	1	1	1	1	1	1	1	1	1	1	1	1	1	1	1	1	1	1	1	1	1	1	1	1
2	1	1	1	1	1	1	1	1	1	1	1	1	1	1	1	2	2	2	2	2	2	2	2	2	2	2	2	2	2	2	2
3	1	1	1	1	1	1	1	2	2	2	2	2	2	2	2	1	1	1	1	1	1	1	1	2	2	2	2	2	2	2	2
4	1	1	1	1	1	1	1	2	2	2	2	2	2	2	2	2	2	2	2	2	2	2	2	1	1	1	1	1	1	1	1
5	1	1	1	2	2	2	2	1	1	1	1	2	2	2	2	1	1	1	1	2	2	2	2	1	1	1	1	2	2	2	2
6	1	1	1	2	2	2	2	1	1	1	1	2	2	2	2	2	2	2	2	1	1	1	1	2	2	2	2	1	1	1	1
7	1	1	1	2	2	2	2	2	2	2	2	1	1	1	1	1	1	1	1	2	2	2	2	2	2	2	2	1	1	1	1
8	1	1	1	2	2	2	2	2	2	2	2	1	1	1	1	2	2	2	2	1	1	1	1	1	1	1	1	2	2	2	2
9	1	2	2	1	1	2	2	1	1	2	2	1	1	2	2	1	1	2	2	1	1	2	2	1	1	2	2	1	1	2	2
10	1	2	2	1	1	2	2	1	1	2	2	1	1	2	2	2	2	1	1	2	2	1	1	2	2	1	1	2	2	1	1
11	1	2	2	1	1	2	2	2	2	1	1	2	2	1	1	1	1	2	2	1	1	2	2	2	2	1	1	2	2	1	1
12	1	2	2	1	1	2	2	2	2	1	1	2	2	1	1	2	2	1	1	2	2	1	1	1	1	2	2	1	1	2	2
13	1	2	2	2	2	1	1	1	1	2	2	2	2	1	1	1	1	2	2	2	2	1	1	1	1	2	2	2	2	1	1
14	1	2	2	2	2	1	1	1	1	2	2	2	2	1	1	2	2	1	1	1	1	2	2	2	2	1	1	1	1	2	2
15	1	2	2	2	2	1	1	2	2	1	1	1	1	2	2	1	1	2	2	2	2	1	1	2	2	1	1	1	1	2	2
16	1	2	2	2	2	1	1	2	2	1	1	1	1	2	2	2	2	1	1	1	1	2	2	1	1	2	2	2	2	1	1
17	2	1	2	1	2	1	2	1	2	1	2	1	2	1	2	1	2	1	2	1	2	1	2	1	2	1	2	1	2	1	2
18	2	1	2	1	2	1	2	1	2	1	2	1	2	1	2	2	1	2	1	2	1	2	1	2	1	2	1	2	1	2	1
19	2	1	2	1	2	1	2	2	1	2	1	2	1	2	1	1	2	1	2	1	2	1	2	2	1	2	1	2	1	2	1
20	2	1	2	1	2	1	2	2	1	2	1	2	1	2	1	2	1	2	1	2	1	2	1	1	2	1	2	1	2	1	2
21	2	1	2	2	1	2	1	1	2	1	2	2	1	2	1	1	2	1	2	2	1	2	1	1	2	1	2	2	1	2	1
22	2	1	2	2	1	2	1	1	2	1	2	2	1	2	1	2	1	2	1	1	2	1	2	2	1	2	1	1	2	1	2
23	2	1	2	2	1	2	1	2	1	2	1	1	2	1	2	1	2	1	2	2	1	2	1	2	1	2	1	1	2	1	2
24	2	1	2	2	1	2	1	2	1	2	1	1	2	1	2	2	1	2	1	1	2	1	2	1	2	1	2	2	1	2	1
25	2	2	1	1	2	2	1	1	2	2	1	1	2	2	1	1	2	2	1	1	2	2	1	1	2	2	1	1	2	2	1
26	2	2	1	1	2	2	1	1	2	2	1	1	2	2	1	2	1	1	2	2	1	1	2	2	1	1	2	2	1	1	2
27	2	2	1	1	2	2	1	2	1	1	2	2	1	1	2	1	2	2	1	1	2	2	1	2	1	1	2	2	1	1	2
28	2	2	1	1	2	2	1	2	1	1	2	2	1	1	2	2	1	1	2	2	1	1	2	1	2	2	1	1	2	2	1
29	2	2	1	2	1	1	2	1	2	2	1	2	1	1	2	1	2	2	1	2	1	1	2	1	2	2	1	2	1	1	2
30	2	2	1	2	1	1	2	1	2	2	1	2	1	1	2	2	1	1	2	1	2	2	1	2	1	1	2	1	2	2	1
31	2	2	1	2	1	1	2	2	1	1	2	1	2	2	1	1	2	2	1	2	1	1	2	2	1	1	2	1	2	2	1
32	2	2	1	2	1	1	2	2	1	1	2	1	2	2	1	2	1	1	2	1	2	2	1	1	2	2	1	2	1	1	2
	a	b	a	c	a	b	a	d	a	b	a	c	a	b	a	e	a	b	a	c	a	b	a	d	a	b	a	c	a	b	a
		b		c	c	b		d	d	b		c	c	b			e	e	b	e	c	c	b	e	d	d	b	d	c	c	b
						c					d		d	d	c				e		e	e	c			e	e	d	e	d	d	c
															d								e				e		e	e	d
																															e

Table C9 Interactions between two columns for Table C8

(Column)	1	2	3	4	5	6	7	8	9	10	11	12	13	14	15	16	17	18	19	20	21	22	23	24	25	26	27	28	29	30	31
(1)		3	2	5	4	7	6	9	8	11	10	13	12	15	14	17	16	19	18	21	20	23	22	25	24	27	26	29	28	31	30
(2)			1	6	7	4	5	10	11	8	9	14	15	12	13	18	19	16	17	22	23	20	21	26	27	24	25	30	31	28	29
(3)				7	6	5	4	11	10	9	8	15	14	13	12	19	18	17	16	23	22	21	20	27	26	25	24	31	30	29	28
(4)					1	2	3	12	13	14	15	8	9	10	11	20	21	22	23	16	17	18	19	28	29	30	31	24	25	26	27
(5)						3	2	13	12	15	14	9	8	11	10	21	20	23	22	17	16	19	18	29	28	31	30	25	24	27	26
(6)							1	14	15	12	13	10	11	8	9	22	23	20	21	18	19	16	17	30	31	28	29	26	27	24	25
(7)								15	14	13	12	11	10	9	8	23	22	21	20	19	18	17	16	31	30	29	28	27	26	25	24
(8)									1	2	3	4	5	6	7	24	25	26	27	28	29	30	31	16	17	18	19	20	21	22	23
(9)										3	2	5	4	7	6	25	24	27	26	29	28	31	30	17	16	19	18	21	20	23	22
(10)											1	6	7	4	5	26	27	24	25	30	31	28	29	18	19	16	17	22	23	20	21
(11)												7	6	5	4	27	26	25	24	31	30	29	28	19	18	17	16	23	22	21	20
(12)													1	2	3	28	29	30	31	24	25	26	27	20	21	22	23	16	17	18	19
(13)														3	2	29	28	31	30	25	24	27	26	21	20	23	22	17	16	19	18
(14)															1	30	31	28	29	26	27	24	25	22	23	20	21	18	19	16	17
(15)																31	30	29	28	27	26	25	24	23	22	21	20	19	18	17	16
(16)																	1	2	3	4	5	6	7	8	9	10	11	12	13	14	15
(17)																		3	2	5	4	7	6	9	8	11	10	13	12	15	14
(18)																			1	6	7	4	5	10	11	8	9	14	15	12	13
(19)																				7	6	5	4	11	10	9	8	15	14	13	12
(20)																					1	2	3	12	13	14	15	8	9	10	11
(21)																						3	2	13	12	15	14	9	8	11	10
(22)																							1	14	15	12	13	10	11	8	9
(23)																								15	14	13	12	11	10	9	8
(24)																									1	2	3	4	5	6	7
(25)																										3	2	5	4	7	6
(26)																											1	6	7	4	5
(27)																												7	6	5	4
(28)																													1	2	3
(29)																														3	2
(30)																															1

421

Table C10 $OA_9(3^4)$

Trial	Column 1	2	3	4
1	1	1	1	1
2	1	2	2	2
3	1	3	3	3
4	2	1	2	3
5	2	2	3	1
6	2	3	1	2
7	3	1	3	2
8	3	2	1	3
9	3	3	2	1
	a	b	ab	ab^2

Table C11   Interactions between two columns for Table C10

(Column)	Column 1	2	3	4
(1)		3 4	2 4	2 3
(2)			1 4	1 3
(3)				1 2

Table C12 $OA_{18}(2^1 \times 3^7)$

Trial	Column 1	2	3	4	5	6	7	8
1	1	1	1	1	1	1	1	1
2	1	1	2	2	2	2	2	2
3	1	1	3	3	3	3	3	3
4	1	2	1	1	2	2	3	3
5	1	2	2	2	3	3	1	1
6	1	2	3	3	1	1	2	2
7	1	3	1	2	1	3	2	3
8	1	3	2	3	2	1	3	1
9	1	3	3	1	3	2	1	2
10	2	1	1	3	3	2	2	1
11	2	1	2	1	1	3	3	2
12	2	1	3	2	2	1	1	3
13	2	2	1	2	3	1	3	2
14	2	2	2	3	1	2	1	3
15	2	2	3	1	2	3	2	1
16	2	3	1	3	2	3	1	2
17	2	3	2	1	3	1	2	3
18	2	3	3	2	1	2	3	1

Note: This is a specially designed array. An interaction is built in between the first two columns. This interaction information can be obtained without sacrificing any other column. Interactions between three-level columns are distributed more or less uniformly to all the other three-level columns, which permits investigation of main effects.

Table C13 $\text{OA}_{27}(3^{13})$

Trial	1	2	3	4	5	6	7	8	9	10	11	12	13
							Column						
1	1	1	1	1	1	1	1	1	1	1	1	1	1
2	1	1	1	1	2	2	2	2	2	2	2	2	2
3	1	1	1	1	3	3	3	3	3	3	3	3	3
4	1	2	2	2	1	1	1	2	2	2	3	3	3
5	1	2	2	2	2	2	2	3	3	3	1	1	1
6	1	2	2	2	3	3	3	1	1	1	2	2	2
7	1	3	3	3	1	1	1	3	3	3	2	2	2
8	1	3	3	3	2	2	2	1	1	1	3	3	3
9	1	3	3	3	3	3	3	2	2	2	1	1	1
10	2	1	2	3	1	2	3	1	2	3	1	2	3
11	2	1	2	3	2	3	1	2	3	1	2	3	1
12	2	1	2	3	3	1	2	3	1	2	3	1	2
13	2	2	3	1	1	2	3	2	3	1	3	1	2
14	2	2	3	1	2	3	1	3	1	2	1	2	3
15	2	2	3	1	3	1	2	1	2	3	2	3	1
16	2	3	1	2	1	2	3	3	1	2	2	3	1
17	2	3	1	2	2	3	1	1	2	3	3	1	2
18	2	3	1	2	3	1	2	2	3	1	1	2	3
19	3	1	3	2	1	3	2	1	3	2	1	3	2
20	3	1	3	2	2	1	3	2	1	3	2	1	3
21	3	1	3	2	3	2	1	3	2	1	3	2	1
22	3	2	1	3	1	3	2	2	1	3	3	2	1
23	3	2	1	3	2	1	3	3	2	1	1	3	2
24	3	2	1	3	3	2	1	1	3	2	2	1	3
25	3	3	2	1	1	3	2	3	2	1	2	1	3
26	3	3	2	1	2	1	3	1	3	2	3	2	1
27	3	3	2	1	3	2	1	2	1	3	1	3	2
	a	b	a b	a b^2	c	a c	a c^2	b c	a b c	a b^2 c^2	b c^2	a b^2 c	a b c^2

Table C14 Interactions between two columns for Table C13

(Column)	1	2	3	4	5	6	7	8	9	10	11	12	13
	(1)	3 4	2 4	2 3	6 7	5 7	5 6	9 10	8 10	8 9	12 13	11 13	11 12
		(2)	1 4	1 3	8 11	9 12	10 13	5 11	6 12	7 13	5 8	6 9	7 10
			(3)	1 2	9 13	10 11	8 12	7 12	5 13	6 11	6 10	7 8	5 9
				(4)	10 12	8 13	9 11	6 13	7 11	5 12	7 9	5 10	6 8
					(5)	1 7	1 6	2 11	3 13	4 12	2 8	4 10	3 9
						(6)	1 5	4 13	2 12	3 11	3 10	2 9	4 8
							(7)	3 12	4 11	2 13	4 9	3 8	2 10
								(8)	1 10	1 9	2 5	3 7	4 6
									(9)	1 8	4 7	2 6	3 5
										(10)	3 6	4 5	2 7
											(11)	1 13	1 12
												(12)	1 11

424

Table C15 $OA_{16}(4^5)$

Trial	Column				
	1	2	3	4	5
1	1	1	1	1	1
2	1	2	2	2	2
3	1	3	3	3	3
4	1	4	4	4	4
5	2	1	2	3	4
6	2	2	1	4	3
7	2	3	4	1	2
8	2	4	3	2	1
9	3	1	3	4	2
10	3	2	4	3	1
11	3	3	1	2	4
12	3	4	2	1	3
13	4	1	4	2	3
14	4	2	3	1	4
15	4	3	2	4	1
16	4	4	1	3	2

Table C16 Interaction between two columns for Table C15

(Column)	Column				
	1	2	3	4	5
	(1)	3	2	2	2
		4	4	3	3
		5	5	5	4
			1	1	1
		(2)	4	3	3
			5	5	4
				1	1
			(3)	2	2
				5	4
					1
				(4)	2
					3

Table C17 $OA_{32}(2^1 \times 4^9)$

Trial	1	2	3	4	5	6	7	8	9	10
					Column					
1	1	1	1	1	1	1	1	1	1	1
2	1	1	2	2	2	2	2	2	2	2
3	1	1	3	3	3	3	3	3	3	3
4	1	1	4	4	4	4	4	4	4	4
5	1	2	1	1	2	2	3	3	4	4
6	1	2	2	2	1	1	4	4	3	3
7	1	2	3	3	4	4	1	1	2	2
8	1	2	4	4	3	3	2	2	1	1
9	1	3	1	2	3	4	1	2	3	4
10	1	3	2	1	4	3	2	1	4	3
11	1	3	3	4	1	2	3	4	1	2
12	1	3	4	3	2	1	4	3	2	1
13	1	4	1	2	4	3	3	4	2	1
14	1	4	2	1	3	4	4	3	1	2
15	1	4	3	4	2	1	1	2	4	3
16	1	4	4	3	1	2	2	1	3	4
17	2	1	1	4	1	4	2	3	2	3
18	2	1	2	3	2	3	1	4	1	4
19	2	1	3	2	3	2	4	1	4	1
20	2	1	4	1	4	1	3	2	3	2
21	2	2	1	4	2	3	4	1	3	2
22	2	2	2	3	1	4	3	2	4	1
23	2	2	3	2	4	1	2	3	1	4
24	2	2	4	1	3	2	1	4	2	3
25	2	3	1	3	3	1	2	4	4	2
26	2	3	2	4	4	2	1	3	3	1
27	2	3	3	1	1	3	4	2	2	4
28	2	3	4	2	2	4	3	1	1	3
29	2	4	1	3	4	2	4	2	1	3
30	2	4	2	4	3	1	3	1	2	4
31	2	4	3	1	2	4	2	4	3	1
32	2	4	4	2	1	3	1	3	4	2

Notes: The interactions between (1) and (2) can be obtained without sacrificing any other column(s).

A two-way interaction between any of the four-level columns is distributed more or less uniformly to the four-level columns.

Table C18 $OA_{25}(5^6)$

Trial	Column 1	2	3	4	5	6
1	1	1	1	1	1	1
2	1	2	2	2	2	2
3	1	3	3	3	3	3
4	1	4	4	4	4	4
5	1	5	5	5	5	5
6	2	1	2	3	4	5
7	2	2	3	4	5	1
8	2	3	4	5	1	2
9	2	4	5	1	2	3
10	2	5	1	2	3	4
11	3	1	3	5	2	4
12	3	2	4	1	3	5
13	3	3	5	2	4	1
14	3	4	1	3	5	2
15	3	5	2	4	1	3
16	4	1	4	2	5	3
17	4	2	5	3	1	4
18	4	3	1	4	2	5
19	4	4	2	5	3	1
20	4	5	3	1	4	2
21	5	1	5	4	3	2
22	5	2	1	5	4	3
23	5	3	2	1	5	4
24	5	4	3	2	1	5
25	5	5	4	3	2	1
	a	b	a b	a b^2	a b^3	a b^4

Table C19 $OA_{50}(2^1 \times 5^{11})$

					Column							
Trial	1	2	3	4	5	6	7	8	9	10	11	12
1	1	1	1	1	1	1	1	1	1	1	1	1
2	1	1	2	2	2	2	2	2	2	2	2	2
3	1	1	3	3	3	3	3	3	3	3	3	3
4	1	1	4	4	4	4	4	4	4	4	4	4
5	1	1	5	5	5	5	5	5	5	5	5	5
6	1	2	1	2	3	4	5	1	2	3	4	5
7	1	2	2	3	4	5	1	2	3	4	5	1
8	1	2	3	4	5	1	2	3	4	5	1	2
9	1	2	4	5	1	2	3	4	5	1	2	3
10	1	2	5	1	2	3	4	5	1	2	3	4
11	1	3	1	3	5	2	4	4	1	3	5	2
12	1	3	2	4	1	3	5	5	2	4	1	3
13	1	3	3	5	2	4	1	1	3	5	2	4
14	1	3	4	1	3	5	2	2	4	1	3	5
15	1	3	5	2	4	1	3	3	5	2	4	1
16	1	4	1	4	2	5	3	5	3	1	4	2
17	1	4	2	5	3	1	4	1	4	2	5	3
18	1	4	3	1	4	2	5	2	5	3	1	4
19	1	4	4	2	5	3	1	3	1	4	2	5
20	1	4	5	3	1	4	2	4	2	5	3	1
21	1	5	1	5	4	3	2	4	3	2	1	5
22	1	5	2	1	5	4	3	5	4	3	2	1
23	1	5	3	2	1	5	4	1	5	4	3	2
24	1	5	4	3	2	1	5	2	1	5	4	3
25	1	5	5	4	3	2	1	3	2	1	5	4
26	2	1	1	1	4	5	4	3	2	5	2	3
27	2	1	2	2	5	1	5	4	3	1	3	4
28	2	1	3	3	1	2	1	5	4	2	4	5
29	2	1	4	4	2	3	2	1	5	3	5	1
30	2	1	5	5	3	4	3	2	1	4	1	2
31	2	2	1	2	1	3	3	2	4	5	5	4
32	2	2	2	3	2	4	4	3	5	1	1	5
33	2	2	3	4	3	5	5	4	1	2	2	1
34	2	2	4	5	4	1	1	5	2	3	3	2
35	2	2	5	1	5	2	2	1	3	4	4	3
36	2	3	1	3	3	1	2	5	5	4	2	4
37	2	3	2	4	4	2	3	1	1	5	3	5
38	2	3	3	5	5	3	4	2	2	1	4	1
39	2	3	4	1	1	4	5	3	3	2	5	2
40	2	3	5	2	2	5	1	4	4	3	1	3
41	2	4	1	4	5	4	1	2	5	2	3	3
42	2	4	2	5	1	5	2	3	1	3	4	4
43	2	4	3	1	2	1	3	4	2	4	5	5
44	2	4	4	2	3	2	4	5	3	5	1	1
45	2	4	5	3	4	3	5	1	4	1	2	2
46	2	5	1	5	2	2	5	3	4	4	3	1
47	2	5	2	1	3	3	1	4	5	5	4	2
48	2	5	3	2	4	4	2	5	1	1	5	3
49	2	5	4	3	5	5	3	1	2	2	1	4
50	2	5	5	4	1	1	4	2	3	3	2	5

Note: Interaction between (1) and (2) can be obtained without sacrificing another column.

Appendix D
Charts and Graph Sheets

This is the way the world ends Not with a bang but a whimper.

T.S. Eliot

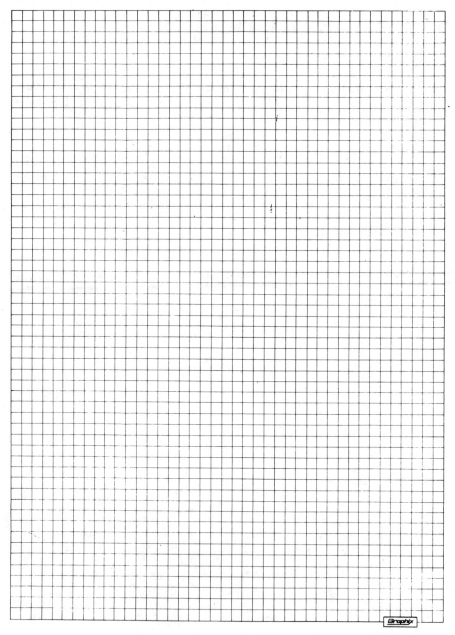

Figure D1   Graph paper

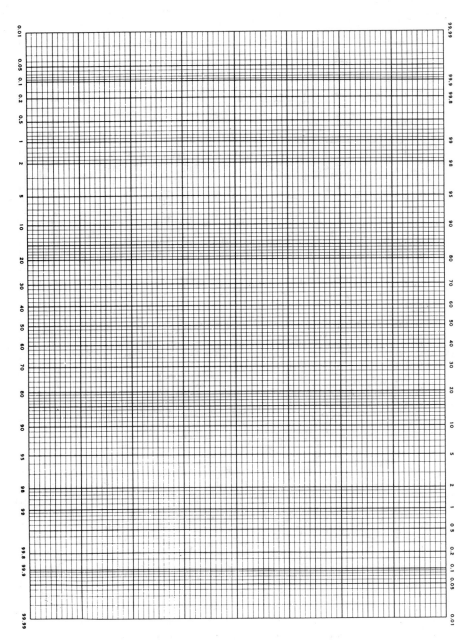

Figure D2 Normal probability paper

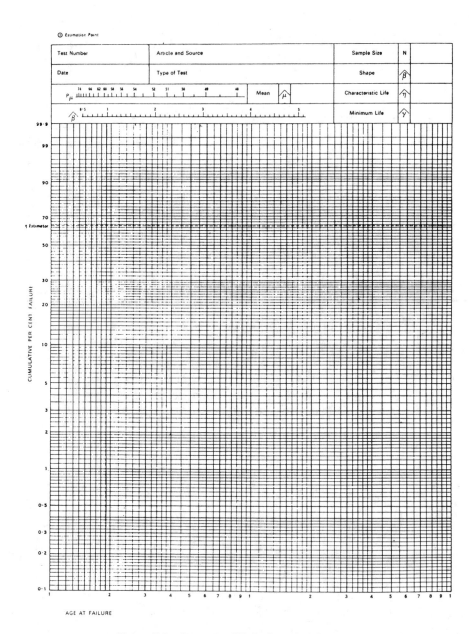

Figure D3 Paper for Weibull probability plot

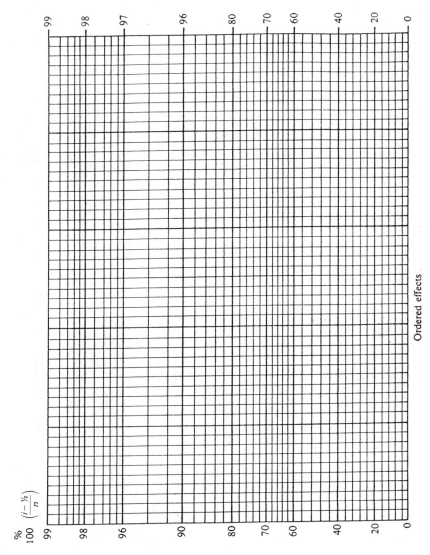

Figure D4 Grid for half-normal plotting (effects each with one degree of freedom)

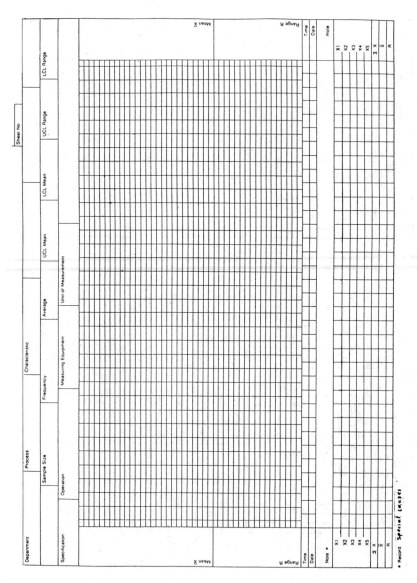

Figure D5 Control chart for variable data (mean/range)

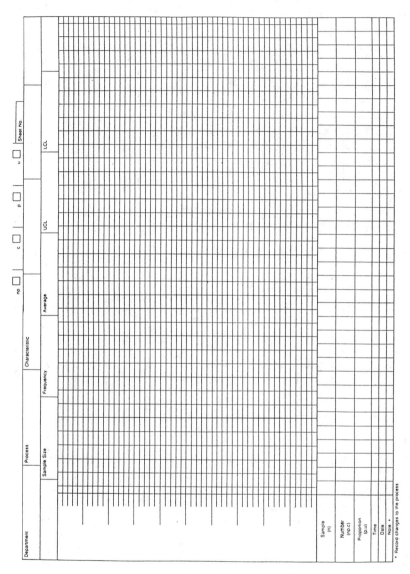

Figure D6 Control chart for attribute data

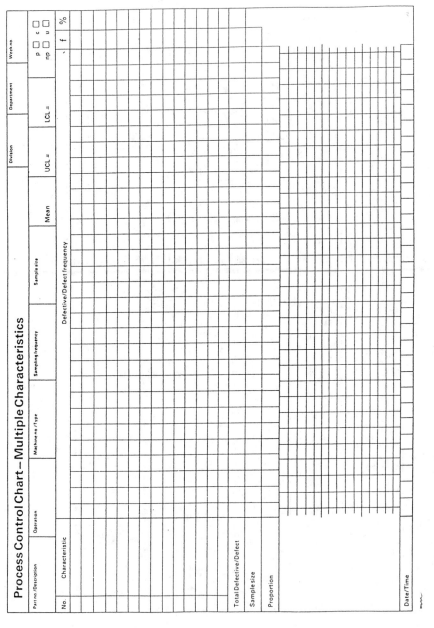

Figure D7 Control chart for multiple characteristics

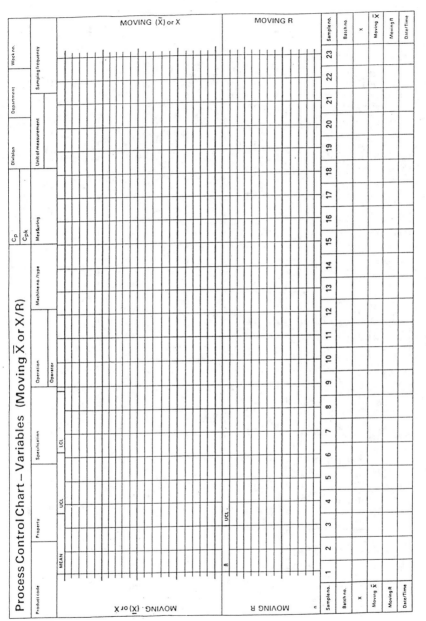

Figure D8 Process control chart: variables (moving $\bar{X}$ or $\bar{X}/R$)

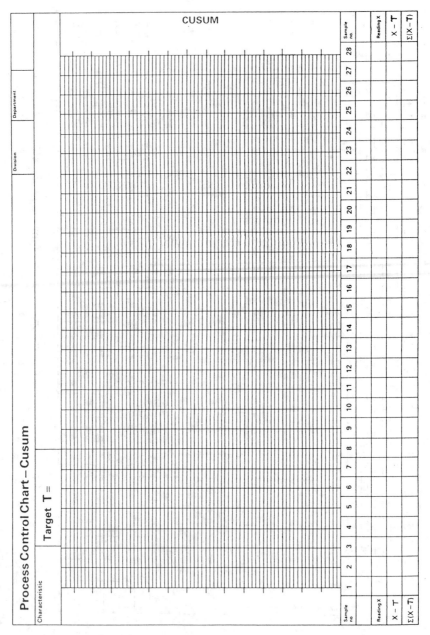

Figure D9 Process control chart: CUSUM

Index

absolutes for quality, 83–5
accumulating analysis, 341, 345, 347–52
action
  component, 198
  limits, 59, 234, 268
  local, 16, 230
  management (on the system), 16, 230,
    246, 257, 289, 308
  plan, 52
  preventive, 234
  rules, 267
additivity, 335, 355
affinity diagram, 189–90
alias group, 167
aliasing, 162–6
  rule, 166
allowance design, 305
alternative hypothesis (definition), 117
analysis of variance (ANOVA), 157,
    161, 174–88 table, 182–3, 316,
    320, 326, 380
appraisal
  costs, 11–12, 95, 207–9
  procedure, 230
arbitrary
  censoring, 221
  targets, 14, 54, 72, 84
Aristotle, xi
attribute
  charts, 231, 250–66
  data, 232
  defectives, 250–7
  defects, 250–1, 257–65
  numbers, 250
  proportions, 250
audits, 65, 72

autonomation, 98
average run length, 276–7
axioms of TQM, 3–10

Bacon, Francis, 154
bad practices, 46
balance (def.), 157
bar chart, 125, 191–2, 206
benefit to cost ratio, 196–7
beta (β) coefficients (*see* discount
    coefficient)
Bhote K. R., 283, 286–7, 391, 396
binary, 374, 376–7, 382
Binomial distribution, 266, 285
block, 156–7, 166
  diagram, 1 93–4
  factor, 167–8, 322, 360
boundary component, 198
brainstorming, 10, 71, 99, 189, 194,
    203, 206, 270, 306, 338, 354,
    360, 396
breakthrough, 19, 49, 62, 64–8, 78, 91,
    339

c-chart, 251, 257, 263–4, 266
capability, 7, 32, 36, 41, 60, 74, 81, 96,
    100, 230–1, 244–5, 266, 283–6
  index, measure, 244, 246, 266,
    287–91
cause
  common, controlled, unassignable
    (def.), 16
  special, uncontrolled, assignable
    (def.), 16
cause and effect diagram, 95, 99,
    194–6, 206, 270